D0948552

Emerging Adults
in America

Emerging Adults in America

Coming of Age in the 21st Century

Edited by Jeffrey Jensen Arnett
and Jennifer Lynn Tanner

American Psychological Association
Washington, DC

Second Printing Dec 2008
Published by
American Psychological Association
750 First Street, NE
Washington, DC 20002
www.apa.org

To order   Tel: (800) 374-2721; Direct: (202) 336-5510
APA Order Department   Fax: (202) 336-5502; TDD/TTY: (202) 336-6123
P.O. Box 92984   Online: www.apa.org/books/
Washington, DC 20090-2984   E-mail: order@apa.org

In the U.K., Europe, Africa, and the Middle East, copies may be ordered from
American Psychological Association
3 Henrietta Street
Covent Garden, London
WC2E 8LU England

Typeset in Century Schoolbook by World Composition Services, Inc., Sterling, VA

Printer: Sheridan Books, Ann Arbor, MI
Cover Designer: Aqueous Studio, Bethesda, MD
Technical/Production Editor: Genevieve Gill

The opinions and statements published are the responsibility of the authors, and such opinions and statements do not necessarily represent the policies of the American Psychological Association.

Library of Congress Cataloging-in-Publication Data

Emerging adults in America: coming of age in the 21st century / edited by Jeffery Jensen Arnett and Jennifer Lynn Tanner.— 1st ed.
    p. cm.— (Decade of behavior)
  Based on a conference held Nov. 2003 at Harvard University.
  Includes bibliographical references and index.
  ISBN 1-59147-329-2
  1. Young adults—United States—Social conditions—21st century—Congresses.
2. Young adults—United States—Psychology—Congresses. 3. Developmental psychology—Congresses. I. Arnett, Jeffrey Jensen. II. Tanner, Jennifer Lynn. III. Series.

  HQ799.7.E63 2005
  305.242′0973—dc22   2005015946

British Library Cataloguing-in-Publication Data
A CIP record is available from the British Library.

Printed in the United States of America
First Edition

APA Science Volumes

Attribution and Social Interaction: The Legacy of Edward E. Jones

Best Methods for the Analysis of Change: Recent Advances, Unanswered Questions, Future Directions

Cardiovascular Reactivity to Psychological Stress and Disease

The Challenge in Mathematics and Science Education: Psychology's Response

Changing Employment Relations: Behavioral and Social Perspectives

Children Exposed to Marital Violence: Theory, Research, and Applied Issues

Cognition: Conceptual and Methodological Issues

Cognitive Bases of Musical Communication

Cognitive Dissonance: Progress on a Pivotal Theory in Social Psychology

Conceptualization and Measurement of Organism–Environment Interaction

Converging Operations in the Study of Visual Selective Attention

Creative Thought: An Investigation of Conceptual Structures and Processes

Developmental Psychoacoustics

Diversity in Work Teams: Research Paradigms for a Changing Workplace

Emotion and Culture: Empirical Studies of Mutual Influence

Emotion, Disclosure, and Health

Evolving Explanations of Development: Ecological Approaches to Organism–Environment Systems

Examining Lives in Context: Perspectives on the Ecology of Human Development

Global Prospects for Education: Development, Culture, and Schooling

Hostility, Coping, and Health

Measuring Patient Changes in Mood, Anxiety, and Personality Disorders: Toward a Core Battery

Occasion Setting: Associative Learning and Cognition in Animals

Organ Donation and Transplantation: Psychological and Behavioral Factors

Origins and Development of Schizophrenia: Advances in Experimental Psychopathology

The Perception of Structure

Perspectives on Socially Shared Cognition

Psychological Testing of Hispanics

Psychology of Women's Health: Progress and Challenges in Research and Application

Researching Community Psychology: Issues of Theory and Methods

The Rising Curve: Long-Term Gains in IQ and Related Measures

Sexism and Stereotypes in Modern Society: The Gender Science of Janet Taylor Spence

Sleep and Cognition
Sleep Onset: Normal and Abnormal Processes
Stereotype Accuracy: Toward Appreciating Group Differences
Stereotyped Movements: Brain and Behavior Relationships
Studying Lives Through Time: Personality and Development
The Suggestibility of Children's Recollections: Implications for Eyewitness Testimony
Taste, Experience, and Feeding: Development and Learning
Temperament: Individual Differences at the Interface of Biology and Behavior
Through the Looking Glass: Issues of Psychological Well-Being in Captive Nonhuman Primates
Uniting Psychology and Biology: Integrative Perspectives on Human Development
Viewing Psychology as a Whole: The Integrative Science of William N. Dember

APA Decade of Behavior Volumes

Acculturation: Advances in Theory, Measurement, and Applied Research
Animal Research and Human Health: Advancing Human Welfare Through Behavioral Science
Behavior Genetics Principles: Perspectives in Development, Personality, and Psychopathology
Categorization Inside and Outside the Laboratory: Essays in Honor of Douglas L. Medin
Children's Peer Relations: From Development to Intervention
Computational Modeling of Behavior in Organizations: The Third Scientific Discipline
Developing Individuality in the Human Brain: A Tribute to Michael I. Posner
Emerging Adults in America: Coming of Age in the 21st Century
Experimental Cognitive Psychology and Its Applications
Family Psychology: Science-Based Interventions
Memory Consolidation: Essays in Honor of James L. McGaugh
Models of Intelligence: International Perspectives
The Nature of Remembering: Essays in Honor of Robert G. Crowder
New Methods for the Analysis of Change
On the Consequences of Meaning Selection: Perspectives on Resolving Lexical Ambiguity
Participatory Community Research: Theories and Methods in Action
Personality Psychology in the Workplace
Perspectivism in Social Psychology: The Yin and Yang of Scientific Progress
Principles of Experimental Psychopathology: Essays in Honor of Brendan A. Maher

Contents

Contributors

Jeffrey Jensen Arnett, Clark University, is the lead editor of the book and the originator of the term *emerging adulthood*. He is the editor of the *Journal of Adolescent Research* and the *Routledge International Encyclopedia of Adolescence* (Vols. 1–4). He has published numerous empirical articles on emerging adulthood and is the author of the book *Emerging Adulthood: The Winding Road From the Late Teens Through the Twenties* (2004).

William S. Aquilino is a professor of human development and family studies at the University of Wisconsin—Madison. His research explores transformations in parent–child relationships during the emerging adulthood phase.

Jane D. Brown, University of North Carolina at Chapel Hill, is the James L. Knight Professor in the School of Journalism and Mass Communication. She studies the role the mass media play in the lives of adolescents and emerging adults. She currently is principal investigator of one of the first longitudinal studies on the uses and effects of sexual content in the media funded by the National Institute of Child Health and Human Development. She is coeditor of *Sexual Teens, Sexual Media* (2002).

Keith B. Burt is a doctoral candidate in clinical and developmental psychology at the University of Minnesota. He is involved with two studies encompassing the transition to adulthood, the Minnesota Longitudinal Study of Parents and Children and Project Competence. His research interests include continuity and change in behavior problems over time, relations between competence and psychopathology, and methodological issues in the analysis of longitudinal data.

W. Andrew Collins, University of Minnesota, is the Morse-Alumni Distinguished Professor of Child Development. He is a principal investigator of the Minnesota Longitudinal Study of Parents and Children, following a sample of individuals from birth to age 28. Past president of the Society for Research on Adolescence, he is coauthor of a textbook on adolescence and numerous empirical and review articles and chapters on adolescence and young adulthood.

James E. Côté is a professor of sociology at the University of Western Ontario, Canada. He is the founding editor of *Identity: An International Journal of Theory and Research* and past-president of the Society for Research on Identity Formation. Dr. Côté is also on the Executive Board of RC34 (Sociology of Youth) of the International Sociological Association, and editor of the *International Bulletin of Youth Research*. He has authored or coauthored five books in identity studies and youth studies, including *Critical Youth Studies: A Canadian Focus*;

Identity Formation, Agency, and Culture: A Social Psychological Synthesis; *Arrested Adulthood: The Changing Nature of Identity and Maturity in the Late-Modern World*; *Adolescent Storm and Stress*; and *Generation on Hold*.

Meghan M. Gillen, Pennsylvania State University, is a doctoral candidate in the Department of Human Development and Family Studies. Her research interests include body image development in adolescence and emerging adulthood.

Mary Agnes Hamilton, Cornell University, studies the ecology of youth development in communities: the principles for youth development; its contexts, activities, and relationships; and the implications for community planning and program implementation. Her ethnographic research focuses on how mentoring relationships build character and competence.

Stephen F. Hamilton, Cornell University, engages in outreach and research on the transition from school to work during emerging adulthood. His 1990 book, *Apprenticeship for Adulthood,* contrasted the apprenticeship system in Germany with the absence of a comparable support system for young people in the United States who do not complete college degrees. In addition to studying education and employment, he does research on service learning and mentoring.

Gisela Labouvie-Vief, Wayne State University, is a pioneer in the area of development of cognition and emotion across the life span. A distinguished researcher in the field, she has had continuous funding through the National Institute on Aging. She has published widely in the area of cognitive, emotional, and self-development and recently received the Distinguished Research Achievement Award from Division 20 (Adult Development and Aging) of the American Psychological Association.

Eva S. Lefkowitz, Pennsylvania State University, is an associate professor of human development and family studies. Her research and publications focus on sexuality and relationships during adolescence and emerging adulthood. She has most recently examined gender role development and sexual behaviors and attitudes during the transition to university among European Americans, African Americans, and Latino Americans.

Ann S. Masten, University of Minnesota, has studied competence and resilience in this period of development in diverse samples, including the Project Competence longitudinal cohort followed for 20 years, who were assessed before, during, and after the emerging adult transition years. She has published numerous theoretical, review, and methodological articles about the meaning and measurement of developmental tasks, risk, and protective processes, including articles in 1998 and 2001 in the *American Psychologist*.

Jelena Obradović is a doctoral candidate in developmental psychology at the Institute of Child Development, University of Minnesota. Her research interests include understanding the effects of extreme life adversity on social and emotional development. She is interested in investigating developmental mechanisms underlying processes of resilience and psychopathology from a dynamic longitudinal perspective.

Jean S. Phinney is a professor of psychology at California State University, Los Angeles. For the past 20 years she has been studying ethnic identity and adaptation among adolescents and emerging adults from diverse ethnic and immigrant groups and has published widely on ethnic identity. She is part of an international team studying adjustment of immigrant adolescents in 13 countries. She is currently conducting a longitudinal study of college persistence among ethnic minority first-generation college students, supported by the National Institutes of Health.

John E. Schulenberg is a professor of developmental psychology at the University of Michigan and a research professor at the University of Michigan's Institute for Social Research and Center for Human Growth and Development. He has published widely on several topics concerning adolescent development and the transition to adulthood, focusing most recently on how developmental transitions and tasks relate to substance use, health risks, and adjustment difficulties.

Jennifer Lynn Tanner is a coeditor of the book and a research assistant professor at Simmons College. Her doctoral work investigated relationships between midlife parents and emerging adults. She was an organizer of the Transition to Adulthood Conference in 1997 at Pennsylvania State University and author of the chapter, "The Economies of Young Adulthood: One Future or Two?" in the book that came out of that conference. Her research focuses on trajectories of development and mental health of emerging adults. She serves on the Executive Council of the Special Interest Group on Emerging Adults.

Manfred van Dulmen is an assistant professor of psychology at Kent State University. His research focuses on understanding behavioral continuity and change from adolescence into young adulthood as well as methodological issues in developmental psychology. His current research program investigates the role of adolescent close relationships as antecedents of continuity and change of antisocial behavior. He is involved as a collaborator in several research projects that study behavioral continuity and change with regard to adolescent competence, adolescent and young adulthood romantic relationships, and the adjustment of adopted children and adolescents. He is coeditor of the *Handbook of Methods in Positive Psychology* (2005).

Nicole R. Zarrett is currently a doctoral candidate in psychology at the University of Michigan, specializing in the study of human development across the life span and within the context of social change. Current research interests include the examination of psychological, social–cultural, and biological factors that influence individuals' interest, achievement, and long-term engagement in both academic and nonacademic activities.

Foreword

In early 1988, the American Psychological Association (APA) Science Directorate began its sponsorship of what would become an exceptionally successful activity in support of psychological science—the APA Scientific Conferences program. This program has showcased some of the most important topics in psychological science and has provided a forum for collaboration among many leading figures in the field.

The program has inspired a series of books that have presented cutting-edge work in all areas of psychology. At the turn of the millennium, the series was renamed the Decade of Behavior Series to help advance the goals of this important initiative. The Decade of Behavior is a major interdisciplinary campaign designed to promote the contributions of the behavioral and social sciences to our most important societal challenges in the decade leading up to 2010. Although a key goal has been to inform the public about these scientific contributions, other activities have been designed to encourage and further collaboration among scientists. Hence, the series that was the "APA Science Series" has continued as the "Decade of Behavior Series." This represents one element in APA's efforts to promote the Decade of Behavior initiative as one of its endorsing organizations. For additional information about the Decade of Behavior, please visit http://www.decadeofbehavior.org.

Over the course of the past years, the Science Conference and Decade of Behavior Series has allowed psychological scientists to share and explore cutting-edge findings in psychology. The APA Science Directorate looks forward to continuing this successful program and to sponsoring other conferences and books in the years ahead. This series has been so successful that we have chosen to extend it to include books that, although they do not arise from conferences, report with the same high quality of scholarship on the latest research.

We are pleased that this important contribution to the literature was supported in part by the Decade of Behavior program. Congratulations to the editors and contributors of this volume on their sterling effort.

Steven J. Breckler, PhD
Executive Director for Science

Virginia E. Holt
Assistant Executive Director for Science

Preface

This is an exciting time for those interested in the study of emerging adulthood. The field is very young, but it has expanded quickly and already has begun to take shape as a distinct area of scholarship. The concept of emerging adulthood was first described in Arnett's (2000) article in the *American Psychologist*. That article described a theory of development from the late teens through the 20s (mainly ages 18–25) and proposed the term *emerging adulthood* for this period. The article was fairly short, and only the outline of a comprehensive theory was presented, but the timing was right. There was a widespread sense among scholars of a need for a developmental understanding of this age period, and a new term for it. Consequently, in a short time *emerging adulthood* has become widely known and used among scholars studying this age period.

In 2004 Arnett published a book-length exposition of the theory, based on research conducted with emerging adults over the past decade (Arnett, 2004). There are numerous other indications of lively scholarly activity on this topic. Many longitudinal studies that began in infancy, childhood, or adolescence now have samples that have reached emerging adulthood (e.g., Aseltine & Gore, 2003; Bachman et al., 2002; Caspi, 2000; Cohen, Kasen, Chen, Hartmark, & Gordon, 2003; Reinherz, Paradis, Giaconia, Stashwick, & Fitzmaurice, 2003; Shiner, Masten, & Tellegen, 2002), and they are providing rich information about the extent to which earlier development is related (or is not related) to development during emerging adulthood. The first emerging adulthood conference, on which most of the chapters in this book are based, was held in November 2003 at Harvard University and drew over twice as many scholars as expected. The second conference on emerging adulthood was held in February 2005 and attracted even more scholars. An Emerging Adulthood Special Interest Group has been established through the Society for Research on Adolescence and is providing a useful venue for scholars interested in emerging adulthood to exchange information and ideas (see http://www.s-r-a.org/easig.html).

Nevertheless, theory and research on emerging adulthood are still in their nascent stages, and much remains to be done to reach the goal of building a new paradigm of emerging adulthood, that is, a shared way of thinking about this age period, including a widely accepted body of knowledge that can guide research and theoretical development. This book represents a major step toward this goal. Twelve scholars present chapters in their area of expertise. All were asked to summarize what is known and to present theoretical ideas about what a paradigm of emerging adulthood might look like with respect to their area. The result is a rich panorama of perspectives on emerging adulthood, covering a wide range of topics.

The book is divided into three main sections—theoretical foundations, individual characteristics, and contexts—followed by a summary chapter. This preface summarizes the chapters briefly to provide an overview of the content of the book.

Part I: Theoretical Foundations

The first two chapters of the book provide an introduction to the theory of emerging adulthood and thereby lay the foundation for the chapters to come. In the first chapter, Jeffrey Jensen Arnett presents a demographic outline of the age period and how it has changed in recent decades (e.g., rising marriage age, broader participation in higher education). He follows this outline with a summary of his theory of emerging adulthood, describing five features he believes distinguish emerging adulthood from other developmental periods (the age of identity explorations, the age of instability, the self-focused age, the age of feeling in-between, and the age of possibilities). Toward the end of the chapter he addresses the challenging issue of the heterogeneity of emerging adulthood. The age period from the late teens through the mid-20s is a time when young people's lives take a great variety of paths, in their living situations, their social relationships, and their status in terms of school and work. Is it possible, then, to characterize emerging adulthood as a developmental period, overall? Arnett answers affirmatively, arguing that the theory of emerging adulthood provides a paradigm that is useful in guiding thinking and research on the age period, as long as the heterogeneity of the age period is kept in mind and investigated as well.

Jennifer Lynn Tanner's chapter focuses on the contribution that the theory of emerging adulthood makes to a general understanding of life span human development. Drawing on life span research, she emphasizes the unique nature and tasks of the years between 18 and 25 compared with the childhood and adolescence that precedes it and the young and later adulthood that follows it. Tanner presents the concept of recentering as the defining process of emerging adulthood from a life span developmental perspective. Bringing together literatures on ego development, separation–individuation, and college student development, she argues that emerging adulthood is not only a stage of human development but a critical turning point in the life span.

Part II: Individual Characteristics

The next five chapters take on issues of cognitive and identity development, ethnic identity, and resilience and mental health during emerging adulthood to provide a window into the individual characteristics that shape the lives of emerging adults. In chapter 3, Gisela Labouvie-Vief introduces the notion that the same contextual and social forces that gave rise to emerging adulthood also created a need for a level of postadolescent cognitive development. This intriguing hypothesis is supported by empirical evidence for a level of adult cognitive development, characterized by abstraction and intersubjectivity, that first appears during the emerging adult years. Included in this chapter are Labouvie-Vief's insights into questions such as, What contexts give rise to this potential for mature levels of adult thinking? and What individual-level factors contribute to this potential?

In chapter 4, James E. Côté examines the extent to which contemporary emerging adulthood represents an extended identity moratorium. Côté draws on Eriksonian theory in his consideration of why and how identity development, once considered the cornerstone of adolescence, has shifted into center stage during emerging adulthood. Côté cites the decline in institutional structures and supports it as the force that has given rise to the exploratory nature of these years. Emphasizing the point that the uncommitted nature of emerging adulthood is an opportunity for some and a challenge or even a morass for others, this chapter highlights the heterogeneity in the experiences of emerging adults.

Jean S. Phinney, in chapter 5, addresses the important issue of differences in the experiences of American ethnic minority groups during emerging adulthood. Phinney explores individual differences in the timing of emerging adulthood by considering how variation in cultural background and immigration status influences how people experience emerging adulthood. Moreover, Phinney addresses how ethnic identity may be shaped by emerging adult experiences. She presents the compelling hypothesis that emerging adulthood may be a time when ethnic identity reaches a new and higher level of awareness because social contexts in emerging adulthood tend to change in ways that may make ethnic identity more salient.

John E. Schulenberg and Nicole R. Zarrett address mental health during emerging adulthood in chapter 6. The authors focus on an interesting question: Why does well-being increase across emerging adulthood for most people in the United States, even though this is the same developmental period during which psychiatric disorders peak? Merging developmental and mental health theories, the authors reframe this question using a person–context interaction perspective to define and discuss adaptation and maladaptation across emerging adulthood. Schulenberg and Zarrett stress the potential for both continuity and discontinuity of trajectories of mental health during turning points in life span human development, and specifically during emerging adulthood. A discussion of the methodological challenges of studying adjustment and well-being across these years is integrated throughout this chapter.

Ann S. Masten, Jelena Obradović, and Keith B. Burt also address pathways of mental health and well-being in chapter 7 but focus specifically on the potential for resilience during emerging adulthood. The challenge of defining *competence* and *resilience* during emerging adulthood is one of the issues these authors address. In addition, Masten and her colleagues offer insight into mechanisms that may be associated with resilience during emerging adulthood. Empirical findings from Masten and colleagues' studies of resilience indicate that emerging adulthood is a developmental period that affords the opportunity for resilience to continue or for new evidence of resilience to appear.

Part III: Contexts

The next five chapters focus on salient contexts of emerging adulthood: family, romantic relationships and peers, sexuality, school and work, and media. William S. Aquilino, in chapter 8, takes a look at the ways family relationships and family supports are important to emerging adult development. Families-of-origin continue to influence development through the emerging adult years.

To some extent parent–child relationships reflect the established patterns of childhood and adolescence but simultaneously transform into something more mutual and adultlike. Aquilino covers a wide range of family characteristics that influence the ways that emerging adults relate to their parents, such as parental divorce, marital conflict, family support, and family socioeconomic status. He concludes with a discussion of the frontier of research in the area of family relationships during emerging adulthood, with an emphasis on the need for work that investigates the diversity of family experiences during this developmental period.

Chapter 9 focuses on emerging adults' relationship experiences with friends and romantic partners. W. Andrew Collins and Manfred van Dulmen provide evidence that emerging adult relationships with friends and romantic partners are both similar and dissimilar from adolescent relationships. Collins and van Dulmen highlight the role of cognitive development underlying changes and shifts that make emerging adult relationships distinct from adolescent relationships. However, continuity in relationship motives, concerns, and expectations reveals connections between interpersonal relationships from adolescence through emerging adulthood.

Sexuality during emerging adulthood, covered by Eva S. Lefkowitz and Meghan M. Gillen in chapter 10, is a central but understudied feature of this age period. This chapter presents empirical data on the norms of sexual behavior in American society during the emerging adult years, including the average number of sexual partners, frequency of sexual relations, and gender differences in sexual behaviors. Sexual attitudes and predictors of sexual attitudes and behavior are discussed. Ethnic differences in sexual behaviors and experiences are addressed, as well as the experiences of lesbian, gay, bisexual, and transgender emerging adults.

Stephen F. Hamilton and Mary Agnes Hamilton, in chapter 11, reflect on how the transition from school to work is a key part of the passage through emerging adulthood. The many divergent paths in school and work that people take after high school in the United States are vividly portrayed. They review the literature on the transition to work and identify the key predictors of productive and satisfying career paths established by emerging adults. Alternatives to current American educational and training programs that might better facilitate the transition from school to work are proposed and discussed.

In chapter 12, Jane D. Brown addresses a unique feature of contemporary emerging adulthood, observing that this cohort of 18- to 25-year-olds is the first to have come of age in a media-saturated world. The mediated lives of American emerging adults include computers, Internet access, magazines, television, and portable electronic music, all of which are part of their daily experience in their homes, schools, and leisure activities. Brown applies the media practice model as a framework for understanding how identity development, a core feature of emerging adulthood, affects and is affected by media use. After laying the groundwork for future research on media use and its effects on emerging adult development and adjustment, Brown concludes the chapter with an international perspective on media use in emerging adulthood.

In the final chapter, Jeffrey Jensen Arnett offers some concluding observations about the field of emerging adulthood as it currently stands. Most of the chapter is devoted to a commentary on each of the preceding chapters of the book, making connections across chapters and identifying new research questions. However, the final section of the chapter focuses on two new issues: emerging adulthood as a worldwide phenomenon and the importance of using qualitative methods in the study of emerging adults. The chapters in this volume focus almost exclusively on emerging adults in the United States and Canada, but here Arnett focuses on how similar demographic patterns are taking place in many other countries with respect to this age period, and how this situation presents the opportunity for and indeed the necessity of studying emerging adulthood worldwide to identify similarities and differences cross-nationally and cross-culturally.

Arnett then argues for the importance of using qualitative methods when studying emerging adults. He cautions against simply taking questionnaires developed for adolescents and applying them to emerging adults, as doing so ignores the potentially important developmental differences between them. The use of qualitative methods can be a way of developing questionnaires that more accurately assess emerging adults. More important, however, the use of qualitative methods allows investigators to make the most of the capacity for self-reflection that is such a notable characteristic of emerging adulthood and to learn from the insights emerging adults have to offer on their lives.

Acknowledgments

We would like to thank the William T. Grant Foundation, the University of Maryland, Simmons College, and the Science Directorate of the American Psychological Association for their support of the first conference on emerging adulthood that was the launching pad for this book. We also wish to thank the persons at the American Psychological Association who were involved in the editorial process and production of the book, specifically Lansing Hays; Mary Lynn Skutley; the development editor, Emily Leonard; and the production editor, Genevieve Gill. Most of all, we would like to thank the authors who contributed to the book. They provided chapters that are remarkably informative, thoughtful, and original. We hope the readers of this book will find their chapters to be as inspiring as we have.

References

Arnett, J. J. (2000). Emerging adulthood: A theory of development from the late teens through the twenties. *American Psychologist, 55,* 469–480.

Arnett, J. J. (2004). *Emerging adulthood: The winding road from the late teens through the twenties.* New York: Oxford University Press.

Aseltine, R. H., & Gore, S. (2003). Race and ethnic differences in depressed mood following the transition from high school. *Journal of Health and Social Behavior, 44,* 370–389.

Bachman, J. G., O'Malley, P. M., Schulenberg, J. E., Johnston, L. D., Bryant, A. L., & Merline, A. C. (2002). *The decline of substance use in young adulthood: Changes in social activities, roles, and beliefs.* Mahwah, NJ: Erlbaum.

Caspi, A. (2000). The child is father to the man: Personality continuities from childhood to adulthood. *Journal of Personality and Social Psychology, 78,* 158–172.

Cohen, P., Kasen, S., Chen, H., Hartmark, C., & Gordon, K. (2003). Variations in patterns of developmental transmissions in the emerging adulthood period. *Developmental Psychology, 39,* 657–669.

Reinherz, H. Z., Paradis, A. D., Giaconia, R. M., Stashwick, C. K., & Fitzmaurice, G. (2003). Childhood and adolescent predictors of major depression in the transition to adulthood. *American Journal of Psychiatry, 160,* 2141–2147.

Shiner, R. L., Masten, A. S., & Tellegen, A. (2002). A developmental perspective on personality in emerging adulthood: Childhood antecedents and concurrent adaptation. *Journal of Personality and Social Psychology, 83,* 1165–1177.

Part I

Theoretical Foundations

1

Emerging Adulthood: Understanding the New Way of Coming of Age

Jeffrey Jensen Arnett

Not long ago an article appeared on the Internet entitled "Top 10 Things to Do Before You Turn 30" (Brodrick, 2003). The list included the following:

- See the world. It's much easier to do when you're 22 and footloose than 35 with two bawling babies in your backpack.
- If you're going to drink a lot, do it when you're young. Get this experimentation out of your system.
- Take risks with your job. Aim for the career you've dreamed of doing. Or just have fun for now. Later, when you've got the mortgage and 2.3 kids and a time share in Cocoa Beach, fun will be the last thing on your mind.
- Do volunteer work. You may be broke, but you can give your sweat and earnestness to a cause in which you believe.
- Use this decade to go to extremes. Climb the tallest mountain you can find. Learn to sail. Road trip to New Orleans for Mardi Gras. [By age 30] people will really be expecting you to act like a grown up. So, you will need some experiences to teach you how to get there.

The article concluded,

> Sounds like your 20s are pretty fun. But don't think this means the rest of your life will be a drag. My point is to take advantage of what you have: energy, idealism, enthusiasm, a willingness to experiment, a lack of encumbrances, a desire to learn and grow. (Broderick, 2003, ¶ 21)

Forty years ago, by age 22 or 23 the typical person in industrialized societies was married, had at least one child, and was well on the way to a mortgage (and perhaps even a time share in Cocoa Beach). It is clear that a great deal has changed in recent decades in what people expect their lives to be like during their 20s. Of course, it has long been true that some young people have been unencumbered and footloose during their 20s (White, 1993). In Europe during the 19th century, at the height of Romanticism, there was an ideal, especially in Germany, of young men having a *Wanderschaft* (traveling period), that is, a period in their late teens or early 20s devoted to travel and self-exploration before they settled into adult commitments. In a similar manner, in Britain many upper-class young men had a "continental tour" or "grand tour" of Europe before entering long-term adult roles. However, these experiences were reserved mainly for the elite and solely for young men (young women would not have been allowed to travel without a chaperone). What is different today is that experiencing the period from the late teens through the mid-20s as a time of exploration and instability is now the norm, something that applies to the majority of young people in industrialized societies, young women as well as young men.

The timing and meaning of coming of age—that is, reaching full adult status—is different today than it was 50 or 100 years ago, different in fact than it has ever been before. The social and institutional structures that once both supported and restricted people in the course of coming of age have weakened, leaving people with greater freedom but less support as they make their way into adulthood. As sociologists have observed, the entry into adulthood has become deinstitutionalized and individualization has increased, meaning that people are required to rely on their own resources and their own sense of agency, for better or worse (Côté, 2000; Heckhausen, 1999; Mayer, 2004). More than ever before, coming of age in the 21st century means learning to stand alone as a self-sufficient person, capable of making choices and decisions independently from among a wide range of possibilities (Arnett, 1998).

In part because the changes in the nature of young people's experiences from their late teens through their mid-20s have happened so recently, this period of life has been little studied by scholars interested in human development. Of course, studies of college students are innumerable, but these studies are usually done without a coherent developmental framework. There have been some notable theoretical efforts by scholars such as Erik Erikson (1950, 1959, 1968), Kenneth Keniston (1971), Gene Bockneck (1986), and James Côté (2000; Côté & Allahar, 1994). However, with the exception of Côté's work, these efforts are decades old and have limited applicability to today's young people.

The theory of emerging adulthood has been offered as a way of conceptualizing the development of today's young people, in American society and in other industrialized societies. It does this in part by recognizing the years from (roughly) 18 to 25 as a distinct period of the life course, different in important ways from the adolescence that precedes it or the young adulthood that follows it. Although numerous articles using the emerging adulthood theory have been published since I first presented an outline of the theory in 2000 (Arnett, 2000a), and I have written a book expanding on the theory and presenting the findings from my own research (Arnett, 2004), this book represents the first attempt to draw together a wide range of scholars in order to provide a comprehensive portrait of development during emerging adulthood.

In this first chapter, I begin by presenting a demographic outline of emerging adulthood. Then I summarize my theory of emerging adulthood by presenting the five features that distinguish it as a developmental period. Finally, I consider the special challenges involved in building a new paradigm of emerging adulthood, given that emerging adults are such a diverse group.

The Demographic Outline of Emerging Adulthood

Fifty years are but a moment in historical terms, so historians of the future will no doubt be amazed when they consider the demographic changes that took place in the last half of the 20th century with respect to the age period from the late teens through the 20s. Especially striking were the changes in the timing of marriage and parenthood, and in participation in higher education.

The median age of marriage rose steeply in every industrialized society from 1960 to the mid-1990s before leveling out. Figure 1.1 shows the pattern for the United States. The pattern for men is parallel to that of women but consistently 2 years later. The pattern for both men and women in other industrialized countries is later than that of the United States, but for them as well marriage usually occurs at some point in the late 20s (Arnett, 2004). Not only has the median age of marriage risen, but the variance has expanded (Modell, 1989). Some people still do get married in their late teens or early 20s, perhaps because of exceptional maturity, conservative religious beliefs, or the spur of an unintended pregnancy, but it is also not unusual for people to marry in their very late 20s or their early 30s, and they are not considered abnormal or even unusual for doing so.

Age at first childbirth has followed a pattern similar to marriage in the United States and other industrialized countries, rising steadily beginning in 1960 and leveling out in the 1990s (Arnett & Taber, 1994). For age at first childbirth as well as for marriage, the variance has expanded as the median age has risen. Some women (although relatively few) still have their first child

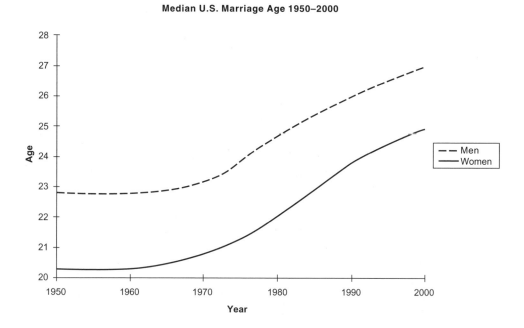

Figure 1.1. Median U.S. marriage age, 1950–2000.

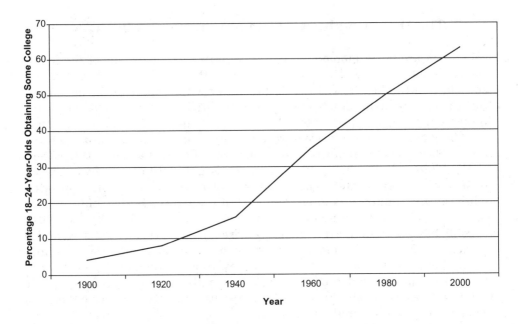

Figure 1.2. College enrollment, 1900–2000.

in their late teens or early 20s, but now it is not uncommon for a woman's first birth to take place in her 30s. Furthermore, marriage has ceased to be the nearly exclusive context for childbirth. In the United States, in 1960 only 7% of children were born to an unmarried mother, but by 2000 this figure had risen to 33% (Bianchi & Casper, 2000). In northern European countries, the percentages of children born to unmarried mothers are even higher (Kiernan, 2002).

Another key part of the demographic outline of emerging adulthood is participation in higher education. One reason many people now wait until at least their late 20s to marry and have their first child is that they are focused before that time on obtaining higher education and then finding a desirable occupation. Participation in higher education has risen substantially during the past century, especially over the past 50 years, as Figure 1.2 shows. The rise of women's participation has been especially notable. Early in the 20th century, young women were discouraged from attending college, no matter how smart they were (Kerber, 1997). Even as recently as 1970, substantially more men than women attended college. Since the late 1980s, however, women have exceeded men in entering college following high school, and today 57% of the undergraduates in American higher education are female (National Center for Education Statistics, 2002). A similar pattern has taken place in other industrialized countries.

One other noteworthy element of the demographic outline of emerging adulthood is the rate of residential change, that is, how often people move from one residence to another. As illustrated in Figure 1.3, the rate of residential change peaks sharply from age 20 to 24, right in the heart of emerging adult-

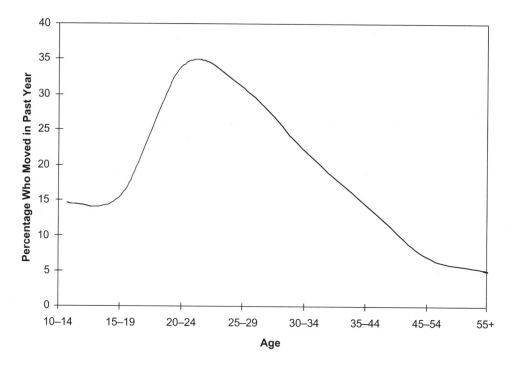

Figure 1.3. Rates of moving by age.

hood. Emerging adults move around a lot in the course of changing their plans regarding love, work, and education.

Overall, what we see from the demographic outline is that in the past half century, the age period from about 18 through the mid-20s has changed from being a time of settling down into adult roles of marriage, parenthood, long-term work, and a long-term residence to being a time that is exceptionally unsettled, a period of exploration and instability, as young people try out various possible futures in love and work before making enduring commitments.

What Is Emerging Adulthood? Five Features

Five main features make emerging adulthood distinct as a developmental period from the adolescence that precedes it or the young adulthood that follows it. These features are based on my research with emerging adults over the past decade (Arnett, 2004): It is the age of identity explorations, especially in the areas of love and work; it is the age of instability; it is the most self-focused age of life; it is the age of feeling in-between, neither adolescent nor adult; and it is the age of possibilities, when optimism is high and people have an unparalleled opportunity to transform their lives. In the following sections I examine each of these features in turn.

The Age of Identity Explorations

Psychologists generally think of identity explorations as a developmental task of adolescence. In his theory of the life course, Erik Erikson (1950) proposed a distinctive crisis for each stage, and identity versus role confusion was the crisis of adolescence. However, even 40 years ago Erikson commented on what he called the "prolonged adolescence" typical of industrialized societies, and the psychosocial moratorium granted to young people in such societies, "during which the young adult through free role experimentation may find a niche in some section of his society" (1968, p. 150). Decades later, this description applies to many more young people than when he wrote it. If adolescence is the period from age 10 to 18 and emerging adulthood is the period from (roughly) age 18 to the mid-20s, most identity exploration now takes place in emerging adulthood rather than adolescence.

Emerging adulthood is the age of identity explorations in the sense that it is the period when people are most likely to be exploring various possibilities for their lives in a variety of areas, especially love and work, as a prelude to making the enduring choices that will set the foundation for their adult lives. In the course of exploring possibilities in love and work, emerging adults clarify their identities, that is, they learn more about who they are and what they want out of life. Emerging adulthood offers the best opportunity for such self-exploration. Emerging adults have become more independent of their parents than they were as adolescents and most of them have left home, but they have not yet entered the stable, enduring commitments typical of adult life, such as a long-term job, marriage, and parenthood. During this interval of years when they are neither beholden to their parents nor committed to a web of adult roles, they have an exceptional opportunity to try out different ways of living and different possible choices in love and work.

Until recently, my research on emerging adults did not include questions or measures on identity, because like most psychologists I was used to thinking of identity formation as an issue pertaining mainly to development during adolescence. However, in my interviews with emerging adults, identity issues have come up over and over again in various forms. In seeking a long-term romantic partner, emerging adults inevitably address identity issues, because to know what person they want to commit themselves to, they have to know what kind of person they are—that is, what their likes and dislikes are and what they want their daily lives to be like in adulthood. In deciding what kind of education to pursue and in looking for a desirable job, identity issues also arise for emerging adults, because in order to know what kind of work will suit them, they have to know who they are—that is, what they enjoy doing and what they are good at. In forming a worldview that addresses questions about values and religious beliefs, emerging adults also address identity issues in these areas, because deciding on their values and beliefs also means deciding who they are and how their worldview is similar to and different from the one held by their parents.

Identity issues may be expected to arise in response to questions about love, work, and ideology or worldviews, the three pillars of identity in Erikson's (1950, 1968) theory, but identity issues come up in response to many other types of questions as well. For example, here is a portion of a 25-year-old African American woman's response to a question about what makes a person an adult (Arnett, 2004):

> Learning about yourself is something that is a really emotional thing because it's like you wake up one day and you think that you're doing this right and you think that you're living the way you want to live, and then the next day you get up and it's like, wait a minute, I'm doing everything wrong. I don't know who I am. And you have to be willing to take that step forward and say, okay, I'm going to get to know myself no matter if it's painful or if it's going to make me happy. I have to dig deep within myself and figure out who I am. And this is a learning process every day. (p. 197)

Identity issues also commonly arise in responses to questions about relationships with parents, expectations for the future, characteristics desired in a romantic partner, and religious beliefs. In short, identity issues are such a salient part of development in emerging adulthood that they arise in response to a wide range of questions, including many that are not directly related to identity.

The Age of Instability

The explorations of emerging adulthood make it not only an exceptionally stimulating and eventful period of life but also an exceptionally unstable one. Figure 1.3, which shows that residential changes in the United States peak during emerging adulthood, illustrates the instability of the age period. Emerging adults' numerous moves reflect their explorations of different possibilities and their frequent changes of direction with respect to love, work, and education.

The high rate of residential change from the late teens through the mid-20s reflects the many profound changes that take place in the lives of emerging adults. For most, the first residential change comes at about age 18 or 19 when they move out of their parents' home, either to go to college or simply to be independent (Goldscheider & Goldscheider, 1999). Other changes soon follow. Those who attend a residential college may move from a dormitory into an apartment after their first year. Many leave college after 1 or 2 years (National Center for Education Statistics, 2004), and when they do a residential change is likely. Most American emerging adults cohabit at some point during their 20s, and residential changes may take place when they initiate cohabitation and when it ends (as happens in 9 out of 10 cohabiting relationships within 5 years; Bumpass & Liu, 2000). About 40% of emerging adults move back home at some point in their early 20s (Goldscheider & Goldscheider, 1999), usually for only a temporary period, after which they move out again. Some emerging adults move to a different part of the country or the world to pursue opportunities in education or work, to accompany a romantic partner, or simply to pursue adventure. The statistic on residential changes during the 20s is emblematic of the instability of emerging adults' lives.

The Self-Focused Age

Emerging adults are not selfish or self-centered, by and large. Having inter-viewed both adolescents and emerging adults in various studies, I have been struck by how much less egocentric emerging adults are, compared with adoles-cents. Emerging adults are more considerate of other people's feelings and better at understanding others' point of view. This quality comes out especially in their relationships with their parents. In emerging adulthood they come to see their parents as persons, not merely parents, and they empathize with them more than they did as adolescents (Arnett, 2004, chap. 3). A change in social cognition seems to take place in the move from adolescence to emerging adulthood that makes people less self-centered.

Nevertheless, emerging adulthood is a distinctly self-focused time of life, which is different than being self-centered. Emerging adults are self-focused in the sense that they have little in the way of social obligations, little in the way of duties and commitments to others, which leaves them with a great deal of autonomy in running their own lives. Children and adolescents typically live with their parents and have to abide by the household rules and routines the parents establish; they spend a substantial proportion of their time in school, where they have to follow the rules and routines set by teachers and school officials. Beyond age 30, most adults have commitments to a spouse, children, and a long-term employer, and all these relationships entail daily requirements and obligations. But in between, during emerging adulthood, most people are relatively free to make independent decisions about their lives (Arnett, 1998).

In one sense, being self-focused is part of the fun of being an emerging adult. They recognize this period as the one time in their lives when they do not have to answer to anyone and can essentially do what they want with their lives, before they enter the permanent (or at least enduring) obligations of adult roles. However, being self-focused has a serious purpose as well. Emerging adults are self-focused with the goal of attaining the self-sufficiency that is at the heart of their view of what it means to be an adult (Arnett, 1998, 2004). Only after attaining self-sufficiency do they feel like they have reached adulthood and begin to view themselves as ready to become more other-focused by entering marriage and parenthood. Identity issues are relevant here; being self-focused allows emerging adults the psychological space to contemplate the "who am I?" questions that are at the heart of identity and to pursue opportunities in love, work, and education that will promote their self-knowledge.

The self-focused quality of emerging adulthood makes it arguably the freest time of life, at least in terms of freedom from social obligations and expectations. However, the flip side of this freedom is that emerging adults spend a consider-able amount of time alone during these self-focused years. According to time-use studies across the life span, emerging adults aged 19 to 29 spend more of their leisure time alone than any other persons except the elderly, and more of their time in productive activities (school and work) alone than any age group under 40 (Larson, 1990). Although most people enjoy having the freedom to be self-focused during their emerging adult years, they do not expect or even desire to be self-focused forever. Rather, they view it as a necessary step before committing themselves to enduring relationships with others, in love and in work.

The Age of Feeling In-Between

One of the reasons I chose the term *emerging adulthood* is that it seemed to fit the way people in their late teens and early 20s describe themselves, developmentally. One of the questions I have asked from my earliest research on this age period is, "Do you feel that you have reached adulthood?" I have found that very few people beyond age 18 consider themselves to be in adolescence, even late adolescence. It is easy to understand why. Unlike adolescents, 18- to 25-year-olds are not in secondary school, they are not going through the biological changes of puberty, and most of them no longer live with their parents. However, most of them do not see themselves as adults, either. In response to the question about whether they feel they have reached adulthood, most 18- to 25-year-olds respond along the lines of "in some ways yes, in some ways no."

Figure 1.4 shows the age pattern derived from the responses to this question in one of my studies (Arnett, 2001). About 60% of emerging adults aged 18 to 25 responded "in some ways yes, in some ways no" when asked, "Do you

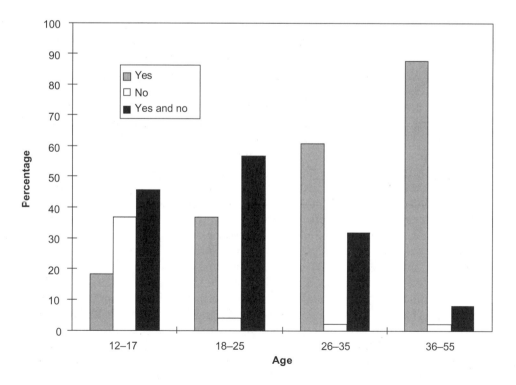

Figure 1.4. Responses to "Do you feel like you have reached adulthood?"

feel like you have reached adulthood?" Once they reach their late 20s and early 30s most Americans feel they have definitely reached adulthood, but even then a substantial proportion, about 30%, still feels in-between. It is only past age 35 that this sense of ambiguity has faded for nearly everyone, and the feeling of being adult is well established.

Thus for most people, the feeling of being fully adult takes a long time to attain, and for a substantial period they feel in-between, as if they are emerging into adulthood but not there yet. The explanation for this phenomenon lies in part in the criteria they consider to be most important for becoming an adult. Emerging adults rarely base their feeling of attaining adulthood on transition events such as finishing their education or getting married, milestones that take place at a specific time and that a person clearly either has or has not reached. On the contrary, the criteria most important to them are reached gradually, so their feeling of becoming an adult is gradual, too. In a variety of regions of the United States and other industrialized countries, in a variety of ethnic groups, in studies using both questionnaires and interviews, people consistently state the following as the top criteria for adulthood (Arnett, 1994, 1997, 1998, 2001, 2003, 2004; Facio & Micocci, 2003; Mayseless & Scharf, 2003; Nelson, Badger, & Wu, 2004):

- Accept responsibility for yourself.
- Make independent decisions.
- Become financially independent.

All three criteria are gradual rather than transition events. As a consequence, although emerging adults begin to feel adult by the time they reach age 18 or 19, most do not feel completely adult until years later, sometime in their mid- to late-20s. By then they have become confident that they have learned to accept responsibility, make their own decisions, and be financially independent. While they are in the process of developing those qualities they feel as if they are in between adolescence and full adulthood.

In contrast to what many other studies have found, a 2003 study by the National Opinion Research Center (NORC) claimed that the top criteria for adulthood were finishing education, obtaining a full-time job, becoming capable of supporting a family, and becoming financially independent (Associated Press, 2003). These results were quite different from other studies on this topic apparently because they gave people only a narrow range of possible choices, mainly transition events (i.e., in addition to *finish education* were *marriage, parenthood,* and *obtaining a full-time job*). If the researchers had given people a broader range of criteria or if they had made the question open-ended, they likely would have found results similar to other studies. I and others have conducted this research numerous times in many parts of the United States with a wide range of ethnic and socioeconomic status (SES) groups, using interviews as well as questionnaires, and the results have been extremely consistent with the pattern I have described here. *Finish education* has consistently ranked near the bottom, so its primacy in the NORC study may well be an artifact of the restrictive method used.

The Age of Possibilities

Emerging adulthood is the age of possibilities in two ways. One is that emerging adulthood is a time of great optimism, of high hopes for the future. In one national survey of 18- to 24-year-old Americans, nearly all—96 %—agreed with the statement "I am very sure that someday I will get to where I want to be in life" (Hornblower, 1997). If this figure seems high, consider that in emerging adulthood high hopes are cheap because they have not yet been firmly tested against reality. Before people get married, it is easy for everyone to believe they are going to end up in a state of permanent marital bliss with their soul mate (Popenoe & Whitehead, 2001, 2002). Before people settle into a long-term job, it is possible for them to believe they are going to find a job that is both well-paying and personally fulfilling, an expression of their identity rather than simply a way to make a living.

Even emerging adults whose backgrounds and current lives do not seem especially promising believe that eventually, and probably sooner rather than later, they are going to "get where they want to be in life." I have found, in fact, that lower SES emerging adults are even more likely than higher SES emerging adults to believe that their lives will be better than their parents' lives (Arnett, 2000b). In emerging adulthood, virtually no one expects to end up with a dreary, dead-end job or join the nearly 50% of Americans whose marriages end in divorce, or make mistakes that drive life into a ditch. Even if their current lives are a struggle, as is the case for many emerging adults, they continue to believe that they will ultimately prevail. During emerging adulthood, high hopes reign.

The second way that emerging adulthood is the age of possibilities is that it represents a crucial opportunity for young people who have experienced difficult conditions in their family lives to move away from home and to steer their lives in a different and more favorable direction before they enter the commitments in love and work that structure adult life. Children and adolescents are at the mercy of their parents to a large degree. The parents determine where the family lives, and consequently who the children's friends are likely to be and where the children go to school. The parents set the structure for daily life in the household, including household rules and customs and the consequences for violating them. If the parents do a reasonably adequate job of providing healthy conditions for development, the children are likely to reap the benefits. But if the parents are dysfunctional, if life goes wrong for them in any of the myriad ways life can go wrong in adulthood—high marital conflict, a bitter divorce, a substance use problem, a mental illness, a physical illness, difficulty finding a decent job, and so on—then the children suffer the consequences along with the parents. There is nothing the children can do about it; they cannot get away.

Until emerging adulthood, that is. Emerging adulthood is the age of possibilities in part because it represents a chance for young people to transform their lives, to free themselves from an unhealthy family environment, and to turn their lives in a new and better direction. Simply being able to leave home is a big part of it. Children and adolescents are unable to leave a destructive environment—it is, in fact, usually illegal for them to leave home unless the state assumes control of them—and if they run away from home they usually put themselves at high risk for numerous other problems (Whitbeck & Hoyt, 1999). But emerging adults have the maturity to live independently, and most do take advantage of this opportunity. There is, subsequently, immense diversity in the directions that people take their lives. In terms of well-being and life satisfaction, young people's lives are more likely to take a turn for the better than for the worse in the course of emerging adulthood (Schulenberg, O'Malley, Bachman, & Johnston, 2005). Thus emerging adulthood represents a great opportunity, even arguably a critical period, for the expression of resilience (see chap. 7).

Even for those who have come from relatively happy and healthy families, emerging adulthood provides an opportunity to transform themselves so that they establish an independent identity and make independent decisions about what kind of person they wish to be and how they wish to live. During emerging adulthood they have an exceptionally wide scope for making their own decisions. Virtually all emerging adults eventually will enter new, long-term obligations in love and work, and once they do their new obligations will set them on paths that resist change and that may continue for the rest of their lives. But while emerging adulthood lasts, they have a chance to change their lives in profound ways.

Regardless of their family background, all emerging adults carry their family influences with them when they leave home, which limits the extent to which they can change what they have become by the end of adolescence. Nevertheless, more than any other period of life, emerging adulthood presents the possibility of change. During this time the fulfillment of all hopes seems possible, because the range of their choices for how to live is greater than it has ever been before and greater than it will ever be again.

The Five Features: Empirical Support

How well do these five features of emerging adulthood hold up empirically? Alan Reifman of Texas Tech has developed a scale called the Inventory of Dimensions of Emerging Adulthood (IDEA; Reifman, Arnett, & Colwell, 2005). There are five subscales based on the features of emerging adulthood presented previously. A sixth subscale, Other-Focused, was created as a counterpoint to the Self-Focused subscale, to test the hypothesis that persons older than emerging adults would be more other-focused than emerging adults are.

In a series of studies (Reifman et al., 2005), exploratory and confirmatory factor analyses supported the coherence of the five features, along with the Other-Focused factor. Internal reliability and test–retest reliability were high. Furthermore, emerging adults were found to be significantly higher on all factors related to the five features (and lower on Other-Focused), compared with older adults, and were also distinct from adolescents (ages 13–17) on most factors. The scale is available at http://www.hs.ttu.edu/hd3317/IDEA.htm.

The Heterogeneity of Emerging Adulthood

Although I have described what I believe to be common patterns for the emerging adulthood age period as a whole, an understanding of subgroup and individual differences is essential to a complete understanding of emerging adulthood, because young people in this age period are extraordinarily diverse. I have proposed, in fact, that emerging adulthood is in part defined by its heterogeneity, that is, it is perhaps the period of life in which variance is greatest, in many aspects of development (Arnett, 2000a). Some emerging adults are in school and some are not; some are employed and some are not; some combine work and school; some are in a committed relationship and some are not; some live with a romantic partner, some live with friends, some live alone, some live with their parents. These variations in turn have implications for the variance that exists among them in psychological variables such as cognitive functioning, emotional well-being, and relationship satisfaction.

The diversity of emerging adults is in part a reflection of their freedom, that is, the lack of social control and the lack of strict norms for what they should be doing with their lives during these years (Arnett, 2005). Social control and social norms set boundaries for what is acceptable and punish behavior that is outside the boundaries. When the boundaries are broad, as they are in emerging adulthood, a wider range of individual differences is allowed expression, on the basis of a wider range of individual tendencies and preferences (see Arnett, 1995, in press). Thus, for example, adolescents are "supposed to be" not yet in a committed long-term romantic relationship and young adults past age 30 are "supposed to be" in one, but it is acceptable for emerging adults to be in a committed relationship, or not to be in one, or to be semi-committed, or any of a wide range of gradations along this continuum. Because of their freedom from social control and the lack of social norms for the 20s, emerging adulthood is the most volitional period of life, the time when people are most likely to be free to follow their own interests and desires, and those interests and desires lead them in an exceptionally wide range of directions.

An important issue arises from this heterogeneity. Given the diversity that exists during the years from ages 18 to 25, is it possible to call it a distinct developmental period with certain common features, as I have done by calling it emerging adulthood? I think it is both possible and desirable to do so, as long as it is recognized that along with the characteristics that are common to many of them, there is also great diversity among them in nearly every aspect of development. To some degree, diversity exists within every developmental period. We describe adolescents as living with their parents and attending secondary school, but of course some are homeless, some live with persons other than their parents, and some have dropped out of school. We describe young adults in their 30s as being married and having children, but some of them are either unmarried or childless or both unmarried and childless. We describe people at midlife as reaching a settled place in life and preparing for their children to leave home, but some people get divorced at midlife and their lives are anything but settled, and some have children who are nowhere near leaving home. We describe people in late adulthood as entering retirement, but many of them continue to work well into their 60s and 70s. For emerging adulthood, I think it can be usefully discussed and described as a developmental period, as long as the many exceptions to any generalization about it are kept in mind.

There is value to thinking about emerging adulthood as a separate developmental period despite its heterogeneity. Paradigms matter. They structure how we as researchers think and what we investigate and how we explain what we find in our research. They lead us toward certain research questions and away from others.

I believe it is because we have had no widely shared paradigm of the years from the late teens through the mid-20s as a separate developmental period that we have neglected it in research until recently. Research that has been done on this age period in the past has mainly conceptualized it as the transition to adulthood, and as a result there is a great deal of research on the timing of transition events such as finishing education, entering marriage, and entering parenthood. But the emerging adulthood paradigm results in a much broader agenda for research. It leads us to ask: What is their cognitive development like? How do their relationships with their parents change, compared with adolescence? How much time do they spend alone, and during their time alone, are they lonely? What are their friendships and romantic relationships like? How much do they use media such as TV and recorded music and the Internet, and for what purposes? And many, many other questions that span the whole range of human experience.

What if someone aged 18 to 25 is not engaged in identity explorations, or is not experiencing instability, or is not self-focused, or does not feel in-between, or does not see a future full of possibilities? Can that person still be considered an emerging adult? Yes, because the features I have proposed as developmentally prominent in emerging adulthood were not proposed as universal features of the age period. The heterogeneity of the age period must always be kept in mind. In our research, we should not only look for general patterns but also investigate different patterns among subgroups of emerging adults.

I look forward to other scholars adding ideas to what I have proposed regarding the salient developmental characteristics of emerging adulthood. This book is an important step in that direction, as the following chapters will show. What seems indisputable is that the median age of entering marriage and parenthood has risen dramatically and is now in the late 20s or beyond in the United States and every other industrialized country, that more people obtain at least some higher education than at any time in the past, and that people change jobs and love partners and residences more frequently in their 20s than in any later period of life. In my view, these facts are enough to merit recognition that a separate period of life now exists between adolescence and young adulthood. (I think *young adulthood* works well for the period following emerging adulthood, lasting until about age 40.) I think *emerging adulthood* works well as a term for this new period, and I have argued that previously proposed terms—*late adolescence, youth, young adulthood,* and *the transition to adulthood*—are all inadequate for various reasons (Arnett, 2004). *Early adulthood* has also been proposed (e.g., Settersten, Furstenberg, & Rumbaut, 2005), but it suffers from liabilities similar to those of the other terms, that is, the lack of a clear meaning that distinguishes it from adolescence or young adulthood. Coming of age in the 21st century is different than it has been in the past, and this new period of life requires a new term with a distinctive meaning, which is why I proposed *emerging adulthood*.

Using the term *emerging adulthood* does not mean embracing everything I have proposed about what it contains. I am committed to *emerging adulthood* as a useful term for 18- to 25-year-olds in industrialized societies, but what precisely this period holds developmentally is an exciting question we have only begun to explore.

Conclusion

Emerging adulthood is a fascinating time of life, full of changes and important decisions that have profound implications for how the rest of the life course will go. It is surprising, then, that it has been given so little attention until now by scholars interested in human development. Fortunately, this neglect has begun to be remedied in recent years, and this book is one reflection of the increased attention and enthusiasm devoted to the study of this age period. What I have put forward in this chapter is intended as one step toward building a new paradigm for emerging adulthood. I hope there will be many more steps to come, as we begin to build this new paradigm together in a community of scholars.

References

Arnett, J. J. (1994). Are college students adults? Their conceptions of the transition to adulthood. *Journal of Adult Development, 1,* 154–168.

Arnett, J. J. (1995). Broad and narrow socialization: The family in the context of a cultural theory. *Journal of Marriage and the Family, 57,* 617–628.

Arnett, J. J. (1997). Young people's conceptions of the transition to adulthood. *Youth & Society, 29,* 1–23.

Arnett, J. J. (1998). Learning to stand alone: The contemporary American transition to adulthood in cultural and historical context. *Human Development, 41,* 295–315.

Arnett, J. J. (2000a). Emerging adulthood: A theory of development from the late teens through the twenties. *American Psychologist, 55,* 469–480.

Arnett, J. J. (2000b). High hopes in a grim world: Emerging adults' views of their futures and of "Generation X." *Youth & Society, 31,* 267–286.

Arnett, J. J. (2001). Conceptions of the transition to adulthood: Perspectives from adolescence to midlife. *Journal of Adult Development, 8,* 133–143.

Arnett, J. J. (2003). Conceptions of the transition to adulthood among emerging adults in American ethnic groups. In J. J. Arnett & N. L Galambos (Eds.), *New directions for child and adolescent development: Vol. 100. Exploring cultural conceptions of the transitions to adulthood* (pp. 63–75). San Francisco: Jossey-Bass.

Arnett, J. J. (2004). *Emerging adulthood: The winding road from the late teens through the twenties.* New York: Oxford University Press.

Arnett, J. J. (2005). The developmental context of substance use in emerging adulthood. *Journal of Drug Issues, 35,* 235–254.

Arnett, J. J. (in press). Socialization in emerging adulthood: From the family to the wider world, from socialization to self-socialization. In J. Grusec & P. Hastings (Eds.), *Handbook of socialization*. New York: Guilford Press.

Arnett, J. J., & Taber, S. (1994). Adolescence terminable and interminable: When does adolescence end? *Journal of Youth and Adolescence, 23,* 517–537.

Associated Press. (2003, May 9). *University of Chicago survey says adulthood begins at age 26.* Retrieved May 9, 2003, from http://www.msnbc.com/news/911377.asp?0cv=CB20

Bianchi, S. M., & Casper, L. M. (2000). American families. *Population Bulletin, 55,* 1–44.

Bockneck, G. (1986). *The young adult: Development after adolescence.* New York: Gardner Press.

Brodrick, C. E. (2003). *Top 10 things to do before you turn 30.* Retrieved September 22, 2003, from http://www.bankrate.com/nsc/news/advice/19990531a.asp?

Bumpass, L. L., & Liu, H. H. (2000). Trends in cohabitation and implications for children's family contexts in the United States. *Population Studies, 54,* 29–41.

Côté, J. (2000). *Arrested adulthood: The changing nature of maturity and identity in the late modern world.* New York: New York University Press.

Côté, J., & Allahar, A. (1994). *Generation on hold: Coming of age in the late 20th century.* New York: New York University Press.

Erikson, E. H. (1950). *Childhood and society.* New York: Norton.

Erikson, E. H. (1959). Identity and the life cycle. *Psychological Issues, 1,* 1–171.

Erikson, E. H. (1968). *Identity: Youth and crisis.* New York: Norton.

Facio, A., & Micocci, E. (2003). Emerging adulthood in Argentina. In J. J. Arnett & N. L Galambos (Eds.), *New directions for child and adolescent development: Vol. 100. Exploring cultural conceptions of the transitions to adulthood* (pp. 21–31). San Francisco: Jossey-Bass.

Goldscheider, F., & Goldscheider, C. (1999). *The changing transition to adulthood: Leaving and returning home.* Thousand Oaks, CA: Sage.

Heckhausen, J. (1999). *Developmental regulation in adulthood: Age-normative sociostructural constraints as adaptive challenges.* New York: Cambridge University Press.

Hornblower, M. (1997, June 9). Great xpectations. *Time, 129*(23), 58–68.

Keniston, K. (1971). *Youth and dissent: The rise of a new opposition.* New York: Harcourt Brace Jovanovich.

Kerber, L. K. (1997). *Toward an intellectual history of women.* Chapel Hill: University of North Carolina Press.

Kiernan, K. (2002). Cohabitation in Western Europe: Trends, issues, and implications. In A. Booth & A. C. Crouter (Eds.), *Just living together: Implications of cohabitation on families, children, and social policy* (pp. 3–31). Mahwah, NJ: Erlbaum.

Larson, R. (1990). The solitary side of life: An examination of the time people spend alone from childhood to old age. *Developmental Review, 10,* 155–183.

Mayer, K. U. (2004). Whose lives? How history, societies, and institutions define and shape life courses. *Research in Human Development, 1,* 161–187.

Mayseless, O., & Scharf, M. (2003). What does it mean to be an adult? The Israeli experience. *New Directions in Child and Adolescent Development, 100,* 5–20.

Modell, J. (1989). *Into one's own: From youth to adulthood in the United States, 1920–1975.* Berkeley: University of California Press.

National Center for Education Statistics (NCES). (2002). *The condition of education, 2002.* Retrieved February 15, 2003, from http://www.nces.gov/pubs2002/2002025.pdf

National Center for Education Statistics (NCES). (2004). *The condition of education, 2004.* Retrieved November 3, 2004, from http://www.nces.gov/pubs2004/2004077.pdf

Nelson, L. J., Badger, S., & Wu, B. (2004). The influence of culture in emerging adulthood: Perspectives of Chinese college students. *International Journal of Behavioral Development, 28,* 26–36.

Popenoe, D., & Whitehead, B. D. (2001). *The state of our unions, 2001: The social health of marriage in America.* Retrieved December 7, 2004, from the National Marriage Project, Rutgers University Web site: http://marriage.rutgers.edu

Popenoe, D., & Whitehead, B. D. (2002). *The state of our unions, 2002.* Retrieved March 23, 2003, from the National Marriage Project, Rutgers University Web site: http://marriage.rutgers.edu

Reifman, A., Arnett, J. J., & Colwell, M. J. (2005). *The IDEA: Inventory of dimensions of emerging adulthood.* Manuscript submitted for publication.

Schulenberg, J. E., O'Malley, P. M., Bachman, J. G., & Johnston, L. D. (2005). Early adult transitions and their relation to well-being and substance use. In R. Settersten, F. Furstenberg, & R. Rumbaut (Eds.), *On the frontier of adulthood: Theory, research, and public policy* (pp. 417–453). Chicago: University of Chicago Press.

Settersten, R. A., Furstenberg, F. F., & Rumbaut, R. G. (2005). *On the frontier of adulthood: Theory, research, and public policy.* Chicago: University of Chicago Press.

Whitbeck, L. B., & Hoyt, D. R. (1999). *Nowhere to grow: Homeless and runaway adolescents and their families.* New York: Aldine de Gruyter.

White, M. (1993). *The material child: Coming of age in Japan and America.* Berkeley: University of California Press.

2

Recentering During Emerging Adulthood: A Critical Turning Point in Life Span Human Development

Jennifer Lynn Tanner

Arnett has proposed the concept of emerging adulthood as a new stage of the life course. His work highlights the force of culture, suggesting that industrialized cultures, predicated on broad socialization practices (Arnett, 1995; Arnett & Taber, 1994), and demographic shifts have created environments in which the life course has expanded to include a new stage of development, one that is unique and distinct from adolescence and young adulthood (Arnett, 1997, 1998, 2000, 2004). In essence, he argued that industrialized countries have institutionalized a preparatory stage that precedes young adulthood and that emerging adults experience as feeling in-between—feeling neither adolescent nor adult.

Arnett's theory offers a cross-sectional perspective of the population features of this era (i.e., the age of instability, identity, possibilities, self-focus, feeling in-between), including a description of the characteristics that 18- to 25-year-olds share as an age group. Arnett's proposition that emerging adulthood is a new developmental stage encourages a theoretical and empirical investigation of his theory from a developmental perspective. The developmental perspective takes the long view—focusing on intraindividual change and stability, variation in individual's developmental trajectories, and influences that modify and optimize development across the human life span (Baltes, Reese, & Nesselroade, 1988). If, indeed, emerging adulthood represents a new stage of the life course, the stage should not only be characterized by unique features but also be linked to prior and later development and adaptation.

The overarching goal of this chapter is to consider how emerging adulthood fits into life span development. The thesis of this chapter is that emerging adulthood is characterized by unique features and that this age period represents not only a stage of life span development but also a critical turning point.

Support for this chapter was provided by the National Institute of Mental health (NIMH R01 MH41569). Special thanks to Jeffrey J. Arnett, Helen Z. Reinherz, and Sasha R. Berger for their support in the development of this chapter.

Drawing on life events research, the first section of this chapter delves into explanations for consistent findings that emerging adulthood represents a peak period of occurrence of significant, marker life events in individuals' lives. These findings support the argument that emerging adulthood is a critical juncture in life span development when the relationship between the individual and society takes on a new meaning.

Toward an integration of emerging adulthood into life span theory, using a developmental systems framework, I propose the concept of recentering as the process that underlies emerging adults' gains in adult sufficiency. The process of recentering is conceptualized as a three-stage process, during which emerging adults make the transition from dependent adolescents to independent young adults. According to a definition that highlights the relational nature of emerging adult development, recentering is the critical and dynamic shift between individual and society that takes place across emerging adulthood during which other-regulated behavior (i.e., behavior regulated by parents, teachers, and society) is replaced with self-regulated behavior toward the goal of adult sufficiency, the ability to meet the demands of adulthood.

This chapter draws on recent empirical work that illustrates the dynamic yet highly variable paths that emerging adults take from dependence toward independence. Moreover, in this chapter, the recentering process is linked to two life span developmental processes (i.e., separation–individuation, ego development) in an effort to elucidate how the unique features of emerging adulthood are embedded within life span development from birth and to explore possible sources of variation in emerging adult development. Last, this chapter explores college as a context for emerging adulthood and asks what we can learn about modification of emerging adult development from the college student development literature. A summary and discussion of future research directions conclude the chapter.

The Critical Years of Emerging Adulthood

What meaning do the years of emerging adulthood hold compared with other decades of life span development? Emerging adulthood represents the years during which the most significant events of people's lives are most likely to occur. Findings from several studies reveal that significant, life-marker events most often occur during the third decade of life. Recent work by Grob, Krings, and Bangerter (2001), drawing on data from three Swiss cohorts, found that life-marker events were most commonly recalled between ages 20 and 29, increasing from infancy through the teens and decreasing in the fourth decade of life (Figure 2.1). Likewise, Fitzgerald and colleagues' work (Fitzgerald, 1984, 1988, 1996) revealed a "reminiscence bump" in memories of significant life-marker events occurring between ages 20 and 29, during emerging adulthood, and of these "benchmark memories" the three most significant life-marker events named were most likely to have occurred during emerging adulthood (Elnick, Margrett, Fitzgerald, & Labouvie-Vief, 1999).

Review of life events research provides insight into why the events of emerging adulthood are most often recalled as the most important. Martin and

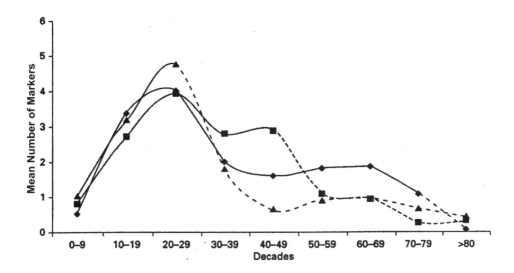

Figure 2.1.   Recall of life-marker events. Mean number of life markers reported for each life decade and cohort. Experienced decades are depicted in bold lines and expected decades in dashed lines. From "Life Markers in Biographical Narratives of People From Three Cohorts: A Life Span Perspective in Its Historical Context," by A. Grob, F. Krings, and A. Bangerter, 2001, *Human Development, 44,* p. 182. Copyright 2001 by Karger. Reprinted with permission.

Smyer (1989) reported similar findings and noted that the majority of significant life events named were traditional transition events such as marriage and first jobs. It is interesting that such life events do not surface as the significant markers of adulthood (Arnett, 1998) but that, with retrospective recall, these events are coded as very meaningful. Why?

Fitzgerald and colleagues concluded that these life events were coded as significant in individuals' memories because they occurred coincident with a key era of self-development. Erikson (1950) suggested that identity development may arise as an important developmental task during adolescence but that some people experience an extended period beyond adolescence during which identity explorations continue. Arnett (2004) contended that it is perhaps during emerging adulthood when identity explorations are most salient and that resolution of identity may be postponed as a function of emerging adult explorations. However, it is Blos (1962) who observed that "the transition from adolescence to adulthood is marked by an intervening phase, postadolescence, which can be claimed rightfully by both, and can be viewed from either of these two stages" (p. 148) and offered a key interpretation of the life events findings. He posited that the adolescent years are marked by explorations of identity, whereas the postadolescent years, which Arnett termed *emerging adulthood,* brings with them the consolidation of identity.

> In terms of ego development . . . the psychic structure has acquired by the
> end of late adolescence a fixity which allows the postadolescent to turn

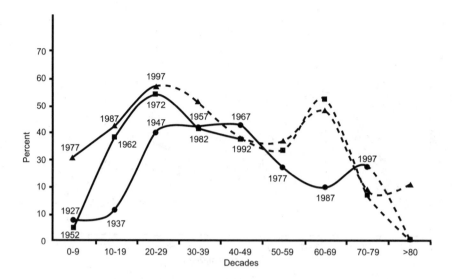

Figure 2.2. Perceptions of control over life marker events. Percentage of personally controlled life markers for each cohort and decade. Experienced decades are depicted in bold lines and expected decades in dashed lines. Historical time is indicated for each experienced decade and cohort. From "Life Markers in Biographical Narratives of People From Three Cohorts: A Life Span Perspective in Its Historical Context," by A. Grob, F. Krings, and A. Bangerter, 2001, *Human Development, 44,* p. 183. Copyright 2001 by Karger. Reprinted with permission.

> to the problem of harmonizing the component parts of personality. This integration comes about gradually. It usually occurs either preparatory to or coincidentally with occupational choice—provided that circumstances allow the individual any choice at all. The integration goes hand in hand with the activation of social role, with courtship, marriage, and parenthood. (p. 149)

Thus, it is at the end of the era of possibilities and exploration that the self consolidates around a set of roles and beliefs that define a relatively stable adult personality. The life events research suggest that this consolidation into an adult self is reflected in the significance of establishing careers, getting married, and becoming parents during these first years of adulthood.

To further investigate why life-marker events were most likely recalled during the 20s, Grob and colleagues considered the role of personal control. It is interesting to note that patterns of perceptions of control over life-marker events took the same shape as did the distribution of significant life events (Figure 2.2). These findings add to an understanding of emerging adulthood as a critical period of life span adjustment. These years represent a period of the life span during which individuals perceive having the most control over the significant events in their lives. In turn, the choices and decisions made during this era are considered life-marker events and define personal biographies across the life span. When findings are pulled together, it is clear that the emerging adult years represent a period during which individuals perceive control over the life events that, in turn, establish adult selves around traditional transitions into adult social roles.

Adulthood begins to take shape during the emerging adult years. Shanahan (2000) remarked that these years are an integral part of biographies that reflect the early experiences of youth and shape the rest of life. In essence, emerging adulthood seems to represent a unique turning point in human development when the exploratory nature of emerging adulthood gives way to commitments to adult roles. Life events research provides insight into the unique features of emerging adulthood from a life span perspective. In addition, interpretation of the findings leads one to consider how life changes from adolescence to emerging adulthood and from these years to young adulthood.

The Process of Emerging Adulthood: A Life Span Perspective

Whereas other scholars have also noted the lengthening of adolescence (Hamburg, 1989) and the increased variability in patterns of adult role transitions into adulthood over the past decades (Booth, Crouter, & Shanahan, 1999; Shanahan, 2000; Shanahan, Sulloway, & Hofer, 2000), Arnett's perspective on these years between 18 and 25 suggests that a new developmental period has emerged. His work (2000, 2004) has specified the population features of these years as the age of identity explorations, self-focus, possibilities, feeling in-between, and instability. If emerging adulthood is indeed a new developmental period then it is imperative to link emerging adulthood with the years that precede and follow this period as this is the way that life span human development is understood. That is, it is important to take a developmental perspective and ask: How does emerging adulthood fit into life span human development? How do these years link adolescence and adulthood?

Although scholars have long been interested in the distinction between adolescence and adulthood, there remains a lack of research on development across these years. One traditional schism that has limited research on development across the emerging adult year is the division of study between preadult (i.e., infant, child, adolescent) and adult development. Textbooks, courses, departments, training, assessment, and licensure in the field of psychology subscribe to this division. For example, the Society for Research in Child Development, the Society for Research on Adolescence,[1] and the Gerontological Society of America are outlets for scholarship on specific age period development—the distinction between research on child and adolescent development and adult development or aging is clear. This distinction and a lack of continuity in understanding development across the transition to adulthood is one barrier that has led to a lack of focus on the developmental processes that bridge adolescence and adulthood. Professional boundaries, rather than theoretically meaningful distinctions, have obfuscated the critical years of emerging adulthood, the years that connect childhood and adolescence to adult development.

---

[1] In 2000, a Special Interest Group on Emerging Adulthood (http://www.s-r-a.org/easig.html) was established through the Society for Research on Adolescence as a forum for the development of scholarship on emerging adult development.

Human developmentalists have sought to unify the study of preadult and adult development by proposing theories and models that coalesce the two developmental epochs. However, a second schism has presented an obstacle in developing an understanding of development postadolescence. Two theoretical camps offer contrasting perspectives on the attainment of adulthood. Life span theory has traditionally represented the psychological perspective, whereas life-course theory has traditionally represented the sociological perspective on development through these years (Mayer, 2003). These two theories have led to a division in work between sociologists' emphasis on transitions to adult roles (Settersten & Mayer, 1997; Smith, 2003) and psychologists' concern with the development of maturity (i.e., cognitive, ego, identity, and moral development; see Tilton-Weaver, Vitunski, & Galambos, 2001) as markers of adult status. Arnett's interdisciplinary model offers a framework for integrating perspectives.

One strength of Arnett's (2000) concept of emerging adulthood is that it incorporates psychological (i.e., identity) and sociological (i.e., geographic and occupational instability) features of this era while emphasizing the role of cultural conditions (i.e., industrialization, secularism) in shaping emerging adult experiences. To maintain the complexity of Arnett's view of this developmental period while taking on the goal of this chapter—to explore how this developmental period fits into life span development—one needs to invoke a lens that not only recognizes the complexity of emerging adulthood but also offers a framework for viewing development through the emerging adult years. The developmental systems perspective (Lerner, 2002) offers such a lens. In this contemporary developmental framework, "the person is not biologized, psychologized, or sociologized" nor culturalized; "rather, the individual is 'systematized'—that is, his or her development is embedded within an integrated matrix of variables derived from multiple levels of organization . . ." (Lerner, 1998, p. 1). In terms of emerging adulthood, the developmental systems perspective highlights the complexity of influences on developmental experiences during this era with particular emphasis on the continuity of individual development influenced by transactions between individuals and their contexts.

Most important, the developmental systems framework stresses the relational nature of development—key to understanding emerging adult development from a life span perspective. Arnett uses the expressions "learning to stand alone," "self-sufficiency," and "independence" to characterize the tasks of emerging adulthood. Data have been presented consistently that indicate that the criteria of adulthood represent progress toward independence rather than transitions to adult roles: The criteria "accept responsibility for one's self," "financial independence," "independent decision-making," "general independence/self-sufficiency," and establishing an "independent household" are the top five (Arnett, 1998, p. 305). However, the relational nature of the criteria of adulthood should not be overlooked.

From the individual's perspective, momentum toward the task of achieving independence is clear. However, from a developmental perspective, which emphasizes the underlying process of becoming adult, the relational nature of this task is striking. What is understated in these characteristics ascribed to adult status is that emerging adulthood is the process of transferring from dependent to independent status in regard to emerging adults' relationships with their parents. That is, emerging adults are involved in the task of becoming responsible for oneself (in contrast to sharing responsibility for one's actions with parents), becoming financially independent from parents, gaining self-sufficiency (in contrast to dependency on parents), and establishing a household independent from parents. In essence, the process of attaining adulthood happens in relation to others and roles important to the emerging adult (i.e., families-of-origin).

Inherent to the developmental systems framework is the centrality of parent–child relations as the most proximal and instrumental shaping force on individual development. The impact of these interactions on emerging adult development is no exception. Unlike theories of family development (i.e., Carter & McGoldrick, 1999), which consider power relations (between parents and children) central to understanding dynamics of both individual and family development, theories of individual development traditionally underemphasize the power shift that occurs at the beginning of the transition to adulthood. However, this very shift "from childlike dependence on the family-of-origin to the autonomies of adulthood" (Shanahan, 2000, p. 2) characterizes the uniqueness of emerging adulthood from a life span developmental systems perspective. At no other period of the life span do the relations between the individual and contexts of development (i.e., family) shift as they do at the beginning of emerging adulthood.

I propose that the heart of this shift is the process of recentering and that recentering is the primary task of emerging adulthood from a life span developmental systems perspective. Recentering constitutes a shift in power, agency, responsibility, and dependence between emerging adults and their social contexts—primarily experienced by emerging adults as a period during which parent regulation is replaced with self-regulation. Building on Arnett's concept of emerging adulthood as the era of learning to stand alone, as well as Blos's (1967) conceptualization of this era as the second separation–individuation process and Ausubel's (1996) model of desatellization, the process of recentering captures and highlights the integrated and relational nature of the process, one that puts at the center of the process the relationship between individual and context. The process can be summarized as a shift in orientation between emerging adults and their environments, during which time they gain self-direction within the systems in which they are involved. A three-stage process of recentering is proposed.

At the end of adolescence and the beginning of emerging adulthood, Stage 1, the individual is embedded within the family-of-origin. Responsibility for the pre-emerging adult child and adolescent remains with parents, teachers, and the community (Figure 2.3a). Prior to emerging adulthood, parents are legally responsible for the behavior, adjustment, development, and care of their dependent children. At age 18 (in American society), social and legal responsibility are transferred to the individual when the individual becomes independent, from the perspective of social responsibility for one's own behavior. Social expectations toward emerging adults begin to change, beginning with the arrival of legal responsibility that emerging adults are forced to take for their behavior. With great variability between emerging adults and across

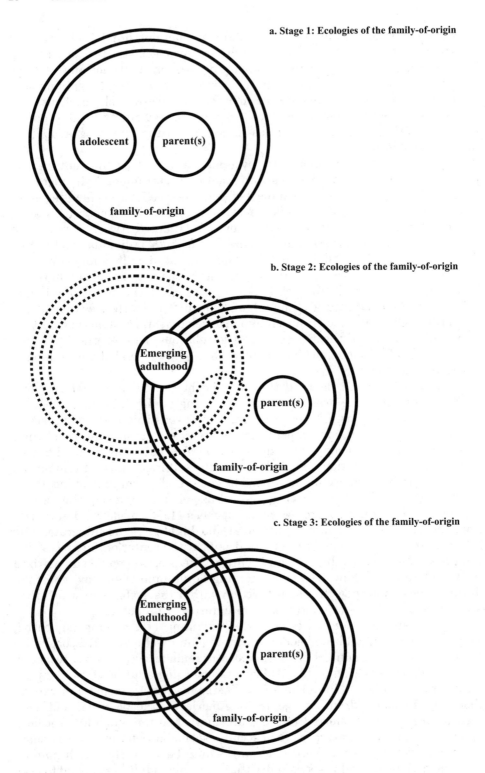

Figure 2.3. The recentering process: Stage 1 (a), Stage 2 (b), and Stage 3 (c).

the contexts in which they are involved, expectations for emerging adults to become self-governing adults (McCandless, 1970) begin to increase at the transition into emerging adulthood. Recentering highlights the intersection of the psychological experience of becoming responsible for self (in the sense of striving to be self-sufficient) and the sociological demand of taking responsibility for self (in the sense of becoming accountable for one's actions).

Gould (1978, p. 45) noted the critical shift between adolescence and emerging adulthood: "until the age of 16 or 18, we have only been the lowly actors in our lives—others have been the producers, directors, and screenwriters." Although the developing person is always an agent (Brandstaedter & Lerner, 1999), at the threshold of emerging adulthood is a gain in self-directedness. Making progress toward financial independence, a set of personal values and beliefs, and equal relationships with parents are characteristics strongly associated with becoming adult in industrialized societies (Arnett, 1997) as these tasks support emerging adults' abilities to progress toward adult sufficiency away from the dependence of adolescence.

Emerging adulthood proper, Stage 2, can be characterized, according to Arnett (2000), by emerging adults' involvements in systems of education, occupation, and intimate relations that are exploratory and temporary in nature. From a developmental systems perspective, "the age of identity explorations and instability" differs from adolescence as it is relatively free from the contextual structures (e.g., family, school) of earlier years. Rather, transitory enrollment in several different college majors and programs, employment in several different types of work, and involvement with different intimate partners reflect the real-life experiences of many emerging adults (Arnett, 2004). Figure 2.3b shows the tenuous nature—denoted by the dashed and incomplete lines—of these system involvements. These commitments to partners and jobs are temporary rather than permanent as they are constructed in response to the exploratory temper of this period. Also, as illustrated, the emerging adult remains connected to, but no longer embedded within, his or her family-of-origin and contexts of adolescence.

During this stage of the recentering process, the parent–child relationship confronts a unique challenge. As the boundaries of an emerging adult's adult self and adult commitments have yet to be confirmed, ties to one's family-of-origin for financial and other support challenge the emerging adult to question, Do I make decisions for myself or according to my parents' directives? In turn, parents are in the process of renegotiating an adult relationship with their emerging adult child, a relationship in which adult children are afforded the freedom to make choices and decisions based on their own values and beliefs. However, emerging adults often require ongoing partial or full financial support from parents, involving them in the lives of their emerging adult children to the extent that the support parents are giving is used in a way that is acceptable to parents. Here murky territory between parents and emerging adults often leads to conflicts different than those of adolescence. Parent–child conflict during adolescence most often revolves around the concrete tasks and rules of daily functioning (i.e., chores, curfew; Smetana, 1989) in terms of adolescents wanting autonomy to set their own rules. In contrast, the conflicts of emerging adulthood revolve more around the psychological component of establishing self as a separate, yet connected, individual (i.e., the separation–individuation process). What may seem like a conflict between parents and an emerging adult child about living arrangements—perhaps whether the emerging adult should come home between semesters or live with friends—has a psychological subtext for both parents and emerging adults: When is the appropriate time for emerging adults to make their own decisions based on their own values and beliefs?

The choices and commitments to adult roles and beliefs that emerging adults make have a dual effect: First, the emerging adult is moving toward lifelong commitments that will characterize one's adulthood; second, the boundaries between the emerging adult and the family-of-origin are becoming more definite. At the same time, emerging adults gain resources to support themselves through a career or other means of adult sufficiency, and boundaries between emerging adults and their families-of-origin gain clarity, which leads to the final stage of the recentering process.

At the close of the recentering process, emerging adulthood gives way to young adulthood, Stage 3, marked by system commitments—firm and long-lasting binders to careers, intimate partners, and (for most but not all) children (Figure 2.3c). These commitments, marked by solid lines to denote the permanence of these ties to others and to roles, stand in contrast to those of emerging adulthood when instability is more characteristic. The effect of these transitions to adult roles is that they place new demands on the young adult. These commitments encourage a young adult to maintain a consistent self, one who meets the expectations of and responsibilities to these system commitments, which replaces the exploratory self of emerging adulthood. In terms of the gains and losses of life span development (Baltes, 1987), giving up the exploratory self, reflected in young adults' fears of getting old, may be the essence of what is traded—the instability of emerging adulthood for the stability underlying the momentum of adulthood.

Indeed, emerging adulthood as the age of identity explorations, instability, possibilities, and self-focus stands in contrast to demands of adult system commitments. As Eccles, Templeton, Barber, and Stone (2003) noted, a new type of relational self-reliance, or adult interdependence, needed for one's own well-being and the parenting of the next generation, brings to a close the emerging adult period. The exploration of emerging adulthood gives way to consolidation of a system organized around the emerging adult's life choices and decisions that structure the starting point of adult pathways. In return, the gains in independence of the individual during emerging adulthood lead to commitments to new systems that mark the beginning of young adulthood. Young adulthood, then, is the stage of the life course during which individuals embark on the first stage of true adulthood, when behavior is regulated toward maintaining self and the systems to which one becomes committed; in return, the systems to which the individual is committed sustain the life of the individual.

The recent empirical work of Cohen, Kasen, Chen, Hartmark, and Gordon (2003) highlights the gradual process of recentering during emerging adulthood. Drawing on data collected from over 200 narrative interviews, the re-

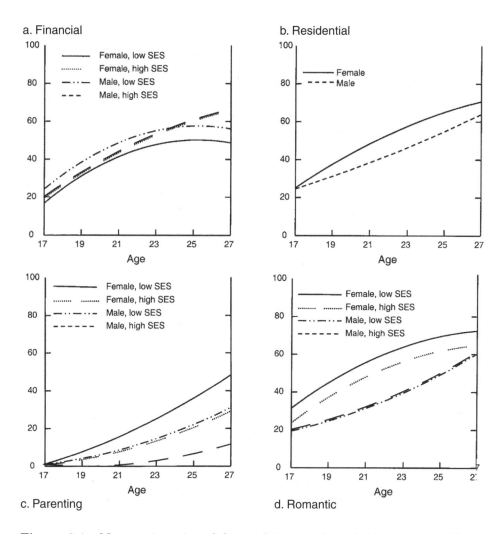

a. Financial

b. Residential

c. Parenting

d. Romantic

Figure 2.4. Mean trajectories of financial (a), residential (b), parenting (c), and romantic (d) domains. From "Variations in Patterns of Developmental Transitions in the Emerging Adulthood Period," by P. Cohen, S. Kasen, H. Chen, C. Hartmark, and K. Gordon, 2003, *Developmental Psychology, 39,* pp. 665–666. Copyright 2003 by the American Psychological Association.

searchers rated emerging adults' behaviors in four domains on a scale from behavior "more like that of a child" to "approximated fully adult role behavior, defined by independence of parental control, expression of own goals and preferences, and assumption of responsibilities" (p. 660). When trajectories of gains in independence from parents from ages 17 to 27 were mapped, findings revealed linear increases in independence from ages 17 to 27 in residential, financial, romantic, and parenting domains for both males and females, illustrated in Figures 2.4a through 2.4d, respectively. These overall trends indicate that, at the crudest level (taking least into account individual trajectories) there is a general trend toward increases in independence[2] for emerging adults as a group.

Beyond the group, or average, trajectories of emerging adult experiences, the complexity and heterogeneity that Arnett suggested is central to the emerging adult experience comes into focus from maps of individual trajectories of emerging adults' progress toward adult system commitments (Figures 2.5a–2.5d). As noted by Cohen et al. (2003), "despite the gradual increase in the extent to which the *average* [emerging adult] had assumed adult roles in these four domains, the actual progression of individuals was much more variable, moving back and forth between increasing and decreasing dependence" (p. 668). These data clearly support Arnett's proposition that emerging adulthood is a period of great variability. Replete with progression and regression, emerging adults make variable progress toward financial and residential independence and marriage and parenthood.

Although progress toward adult independence and roles is highly differential within the population of emerging adults, census data (U.S. Bureau of the Census, 2000) indicate that by age 30 the majority of the emerging adult population has made transitions to marriage and parenthood. These transitions to adult roles, in turn, affect individuals' senses of reaching adulthood (Arnett, 1998, 2001; Greene, Wheatley, & Aldava, 1992). As indicated by Arnett's work (2000), by the late 20s and early 30s only a small percentage of respondents do not see themselves as adults and approximately one third report "both yes and no."

These data tell a story of increasing independence during emerging adulthood and emphasize the variance in individual pathways that emerging adults take moving into adulthood. Altogether, this empirical work validates emerging adulthood as a critical turning point in the human life span. Review of these findings reveals that the emerging adult years are marked by gradual, linear gains in independence toward control over one's life and a gradual shift away from childlike dependence in terms of educational and occupational events and changes with families and relationships. Review also reveals great variability in recentering.

But why such variation? Taking a life span developmental systems perspective supports the investigation of this question by the consideration of the factors that influence the development of the individual prior to emerging

---

[2] Cohen et al. (2003) provided additional analysis of the breakdown in trajectories of independence by sex and by socioeconomic status. Although not germane to this chapter it is worth noting several broad findings of interest: (a) young women showed earlier residential independence associated with earlier financial independence, but young women never ascended to the same level of financial independence as men because support from partners became a substantial contributor to their financial independence; (b) there were no differences in residential independence between low and high SES groups although the two groups may have achieved independence differently; that is, higher SES emerging adults move out of the home sooner, but to semi-independent statuses (i.e., college) and lower SES emerging adults move out later, but also to semi-independence through financial contributions to the household; and (c) higher SES emerging adults were significantly slower to take on marriage and parent roles.

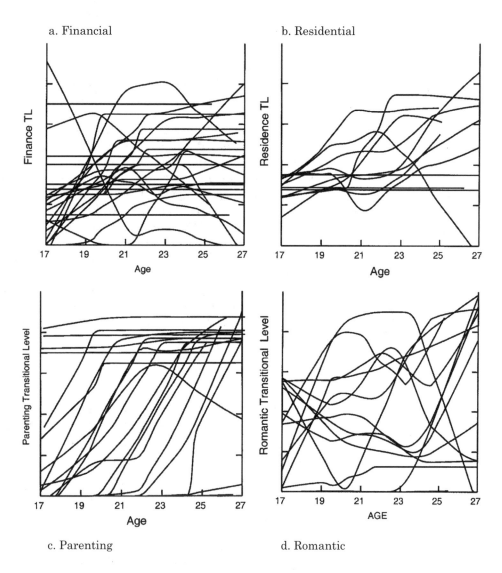

a. Financial

b. Residential

c. Parenting

d. Romantic

Figure 2.5. Individual trajectories of financial (a), residential (b), parenting (c), and romantic (d) domains. From "Variations in Patterns of Developmental Transitions in the Emerging Adulthood Period," by P. Cohen, S. Kasen, H. Chen, C. Hartmark, and K. Gordon, 2003, *Developmental Psychology, 39,* pp. 665–666. Copyright 2003 by the American Psychological Association.

adulthood. Going back to the hypothesis that the process underlying the transition to adulthood is recentering, the following section reviews research that explores variation in emerging adult development from two sources, family (i.e., separation–individuation) and individual (i.e., ego development) characteristics. The chapter now turns to a discussion of how the recentering process relates to separation–individuation and ego development.

Variation in Emerging Adulthood

Central to the thesis of this chapter, that emerging adulthood is a critical period of life span development, is the notion that emerging adult development builds on all previous and affects all future development. Following from this proposition, in this section of the chapter I tie the recentering process to the life span processes of parent–child separation–individuation and psychosocial development (i.e., ego development). The goal of linking the primary developmental task of emerging adulthood to these life span processes is to bring attention to two likely sources of variation in emerging adult experiences. Not all emerging adulthoods are created equal. Those emerging adults with developmental histories that have prepared them for recentering approach adulthood with a different set of resources than do those emerging adults with compromised developmental histories. At the threshold of these years, past experiences of self in relation to society have been established and account for individual differences in approaches to the task of recentering. Two literatures—separation–individuation (a family-level characteristic) and ego development (an individual-level characteristic)—provide insight into associations between past developmental experiences and variation in emerging adults' abilities to recenter toward adult sufficiency.

Separation–Individuation

As noted, recentering takes center stage as the critical developmental task during emerging adulthood, a task that involves a relational restructuring between the emerging adult and his or her family-of-origin. The concept of recentering closely resembles the separation–individuation process, which

> minimally involves a renegotiation of relationships with caregivers. The press toward individuation requires the young adult to shed parental dependencies, yet this should not come at the expense of close familial ties. Rather, the goal of individuation is relational autonomy, whereby independence and self-governance are affirmed within the content of continuous, mutually validating relationships. (from Josselson, 1988, as quoted in Lapsley & Edgerton, 2002, p. 485)

The difference is that the process of recentering is embedded in a developmental systems framework, to highlight the relational, the give and take, between the emerging adult and his or her contexts.[3]

---

[3]The difference between the concepts is that recentering maintains that the process is relational. A measure of recentering is, by definition, relational and a systems-level variable that describes the extent to which an emerging adult is embedded within the family-of-origin and how established new system commitments are. Recentering takes into account relations both to one's past systems (i.e., parents, school) and to one's future systems (i.e., work, partners, children). Separation–individuation, in contrast, is generally considered an individual-level variable that describes a level of differentiation of self from family.

Findings from a longitudinal study of associations between parent support for and adolescent progress toward separation–individuation reveal that healthy separation–individuation predicts adjustment and the ability to gain adult-sufficiency in emerging adulthood. O'Connor, Allen, Bell, and Hauser (1996) found that adolescents who had difficulty establishing relations with parents characterized by balanced separation and individuation (at age 16; note that the authors refer to this process as autonomous-relatedness) reported very close contact (e.g., not characteristic of healthy emerging adult individuation) with their parents as young adults and lower relationship satisfaction with fathers (at age 25). In the same study, separation–individuation (at age 14) was associated with educational attainment and occupational prestige during emerging adulthood (Bell, Allen, Hauser, & O'Connor, 1996). And again, data from the same longitudinal study revealed that having a secure attachment style, associated with the ability to establish healthy and well-functioning intimate relationships during emerging adulthood (age 25), was associated with progress toward separation–individuation during adolescence (age 14; Allen & Hauser, 1996). Separation–individuation seems to predict not only intimate relationships but also adjustment to marriage for emerging adults. These findings indicate that the separation–individuation process that begins in adolescence and is usually resolved as a task of emerging adulthood is highly predictive of variation in emerging adults' progress toward recentering and adult-sufficiency. Close relations with parents that border on enmeshment and a lack of educational and occupational resources clearly impede an emerging adult's ability to recenter and make progress toward the establishment of adult system commitments (i.e., intimate relationships). It can be extrapolated from this research that some emerging adults, those characterized by parents who support separation–individuation, look different from emerging adults with parents who do not support separation–individuation, which explains some of the variation in emerging adults' abilities to recenter and gain adult sufficiency.

The majority of studies that have investigated links between separation–individuation and adjustment during emerging adulthood have relied on college student samples. Given the limitation of reliance on this specialized group of emerging adults, the literature on separation–individuation of college students clearly illustrates the association between feeling individuated from one's family and feeling like an adult. Moore's (1987) research based on 391 college students' endorsement of the importance of 34 items in describing the extent to which they had separated and individuated from their parents revealed that Self-Governance was the factor most strongly associated with feeling that one had established a self separate from parents. Items that loaded onto the self-governance factor were Feeling Mature Enough, Feeling Like an Adult, Having To Do Things for Self Now, Being Independent, Making My Own Decisions, and Having To Take Care of Myself. In contrast, emotional detachment from parents (i.e., No Longer Being Attached to Family, Not Feeling Close to Family, Breaking Ties to Family, Feeling of not Belonging at Home Anymore, Feeling of Being a Visitor When at Home, Not Seeing Family Very Often) was least associated with feeling individuated from one's parents, underscoring the relational nature of the recentering process. Note that relations with one's family-of-origin are maintained in the developmental process.

In another foundation study that linked separation–individuation to college student adjustment, Lapsley, Rice, and Shadid (1989) reported that separation–individuation from parents occurs along multiple dimensions,[4] that increases in separation–individuation occur from freshman to senior year of college (although not uniformly), and that there are sex differences in separation–individuation between mothers and fathers and daughters and sons. Drawing on a sample of undergraduate emerging adults, Perosa, Perosa, and Tam (2002) found that indices of emerging adults' sense of individuation from family were associated with 32% to 55% of the variance in identity development. Using the same measure (Personal Authority in the Family System Questionnaire; Bray, Williamson, & Malone, 1984), Fraser and Tucker (1997) found that individuation was associated with problem-solving abilities in college students and concluded that "highly individuated college students and students who are good problem solvers may share certain characteristics. Perhaps parents who allow their children to achieve optimal levels of individuation also promote a strong sense of responsibility, self-confidence, and optimism in their children that leads to their adeptness at problem-solving" (p. 466). In sum, findings from research with college students reveal that separation–individuation is associated with resources that will help emerging adults make strides toward adult-sufficiency.

Although the process of recentering is central to emerging adulthood, it is important to note that separation–individuation is a life span process that begins at birth (Mahler, 1975; Spitz, 1959). In addition, these early experiences bring about transformations in parent–child relationships through adolescence and emerging adulthood, and result in parent–adult child relationships defined more by mutuality than hierarchy (Hill & Holmbeck, 1986). As Stierlin (1974) noted, "we conceive of separation in adolescence as part of a continuous movement toward relative mutual individuation in which parents and children participate. The ultimate aim is mature interdependence of the parties" (p. 173). Stierlin's seminal contributions to the literature on the effects of parent interactions on adolescent and emerging adult development were predicated on the hypothesis that parents' constraining interactions (i.e., withholding, overindulgence) inhibit, whereas parents' enabling interactions (i.e., explaining, empathy) support maturation and by *maturation,* Stierlin was referring to ego development. Ego development is a life span developmental process, one that describes individuals' orientations toward autonomy and independence

---

[4]Hoffman (1984) published the Psychological Separation Inventory, a widely used measure of separation–individuation. The measure has been successfully used to demonstrate four dimensions of separation–individuation from parents: Functional Independence (the ability to manage and direct one's personal and practical affairs with minimal assistance from parents), Emotional Independence (freedom from excessive need for approval, closeness, and emotional support in relation to parents), Conflictual Independence (freedom from excessive guilt, anxiety, resentment, responsibility, and anger in relation to parents), and Attitudinal Independence (the image of oneself as unique from parents and having one's own set of beliefs, values, and attitudes); the subscales were differentially associated with adjustment (Moore, 1987).

that represents a second source of variation (an individual-level characteristic) in emerging adults' pathways and progress toward adult sufficiency.

Ego Development

Ego development is a life span process that has roots at birth and is influenced by parenting behaviors during childhood (Dubow, Huesmann, & Eron, 1987; Kremen & Block, 1998) and adolescence (Hauser, Powers, Noam, Jacobson, Weiss, & Follansbee, 1984). Ego development is a master trait (Loevinger, 1976) that integrates previous interactions and guides future interactions between the individual and the environment. Second only in importance to intelligence in explaining human functioning, the theory of ego development integrates multiple perspectives of human development (i.e., Sullivan, Freud, & Piaget; see Hauser, 1993) and is proposed as an index of individuals' psychological mindedness (ability to understand self and world in psychological terms; i.e., "my work is part of my identity" vs. "I work to make money"), integration and synthesis of perceptions and cognitions, and agency or active mastery (Hauser, 1993).

> Trends in ego development can be discerned in terms of increases in internalization of rules of social intercourse, cognitive complexity, tolerance of ambiguity, and objectivity. In addition, the individual's impulse control becomes progressively guided by self-chosen, long-term intentions, accompanied by an enhanced respect for individual autonomy and an interest in genuine mutuality. (Hauser, Borman, Jacobson, Powers, & Noam, 1991, p. 98)

The task of recentering requires the emerging adult to organize and self-regulate one's efforts toward the task of gaining adult sufficiency. Whereas progress toward the developmental tasks of childhood and adolescence (i.e., moral development and educational progress) is scaffolded by institutions (i.e., family, school), emerging adults are challenged to scaffold their own progress from adolescence to adulthood. Because of the importance of agency, active mastery, self-regulation, and impulse control as predictors of adult sufficiency, higher levels of ego development should be considered a core component in understanding differences between those who do well in emerging adulthood and those who flounder. In sum, ego development can be considered an underlying, life span developmental characteristic predictive of emerging adults' potentials to learn to stand alone.

Over the course of the individual life span, experiences are integrated and consolidated by ego development, which results in variation in individuals' senses of mastery over the environment and abilities to cope with and be flexible in relation to the environment. After adolescence, the emerging adult stands related to, but no longer nested within, the family-of-origin. As emerging adults recenter toward adult sufficiency, they stand at the beginning of emerging adulthood with all previous interactions and experiences between self and environment neatly organized in the ego (Bockneck & Perna, 1994, p. 30). It follows that higher levels of ego development should be associated with the ability to take on the task of recentering and adult sufficiency.

Exhibit 2.1. Emerging Adults' Autonomy Strivings as a Function of Ego Development

Preconformist EAs	Conformist EAs	Postconformist EAs
"the needy and volatile affect was striking. . . . These girls felt inadequate, insecure, and not in control of themselves or their lives. . . . Although they all had handled the academic challenges of high school, none seemed confident in her ability to function independently in college." (p. 328)	"felt that it was necessary to submerge their real thoughts and feelings [about going away to college] in order to maintain their attachment to their parents. . . . These adolescents were struggling to separate and individuate from their families, yet appeared caught in inner conflicts that mitigated against their autonomous development." (p. 335)	"felt eager to move on to the next phase of their lives . . . appeared to feel confident about their adequacy to function autonomously, while still recognizing their sadness about leaving home." (p. 341)

Note. EA = emerging adult. Data from Lasser and Snarey (1989).

Linking life span ego development to emerging adult experiences contributes a frame for understanding variation in emerging adults' orientation toward autonomy and independence. Qualitative findings from Lasser and Snarey's (1989) study of female high school seniors' strivings for autonomy when making the transition to college revealed significant differences between emerging adults' pathways toward independence as a function of ego development. The authors compared three groups of emerging adults: those with immature (preconformist), moderate (conformist), and mature (postconformist) levels of ego development. It was expected that higher levels of ego development would be associated with healthier autonomy strivings and greater adaptation to the challenge of transition to college. Indeed, emerging adults with higher levels of ego development were more comfortable with the task of learning to stand alone, whereas emerging adults at lower levels of ego development were less comfortable. Exhibit 2.1 illustrates differences in emerging adults' orientations toward autonomy and ego development.

The quotations in Exhibit 2.1 clearly indicate differences in emerging adults' capacities for and orientations toward adult sufficiency. Those emerging adults less mature in terms of their ego development are much less prepared to take on the task of a large step toward independence, the transition to college. In contrast, those at more mature levels of ego development recognize the losses associated with the gains in independence that will come their way as a result of the transition. Furthermore, these findings link a developmental process, ego development, to the core task of emerging adulthood, recentering, highlighting the developmental strand that links earlier life experiences to emerging adult experiences. Ego development, therefore, that occurs prior to emerging adulthood has some predictive validity in determining emerging adults' initial orientations toward experiences of gaining adult sufficiency.

There is evidence to indicate that ego development is also predictive of the ability to apply skills and resources that support emerging adults' abilities to engage in exploratory commitments (i.e., relationship and friendships). In terms of emerging adults' interpersonal relations, Schultz and Selman (1998) found that, at age 23, higher levels of ego development were related to greater skill negotiating needs for autonomy and relatedness and balancing these relationship dimensions in close peer and intimate relationships. The authors noted that individuals at "lower stages of ego development have limited abilities to relate to others, with a progression to higher levels at which individuals have strengths that facilitate intimate, collaborative relationships . . ." (Schultz & Selman, 1998, p. 181). As well, Hennighausen, Hauser, Billings, Schultz, and Allen (2004) reported that those emerging adults who had reached higher levels of ego development during adolescence were rated as more flexible and less hostile by their peers and reported more complex and maturing interpersonal styles at age 25. In sum, those emerging adults with higher levels of ego development are better at developing the relational, temporary system commitments that allow emerging adults to explore their identities and possibilities.

In addition, Helson and Roberts (1994) linked ego development at age 21 to higher levels of and increases in characteristics associated with maturation toward adult sufficiency not only during emerging adulthood but into midlife as well. As can be seen from Figure 2.6, higher scores on ego development were associated with Responsibility and Achievement via Independence. Individuals who score high on responsibility are more reasonable and responsible and take their duties more seriously than do those low on this measure. Those who score high on Achievement via Independence have stronger drives to do well and like to work in environments that encourage individual initiative than do those lower on this index. Both of these characteristics, associated with higher levels of ego development, have clear implications for success in meeting the tasks of emerging adulthood.

These studies underscore the significance of ego development during emerging adulthood and the impact that ego development has on critical features of emerging adulthood—educational and occupational achievement, interpersonal functioning, and personality characteristics associated with adult sufficiency. Research on associations between life span ego development and emerging adult resources and adjustment indicates that ego development prior to emerging adulthood predicts emerging adults' abilities to take on the tasks of this developmental period and meet them with success. The following section highlights the continuity of ego development during emerging adulthood and the important role that ego development plays in shaping success and adaptation through emerging adulthood into young adulthood.

Ego Development and Life Goals

As emerging adults make strides toward adult sufficiency, the need to structure and guide their own life increases and the ability to do so motivates them to formulate life plans that guide them through emerging adulthood into young

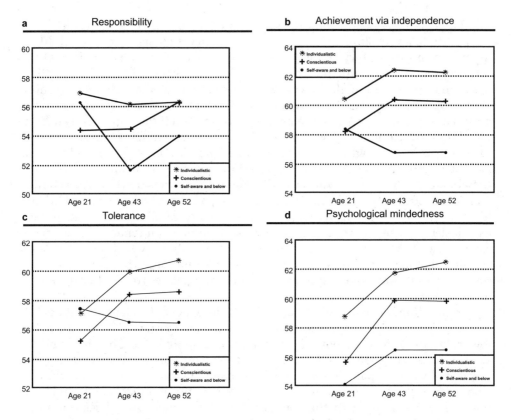

Figure 2.6. Ego development from emerging adulthood to midlife. Panels a–d: Change shown by ego-level groups in responsibility, tolerance, achievement via independence, and psychological mindedness. Means are given in standard score form (M = 50, SD = 10), on the basis of norms from a representative sample of 2,000 men and women (Gough, 1987). From "Ego Development and Personality Change in Adulthood," by R. Helson and B. W. Roberts, 1994, *Journal of Personality and Social Psychology, 66,* pp. 911–920. Copyright 1994 by the American Psychological Association.

adulthood. In light of the link between the tasks of emerging adulthood and life span development, the ego takes on a new task of emerging adulthood— laying out a life plan toward adult sufficiency:

> At late adolescence, these [ego] processes lead to a delimitation of goals definable as life tasks; while at postadolescence, the implementation of these goals in terms of relationships, roles, milieu choices become the foremost concern. The ego . . . now becomes conspicuously and increasingly absorbed by these endeavors. (Blos, 1962, p. 151)

Arnett (2004) drew attention to the importance of the plan during emerging adulthood. It is during these years that emerging adults lay out life plans, or dreams, for their futures. Others, as well, have suggested that the formation of this life plan is critical to the postadolescent years. For example, Wittenberg

(1968) labeled this process the establishment of a *weltanschauung*, or a life philosophy that was used to guide individuals through adulthood. This same notion, that the landscape of emerging adulthood motivates individuals to formulate a life dream, is described in Daniel Levinson's stage theory of adult development.

Levinson's (1978) original intent, which resulted in his well-known theory of adult development, was to study midlife development. However, interviews with midlife men revealed the importance of the emerging adult years in establishing adult pathways. He concluded that during the emerging adult years, which he called the novice phase, formation of a dream, "a vague sense of self-in-adult-world" (p. 91), is developed and that the task of the following years is "giving it [the dream] greater definition and finding ways to live it out" (p. 91). Although Levinson's (1996) adult study of women's development did not emphasize the dream for women as it did for men, Plunkett's (2001) analysis of women's career development postcollege emphasized the salience of women's inner scripts as guides across these critical years.

Nurmi (1993) proposed a systems perspective to describe how emerging adults formulate life plans by focusing on the construction of personal goals. Personal goals are defined as individuals' motivations for certain goals that will meet individuals' needs and have the potential to be actualized in regard to opportunities available (see Pulkkinen, Nurmi, & Kokko, 2002). Noting both personal agency and opportunity structure as defining influences, Nurmi (1993) suggested that emerging adults set goals that reflect the specific tasks (Havighurst, 1972) of the developmental period. Roisman, Masten, Coatsworth, and Tellegen (2004) have since presented evidence that the developmental tasks of emerging adulthood include both salient (i.e., friendship, academic, and conduct) and emerging (i.e., occupational and romantic) developmental tasks.

During the emerging adult years, possibilities are explored and goals are established. Constructing a set of goals, activating the goals, evaluating goals and achievements, and reflecting on one's progress are the four stages of the self-definition process that is activated during life transitions (Nurmi, 1997). In turn, this model (Figure 2.7) suggests that individual's abilities to deal with the goal construction, actualization, and evaluation of one's life have implications for success and mental health during this developmental period. In sum, the extent to which emerging adults are able to establish life plans during emerging adulthood—that is, an emerging adult's ability to meet the developmental challenge to the ego for this developmental stage—should be associated with adjustment. Future research that explores associations between emerging adults plans for the future, agency in carrying out the plan, and adjustment will help to shed light on the salience of the plan during this developmental period.

In regard to the developmental systems framework, the notion of the individual-in-context arises when considering the developmental task that lies in front of emerging adults: to establish a plan that leads to adult sufficiency and to carry out this plan. The context that is most often associated with emerging adulthood is the college environment. Acknowledging that institutional contexts are established to support the developmental needs of age groups (i.e., nursery schools for preschool children, nursing homes for the

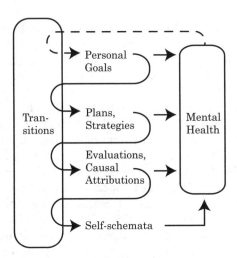

Figure 2.7. Nurmi's model of self-development and mental health. From *Health Risks and Developmental Transition During Adolescence* (p. 397), edited by J. Schulenberg, J. L. Maggs, and K. Hurrelmann, 1999, New York: Cambridge University Press. Copyright 1997 by Cambridge University Press. Reprinted with permission.

elderly), the college context, often considered a dominion of self-exploration, is most commonly associated with the emerging adult period. If some emerging adults are afforded the opportunity to attend college and some are not, and college is an environment that supports emerging adult development (i.e., exploration, identity, possibilities, establishing life plans), then exploration of the differences between emerging adults enrolled in college versus those who are not enrolled is a worthy avenue for exploring variation in emerging adult development.

College as a Context of Emerging Adulthood

The questions that arise are as follows: In light of the variation in experience of emerging adults, do contextual opportunities available (e.g., cultural, historical) define whether an individual will have an emerging adulthood? Moreover, do contextual opportunities available define the length of an individual's emerging adulthood? Last, do opportunities available predict emerging adult adjustment?

Arnett's work suggests "in some respects yes, in some respects no." He acknowledged that education, both undergraduate and graduate training, supports exploration and delay of adult role commitments—key elements of emerging adulthood. However, Arnett also suggested that emerging adulthood is a concept useful for understanding the experiences of the "forgotten half"—those who do not attend college after high school (W. T. Grant Foundation, 1988)— as well as the experiences of postcollege young adults prior to an individual's engagement in adult roles. Arnett's goal in presenting the theory of emerging adulthood is to bring scholarly attention to an age period that has previously been studied almost exclusively with college student samples, which suggests that there are universal developmental principles that bridge the college and noncollege populations during this age period. Are there?

Teasing apart the role of context in emerging adulthood from the characteristics of the age period is important. If the concept of emerging adulthood is inextricably linked to the college student experience, the concept of emerging adulthood adds little to the body of knowledge of development between ages 18 and 25 above and beyond that established in the college student development literature[5] (Chickering, 1969; see Evans, Forney, & Guido-DiBrito, 1998). However, if the concept of emerging adulthood can be disentangled from the college student experience, then how is the college experience, and education in general, associated with emerging adult development?

To address this important question, one needs to distinguish the developmental features of this period from the contexts of emerging adulthood, highlighting the variation in development that can occur as a function of emerging adults' involvements with different (college vs. noncollege) contexts. Research that offers comparisons of developmental outcomes between college and noncollege emerging adults should offer insight. One study by Klerman and Karoly (1994) reported findings from the National Longitudinal Study of Youth (NLSY) of emerging adult men comparing the two groups. Drawing on a subsample of males who participated in the NLSY, males who entered the labor market before high school graduation were compared with males who entered the labor market after high school graduation and after completion of college in regard to their occupational stability. Results revealed that, regardless of highest level of education completed (i.e., high school dropout, high school graduate, some college, college graduate), all emerging adults experienced a period of "milling about" and multiple job transitions after educational completion. It is interesting to note that those emerging adults with the least education experienced the greatest number of job transitions. This finding suggests that one population feature of emerging adulthood as proposed by Arnett (2000)—instability in terms of occupational transitions—holds true for both college-student and non-college-student emerging adults.

A second finding from this same study further indicates that educational attainment has an impact on the age of instability in that it seems to curtail the exploration associated with emerging adulthood. Klerman and Karoly (1994) found that as soon as it was feasible (i.e., posteducational completion), those with the most education reported the highest job stability (i.e., length of time in same job). In some respects, those with the least education experienced the longest period of occupational instability; in other words, higher academic attainment was associated with accelerated commitments to careers.

Also offering comparisons between college-bound and non-college-bound emerging adults, Gore and colleagues (Gore, Aseltine, Colton, & Lin, 1997)

---

[5]For example, models of psychosocial (Chickering, 1969) and cognitive–structural (Perry, 1968) development have been advanced as theoretical frameworks for understanding college student development.

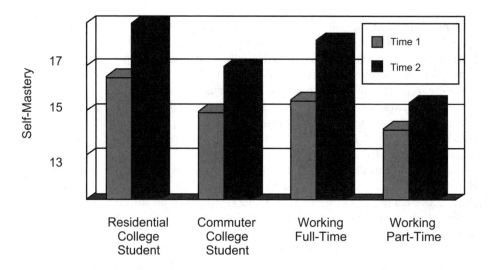

Figure 2.8. Self-mastery change post-high-school. From *Stress and Adversity Over the Life Course* (p. 206), edited by I. H. Gotlib and B. Wheaton, 1997, New York: Cambridge University Press. Copyright 1997 by Cambridge University Press. Adapted with permission.

investigated changes in sense of mastery from high school (Time 1) to 2 years post-high-school (Time 2). The authors used Sense of Mastery as the index of adaptation, interpreting emerging adults' perceptions of agency as a measure of competence. They investigated whether emerging adults' sense of mastery increased over time and whether or not it was associated with their post-high-school role commitments. The findings were interesting. As can be seen in Figure 2.8, there was a significant overall increase in self-mastery after high school graduation across groups. This finding is consistent with the earlier reviewed life events research that indicated increases in sense of control following adolescence. Second, these findings indicated that increases in self-mastery are significantly higher in the groups that made the transition to full-time college and those who made the transition to full-time work compared with part-time commuter students and part-time and unemployed groups. It can be inferred from this research that gains in self-mastery are optimized by contexts that afford full-time gains in self-governance.

In sum, the population features of emerging adulthood seem to hold true for both college-student and non-college-student emerging adults in terms of their progress toward increasing self-governance. Such findings indicate that taking on roles that support gains in self-sufficiency from parents—whether it is the geographical distance of college or the financial independence of a paycheck—promotes the primary developmental task of emerging adulthood. What is important about these studies, toward understanding variation in emerging adult experiences, is that, in contrast to sharing population features of emerging adulthood (i.e., instability, gains in control), college-bound and non-college-bound emerging adults, by definition, do not share contexts of emerging adulthood. These studies support Arnett's claim that the population features of emerging adulthood cut across both college-student and non-college-student emerging adults. There is also evidence, however, that the context of college may impact pathways of emerging adult development. That is, whereas college and noncollege emerging adults may look alike in terms of the population features of the developmental period (e.g., feeling in-between, explorations), the different contexts in which they are involved during this developmental era may be associated with differences in their development and adjustment both during and following this age period.

According to the literature available, several features of the college-bound trajectory are linked with features of emerging adulthood that do not hold true for non-college-bound youth. First, college has an indirect effect on development because educational involvement during these years delays system commitments. College and graduate student enrollment delays transitions to marriage (Gaughan, 2002; Thornton, Axinn, & Teachman, 1995) and parenthood (Marini, 1984; Wu & Macneill, 2002). Such delays in system commitments (i.e., marriage and parenthood) extend the period of emerging adulthood, protracting the period of exploration. In turn, some research suggests that delay of system commitments or exploration before commitment is associated with adjustment across adulthood.

In addition to the indirect effect of college—extending emerging adulthood—college also has a direct effect on development (Arnstein, 1980; see Pascarella & Terenzini, 1991, for a review). College experience has been associated with ego development (Whitbourne & Tesch, 1985), identity development (Hood, Riahinejad, & White, 1986), moral development (Rest & Navarez, 1991), and cognitive development (Pascarella, Bohr, Nora, & Terenzini, 1995). Although more research needs to be conducted to flesh out preexisting differences in college-bound versus non-college-bound enrolled emerging adults that are sometimes attributed to differences between the two groups associated with college, college experience is positively and significantly related to increases in psychosocial development.

In his well known model of college student development, Chickering (1969) suggested that the college context supports development along seven vectors: developing competence, managing emotions, moving through autonomy toward interdependence, developing mature interpersonal relationships, establishing identity, developing purpose, and developing integrity. It is interesting to note that these vectors of development map onto the master trait of ego development. If the theoretical proposition holds true, that differences between college- and non-college-educated adults will be reflected in developmental differences, this proposition should be supported by empirical findings. Indeed, Holt's (1980) empirical comparison of college and noncollege emerging adults (ages 16–25) revealed that the proportion of emerging adults rated at the higher levels of ego development were more likely to have attended college. As can be seen in Figure 2.9, emerging adults were more likely to be at higher levels of ego development if they had attended college.

This latter finding supports the hypothesis that college has a significant effect on emerging adult development. Consistent with the proposition that emerging adulthood is an extension of prior experience, inherent differences

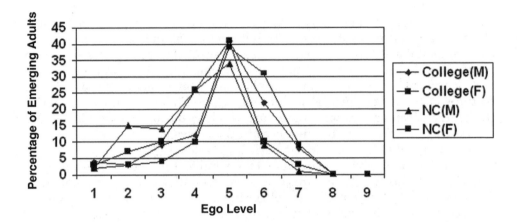

Figure 2.9. Comparison of ego development between college and non-college emerging adults. Data adapted from "Loevinger's Measure of Ego Development: Reliability and National Norms for Male and Female Short Forms," by R. R. Holt, 1980, *Journal of Personality and Social Psychology, 39*, pp. 909–920. Copyright 1980 by the American Psychological Association.

between college- and non-college-bound emerging adults exist prior to these years that, in turn, determine who does and does not attend college. In addition to adolescent-era characteristics that differentiate college-bound from non-college-bound individuals, there is evidence that these differences in trajectories of individuals who will and will not be exposed to the development-promoting effects of college during emerging adulthood are established in the earliest years of life. For example, Duncan and colleagues' work (see Duncan & Brooks-Gunn, 2000), drawn from the Panel Study of Income Dynamics, revealed that highest level of educational attainment was significantly predicted by family income—not family income during adolescence, but during the first 5 years of life—after controlling for a variety of other family factors. It is important to keep in mind that differences between emerging adults may be meaningful in terms of both concurrent and future adjustment, but in many cases, the roots of these differences are developmental and lie in the earliest years of life.

Teasing apart the context of college and emerging adult development is important because although the features of emerging adulthood may be the same for college- and non-college-enrolled emerging adults, experiences and developmental trajectories may be different. Put forth as one hypothesis in this chapter, I argue here that beyond variation in emerging adults at the beginning of emerging adulthood (i.e., parent–child interactions, ego development, parent socioeconomic status [SES]), differences in contexts of emerging adulthood (i.e., college vs. no college) increase the spread, or variability, in emerging adult differences already visible before emerging adulthood. Individual differences in preparedness for the tasks of emerging adulthood may explain some variation in the pathways that emerging adults take from adolescence to adulthood toward adult sufficiency. Simply put, some emerging adults have more resources (i.e., developmental, financial) that help them to recenter than do others. These same resources (i.e., autonomy, identity, self-esteem, family SES), in turn, influence whether development is supported by an emerging adult's context. Together, differences in starting points before emerging adulthood as well as experiences during emerging adulthood interact to increase the spread between those who go into emerging adulthood more or less advantaged. In sum, it is possible that early factors can predict who becomes forgotten during emerging adulthood and that contexts of emerging adulthood that do not continue to promote development further divides emerging adult populations. Research that tests this spread hypothesis will help indicate whether support for emerging adult development and adjustment should be aimed at adolescents (or even children) or whether interventions with emerging adults are the most fruitful for helping them achieve their potentials.

Taking the perspective that the forgotten half may be left behind long before emerging adulthood has implications for how we, as professionals, think about shaping lives and fostering development during these years. The W. T. Grant Foundation (1988) has urged researchers to think about the challenges that the forgotten half face during the transition to adulthood. The Annie E. Casey Foundation (2004) recently drew attention to specific non-college-bound groups (i.e., teens in foster care, youth involved in the juvenile justice system, teen parents, and high school dropouts) who are especially vulnerable because they are disconnected from institutions that foster development and adjustment during the transition to adulthood. The spirit of working toward a greater understanding of emerging adult development emphasizes the significance of supporting the potential of all emerging adults, rather than a restricted focus on college student development and adjustment. Keeping with the goals of developmental science, I consider in the following section whether elucidating how the college environment meets the needs of emerging adults might lead to an understanding of ways that development can be supported, even optimized, during this period.

Modifying and Optimizing Emerging Adult Development

Because emerging adulthood is a critical turning point in human development, the extent to which these years coincide with development before taking on system commitments has implications for life span development. In short, emerging adulthood may further accentuate the differences between college-bound youth and the forgotten half. Emphasizing the association between emerging adulthood as a developmental stage and college as a context of emerging adulthood furthers an understanding of how the college environment, for example, is a modifier of emerging adult development rather than a defining feature of this period.

From this perspective, college is one ecological niche available to individuals who have the resources to delay entry into adult roles, rather than a niche that defines emerging adulthood. Emerging adulthood is the age of feeling in-between, instability, identity explorations, self-focus, and possibilities (Arnett,

2004). In addition, the college environment has the potential, for some, to facilitate explorations, soul-searching, and optimism about one's potential to change the world. College has this effect on emerging adults, it is widely believed, because it is in this supportive context that emerging adults are exposed to people, ideas, and experiences that challenge their expectations and worldviews. Much like the formula for healthy parenting, effective teaching, successful management, and coaching, the college environment has the potential to buttress emerging adult development by simultaneously providing support and challenge, which results in more advanced identity and ego development. Although the existence of college environments that combine support and challenge may not characterize the college experience for all (or even most) students, it is important to observe that that these are the elements of a successful college experience, one that promotes optimal development during these years.

If this formula supports emerging adult development, can these factors converge in noncollege contexts? Yes. According to the mentoring literature (e.g., Parks, 2000), one special relationship can define an emerging adult's trajectory toward success (Handel, 1990). Levinson (1978) underscored the significance of men establishing a mentor relationship during the emerging adult years, with mentors who would champion their careers and support them in the challenging climb up the corporate ladder. Referring back to Klerman and Karoly's (1994) work, non-college-bound emerging adults' exposure to multiple jobs should increase their opportunities for gaining a mentor, one who helps the individual and guides the individual toward adult stability. In one potential solution to a lack of scaffolding for noncollege adults, the forgotten half may benefit the most from an institutional and cultural shift that encourages and rewards adults for mentoring emerging adults. Although currently society is not structured to mentor emerging adults into young adulthood, the college student development model combined with meaningful interactions with mentors is one potential model for supporting development of both college- and non-college-enrolled emerging adults. Understanding that emerging adulthood is a developmental period during which individuals benefit from exploring themselves and possibilities in love and work before they make commitments implies that resources should be established (e.g., public policies, workplace initiatives, counseling opportunities) to encourage the developmental and adjustment of all emerging adults. In this critical turning point in the life span, the years during which adult pathways are established, all emerging adults should be encouraged to develop a plan and accrue resources that will help them to carry out their plan toward adult self-sufficiency.

Conclusion: Emerging Adulthood as a Critical Turning Point in the Human Life Span

The first steps of adulthood are taken during the emerging adult years. According to life events research, these first steps significantly affect pathways of adulthood, leaving indelible marks on individuals' memories from these critical years. In light of the significance of this era on life span development, it is important to understand how development occurs during this age period and the influences that support both emerging adult and life span adjustment.

To elucidate the developmental processes that come into play during this critical era of development, I have made the overarching goal of this chapter to link population features of emerging adulthood to theoretical and empirical notions of the ways that emerging adults change between adolescence and emerging adulthood. The key idea presented is that recentering is the process that defines individual change during emerging adulthood and that life span processes underlie individual variation.

The significant feature of this critical turning point is the changing nature of the relationship between the individual and society. Prior to emerging adulthood, the individual is dependent on and regulated by parents, teachers, and the laws of society. During emerging adulthood, the individual accrues experience and prepares for self-governance with variable amounts of support still available from parents (i.e., financial gifts) and institutions (i.e., college). As resources from parents decline and the emerging adult ages out of institutions that structure the development and goals of emerging adults (this can be high school or college), there is a push and a pull for emerging adults to make commitments to systems that afford them a way to support themselves. Indeed, this absence of control (i.e., parental) and presence of strain (i.e., need to financially support oneself) has been associated with commitments to adult roles (Hagan & Wheaton, 1993). Thus, the earlier that support for development ends, the shorter the emerging adult period and the earlier young adulthood begins. In turn, the amount and quality of exploration, linked to development during emerging adulthood, has implications for development and adjustment across the adult years.

By establishing the task of recentering as the primary developmental task of emerging adulthood, we, in the field, can begin to focus on forces that shape and influence emerging adults' success and adaptation. Future research should elucidate early precursors to healthy emerging adult development and adjustment—that is, the characteristics and experiences of childhood and adolescence that are most related to healthy emerging adult development. Although this chapter has linked family individuation and ego development to emerging adult adjustment, a good deal remains to be learned about the influence of cognitive, social, interpersonal, physical, moral, spiritual, and self-development during childhood and adolescence on emerging adult experience.

Over a decade ago, Nurmi (1993) reviewed Greene and colleagues' (1992) research on adolescents' perceptions of adult status and observed that "no research has so far been carried out on the extent to which these beliefs [about adult status] influence how young people set personal goals, plan their future lives, and evaluate pertinent goal attainment" (pp. 179–180). This gap remains; very little is known about pathways through emerging adulthood—how individuals get from adolescence to young adulthood. The three-stage process of recentering offers a framework for understanding how individuals make the transition into emerging adulthood, experience the developmental period of emerging adulthood, and transition from emerging adulthood into young and later adulthood. Research that focuses on the plans that adolescents make for themselves, revise in emerging adulthood, and carry out in young adulthood should provide insight into more and less adaptive pathways through this critical age period.

Taking a life span perspective on emerging adulthood reveals many frontiers of research. For instance, Cohen et al.'s (2003) work on gains and variability in independence from ages 17 to 27 lend support to the proposition that the key developmental process of emerging adulthood is recentering—the reestablishment of self-in-adult-system, committed to social contexts that, in turn, support adult development and adjustment. What is not known is whether these gains in independence are the steepest between ages 18 and 25. For example, midlife and later life may represent steep increases in independence from commitments established during the emerging adult years (i.e., commitments to careers, intimate relationships, and adult children). To compare trajectories toward independence, one needs to rely on longitudinal data that can describe pathways into, across, and from emerging adulthood.

Also, because the concept of emerging adulthood has only recently been proposed, can it be assumed that the contemporary features of development between ages 18 and 25 are associated with the same pathways of life span adjustment that past cohorts experienced or future cohorts will experience? That is, what impact does an elongated emerging adulthood have on life span adjustment? One hypothesis is that greater exploration during the emerging adult years may lead to system commitments characterized by better fit than were system commitments made during the early 20s. However, the opposite may be true. Perhaps delayed commitments to marriage and parenthood represent risk factors for poor mental health. Because previous research suggests that marriage promotes stability, which, in turn, fosters mental health (Horwitz, Raskin-White, & Howell-White, 1996), delayed marriage may postpone the protective nature of a committed relationship. Given the contemporary landscape of the years between ages 18 and 25, the association between exploration and commitment has the potential to be further complicated. For example, delayed commitments to marriage ultimately are tied to a greater number of partners, greater personal identity development, and a longer time to establish habits and preferences that are unique to the individual—all experiences that may lead to difficulties compromising and prioritizing others over self, key components of healthy marriages and partnerships. Because delay of transitions to adult roles may have been different for past versus contemporary generations, it will be important to examine how emerging adult experiences prior to system commitments affect adjustment during young adulthood.

Past research has been skewed toward understanding the development and adjustment of college students. Parsing apart the context of college from emerging adult development leads one to look at the viability of models designed to support college student development and adjustment and to ask whether these same models can be used to support the development of non-college-bound adults. Or do alternative models need to be developed to support the recentering of this latter group? Arnett's contribution of the concept of emerging adulthood supports such investigations and progress to be made in the direction of understanding the complex intersection between emerging adults and their contexts, and cultural and subcultural variations.

In sum, I have argued that emerging adulthood is a unique period of life span human development. Variations in emerging adults' abilities to recenter, to learn to stand alone, have been linked to the process of life span ego development. In turn, the roots of emerging adulthood have been exposed, as they are planted in early family experiences. Moreover, I have argued that the lack of ecological constraints frees up an emerging adult to explore possibilities and spend time focusing on self-development and that, in contrast, system commitments to adult roles and relationships change the association between age and development at this critical turning point.

In light of the critical nature of these years, it is striking that more empirical work has not focused on these pivotal years. Arnett's contribution has opened a dialogue about the complexity and salience of the third decade of life, the launching pad of adulthood. I have sought, in this chapter, to make a strong case for emerging adulthood as a unique stage of development, one that poses a specific task to the ego—to gain self-governance. It is my hope that this work can bring to light the importance of interactions with emerging adults and lead the field to consider ways to scaffold their development and facilitate the understanding of the importance of this period, when adult pathways begin.

References

Allen, J. P., & Hauser, S. T. (1996). Autonomy and relatedness in adolescent-family interactions as predictors of young adults' states of mind regarding attachment. *Development and Psychopathology, 8,* 793–809.

Annie E. Casey Foundation. (2004). Moving youth from risk to opportunity. *Kids Count 2004 data book online.* Baltimore: Author.

Arnett, J. J. (1995). Broad and narrow socialization: The family in the context of a cultural theory. *Journal of Marriage and the Family, 57,* 617–628.

Arnett, J. J. (1997). Young people's conception of the transition to adulthood. *Youth & Society, 29,* 1–23.

Arnett, J. J. (1998). Learning to stand alone: The contemporary American transition to adulthood in cultural and historical context. *Human Development, 41,* 295–315.

Arnett, J. J. (2000). Emerging adulthood: A theory of development from the late teens through the twenties. *American Psychologist, 55,* 469–480.

Arnett, J. J. (2001). Conceptions of the transition to adulthood: Perspectives from adolescence to midlife. *Journal of Adult Development, 8,* 133–143.

Arnett, J. J. (2004). *Emerging adulthood: The winding road from the late teens through the twenties.* New York: Oxford University Press.

Arnett, J. J., & Taber, S. (1994). Adolescence terminable and interminable: When does adolescence end? *Journal of Youth and Adolescence, 23,* 517–537.

Arnstein, R. L. (1980). The student, the family, the university, and the transition to adulthood. *Adolescent Psychiatry, 8,* 160–172.

Ausubel, D. (1996). *Ego development and psychopathology.* New Brunswick, NJ: Transaction.

Baltes, P. B. (1987). Theoretical propositions of life-span developmental psychology: On the dynamics between growth and decline. *Developmental Psychology, 23,* 611–626.

Baltes, P. B., Reese, H. W., & Nesselroade, J. R. (1988). *Life-span developmental psychology: Introduction to research methods.* Hillsdale, NJ: Erlbaum.

Bell, K. L., Allen, J. P., Hauser, S. T., & O'Connor, T. G. (1996). Family factors and young adult transitions: Educational attainment and occupational prestige. In J. A. Graber & J. Brooks-

Gunn (Eds.), *Transitions through adolescence: Interpersonal domains and context* (pp. 345–366). Hillsdale, NJ: Erlbaum.

Blos, P. (1962). *On adolescence: A psychoanalytic interpretation.* New York: Free Press.

Blos, P. (1967). The second individuation of adolescence. *Psychoanalytic Study of the Child, 22,* 162–186.

Bockneck, G., & Perna, F. (1994). Studies in self-representation beyond childhood. In J. M. Masling & R. F. Bornstein (Eds.), *Empirical perspectives on object relations* (pp. 29–58). Washington, DC: American Psychological Association.

Booth, A., Crouter, A. C., & Shanahan, M. J. (Eds.). (1999). *Transitions to adulthood in a changing economy: No work, no family, no future?* Westport, CT: Praeger Publishers.

Brandstaedter, J., & Lerner, R. M. (1999). *Action and self-development: Theory and research through the life span.* Thousand Oaks, CA: Sage.

Bray, J. H., Williamson, D. S., & Malone, P. E. (1984). Personal authority in the family system: Development of a questionnaire to measure personal authority in intergenerational family processes. *Journal of Marital and Family Therapy, 10,* 167–178.

Carter, B., & McGoldrick, M. (1999). Overview: The expanded family life cycle: Individual, family, and social perspectives. In B. Carter & M. McGoldrick (Eds.), *The expanded family life cycle: Individual, family, and social perspectives* (pp. 1–26). Boston: Allyn & Bacon.

Chickering, A. W. (1969). *Education and identity.* San Francisco: Jossey-Bass.

Cohen, P., Kasen, S., Chen, H., Hartmark, C., & Gordon, K. (2003). Variations in patterns of developmental transitions in the emerging adulthood period. *Developmental Psychology, 39,* 657–669.

Dubow, E. F., Huesmann, L. R., & Eron, L. D. (1987). Childhood correlates of adult ego development. *Child Development, 58,* 859–869.

Duncan, G. J., & Brooks-Gunn, J. (2000). Family poverty, welfare reform, and child development. *Child Development, 71,* 188–196.

Eccles, J., Templeton, J., Barber, B., & Stone, M. (2003). Adolescence and emerging adulthood: The critical passage ways to adulthood. In M. H. Bornstein, L. Davidson, C. L. M. Keyes, & K. A. Moore (Eds.), *Well-being: Positive development across the life course* (pp. 343–406). Mahwah, NJ: Erlbaum.

Elnick, A. B., Margrett, J. A., Fitzgerald, J. M., & Labouvie-Vief, G. (1999). Benchmark memories in adulthood: Central domains and predictors of their frequency. *Journal of Adult Development, 6,* 45–59.

Erikson, E. (1950). *Childhood and society.* New York: Norton.

Evans, N. J., Forney, D. S., & Guido-DiBrito, F. (1998). *Student development in college: Theory, research, and practice.* San Francisco: Jossey-Bass.

Fitzgerald, J. M. (1984). Autobiographical memory across the lifespan. *Journal of Gerontology, 39,* 692–698.

Fitzgerald, J. M. (1988). Vivid memories and the reminiscence phenomenon: The role of a self narrative. *Human Development, 31,* 261–273.

Fitzgerald, J. M. (1996). Intersecting meanings of reminiscence in adult development and aging. In D. C. Rubin (Ed.), *Remembering our past: Studies in autobiographical memory* (pp. 360–383). New York: Cambridge University Press.

Fraser, K. P., & Tucker, C. M. (1997). Individuation, stress, and problem-solving abilities of college students. *Journal of College Student Development, 38,* 461–468.

Gaughan, M. (2002). The substitution hypothesis: The impact of premarital liaisons and human capital on marital timing. *Journal of Marriage and the Family, 64,* 407–419.

Gore, S., Aseltine, R., Colton, M. E., & Lin, B. (1997). Life after high school: Development stress, and well-being. In I. H. Gotlib & B. Wheaton (Eds.), *Stress and adversity over the life course* (pp. 197–214). New York: Cambridge University Press.

Gough, H. G. (1987). *Manual for the California Psychological Inventory.* Palo Alto, CA: Consulting Psychologists Press. (Original work published 1957)

Gould, R. (1978). *Transformations.* New York: Simon & Schuster.

Greene, A. L., Wheatley, S. M., & Aldava, J. F. (1992). Stages on life's way: Adolescents' implicit theories of the life course. *Journal of Adolescent Research, 7,* 364–381.

Grob, A., Krings, F., & Bangerter, A. (2001). Life markers in biographical narratives of people from three cohorts: A life span perspective in its historical context. *Human Development, 44,* 171–190.

Hagan, J., & Wheaton, B. (1993). The search for adolescent role exits and the transition to adulthood. *Social Forces, 71,* 955–980.

Hamburg, D. (1989). Preparing for life: The critical transition of adolescence. *Crisis, 10,* 4–15.

Handel, A. (1990). Formative encounters in early adulthood: Mentoring relationships in a writer's autobiographical reconstruction of his past self. *Human Development, 33,* 289–303.

Hauser, S. T. (1993). Loevinger's model and measure of ego development: A critical review: II. *Psychological Inquiry, 4*(1), 23–30.

Hauser, S. T., Borman, E. H., Jacobson, A. M., Powers, S. I., & Noam, G. G. (1991). Understanding family contexts of adolescent coping: A study of parental ego development and adolescent coping strategies. *Journal of Early Adolescence, 11,* 96–124.

Hauser, S. T., Powers, S. I., Noam, G. G., Jacobson, A. M., Weiss, B., & Follansbee, D. J. (1984). Familial contexts of adolescent ego development. *Child Development, 55,* 195–213.

Havighurst, R. J. (1972). *Developmental tasks and education.* New York: David McKay.

Helson, R., & Roberts, B. W. (1994). Ego development and personality change in adulthood. *Journal of Personality and Social Psychology, 66,* 911–920.

Hennighausen, K. H., Hauser, S. T., Billings, R. L., Schultz, L. H., & Allen, J. P. (2004). Adolescent ego-development trajectories and young adult relationship outcomes. *Journal of Early Adolescence, 24,* 29–44.

Hill, J. P., & Holmbeck, G. N. (1986). Attachment and autonomy during adolescence. *Annals of Child Development, 3,* 145–189.

Hoffman, J. A. (1984). Psychological separation of late adolescents from their parents. *Journal of Counseling Psychology, 31,* 170–178.

Holt, R. R. (1980). Loevinger's measure of ego development: Reliability and national norms for male and female short forms. *Journal of Personality and Social Psychology, 39,* 909–920.

Hood, A. B., Riahinejad, A. R., & White, D. B. (1986). Changes in ego identity during the college years. *Journal of College Student Personnel, 27,* 107–113.

Horwitz, A. V., Raskin-White, H., & Howell-White, S. (1996). Becoming married and mental health: A longitudinal study of a cohort of young adults. *Journal of Marriage and the Family, 58,* 895–907.

Josselson, R. (1988). The embedded self: I and thou revisited. In D. K. Lapsley & F. C. Power (Eds.), *Self, ego, identity: Integrative processes too* (pp. 91–108). New York: Springer.

Klerman, J. A., & Karoly, L. A. (1994). Young men and the transition to stable employment. *Monthly Labor Review, 117,* 31–48.

Kremen, A. M., & Block, J. (1998). The roots of ego-control in young adulthood: Links with parenting in early childhood. *Journal of Personality and Social Psychology, 75,* 1062–1075.

Lapsley, D. K., & Edgerton, J. (2002). Separation–individuation, adult attachment style, and college adjustment. *Journal of Counseling and Development, 80,* 484–493.

Lapsley, D. K., Rice, K. G., & Shadid, G. (1989). Psychological separation and adjustment to college. *Journal of Counseling Psychology, 36,* 286–294.

Lasser, V., & Snarey, J. (1989). Ego development and perceptions of parent behavior in adolescent girls: A qualitative study of the transition from high school to college. *Journal of Adolescent Research, 4,* 319–355.

Lerner, R. M. (1998). Theories of human development: Contemporary perspectives. In W. Damon (Series Ed.) & R. M. Lerner (Vol. Ed.), *Handbook of child psychology: Vol. 1* (5th ed., pp. 1–4). New York: Wiley.

Lerner, R. M. (2002). *Concepts and theories of human development.* Mahwah, NJ: Erlbaum.

Levinson, D. (1978). *The seasons of a man's life.* New York: Knopf.

Levinson, D. (1996). *The seasons of a woman's life.* New York: Knopf.

Loevinger, J. (1976). *Ego development: Conceptions and theories.* San Francisco: Jossey-Bass.

Mahler, M. (1975). *The psychological birth of the human infant.* New York: Basic Books.

Marini, M. M. (1984). Women's educational attainment and the timing of entry into parenthood. *American Sociological Review, 49,* 491–511.

Martin, P., & Smyer, M. A. (1989). The experience of micro- and macroevents: A life span analysis. *Research on Aging, 12,* 294–310.

Mayer, K. (2003). The sociology of the life course and life span psychology—Diverging or converging pathways? In U. M. Staudinger & U. Lindenberger (Eds.), *Understanding human development: Lifespan psychology in exchange with other disciplines* (pp. 463–481). Dordrecht, the Netherlands: Kluwer Academic.

McCandless, B. R. (1970). *Adolescents: Behavior and development.* Hinsdale, IL: Dryden Press.

Moore, D. (1987). Parent–adolescent separation: The construction of adulthood by late adolescents. *Developmental Psychology, 23,* 298–307.

Nurmi, J.-E. (1993). Adolescent development in an age-graded context: The role of personal beliefs, goals and strategies in the tackling of developmental tasks and standards. *International Journal of Behavioral Development, 16,* 169–189.

Nurmi, J.-E. (1997). Self-definition and mental health during adolescence and young adulthood. In J. Schulenberg, J. L. Maggs, & K. Hurrelmann (Eds.), *Health risks and developmental transitions during adolescence* (pp. 395–419). New York: Cambridge University Press.

O'Connor, T. G., Allen, J. P., Bell, K. L., & Hauser, S. T. (1996). Adolescent–parent relationships and leaving home in young adulthood. In J. A. Graber & J. S. Dubas (Eds.), *Leaving home: Understanding the transition to adulthood* (pp. 39–52). San Francisco: Jossey-Bass.

Parks, S. D. (2000). *Big questions, worthy dreams: Mentoring young adults in their search for meaning, purpose, and faith.* San Francisco: Jossey-Bass.

Pascarella, E., Bohr, L., Nora, A., & Terenzini, P. (1995). Cognitive effects of 2-year and 4-year colleges: New evidence. *Educational Evaluation & Policy Analysis, 17,* 83–96.

Pascarella, E. T., & Terenzini, P. T. (1991). How college makes a difference: A summary. In E. T. Pascarella & P. T. Terenzini (Eds.), *How college affects students: Findings and insights from twenty years of research* (pp. 556–635). San Francisco: Jossey-Bass.

Perosa, L. M., Perosa, S. L., & Tam, H. P. (2002). Intergenerational systems theory and identity development in young adult women. *Journal of Adolescent Research, 17,* 235–259.

Perry, W. G., Jr. (1968). *Forms of intellectual and ethical development in the college years: A scheme.* New York: Holt, Rinehart & Winston.

Plunkett, M. (2001). Serendipity and agency in narratives of transition: Young adult women and their careers. In D. P. McAdams, R. Josselson, & A. Lieblich (Eds.), *Turns in the road: Narrative studies of lives in transition* (pp. 151–176). Washington, DC: American Psychological Association.

Pulkinen, L., Nurmi, J.-E., & Kokko, K. (2002). Individual differences in personal goals in mid-thirties. In L. Pulkkinen & A. Caspi (Eds.), *Paths to successful development* (pp. 331–352). New York: Cambridge University Press.

Rest, J., & Navarez, D. (1991). The college experience and moral development. In W. M. Kurtines & J. L. Gewitz (Eds.), *Handbook of moral behavior and development, Vol. 2: Research* (pp. 230–245). Hillsdale, NJ: Erlbaum.

Roisman, G. I., Masten, A. S., Coatsworth, J. D., & Tellegen, A. (2004). Salient and emerging developmental tasks in the transition to adulthood. *Child Development, 75,* 123–133.

Schultz, L. H., & Selman, R. L. (1998). Ego development and interpersonal development in young adulthood: A between-model comparison. In P. M. Westenberg, A. Blasi, & L. D. Cohn (Eds.), *Personality development: Theoretical, empirical, and clinical investigations of Loevinger's conception of ego development* (pp. 181–202). Mahwah, NJ: Erlbaum.

Settersten, R. A., Jr., & Mayer, K. U. (1997). The measurement of age, age structure, and the life course. *Annual Review of Sociology, 23,* 233–261.

Shanahan, M. J. (2000). Pathways to adulthood: Variability and mechanisms in life course perspective. *Annual Review of Sociology, 26,* 667–692.

Shanahan, M. J., Sulloway, F. J., & Hofer, S. M. (2000). Conceptual models of context in developmental studies. *International Journal of Behavioral Development, 24,* 421–427.

Smetana, J. (1989). Adolescents' and parents' reasoning about actual family conflict. *Child Development, 59,* 1052–1067.

Smith, T. (2003). *Coming of age in 21st century America: Public attitudes towards the importance and timing of transitions to adulthood* (GSS Topical Report No. 35). Chicago: University of Chicago, National Opinion Research Center.

Spitz, R. (1959). *No and yes: On the beginnings of human communication*. New York: International Universities Press.

Stierlin, H. (1974). *Separating, parents and adolescents*. New York: Quadrangle.

Thornton, A., Axinn, W. G., & Teachman, J. D. (1995). The influence of school enrollment and accumulation on cohabitation and marriage in early adulthood. *American Sociological Review, 60,* 762–774.

Tilton-Weaver, L. C., Vitunski, E. T., & Galambos, N. (2001). Five images of maturity in adolescence: What does "grown up" mean? *Journal of Adolescence, 24*(2), 143–158.

U.S. Bureau of the Census. (2000). *Statistical abstracts of the United States: 2000*. Washington, DC: Author.

Whitbourne, S. K., & Tesch, S. A. (1985). A comparison of identity and intimacy statuses in college students and alumni. *Developmental Psychology, 21,* 1039–1044.

Wittenberg, R. (1968). *Postadolescence*. New York: Grune & Stratton.

W. T. Grant Foundation. (1988). *The forgotten half: Non-college youth in America: An interim report on the school-to-work transition*. Washington, DC: Author.

Wu, Z., & Macneill, L. (2002). Education, work, and childbearing after age 30. *Journal of Comparative Family Studies, 33,* 191–213.

Part II

Individual Characteristics

3

Emerging Structures
of Adult Thought

Gisela Labouvie-Vief

Several writers of the past century called attention to the fact that contemporary life has transformed the entry into adulthood. In *Culture and Commitment*, for example, Margaret Mead (1970) argued that if once lives had been firmly grounded in secure roles, such roles were beginning to break down; as a result, individuals had begun to experience a dislocation from a self whose life course was prefigured by his or her predecessors in a predictable generational sequence. Modern times, she suggested instead, were witnessing the emergence of a postfigurative self that could no longer rely on such clear plans. Indeed, the very notions of commitment and identity, according to Mead, sprang up because of this move toward a postfigurative society.

The uprooting of individuals from a sense of secure grounding in an intergenerational flow has become even more pronounced as the worldwide pluralism in political ideologies, religions, and ethnicities has become a source of global concern. The need to deal with such a complex world demands complex cognitive skills, as individuals need to reconstruct their intuitive sense of what is firm and secure at a much more abstract level (Kegan, 1982). Even though most adolescents and youth who enter this transition appear to be developmentally prepared to acquire such abstract skills, they are highly dependent on the availability of contexts that nurture those skills.

This chapter, as a consequence, deals with emergence in two senses. The first is that the social and intellectual transformations of the past century created the need to address new forms of thinking and being. Until the turn of the 20th century, thinking had been described in terms of certainty, stable outcomes, and rational processes; in the 20th century interest arose in processes of thinking that deal with the uncertain and changing nature of knowledge, the acknowledgment of diversity, and the importance of nonrational (e.g., automatic and affective) processes in decision making. In cognitive–developmental psychology, too, this search emerged as the attempt to question available notions of growth from childhood to adolescence, especially as embodied in the

Preparation of this work was supported by National Institute on Aging Grant AG09203.

theory of Jean Piaget. Around the year of 1980, a flurry of writings appeared suggesting that beginning in later adolescence or perhaps even following adolescence, many individuals experience a disequilibration of their thinking that can lead to a significant expansion of thinking, indeed a new level or stage, or even series of stages.

The second sense of emergence deals more specifically with the life stage discussed in this volume—the question of how these emerging structures of thought map into the period of emerging adulthood. I present data to show that indeed, the capacity for new and complex forms of thinking emerges after adolescence and matures rapidly during emerging adulthood. But even so, I suggest that this period appears to present a kind of critical stage in which these thought structures get launched but are not necessarily brought to fruition.

In this chapter, I present theory and research on the emergence of these more complex adult thought structures as individuals enter adulthood. In the first section of the chapter I locate the origin of these proposals in movements in contemporary thinking about development. In the second section, I summarize some of the major proposals concerning the emergence of adult thought structures and present data to suggest that they begin to appear at the entry into emerging adulthood. These data also suggest that because many individuals at this developmental stage are in transition, the support of appropriate contexts (such as those related to education and work) is of great importance. This role of contexts, both inner and outer, in emerging thought structures is the topic of the third section, in which I discuss the variability of thinking in the period of emerging adulthood.

The Emergence of Relativism

The topic of emerging adult thought structures—and the possibility of a new stage they imply—moved on the stage of developmental theory some 40 years ago with the work of Lawrence Kohlberg (e.g., 1969, 1973). Inspired by Piaget's (Inhelder & Piaget, 1958) theory of the development of thought structures, Kohlberg (1969) began in the 1960s to outline a general cognitive–developmental framework proposing that cognitive growth reorganized individuals' understanding of self and reality as reflected in such domains as morality, authority, laws, rights, and norms. Following Piaget's conviction that the development of structures of thinking reorganizes children's understanding of concepts of physical laws, moral issues, and emotions, Kohlberg laid out a broad cognitive–developmental theory proposing general levels (or stages) of complexity that undergird individuals' understanding of social reality at different points of development. Like Piaget, Kohlberg assumed that underlying the understanding of these diverse domains was a naïve epistemology (see also Broughton, 1980), an evolving awareness of how humans can know and judge important issues of life.

In 1969, in an article with Kramer (Kohlberg & Kramer, 1969), Kohlberg reported on a follow-up of his original standardization sample into early adulthood and noted that many individuals who in their late adolescence had appeared to have acquired a principled and universal sense of morality appeared to have regressed some years later, after entering college. Many of these youth had begun to show signs of relativism and questioning the firm values they had previously held. Kohlberg and Kramer did not, at first, conclude that this increase in relativistic thinking signaled the entry into a new stage of thinking about moral issues. Instead, they proposed that it reflected a retrogression.

This regressive interpretation came at a time when traditional concepts of rationality were being thoroughly revised. In science and philosophy, the notion that universal truths could be arrived at by rational analysis from axiomatic ground principles was being overturned. Instead, context, interpretation, perspective, and change all were being acknowledged as part and parcel of truth claims (e.g., Baynes, Bohman, & McCarthy, 1987; DeLong, 1970; Wittgenstein, 1953). For some writers, this led to the rejection of the very concept of rationality and to the belief in the radical relativity of all knowledge. But others (see Habermas, 1984) suggested that the notion of rationality was not so much outdated; rather, it was being transformed from something that could be concretely grasped by the individual mind to something that emerges out of the confrontation and coordination of multiple perspectives. Thus laws and truths were more like complex systems that change, like coming-into-being of forms that are the subject of evolution.

In developmental psychology, too, contextualism rose as an important theoretical stance as the roles of context (Labouvie-Vief & Chandler, 1978; Riegel, 1976) and cohort (Schaie & Labouvie-Vief, 1974) were being proposed as important factors in development. Following this emerging zeitgeist of contextualism and postmodernism, Kohlberg (1973) and Turiel (1974) eventually proposed that these college students had not really regressed. Rather, they had begun to question earlier views that were quite absolutist. Turiel suggested that this phase of relativism represented an opening up of an earlier view of morality that, even though it claimed universal validity, was too much rooted in conventional social practices. Thus what at first had seemed a kind of regressive movement, he proposed, might actually reflect a disequilibration of a closed form of thinking—a disequilibration that eventually could lead to further structural advances in adult thinking.

Almost simultaneously with Kohlberg's grappling with issues of relativity, William Perry (1968) had begun to study relativism in Harvard students as they progressed through the college years. Perry suggested that when they entered college, these individuals held a particular view of the nature of knowledge that fit quite well with the traditional concept of rationality. They believed that they were in college to learn what was right or true. This notion led them to polarize the world into right and wrong, a dualism that was extended not only to matters intellectual but also to those who held the views—especially professors and other authorities.

Taken aback at first by the coexistence of so many truth claims, many of these students soon came to understand that the source of their confusion was their own dualistic view of the nature of knowledge. Thus, the sense that there were safe, objective facts that were somehow outside the realm of human subjectivity began to crumble, giving way to a position of relativism.

Perry noted that relativism not only can move the bottom of certainty out from under youth but also can lead them to a new and transformed model of rationality, one in which the old notion of objective knowledge is wedded to subjective engagement and commitment (see also Belenky, Clinchy, Gold-berger, & Tarule, 1986). The individual now can become a much more active participant in the process of knowledge. There is vastly increased tolerance for diversity, yet the self can be securely anchored in its own viewpoint that is understood to have strong subjective elements. Thus, subjectivity in self and others is understood to be valid and necessary.

The work of Kohlberg and Perry was extremely influential because it set the stage for subsequent inquiries into changes in thinking as individuals move from adolescence into adulthood. Kohlberg's subsequent revision of his coding system (see Colby & Kohlberg, 1987) indeed suggested that the emergence of relativism prefigured the development of more mature adult thinking. Most of the writers thereafter would agree that the relativism emerging sometime in late adolescence prefigured a more complex way of thinking whose significance was extremely broad, stretching from general assumptions about the nature of morality, truth, and reality to understanding of self, others, and emotions.

Despite much criticism, this cognitive–developmental stance has survived and matured as it absorbed the confrontation with contextual diversity. Current adherents of this approach (e.g., Commons, Richards, & Armon, 1984; Dawson, 2002; Dawson, Xie, & Wilson, 2003; Fischer & Yan, 2002; Fischer, Yan, & Stewart, 2003; Karmiloff-Smith, 1998; Labouvie-Vief, 2003; Pascual-Leone, 1984) adopt much more dynamic views of the evolution of cognitive structures in which context and variability play important roles. Even so, the notion that there are structures of thinking that pervade many domains of life has persisted; one could even say it has become reinvigorated. However, as I point out in the following section, most researchers working in the field prefer to talk about levels rather than stages, indicating a current belief that orders of complexity are logically independent from age or the time at which they enter into the individuals' repertoire.

Levels of Adult Thought

Since the early work of Kohlberg and Perry, research on cognitive development in emerging adulthood has blossomed and suggested a rather coherent picture. In this section, I outline this research, which indicates that emerging adulthood may be a period that is highly significant for the launching and even solidification of these complex forms of thinking.

Kohlberg's Stages of Moral Judgment

It would be impossible to discuss work on the emergence of structures of adult thought without detailing the contribution of Kohlberg. At the core of his theory was an extension of the physicalistic model of reality of Piaget's theory—of the child as scientist. Kohlberg's core assumption was that our social reality as humans is interpersonally constituted. Adopting from James Mark Baldwin (1906) and George Herbert Mead (1934) the assumption that the self develops

Table 3.1.   Adult Stages of Moral Judgment

Stage	Social perspective
Conventional	
3 (Interpersonal expectations & conformity)	Perspective of the individual in relation with other individuals; Aware of shared feelings, agreements, and expectations that take primacy over individual interests; Relates points of view through the concrete Golden Rule, "putting yourself in the other guy's shoes;" Does not consider generalized system perspective.
4 (Social system & conscience)	Differentiates societal point of view from interpersonal agreement or motives; Takes the point of view of the system that defines roles and rules; Considers individual relations in terms of place in the system.
Postconventional	
5 (Social contract & individual rights)	Prior-to-society perspective; Perspective of values and rights prior to social attachments and contracts; Integrates perspectives by formal mechanisms of agreement, contract, objective impartiality, and due process; Considers moral and legal points of view; recognizes that they sometimes conflict and finds it difficult to integrate them.
6 (Universal ethical principles)	Perspective of moral point of view from which social arrangements derive; Perspective is that of an individual recognizing the nature of morality or the fact persons are ends in themselves and must be treated as such.

in a shared matrix with other selves, Kohlberg (see also Selman, 1980) posited a series of general stages outlining how individuals deal with successively more complex ways of understanding reciprocity and equality. Kohlberg was less concerned with subject–object relations than with between-subject relations, or intersubjectivity. In a sense, one could say that he laid out a series of increasingly complex forms of intersubjectivity that can guide individuals' thinking and behavior.

At Kohlberg's preconventional level, the rules that organize human understanding are related to individuals' immediate experience vis-à-vis others—such as parents—who are seen as powerful and whom individuals' aim to please. The ability to relate to more abstract norms and rules emerges at the conventional and postconventional levels, which are displayed in Table 3.1. At the conventional level, individuals begin to understand that a more abstract shared reality of common rules and norms superordinates the concrete preconventional reality. This is first evident at Stage 3 as a sense that group expectations take precedence over individual feelings. At Stage 4, a more complex societal perspective emerges in which a more generalized social-systems perspective of formalized laws takes precedence even over the rules of one's immediate group. At Level 3, the postconventional level, this social-systems perspective becomes widened further into a perspective that involves change and diversity. Postconventional thinking at first appears to be initiated by a sense of doubt about whether the laws and truths one has come to accept are, indeed, unalterable, and the suspicion that context and history matter. Such transitional doubt further leads individuals to wonder if such change and diversity can be orderly and principled. This doubt matures into the conviction, at Stage 5, that change can come about in an ordered way if individuals integrate their varying perspectives by formal mechanisms of agreement, contract, objective impartiality, and due process. In this way, it is possible to critique the validity of laws in terms of the degree to which they preserve and protect fundamental rights and values; thus the sense of right and wrong is more procedural. At Stage 6, finally, individuals adopt a more universalizing perspective affirming the equality and dignity of human beings. Thus social agreements are valid to the extent that they honor such general principles.

Colby, Kohlberg, Gibbs, and Lieberman (1983) studied these adult stages of moral reasoning in a sample of 84 boys ages 10, 13, and 16 years and followed longitudinally for 20 years. Between the ages of about 18 and 28, there was a noted decline in the proportion of Stage 3 responses and a corresponding increase in Stage 4 responses, indicating a social-systems perspective. Stage 4 thinking was virtually absent before late adolescence; in fact, only one individual younger than 18 displayed it. Stage 4 responses then rose systematically throughout adulthood, reaching about 60% at the oldest age level, 36. The transition to Stage 5 occurred even later, about the mid-20s; but Stage 5 responses never rose above 10%. Overall, the pattern looks quite similar for high socioeconomic status (SES) and low SES individuals, although that of the high SES individuals looks somewhat more favorable.

Overall, then, Kohlberg's data suggested that the period of emerging adulthood constitutes a critical phase for the beginning of individuals' ability to think beyond a purely interpersonal–conventional perspective and to embrace a conventional abstract systems perspective. A similar picture has also emerged in a recent reanalysis of several Kohlbergian studies (Dawson, 2002), although this reanalysis also suggested that during emerging adulthood, most individuals may just begin to elaborate such a perspective, as many of them score in the transitional level.

I think it is difficult to overestimate Kohlberg's view of the prior-to-society perspective for the emergence of adult thought, from both a philosophical and a psychological point of view. To a radical postmodern relativism that maintains that different abstract perspectives are incommensurable, it proposes that they can be intercoordinated and related at a more complex level that involves negotiation and communication. This view underlies an ideal vision of political process but also of scientific inquiry; it is a perspective that allows a vision of ordered change rather than one directed by mere convention or social power. On a more concrete level, it can permit individuals to resolve the conflict or even clash between the role expectations (e.g., ones related to one's religion, political conviction, or gender roles) of the group in which one is embedded and those that are formalized in more legal systems. Perry's work had ended on a note of a relativism that left room for a more complex view of objectivity. But Kohlberg affirmed that relativism does not necessarily suspend rational discourse nor justify a more abstract form of individualism. As is true of the work of Habermas, Kohlberg suggested that individuals continue to search for new levels of intersubjectivity that interrelate and coordinate perspectives.

Most subsequent writers were profoundly influenced by both Kohlberg and Perry, but most agreed with Kohlberg that relativism does not form the most mature form of knowledge. Broughton's (e.g., 1980) work, for example, suggested that relativism is superseded by a new form of objectivity in which the self cocreates knowledge through an active, dialectical, social process. This theme became the topic of a number of theoretical and empirical investigations that addressed how individuals began to interrelate subjective and objective aspects of knowledge. Basseches (1984a, 1984b), Kramer (1983), Labouvie-Vief (1984, 1994), and Sinnott (1984, 1989) all suggested that the discovery of seemingly incompatible and contradictory systems of knowledge confronted young adults with issues of interpretation and perspective; and all agreed that young adults eventually resolve these contradictions as they integrate them into an "overriding more inclusive whole made up of two or more formally consistent systems" (Kramer, 1983, p. 93).

Levels of Thinking in Emerging Adults

That the period of emerging adulthood marks the beginning of a more complex way of thinking—one that is better able to deal with contradiction, diversity, and the individual's own role in the process of knowledge—has been confirmed by a number of authors who have charted individuals' emerging ability to differentiate and reintegrate such dualities as objective and subjective, information and interpretation, individual and generalized perspectives, and so forth (Basseches, 1984a; Blanchard-Fields, 1986; Kramer, 1983; D. Kuhn, Pennington, & Leadbeater, 1983; Labouvie-Vief, 1980, 1994; Sinnott, 1989). The various proposals for such thought structures have covered a variety of different domains, but the most general theory is probably that developed by Michael Commons (Commons et al., 1984) and Kurt Fischer (Fischer, 1980; Fischer et al., 2003). Both theories describe successive levels as increasingly complex intercoordination of representations and skills that in many ways extend the analyses of formal thinking Piaget had offered. Fischer, in particular, has worked on applying such general levels of abstractions to a variety of domains, from reflective thinking to emotions and interpersonal representations. This work has most recently resulted in a general system for analyzing the developmental complexity of representations as they may occur in many domains of thinking.

One example of how this theory is used is its application to a study of critical thinking by Kitchener and King (King & Kitchener, 1994; Kitchener & King, 1981). These authors worked with individuals ranging in age from 16 to 34. The research participants were given problems that required making judgments about controversial issues. One problem, for example, asked that they take a stand on the controversy of religious versus scientific accounts of evolution: Did they believe the creationist teaching that God had created all life in a single instant, or did they believe the scientific account of gradual biological evolution?

Table 3.2. King and Kitchner (1994): Reflective Judgment

Stage	Description	Example
1	Knowing is limited to single concrete observations: what a person observes is true.	"I know what I have seen."
2	Two categories for knowing: right answers and wrong answers. Good authorities have knowledge; bad authorities lack knowledge.	"If it is on the news, it has to be true."
3	In some areas, knowledge is certain and authorities have that knowledge. In other areas, knowledge is temporarily uncertain. Only personal beliefs can be known.	"When there is evidence that people can give to convince everybody one way or another, then it will be knowledge; until then, it's just a guess."
4	Concept that knowledge is unknown in several specific cases leads to the abstract generalization that knowledge is uncertain.	"I'd be more inclined to believe evolution if they had proof. It's just like the pyramids: I don't think we'll ever know. Who are you going to ask? No one was there."
5	Knowledge is uncertain and must be understood within a context; thus justification is content specific.	"People think differently and so they attack the problem differently. Other theories could be as true as my own, but based on different evidence."
6	Knowledge is uncertain but constructed by comparing evidence and opinion on different sides of an issue or across contexts.	"It's very difficult in this life to be sure. There are degrees of sureness. You come to a point at which you are sure enough for a personal stance on the issue."
7	Knowledge is the outcome of a process of reasonable inquiry. This view is equivalent to a general principle that is consistent across domains.	"One can judge an argument by how well thought-out the positions are, what kinds of reasoning and evidence are used to support it, and how consistent the way one argues on this topic is as compared with other topics."

Note. Data from King and Kitchener (1994).

Kitchener and King scored individuals' justification of knowledge claims into seven stages (Table 3.2). The first of those are prereflective, as individuals do not recognize a need to justify knowledge claims. They assume that truth is simply what one observes or believes in, and no justification is necessary; in a somewhat more complex fashion, individuals juxtapose right views with wrong ones, and right or wrong is adjudicated by authority. For example, at Stages 3 and 4, individuals master a single first-order abstraction, such as *truth*, but cannot clearly understand (even though they may have intuitive hunches) that truth can be affected by one's perspective, nor are they able to elaborate how. In contrast, at Stage 5 they begin to display a second-order abstract perspective that compares arguments and viewpoints and relates them to their contexts. Stages 6 and 7 bring the individual beyond a simple contextualist–relativist perspective as they begin to search for a principle that can examine and perhaps compare and even unify different perspectives. The third-order abstractions of Stage 6 bring the realization that comparison is possible, but only the fourth-order abstractions of Stage 7 permit the individual to reconcile notions of relativity with systematic standards of how evidence can be compared. Rather than being identified with concrete positions, notions of truth come to be based on procedural criteria such as the adequacy of methods of inquiry. Here, then, individuals realize that truth does not so much have to do with objective facts but rather with an attitude of critical thinking, careful evaluation, and openness to falsification and change—the complex intersubjective perspective Kohlberg outlined for Stage 5 thinking.

Kitchener and King's work has been widely replicated, and the authors (King & Kitchener, 1994) report the results of reflective judgment scores on more that 1,300 individuals. Data indicate that scores increase as individuals progress through the educational system; they approach Stage 4 relativism at the end of high school and the beginning of the college years and increase through the college years, graduate school, and postgraduate training. Even so, the very highest levels are relatively rare even among individuals with the most advanced education.

How general are patterns of intellectual evolution such as those outlined by Kohlberg in the moral domain and by Kitchener and King in the domain of reflective thinking? In a series of recent papers, Dawson (2002; Dawson et al., 2003) used the Commons–Fischer general scheme of levels of abstraction to develop a general, content-independent scoring method in which the complexity of individuals' verbal statements is coded. Applying her analysis to several studies of Kohlberg's moral levels coding, for example, she finds a correlation of .92 between this latent complexity dimension and moral stages. Relationships to age and education show the usual patterns: Age shows a monotonically increasing quadratic relation to complexity scores, whereas education and level are correlated in a linear fashion with a correlation of .80. I discuss the possible implication of this strong relationship to education in the third section of this chapter.

Self and Emotions

Epistemological assumptions about the nature of truth are not the only kinds of cognitions that mark the entry into adulthood. Rather, the assumptions inherent in them about the nature of right and wrong are carried into daily experiences of individuals and expand their emotions and their sense of self and reality. These expansions are important in how individuals deal with the polarizations that often occur when thinking about self and others in such arenas as roles and responsibilities and ways of interacting with others (Kegan, 1982). They are also important in the religious arena (Fowler, 1981) in which the evolution of more complex forms of thinking affords individuals the under-standing that diversity in belief does not contradict the notion of abiding faith and religious commitment. Such social–cognitive forms of cognition form an important component of the general cognitive changes outlined so far.

How individuals' thinking about self and emotions develops is the topic of an ongoing longitudinal–sequential study of individuals from 10 years to over 80 years of age (Labouvie-Vief, Chiodo, Goguen, Diehl, & Orwoll, 1995; Labouvie-Vief & Medler, 2002). This study involved the follow-up of an original sample of 400 community-living individuals randomly selected from three sub-urban communities of a Midwestern metropolitan area on the basis of 1990 Census information. Along with completing an extensive battery of cognitive and socioemotional measures, individuals wrote a brief narrative describing the self—likes and dislikes as well as thoughts. These narratives were tran-scribed and coded into four levels of adult emotional and self-development (see Table 3.3).

At Level 1, individuals describe the self in terms of the values of the immediate social group, such as their relationships and the immediate social network. They emphasize features of the self and others that make for immedi-ate group acceptance. (e.g., "I am outgoing and friendly"). At Level 2, one finds self-descriptions that reflect a more individualized, differentiated, and inner sense of self. For example, the self is described in terms of fairly self-directed values and goals, often related to achievement and institutionalized social roles. However, the individual accepts these roles rather than reflects on them (e.g., "I am family oriented and active in my community"). In contrast, individu-als of Level 3 have a more contextual view of the self. Their descriptions often are critical of conventions as institutional goals are reexamined and placed in historical perspective, including reflections of how they have shaped the self. One now finds more dynamic self-descriptions that emphasize the role of histori-cal and psychological factors, with many references to processes and contrasts over time (e.g., "I am relearning who I am"). Finally, at Level 4 these descrip-tions are even more multifaceted as individuals describe themselves in the most complex way in terms of underlying, unconscious motivations and reciprocal interactions. The view of self is truly dynamic as individuals realize that activi-ties and goals are subject to continual revision as one gains knowledge of self and others. Overall, the sense of self conveyed is one of process, becoming, and emergence. Thus identity is viewed as transforming over time as a result of an inner psychological reorganization.

Our results show, as one might expect, that most of the adolescents' re-sponses, about 90%, are coded below Level 2. In contrast, for 20- to 29-year-olds the percentage of these lower level responses drops by about 50%; instead, they show an increase of about 40% of responses that are Level 2 or higher. This level stays virtually unchanged for the 30- to 45-year-olds but is highest for those aged 46 to 59. Even so, my analyses in the next section suggest that emerging adults find it difficult to integrate their complex thinking, and that integration is not achieved until later in adulthood. In turn, the age groups over 60 show a dramatic increase in lower level responses.

These results reflect that individuals of the emerging adulthood period begin to profoundly restructure their sense of self. As Jung proposed (see

Table 3.3. Levels of Self-Representation

Level	Description	Example
0 (concrete–presystemic)	The language used is simple and concrete. Characteristics and physical traits are seen as global. Events are detailed in simple seriation. Action-oriented behaviors describe activities. No references to goals or psychological processes occur.	I am an engineer. I am physically robust, strong, (6 ft, 280 lbs). I am tall. I am nice. I am pretty. I have two sisters.
1 (interpersonal–protosystemic)	Simple evaluations are made that reflect the values of the immediate social group. Traits described are nondifferentiated. Individuals are described in terms of relationships (simple descriptors) and social networks. Emphasis is on features of the self or others that make for in-group acceptance.	I like to fool around and make my friends laugh. I am outgoing and friendly. I love my family. I am fun to be with. I have lots of friends. I am involved in many clubs at school.
2 (institutional–intrasystemic)	Interpersonal descriptors indicate a clearer sense of the individual within the social group. Traits at this level indicate a more self-directed and goal-directed individual whose evaluations are guided by achievement-oriented and conventional goals, values, and roles. Achievement of these goals and values is a frequent theme.	I am family-oriented and active in my community. I am effective as a mother. I am empathic and a committed friend. I have not been successful in my life. I work hard to support my children and really love them. I have tried, with some success, to develop the patience of my father and devotion of my mother.

(continued)

Table 3.3. *(Continued)*

Level	Description	Example
3 (contextual–intersystemic)	Descriptions are critical of convention, involve an awareness of how traits change, and give a sense of individuals with their own value system. Institutional goals are reexamined and put into historical or psychological perspective. Descriptions involve references to processes and contrasts over time.	I am a singer, an actress, and a writer and want to use these talents more creatively than I do now. I get along well with all people but need to develop more insight as to what motivates other people. I am relearning who I am. I am adding new dimensions to my life in as many ways as possible.
4 (dynamic–intersubjective)	Roles and traits are described at a complex psychological level and reflect awareness of underlying, often unconscious motivation and reciprocal interaction. Activities and goals are seen as subject to continual revision as one gains knowledge of oneself and others. Reference is to multiple dimensions of life history and an emphasis on process, becoming, and emergence.	I struggle with the concept of who I am and have been identified as all-giving mother, self-sufficient, religious, and I think, feeling the need to be a more individualized woman with specific needs and desires. I work for profit rather than for satisfaction, partly because of my (guilty) need to continue to support my family. At this point in my life and my parents' lives, they are becoming dependent, and I find myself reliving the tensions of struggling to remain my adult self but getting pulled back to my younger self as I have spent more time with them.

Note. From "Representations of Self Across the Life Span," by G. Labouvie-Vief, L. M. Chiodo, L. A. Goguen, M. Diehl, and L. Orwoll, 1995, *Psychology and Aging, 10,* p. 407. Copyright 1995 by the American Psychological Association.

Whitmont, 1969), early adulthood is a period in which the role of institutions in development is powerful in shaping the sense of self, and my findings do suggest that this process begins approximately at the transition from adolescence to emerging adulthood and demonstrates the most dramatic growth during that period.

In sum, there is ample evidence that the period of emerging adulthood, from about the age of 18 to around 30, is a significant time for the development of mature thought structures. These thought structures appear to permeate many dimensions of individuals' lives. They permit them to project self into the future and into complex roles and communal activities and to participate creatively in many activities of adult life. At the same time, research indicates that this period appears to mark the emergence of these structures rather than their culmination, and that only a portion of individuals may come to master them.

One aspect of this emergence of adult thought is potentially troubling, however: Again and again, studies demonstrate that whether or not individuals begin to evolve more mature forms of thinking in emerging adulthood is strongly dependent on education. One might conclude from this strong linkage that these forms represent somewhat esoteric ways of thinking that do not necessarily illuminate a general developmental process. Instead, I suggest that the diversity of forms of thinking that is evident in emerging adulthood—and indeed at any stage of development—can be more profitably viewed if they are placed in a broader social context and their role in adult life is examined, more generally. That is, what are the conditions that foster or hinder their growth, and what are their relations to adjusting to the demands of adulthood?

Variations in Cognitive Growth

The preceding review suggests that during the period of emerging adulthood, thinking begins to change in profound ways. In general, the capacity emerges to think beyond the conventional and accustomed and to develop more system-oriented views about reality. Although research has not addressed the specific time at which these higher order forms of thinking emerge, they do appear to mark the end of adolescence and transition into emerging adulthood. At the same time, it is evident that mature adult structures of thought begin to emerge only after late adolescence, and neither the emergence nor the continued development of mature thought are givens. Rather, they appear to constitute a potentiality that needs to meet certain conditions if it is to be realized. Many individuals may continue to function in ways that are very concrete and conventional.

This period of emerging adulthood might be thought of, then, in Eriksonian terms as a crisis. The ideal outcome of that crisis is the ability to contribute to society in a principled manner—in a way that reflects not only the internalization of cultural values and roles but also a capacity to reflect on them and a creative ability to work with them and transform them. Yet this outcome remains just that—an ideal—and the lives of many individuals may require that they function in ways that are more concrete and conventional. In some cases, such conventionality may be a result of temperament or endowment, but in others, it may mirror the structure of the embedding environment. What, then, are factors that promote or discourage complex, mature thought?

Dynamics of Cognition

One major reason that individuals may not evidence high-level thinking is that cognitive structures appear to be responsive to a set of dynamic circumstances. The conventional view of the development of thought structures held that they emerged quite inevitably in a step-like sequence of stages, at least in a good-enough environment. Each stage was assumed to form a *structure d'ensemble* pervading many or even most domains of life. Many current views of cognitive growth have abandoned this view in favor of one more compatible with modern dynamic-systems thinking (e.g., Dawson, 2002; Fischer, 1980; Karmiloff-Smith, 1998; Labouvie-Vief & Márquez Gonzalez, 2004). One core feature of more dynamic views is that they tend to replace the notion of age- or life-period-correlated stages with that of levels. Levels are a more abstract ordering principle that may or may not be highly correlated with age, and may or may not form a domain-general sequence of development. Thus, although the general structure of levels can be applied to many domains, individuals' behavioral repertoire across different domains can consist of many different levels simultaneously. Such a structure is called "a web" by Fischer (e.g., Fischer et al., 2003). In a web, there may be many developmental strands (or domains), each of a different level of complexity, depending on the specific contexts and activities. In addition to such across-strand variability will be within-strand variability depending on whether certain supporting conditions are available. Thus even within a domain, performance can vary along several levels, forming a range of levels or developmental range.

According to this dynamic view of levels, it is not necessarily problematic that levels of cognitive–emotional development are somewhat idealized and reached by only relatively few individuals. In fact, it is possible to see the use of idealized levels not so much as a prescription for what one would expect most individuals to accomplish, but rather as a diagnostic tool that can be used to determine their current performance and the pattern of causes associated with it. In that sense, the use of cognitive levels could be said to be more akin to the use of an idealized standard of perfect health. Such a standard does not demand that most individuals possess perfect health; rather, it serves to diagnose why individuals differ from this idealized standard, each in their own unique way. Indeed, without such a standard, it would not be possible to determine deviations from it, nor prescribe possible courses of actions that might bring individuals closer to it. In that way, I suggest that instead of expecting high levels of thinking to be achieved by all individuals under all circumstances, those of us in the field should focus on systematically examining how and why individuals differ in the level of their cognitive functioning (see Labouvie-Vief, 1994).

In the context of adult cognitive levels, Kitchener, Lynch, Fischer, and Wood (1993) applied this notion to the reflective judgment task in individuals aged 14 to 28 when performance was assessed under different conditions. One was the usual condition in which individuals performed under standard instructions, without any special support. In contrast, a second condition was one of high support—individuals read a prototypical statement of each level and then responded to a series of questions about each level. These questions highlighted basic concepts, and individuals' attention was directed to the critical aspects of those. Finally, respondents summarized the prototypic statements in their own words, and scores for these summaries were derived.

The results of this study showed that under the high-support condition, individuals achieved significantly higher scores than they did under the standard condition. For example, stage 6 responses appeared to spurt at about the age of 20, when about 50% of responses were scored at this level; another spurt at about age 25 raised the percentage to nearly 100. As Fischer et al. (2003) noted, data such as these suggest that one's functional level may lag considerably under one's optimal level—in fact, a level may not become functional until the next higher level emerges under optimal (high support) conditions. Thus, support and scaffolding are inherent conditions for the development of reflective thinking—and higher order reflective thinking clearly appears in the period of emerging adulthood.

Findings such as these are important in interpreting the relation of higher level thinking to education. I have noted throughout that levels of complexity of thinking are strongly correlated with education: Colby et al. (1983) reported a correlation of .54 between moral reasoning and education, but Dawson (2002) reported one as high as .80. Such high correlations with education and a developmental outcome are often considered problematic because they may indicate dependence on verbal output that should be parceled out. In contrast, I suggest that education reflects a critical theoretical variable from both a cultural psychology and a neurobiological perspective on development because education is the very process or means by which culture imparts knowledge to the younger generations. The development of younger generations is embedded into a system of knowledge provided by current and prior generations of mature adults. Thus education forms the very mechanism by which individuals are initiated into the storehouse of cultural knowledge. Just as research suggests a period of emerging structures of mature thought at the transition into adulthood, so it also suggests that the middle-aged generation manages this storehouse; they are the carriers of the most complex thought structures integrating high-level knowledge.

The presence of mature adults, then, provides knowledge in highly organized, well-structured form, an essential ingredient of effective education. Even though Piaget described the individual as a discoverer of knowledge, many of the skills he described—such as knowing the laws of balances, pendulums, and hydraulic presses—would hardly emerge on the same time frame unless the laws underlying them were already part of a culture in which competent adults can aid adolescents in breaking down the critical parameters of such problems. In fact, the typical Piagetian experiment often amounts to a teaching situation in which the youngster's attention is directed to a few well-isolated critical variables. It would be impossible to acquire these laws—which, after all, may have required the lives of generation of scientists of the past to formalize—on their own. Rather, much as Gould (1977) has suggested that biological development in many ways incorporates the results of the evolution of prior generations, so individual psychological development is nested in a process of cultural evolution of which the middle-aged generation represents the culmination. Younger generations are not just knowledge builders but also are novices mentored by more skilled knowers. Thus, their continued development depends on the presence of an informational differential or gradient provided by more mature generations.

The dependence of knowledge acquisition on the guidance of more mature adults has been well noted by child developmentalists (e.g., Rogoff, 1990; Vygotsky, 1978) who have examined processes of knowledge transmission of adults to children. This dependence very much continues into adulthood, yet only a few researchers on youth and adulthood have examined this continuing dependence. One of the theorists who commented on it was Jung (see Whitmont, 1969), who saw the period of emerging adulthood (indeed the whole beginning of the life span) as a process of becoming entrenched in society's institutions. On a more positive note, Caspi and Roberts (2001) recently noted that as young adults begin to make commitments to and invest in those institutions, they also evidence a profile of improved and more stable adjustment; Helson (1999), in her longitudinal study of Mills College women, also noted that between college age and early adulthood, the women increased in norm-orientation, which suggests greater institutional and role commitment.

Nobody recognized the necessary alliance between individuals entering adulthood and mature adults who master the tasks of adulthood better than did Erikson, who suggested that the entry into adulthood depended on the presence of knowledgeable and generative adults. Erikson's point is especially important as many of the tasks of adulthood are no longer so well-structured but move into arenas in which knowledge must be applied in ill-defined situations, or even created anew as one goes along. Such ill-structured problems place increasingly high demands on personal and emotional factors as individuals tolerate ambiguity inherent in a knowledge process that is open-ended and uncertain.

To be sure, not all institutions have the primary goal of fostering such a pattern of principled autonomy; in fact, as Kohn and Schooler (1978) showed, institutions can invest in creating conformity and dependency for a group of adults, such as those of low socioeconomic status, who will work in highly structured institutional settings. In such settings, autonomy and critical thinking can be considered a liability rather than an asset. As a consequence, questions of continued cognitive growth throughout the period of emerging adulthood and thereafter are inextricably intertwined with aspects of social stratification and the degree to which it affects participation in higher education (Schooler, 1987).

Affective Complexity

The importance of adults who manage knowledge systems also highlights the emotional dimensions of knowledge. Even complex institutionalized knowledge systems, as T. S. Kuhn (1970) pointed out, serve not only informational and scientific functions but also social-regulatory and emotional functions; they define networks of power and authority that affirm congruent claims and suppress ones that challenge them. Thus individuals sometimes experience a conflict between their need to feel socially affirmed and appropriate and potentially important insights they may develop.

Erikson (1984) described how such conflicts ideally are held at bay because of a common generational bond young and mature adults share. He suggested that young adults need mature adults to help them maintain a sense of coherence as they mirror their growing competencies and to affirm for them an ideology worth investing in. However, middle adults, in taking on roles of authority—parent, teacher, religious, or political leader—need to feel affirmed by youth that they are, in the eyes of youth, numinous models who transmit ideals and values. Yet this generational linkage, like that between parent and children, has its dark side and can breed what he termed *totalism* and *authoritism,* in which a complex world picture yields to the need to be accepted by a charismatic leader. How individuals understand emotional processes is likely to affect the degree to which they are vulnerable to such social influences.

In recent work by my colleagues and me (Labouvie-Vief, 2003; Labouvie-Vief & Márquez Gonzalez, 2004; Labouvie-Vief & Medler, 2002), we have begun to explore how individuals are able to dynamically coordinate the demands of conceptual complexity and social acceptance. It has been a strength of cognitive–developmental theories (e.g., Kohlberg, 1969; Piaget, 1980) that they proposed a transformative view of emotions, somewhat in contradiction to prevalent theories that emphasize primary emotions (e.g., Ekman, 1984; Izard, 1997). According to this transformative view of emotions, emerging cognitive capacities transform the very functioning of emotions, even causing at times the emergence of new emotions that appear to be linked to higher levels of complexity. An example is the emergence of self-conscious emotions such as shame or pride that already presume a capacity to represent others' evaluation of one's own behavior (Lewis, 2000; Schore, 1994). Even so, this reflective emotion processing system is but one route to emotional processing—one that LeDoux (1996) called the high or cortical road. In contrast, many situations require emotions to be processed through a low or limbic road that secures successful emotion regulation in emergency situations that do not permit resource-rich reflective processes. Thus high levels of emotion understanding and regulation remain quite vulnerable to the potentially disruptive effects of emotions.

Although the road of reflection, then, increases the adaptive repertoire of individuals, it does not guarantee good adaptation. Indeed, a large body of research indicates that measures of conceptual complexity are quite independent of measures of emotional adjustment. That is, high levels of conceptual complexity can also serve maladaptive functions such as distortion of reality in defensive maneuvers. For this reason, in my own work I have emphasized that successful adaptation requires individuals to coordinate a concern with complexity and high-level reflective control with the ability to maintain sufficiently positive levels of positive affect and to ward off extreme levels of negative affect. In recent work, I referred to these different strategies as *differentiation* and *optimization.*

To describe such a dynamic between differentiation and optimization, my collaborators and I (Labouvie-Vief, 2003; Labouvie-Vief & Márquez Gonzalez, 2004) expanded Piaget's concept of an interplay between two core strategies of processing information (assimilation and accommodation) through a generalization of the Yerkes–Dodson law (Metcalfe & Mischel, 1999). This law postulates a compensatory and curvilinear relationship between an individual's level of emotional activation or arousal and the degree to which complex, integrated behavior is possible. Slight elevations of activation foster integrated, well-ordered thinking and behavior. However, when activation rises to extremely high levels, it tends to disrupt or degrade integration. At high levels of activation, automated nonconscious thoughts and behaviors, which are less easily disrupted by high arousal or activation, take over in an effort to maintain affect in a sufficiently positive range.

For an example of such degradation, think about common reactions to a frightening event, such as the terrorist attacks on September 11, 2001. The reactions to these attacks involved not only an increase in patriotic feelings and an emphasis on family values but also increases in racial and ethnic stereotyping. This example shows that the degradation of complex thinking due to high emotional activation does not necessarily result in complete fragmentation but can be relatively coherent or graceful. First, behavior becomes more automatic and schematized (Metcalfe & Mischel, 1999). Second, the ability to coordinate positive and negative aspects about self and others is disrupted, which leads to a positivity bias in which attention is diverted from negative information about the self. In contrast, negative affect and information often are projected on others, resulting in increased black-and-white thinking, stereotyping, and polarization among in-groups and out-groups (e.g., Paulhus & Lim, 1994). In a sense, trading off differentiation and complexity in favor of optimizing positive emotions makes good sense in situations that pose a threat to the well-being and survival of the self. Such situations stimulate emergency responses in which resources are focused on the self-protective task of restoring equilibrium and securing survival (Bodenhausen, 1992). However, as Erikson (1984) has discussed, this self-protective response also has a dark side—the exclusion of others from the circle of humanity in which one includes oneself.

The principle of dynamic integration usually works flexibly in response to situational demands, creating a dynamic cognitive–affective system that adjusts its level to the flow of circumstances. However, such flexibility can be relatively permanently altered by two sets of circumstances. First, normal developmental changes in cognitive resources can alter vulnerability to degradation. As these resources grow, individuals are better able to maintain integrated behavior even when levels of activation are high. In contrast, as long as these cognitive resources remain relatively low, individuals are more strongly affected by overactivation (Labouvie-Vief & Márquez Gonzalez, 2004; Metcalfe & Mischel, 1999). Second, if development does not proceed in a context of relatively low and well-regulated arousal or activation, individuals are likely to develop poor strategies of affect regulation; these strategies, in turn, should render the individuals particularly vulnerable to the degrading affects of overactivation.

To examine differing strategies of how individuals regulate their emotions, my colleagues and I defined different ways in which individuals can deviate from well-regulated, integrated functioning (Labouvie-Vief & Márquez Gonzalez, 2004; Labouvie-Vief & Medler, 2002). Following Werner (1957), we identified an integrated style that permits individuals to do so with relative ease. But we also defined two major deviations from an integrated style. One was a self-protective style in which individuals trade off complexity for positive affect by simplifying their representation of affect, focusing positive affect on the self and the immediate social network but negative affect on the out-group. We contrasted this with a complex style in which individuals traded off positive affect and social relations for conceptual complexity and individuation—hence, while attempting to maintain a complex and objective view, they experience lowered levels of positive affect and higher levels of negative affect and depression. Finally, we identified a dysregulated regulation style that showed aspects of both.

Self-protective individuals aim to maximize positive and minimize negative emotion but do so by engaging in thinking of low complexity. These individuals are high in self-acceptance but low in self-doubt and value the importance of social network, self-control, and social conformance; they place relatively low emphasis on personal growth and score low in empathy. In contrast, complex individuals, although high in cognitive–affective complexity, also score higher on negative affect and depression. They value intellectuality, openness, and independence and score high in empathy. Thus whereas one group values smooth adaptation to the social world (Erikson's world of pseudospeciation), the other group values growth and independence from normative values.

Each confers different sets of not only vulnerabilities but also strengths. The strength of the self-protective style is to foster a sense of group cohesion and to act quickly in emergency situations; its weakness is a tendency toward black-and-white thinking. The core strength of the complex style is its ability to maintain a differentiated and objective view of reality; its intellectuality, independence, and openness to psychological depth often have been associated with high levels of creativity, but also with a number of psychological vulnerabilities such as increased neuroticism and depression (Helson, 1999). These diverging affective patterns appear to indicate different identity styles, each reflecting characteristic variations in how individuals integrate the need for hedonic balance with that for complexity, openness, and objectivity (see Helson & Srivastava, 2001).

Table 3.4 presents the data from our research, classifying individuals from seven separate age intervals according to integrated, self-protective, complex, and dysregulated styles. The distribution by age shows a pattern highly consistent with what one would expect from other developmental findings (for review, see Harter, 1999). Our data indicate that preadolescents fall primarily into the self-protective group: They tend to give simple descriptions biased toward positivity; those not fitting this pattern are classified as dysregulated. For adolescents, the percentage of self-protective individuals declines considerably, but that of dysregulated individuals increases; this pattern suggests that individuals now begin to process more negative affect but do not yet have complex

Table 3.4. Distribution of Regulation Styles (% Within Age Category)

Age	Integrated	Self-Protective	Complex	Dysregulated
Preadolescents				
(11.00–14.99)	0.0	75.0	0.0	25.0
Adolescents				
(15.00–19.99)	0.0	23.1	7.7	69.2
Emerging adults				
(20.00–29.99)	8.3	20.8	37.5	33.3
Adults				
(30.00–45.99)	34.2	18.4	26.3	21.1
Middle-aged adults				
(46.00–59.99)	33.3	21.2	36.4	9.1
Older adults				
(60.00–69.99)	33.3	33.3	20.8	12.5
Elderly adults				
(70.00–85.99)	33.3	12.5	20.8	33.3

structures to begin integrating it (see Harter & Monsour, 1992). Thus they are likely to be overwhelmed. In contrast, the emerging adults show a much lower percentage of overwhelmed individuals but a much higher percentage of complex individuals. This finding suggests that complex thinking about affect rises dramatically; yet the high percentage of dysregulated and the low percentage of integrated individuals indicate that emerging adults are unlikely to integrate complexity and thus they continue to show high levels of negative affect and a sense of fragmentation overall. However, the next age period of adults over the age of 30 shows a dramatic rise in integrated individuals, and the pattern of styles remains fairly constant for the remainder of adulthood.

These findings are in line with the frequent report that the period of emerging adulthood may be wrought with complex and difficult emotions and attending high levels of negative affect and depression (see Reinherz, Gianconia, Wasserman, Silverman, & Burton, 1999); thus, even those of high complexity have a difficult time integrating their complex view of the world. Even though this age group shows an improved pattern of affect compared with the adolescents (see also Roberts, Caspi, & Moffit, 2001), this period also is clearly set off from adulthood proper. Indeed, this period has been called the nadir of adulthood from an affective perspective (Mroczek & Kolarz, 1998). In contrast, the patterns for the postemerging adulthood individuals suggest a better ability to live more comfortably with complexity. This trend, which suggests increasing consolidation of more complex cognitive–affective structures, continues at least until midlife. Thus emerging adulthood truly does emerge as a somewhat crucial period of the life span.

I commented in the previous section that complex, critical, and relativizing thinking emerges only in the 20s (approximately), and this fact suggests that emerging adults continue to display emotional problems resulting from polarizing thinking with attendant dependence on norms and social acceptance. A considerable body of research supports this suggestion. For example, in a series of studies, Blanchard-Fields and colleagues observed that adolescents made less differentiated or dialectical attributional explanations than did young and middle-aged adults and had more difficulty integrating discrepant information presented by different protagonists (Blanchard-Fields, 1986; Blanchard-Fields, Baldi, & Stein, 1999). Emerging adults have difficulty maintaining balanced cognitive–emotional representations especially if emotions are strongly activated, as when issues of security and survival are activated. Research on terror management theory, thus far performed primarily with college students, supports this prediction (Pyszczynski, Greenberg, & Solomon, 1999). Thus, when death-related fears are aroused, college students are more likely to give harsh evaluations of moral transgressors (Florian & Mikulincer, 1997) while increasing the favorableness of ratings of individuals who praise their own cultural standards (Greenberg et al., 1990; Greenberg, Pyszczynski, Solomon, Simon, & Breus, 1994; Pyszczynski et al., 1996). Death-related threat is also likely to increase racist attitudes (Greenberg, Schimel, Martens, Solomon, & Pyszczynski, 2001).

Findings such as those are consistent with my view that emerging adults are still easily swayed by their emotions to distort their thinking in self-serving and self-protective ways. Still, my results suggest that such distortion would be less likely for the subgroup of emerging adults who evidence more complex thinking—the complex and integrated. My own research is suggestive in that regard, as these two groups are high in empathy, flexibility, and autonomy. In a similar fashion, Greenberg and collaborators (Greenberg, Simon, Pyszczynski, Solomon, & Chatel, 1992) showed that priming death-related threat increases the acceptance of dissimilar others by individuals with tolerant values, especially if these values have been recently primed.

What causes individuals to embark on one or the other deviation from a more integrated pathway? Individual differences in temperament (Rothbart, Ahadi, & Evans, 2000), attachment history (Mikulincer & Shaver, 2001), or difficult life situations beyond one's control (Labouvie-Vief, Zhang, & Jain, 2003) all may be critical factors. Again, little precise information about these factors is available, but research on attachment styles and emotion regulation suggests that securely attached emerging adults (who are also more likely to be integrated and complex) behave quite differently in many tasks of emotion and emotion representation than do insecurely attached ones. For example, they have less well-balanced self-representations, either overvaluing the self while projecting negative attributes on others as in the case of dismissing individuals, or undervaluing the self as in the case of anxious individuals (Mikulincer, 1998; Mikulincer, Florian, & Tolmacz, 1990; Mikulincer, Orbach, & Iavnieli, 1998). Securely attached emerging adults also are less likely to distort their judgment of others in response to mortality salience, judging the transgressions of protagonists as less severe and showing less movement toward adherence to prevalent cultural values under conditions of stress (Florian & Mikulincer, 1998).

These findings suggest that even in emerging adulthood, individual differences are pronounced. They also suggest, however, that the problems of integration suggested by research with college students may be somewhat specific to this age period. In contrast, one would predict that the ability for balanced presentation increases well into midlife—although it is important to note that better than 50% of individuals tend to respond in ways that are not well integrated. These findings, again, point to the role of middle-aged adults whose levels of integration play a critical role. Does this generation of mentors provide models of openness and disciplined change? Are they able to teach those emerging into adulthood in ways that are generative, or do they do so in ways that serve needs of personal aggrandizement? Questions such as these are important for future investigations.

Conclusion

In sum, this chapter has presented evidence of emerging structures of adult thought that begin to appear after the end of adolescence and show rapid growth during the period of emerging adulthood. These thought structures can be described in terms of abstract levels of complexity, but go beyond high-level formal thinking, per se. A common thread that combines them is the understanding of forms of intersubjectivity that can extend beyond institutional boundaries and reach toward constructive change. The understanding of such complex forms of intersubjectivity forms the basis of many important adult accomplishments, such as the formation of identity, the establishment of personal and institutional bonds, and the extent and style of participation in educational, economic, political, and religious life.

This review also has shown that these forms of thinking remain a potentiality for many, a promise rather than a reality. Embedded as they are in a process of generational transmission, they require the support of the more encompassing knowledge systems administered by mature adults who are the carriers of complex knowledge. In this way, emerging adulthood can be seen as a period critical for the establishment of mature structures of thinking, yet also vulnerable to stabilizing distortive forms of thinking if important familial and cultural supports are not available.

References

Baldwin, J. M. (1906). *Thought and things: A study of the development and meaning of thought, or genetic logic.* New York: Macmillan.

Basseches, M. (1984a). *Dialectical thinking and adult development.* Norwood, NJ: Ablex.

Basseches, M. (1984b). Dialectical thinking as a metasystematic form of cognitive organization. In M. L. Commons, F. A. Richards, & C. Armon (Eds.), *Beyond formal operations: Late adolescent and adult cognitive development* (pp. 216–238). New York: Praeger Publishers.

Baynes, K., Bohman, J., & McCarthy, T. (1987). *Philosophy: End or transformation.* Cambridge, MA: MIT Press.

Belenky, M. F., Clinchy, B. M., Goldberger, N. R., & Tarule, J. M. (1986). *Women's ways of knowing.* New York: Basic Books.

Blanchard-Fields, F. (1986). Reasoning on social dilemmas varying in emotional saliency: An adult developmental perspective. *Psychology and Aging, 1,* 325–333.

Blanchard-Fields, F., Baldi, R., & Stein, R. (1999). Age relevance and context effects on attributions across the adult lifespan. *International Journal of Behavioral Development, 23,* 665–683.

Bodenhausen, G. V. (1992). Identity and cooperative social behavior: Pseudospeciation or human integration? In A. Combs (Ed.), *Cooperation: Beyond the age of competition* (pp. 12–23). Philadelphia: Gordon & Breach.

Broughton, J. M. (1980). Genetic metaphysics: The developmental psychology of mind-body concepts. In R. W. Rieber (Ed.), *Body and mind: Past, present, and future* (pp. 177–221). New York: Academic Press.

Caspi, A., & Roberts, B. W. (2001). Personality development across the life course: The argument for change and continuity. *Psychological Inquiry, 12,* 49–66.

Colby, A., & Kohlberg, L. (1987). *The measurement of moral judgment.* New York: Cambridge University Press.

Colby, A., Kohlberg, L., Gibbs, J., & Lieberman, M. (1983). A longitudinal study of moral judgment. *Monographs of the Society for Research in Child Development, 48,* 1–124.

Commons, M. L., Richards, F. A., & Armon, C. (1984). *Beyond formal operations: Late adolescent and adult cognitive development.* New York: Praeger Publishers.

Dawson, T. L. (2002). New tools, new insights: Kohlberg's moral judgment stages revisited. *International Journal of Behavioral Development, 26,* 154–166.

Dawson, T. L., Xie, Y. Y., & Wilson, M. (2003). Domain-general and domain-specific developmental assessments: Do they measure the same thing? *Cognitive Development, 18,* 61–78.

DeLong, H. (1970). *A profile of mathematical logic.* Reading, MA: Addison-Wesley.

Ekman, P. (1984). Expression and the nature of emotion. In K. R. Scherer & P. Ekman (Eds.), *Approaches to emotion* (pp. 319–343). Hillsdale, NJ: Erlbaum.

Erikson, E. H. (1984). *The life cycle completed: A review.* New York: Norton.

Fischer, K. W. (1980). A theory of cognitive development: The control and construction of hierarchies of skills. *Psychological Review, 87,* 477–531.

Fischer, K. W., & Yan, Z. (2002). Darwin's construction of the theory of evolution: Microdevelopment of explanations of variation and change in species. In N. Granott & J. Parziale (Eds.), *Microdevelopment: Transition processes in development and learning* (pp. 294–318). New York: Cambridge University Press.

Fischer, K. W., Yan, Z., & Stewart, J. (2003). Adult cognitive development: Dynamics in the developmental web. In J. Valsiner & K. Connolly (Eds.), *Handbook of developmental psychology* (pp. 491–516). Thousand Oaks, CA: Sage.

Florian, V., & Mikulincer, M. (1997). Fear of death and the judgment of social transgressions: A multidimensional test of terror management theory. *Journal of Personality and Social Psychology, 73,* 369–380.

Florian, V., & Mikulincer, M. (1998). Symbolic immortality and the management of the terror of death: The moderating role of attachment style. *Journal of Personality and Social Psychology, 74,* 725–734.

Fowler, J. W. (1981). *Stages of faith: The psychology of human development and the quest for meaning.* San Francisco: Harper & Row.

Gould, S. J. (1977). *Ontogeny and phylogeny.* Cambridge, MA: Belknap Press.

Greenberg, J., Pyszczynski, T., Solomon, S., Rosenblatt, A., Veeder, M., Kirkland, S., & Lyon, D. (1990). Evidence for terror management theory II: The effects of mortality salience on reactions to those who threaten or bolster the cultural worldview. *Journal of Personality and Social Psychology, 58,* 308–318.

Greenberg, J., Pyszczynski, T., Solomon, S., Simon, L., & Breus, M. (1994). Role of consciousness and accessibility of death-related thoughts in mortality salience effects. *Journal of Personality and Social Psychology, 67,* 627–637.

Greenberg, J., Schimel, J., Martens, A., Solomon, S., & Pyszczynski, T. (2001). Sympathy for the devil: Evidence that reminding Whites of their mortality promotes more favorable reactions to White racists. *Motivation and Emotion, 25,* 113–133.

Greenberg, J., Simon, L., Pyszczynski, T., Solomon, S., & Chatel, D. (1992). Terror management and tolerance: Does mortality salience always intensify negative reactions to others who threaten one's worldview? *Journal of Personality and Social Psychology, 63,* 212–220.

Habermas, J. (1984). *The theory of communicative action: Vol. 1. Reason and the rationalization of society* (T. McCarthy, Trans.). Boston: Beacon Press.

Harter, S. (1999). *The construction of the self: A developmental perspective.* New York: Guilford Press.

Harter, S., & Monsour, A. (1992). Developmental analysis of conflict caused by opposing attributes in the adolescent self-portrait. *Developmental Psychology, 28,* 251–260.

Helson, R. (1999). A longitudinal study of creative personality in women. *Creativity Research Journal, 12,* 89–101.

Helson, R., & Srivastava, S. (2001). Three paths of adult development: Conservers, seekers, and achievers. *Journal of Personality and Social Psychology, 80,* 995–1010.

Inhelder, B., & Piaget, J. (1958). *The growth of logical thinking from childhood to adolescence* (A. P. S. Seagrim, Trans.) New York: Basic Books.

Izard, C. E. (1997). *Human emotions.* New York: Plenum Press.

Karmiloff-Smith, A. (1998). Is atypical development necessarily a window on the normal mind/brain? The case of Williams syndrome. *Developmental Science, 1,* 273–277.

Kegan, J. (1982). *The evolving self.* Cambridge, MA: Harvard University Press.

King, P. M., & Kitchener, K. S. (1994). *Developing reflective judgment: Understanding and promoting intellectual growth and critical thinking in adolescents and adults.* San Francisco: Jossey-Bass.

Kitchener, K. S., & King, P. M. (1981). Reflective judgment: Concepts of justification and their relationship to age and education. *Journal of Applied Developmental Psychology, 2,* 89–116.

Kitchener, K. S., Lynch, C. L., Fischer, K. W., & Wood, P. K. (1993). Developmental range of reflective judgment: The effect of contextual support and practice on developmental stage. *Developmental Psychology, 29,* 893–906.

Kohlberg, L. (1969). Stage and sequence: The cognitive-developmental approach to socialization. In D. A. Goslin (Ed.), *Handbook of socialization theory and research* (pp. 347–380). Chicago: University of Chicago Press.

Kohlberg, L. (1973). Stages and aging in moral development: Some speculations. *Gerontologist, 13,* 497–502.

Kohlberg, L., & Kramer, R. (1969). Continuities and discontinuities in childhood and adult moral development. *Human Development, 12,* 3–120.

Kohn, M. L., & Schooler, C. (1978). The reciprocal effects of the substantive complexity of work and intellectual flexibility: A longitudinal assessment. *American Journal of Sociology, 84,* 24–52.

Kramer, D. A. (1983). Post-formal operations? A need for further conceptualization. *Human Development, 26,* 91–105.

Kuhn, D., Pennington, N., & Leadbeater, B. (1983). Adult thinking in developmental perspective. In P. B. Baltes & O. G. Brim Jr. (Eds.), *Life-span development and behavior: Vol. 5* (pp. 158–195). New York: Academic Press.

Kuhn, T. S. (1970). *The structure of scientific revolutions* (2nd ed.). Chicago: University of Chicago Press.

Labouvie-Vief, G. (1980). Beyond formal operations: Uses and limits of pure logic in life-span development. *Human Development, 23,* 141–161.

Labouvie-Vief, G. (1984). Culture, language, and mature rationality. In H. W. Reese & K. A. McCluskey (Eds.), *Life-span developmental psychology: Historical and generational effects* (pp. 109–128). New York: Academic Press.

Labouvie-Vief, G. (1994). *Psyche and Eros: Mind and gender in the life course.* New York: Cambridge University Press.

Labouvie-Vief, G. (2003). Dynamic integration: Affect, cognition, and the self in adulthood. *Current Directions in Psychological Science, 12,* 201–206.

Labouvie-Vief, G., & Chandler, M. J. (1978). Cognitive development and life-span developmental theory: Idealistic versus contextual perspectives. In P. B. Baltes (Ed.), *Life-span development and behavior* (pp. 181–210). New York: Academic Press.

Labouvie-Vief, G., Chiodo, L. M., Goguen, L. A., Diehl, M., & Orwoll, L. (1995). Representations of self across the life span. *Psychology and Aging, 10,* 404–415.

Labouvie-Vief, G., & Márquez Gonzalez, M. (2004). Dynamic integration: Affect optimization and differentiation in development. In D. Y. Dai & R. J. Sternberg (Eds.), *Motivation, emotion, and cognition: Integrative perspectives on intellectual functioning and development* (pp. 237–272). Mahwah, NJ: Erlbaum.

Labouvie-Vief, G., & Medler, M. (2002). Affect optimization and affect complexity: Modes and styles of regulation in adulthood. *Psychology and Aging, 17,* 571–587.

Labouvie-Vief, G., Zhang, F., & Jain, E. (2003). *Affect complexity and affect optimization: Cross-sectional validation and longitudinal examination*. Unpublished manuscript, Wayne State University, Detroit, MI.

LeDoux, J. E. (1996). *The emotional brain: The mysterious underpinnings of emotional life*. New York: Simon & Schuster.

Lewis, M. (2000). The emergence of human emotions. In M. Lewis & J. M. Haviland-Jones (Eds.), *Handbook of emotions* (2nd ed., pp. 265–280). New York: Guilford Press.

Mead, G. H. (1934). *Mind, self, and society from the standpoint of a social behaviorist*. Chicago: University of Chicago Press.

Mead, M. (1970). *Culture and commitment: A study of the generation gap*. Garden City, NY: Natural History Press/Doubleday.

Metcalfe, J., & Mischel, W. (1999). A hot/cool-system analysis of delay of gratification: Dynamics of willpower. *Psychological Review, 106*, 3–19.

Mikulincer, M. (1998). Adult attachment style and affect regulation: Strategic variations in self-appraisals. *Journal of Personality and Social Psychology, 75*, 420–435.

Mikulincer, M., Florian, V., & Tolmacz, R. (1990). Attachment styles and fear of personal death: A case study of affect regulation. *Journal of Personality and Social Psychology, 58*, 273–280.

Mikulincer, M., Orbach, I., & Iavnieli, D. (1998). Adult attachment style and affect regulation: Strategic variations in subjective self-other similarity. *Journal of Personality and Social Psychology, 75*, 436–448.

Mikulincer, M., & Shaver, P. R. (2001). Attachment theory and intergroup bias: Evidence that priming the secure base schema attenuates negative reactions to out-groups. *Journal of Personality and Social Psychology, 81*, 97–115.

Mroczek, D. K., & Kolarz, C. M. (1998). The effect of age on positive and negative affect: A developmental perspective on happiness. *Journal of Personality and Social Psychology, 75*, 1333–1349.

Pascual-Leone, J. (1984). Attentional, dialectic and mental effort: Towards an organismic theory of life stages. In M. L. Commons, F. A. Richards, & G. Armon (Eds.), *Beyond formal operations: Late adolescence and adult cognitive development* (pp. 182–215). New York: Praeger Publishers.

Paulhus, D. L., & Lim, D. T. K. (1994). Arousal and evaluative extremity in social judgments: A dynamic complexity model. *European Journal of Social Psychology, 24*, 89–99.

Perry, W. G. (1968). *Forms of intellectual and ethical development in the college years*. New York: Holt, Rinehart & Winston.

Piaget, J. (1980). *Experiments in contradiction* (D. Coleman, Trans.). Chicago: University of Chicago Press.

Pyszczynski, T., Greenberg, J., & Solomon, S. (1999). A dual-process model of defense against conscious and unconscious death-related thoughts: An extension of terror management theory. *Psychological Review, 106*, 835–845.

Pyszczynski, T., Wicklund, R. A., Floresku, S., Koch, H., Gauch, G., Solomon, S., & Greenberg, J. (1996). Whistling in the dark: Exaggerated consensus estimates in response to incidental reminders of mortality. *Psychological Science, 7*, 332–336.

Reinherz, H. Z., Gianconia, R. M., Wasserman, M. S., Silverman, A. B., & Burton, L. (1999). Coming of age in the 1990s: Influences of contemporary stressors on major depression in young adults. In P. Cohen, C. Slomkowski, & L. N. Robins (Eds.), *Historical and geographical influences on psychopathology* (pp. 141–161). Mahwah, NJ: Erlbaum.

Riegel, K. F. (1976). The dialectics of human development. *American Psychologist, 31*, 679–700.

Roberts, B. W., Caspi, A., & Moffit, T. E. (2001). The kids are alright: Growth and stability in personality development from adolescence to adulthood. *Journal of Personality and Social Psychology, 81*, 670–683.

Rogoff, B. (1990). *Apprenticeship in thinking: Cognitive development in social context*. New York: Oxford University Press.

Rothbart, M. K., Ahadi, S. A., & Evans, D. E. (2000). Temperament and personality: Origins and outcomes. *Journal of Personality and Social Psychology, 78*, 122–135.

Schaie, K. W., & Labouvie-Vief, G. (1974). Generational versus ontogenetic components of change in adult cognitive behavior: A fourteen-year cross-sequential study. *Developmental Psychology, 10*, 305–320.

Schooler, C. (1987). Psychological effects of complex environments during the life span: A review and theory. In C. Schooler & K. W. Schaie (Eds.), *Cognitive functioning and social structure over the life course* (pp. 24–49). Norwood, NJ: Ablex.

Schore, A. N. (1994). *Affect regulation and the origin of the self: The neurobiology of emotional development.* Hillsdale, NJ: Erlbaum.

Selman, R. L. (1980). *The growth of interpersonal understanding: Developmental and clinical analyses.* New York: Academic Press.

Sinnott, J. D. (1984). Postformal reasoning: The relativistic stage. In M. L. Commons, F. A. Richards, & C. Armon (Eds.), *Beyond formal operations: Late adolescent and adult development* (pp. 298–325). New York: Praeger Publishers.

Sinnott, J. D. (1989). Life-span relativistic post-formal thought: Methodology and data from every day problem solving studies. In M. L. Commons, J. D. Sinnott, F. A. Richards, & C. Armon (Eds.), *Adult development: Vol. 1. Comparisons and applications of developmental models* (pp. 239–278). New York: Praeger Publishers.

Turiel, E. (1974). Conflict and transition in adolescent moral development. *Child Development, 45,* 14–29.

Vygotsky, L. S. (1978). *Mind in society: The development of higher psychological processes.* Cambridge, MA: Harvard University Press.

Werner, H. (1957). *Comparative psychology of mental development.* New York: International Universities Press.

Whitmont, E. C. (1969). *The symbolic quest: Basic concepts of analytical psychology.* Princeton, NJ: Princeton University Press.

Wittgenstein, L. (1953). *Philosophical investigations.* Oxford, England: Blackwell Publishers.

4

Emerging Adulthood as an Institutionalized Moratorium: Risks and Benefits to Identity Formation

James E. Côté

> Adulthood is the ever-shrinking period between childhood and old age. It is the apparent aim of modern industrial societies to reduce this period to a minimum.
>
> —Thomas Szasz (1973, p. 54)

Two of the least contested issues in contemporary adolescent psychology and youth studies are that (a) important aspects of identity formation, one of the pillars of human development, take place during the transition to adulthood, and (b) the transition to adulthood is now taking far longer than in the past, delayed until the late 20s for a significant proportion of the population. In this chapter, I deal with these two issues simultaneously, examining what is known about the changes in identity formation during the now prolonged transition to adulthood, with a focus on research examining identity changes during the period designated as emerging adulthood.[1] This task goes beyond the conventional view that most identity formation occurs primarily during adolescence to deal with contemporary realities where key identity issues are not resolved for many people until well beyond the teens, during what is referred to in this volume as emerging adulthood.

The theoretical basis of this chapter is Erik Erikson's identity theory and his proposal that, as part of the transition to adulthood, societies can offer their young people *institutionalized moratoria*—structured contexts for working through identity confusion and resolving an identity crisis. After reviewing

---

[1]According to Snarey, Kohlberg, and Noam (1983), emerging adulthood is a cultural age, like adolescence, because there is an emphasis "on quantitative changes in age, mastery, performance, knowledge, rights, and responsibilities" (p. 328). Erikson's identity stage constitutes a functional phase because there is both a qualitative change in identity structure and a quantitative change in social status (from adolescence to adulthood) upon resolution of the stage. The fact that the identity stage now takes longer does not mean that emerging adulthood is a functional phase, because in a functional phase qualitative changes must take place if subsequent development is to take place.

Erikson's theory and noting its basis in the mid-20th-century America about which he wrote, I characterize the recent prolongation of youth in terms of (a) the changed education-to-work transition whereby large numbers of youth are now required to postpone aspects of their identity formation, and (b) the diminished normative structure governing the transition to adulthood. With this theoretical background, I review the empirical identity status literature in terms of what identity development might take place during the age range of 18 to 29. Findings from a longitudinal study involving measures of identity stage resolution (Côté, 2002), identity status (Adams, Bennion, & Huh, 1987), and identity confusion (Steinberg & Schnall, 2000) are then discussed in terms of their Eriksonian and sociological implications. Finally, unanswered questions regarding the identity-formation benefits and liabilities of a prolonged institutionalized moratorium are posed, and directions for future research needed to answer these questions are presented, along with a suggested classification of the new life-course options associated with a prolonged transition to adulthood.

The Original Theory: Erikson

Erik Erikson is the recognized pioneer of identity theory in the social sciences (Weigert, Teitge, & Teitge, 1986) and the father of the identity crisis ("Psychoanalyst Coined Identity Crisis," 1994). In his well-known eight-stage theory of the life cycle, the psychosocial task of identity formation was identified as a normative event, in the sense that it typically occurred within adolescence (or the equivalent of adolescence-like rites of passage, depending on the culture; e.g., Erikson, 1950). However, Erikson also pointed out ways in which significant identity formation can take place after adolescence, for certain people in certain cultural and historical contexts (e.g., Erikson, 1958). At the time of his writing some 50 years ago, these extensions of the identity stage were thought to be exceptions to the normative event of adolescent identity formation. However, the extension of the identity stage beyond adolescence now appears to be a normative event in postindustrial societies, in which the workforce participation of adolescents and emerging adults has become a source of cheap labor and higher educational credentials are essential for stable employment (Côté & Allahar, 1996; Tannock, 2001). This prolonged education-to-work transition delays the assumption of adult roles and hence the reality-based resolution of the identity stage. In doing so, it can aggravate the identity crisis, create identity confusion, and interfere with the development of a stable sense of ego identity.[2]

---

[2]It is not possible to provide a single definition of *identity* because of its multidimensionality. Côté and Levine (2002) showed how three levels of analysis can represent this multidimensionality (ego identity, personal identity, and social identity) and called for the development of, and adherence to, a taxonomy of identity concepts to reverse the tendency in the literature toward a proliferation of definitions of *identity* that do not take into account these three levels of analysis and that do not distinguish among process, content, and structure. Côté and Levine suggested the following characterization of the multidimensionality of identity formation that is useful for understanding what might take place during adolescence and emerging adulthood:

The Institutionalized Moratorium

As with many of the identity concepts now in usage, Erikson (1968) was the first to speak of the institutionalized moratorium. His general theory of the life cycle proposed that each stage has some sort of psychosocial moratorium that gives each novitiate some extra time to master that stage. Some stages also provide structured or institutionalized contexts to provide guidance to those in a psychosocial moratorium. He wrote most about the moratorium of the identity stage, arguing that most cultures provide their new members with some sort of social structural guidance to take them from childhood to adulthood (the institutionalized part of the concept), as well as a time-out from certain social responsibilities that constitutes a delay in the transition (the moratorium part). Erikson thus argued that most cultures historically provide their young people with some sort of structured delay from adult responsibilities, during which novitiates can take time to develop their adult identities within guiding social structures. In his words,

> Societies offer, as individuals require, a more or less sanctioned intermediary period between childhood and adulthood, *institutionalized moratoria,* during which a lasting pattern of "inner identity" is scheduled for relative completion. (1980, p. 110)

These identity moratoria[3] usually grant adolescents and emerging adults the license to experiment with various roles, if they so wish, without them being expected to accept or carry permanent responsibilities and commitments. This experimentation can take various forms of exploration, including travel (the *Wanderschaft*), military service (or programs such as the Peace Corps), schooling, or even just "dropping out" for a while (cf. Erikson, 1968, p. 157). In the 1950s, Erikson (1958) believed that this moratorium could sometimes last until age 24, especially among college students, but at that time it was more commonly a late-adolescent phenomenon. Erikson (Evans, 1969) also acknowledged that societies vary in terms of the degree to which they structure identity moratoria and in terms of how much conformity they demand to the norms and values of adult society during that moratorium. For example, military service is tightly structured, whereas the Wanderschaft is loosely structured.

---

(1) the subjective/psychological dimension, or ego identity *qua* a sense of temporal-spatial continuity and its concomitants; (2) the personal dimension, or a behavioral and character repertoire that differentiates individuals; and (3) the social dimension, or recognized roles within a community. . . . [T]hese components need to come together during the identity stage, and when they do not, or as they are doing so, an identity crisis is evident. Such an identity crisis is characterized by a subjective sense of identity confusion, a behavioral and character-ological disarray, and a lack of commitment to recognized roles in a community. Accordingly, resolution of the identity stage is facilitated when the three dimensions dovetail: when (1) a relatively firm sense of ego identity is developed, (2) behavior and character become stabilized, and (3) community-sanctioned roles are acquired. . . . (p. 15)

[3] I refer to the general period of delay of adulthood as the identity moratorium because a moratorium does not necessarily take place within an institutionalized setting; people can create their own or experience it by default (Erikson, 1968).

The Identity Crisis

Erikson argued that the moratorium period can provide an essential interlude during which identity crisis can be resolved in ways compatible with the specific needs of the person experiencing it. Institutionalized, as opposed to self-constructed, moratoria can provide contexts in which the crisis can be resolved in relative safety, especially in providing tolerance for the playing out of old unresolved conflicts from previous stages and exploring an expanded social world in which to function in a less conflicted way.

Erikson referred to a variety of forms that identity crises can take, pointing out that they can vary in terms of their severity (e.g., 1958, p. 47), prolongation (e.g., 1968, p. 17), and aggravation (e.g., 1975, pp. 20–22). For Erikson, the severity of an identity crisis is proportionate to the degree to which the sense of identity confusion upsets and outbalances the sense of ego identity. When this happens, an individual's personal and social role repertoires can be unstable. A prolonged identity crisis is manifested when the role repertoire remains unstable over long periods. Finally, an aggravated identity crisis involves repeated but unsuccessful attempts to establish a stable and viable personal and social role repertoire.

Identity Confusion

For Erikson, people can experience a psychological limbo or void during the identity crisis, along with oscillations between the senses of ego identity (temporal–spatial continuity in the sense of self) and identity confusion (dissociations of self in of time and space). In Erikson's words, "as long as the establishment of identity is incomplete a crisis exists which . . . amounts to an identity-confusion" (1959, p. 68). This identity confusion can be manifested in terms of "contradictory self images or aspirations" (Erikson, 1975, p. 46) and "a loss of center" (Erikson, 1968, p. 212). In its more obvious manifestations, identity confusion can be observed "[1] in excessively prolonged moratoria . . . [2] in repeated impulsive attempts to end the moratorium with sudden choices . . . [along with a denial] that some reversible commitment has already taken place, or [3] sometimes in severe regressive pathology" (Erikson, 1968, p. 246). Along with unconscious conflicts, Erikson (1968) thought that contradictory roles or opportunities are often a source of identity confusion.

The Contemporary Moratorium: An Education-to-Work Transition Perspective

Sociological circumstances associated with the transition to adulthood have changed over the 50 years since Erikson formulated his theory, in ways that have undoubtedly affected how the identity moratorium is experienced and adult identities are formed. One way to understand these sociological changes is to look at the opportunities in the labor market for those in their late teens and early 20s. In countries that could be counted as postindustrial societies, the youth labor market collapsed in the 1980s as the relatively well-paying manufacturing sector gave way to the less well-paid service sector, caricatured in terms of the McJob (e.g., Furlong & Cartmel, 1997; Tannock, 2001). Youth participation rates in the workforce have decreased dramatically and youth unemployment rates have increased (Bowlby & Jennings, 1999). At the same time, the major corporate restructurings of the labor force since the 1980s left many adolescents and emerging adults in a position of economic disadvantage. Now, it is commonplace for adolescents and emerging adults to have access mainly to dead-end, low paying jobs (often part-time or contractual) that make it very difficult to attain financial self-sufficiency (e.g., Côté & Allahar, 1996; Tannock, 2001). In the face of poorer entry-level job prospects, more adolescents and emerging adults have sought postsecondary educational credentials in the hope of gaining an advantage in access to better paying jobs[4] by bypassing those attempting to climb internal career ladders through the more traditional noncollege routes.[5] In response, colleges and universities in postindustrial societies have expanded to include significant proportions of their youth populations. Countries such as the United States and Canada now have almost one-half of their citizens in their early 20s attending educational institutions full-time (e.g., Montgomery & Côté, 2003), and the estimated duration of the cohort school-to-work transition is now 8 years and growing—beginning at 16 and ending at 23—2 years longer than it was in 1985 (Bowlby, 2000).[6]

For some historical context to the education-to-work perspective from sociology, consider that in 2000 some 40% of young Canadians aged 20 to 24 were attending school full-time (Statistics Canada, 2003a). In the 1950s, when Erikson developed his adolescence-based identity theory, this was the approximate percentage of young Canadians aged 15 to 19 attending school full-time, whereas only about 5% of those in their early 20s were doing so (Normand, 1995). The educational experiences of those now in their early 20s resemble those who were in their late teens 50 years ago, which suggests that since Erikson first wrote about identity formation, adolescence has undergone a metamorphosis to produce a second age-period of relative dependency that is now called *emerging adulthood.*

Although those with higher credentials do in fact experience an advantage over the less educated in terms of workplace opportunities (higher salaries and less unemployment), it appears that much of this advantage is at the expense of those not fortunate enough to gain higher credentials. For example, between 1980 and 2000, whereas (inflation-adjusted) average incomes of young university graduates in Canada remained about the same (the decline of the 1980s

---

[4] See Lapsley, Enright, and Serlin (1985) for data indicating that historically, educational participation drops dramatically when good jobs are available to young people and increases when youth labor is not needed.

[5] According to Butlin (1999), a minimum of 17 years of education is now required for about one half of new jobs in the Canadian economy. During the 21st century, the level of required education is predicted to increase to the point where most new jobs will require some postsecondary schooling (Allen, Harris, & Butlin, 2001).

[6] The cohort school-to-work transition begins at the point where more young people are studying without working and ends at the point where the majority is working without studying.

was reversed in the 1990s), the incomes of high school graduates dropped some 10% to 15% (Statistics Canada, 2003b). In the United States between 1979 and 1994, baccalaureate graduate real earnings increased by 5%, whereas those of high school graduates fell by 20% (Morris & Western, 1999). Considered as a whole, the incomes of the "forgotten half" (all those who do not use the college route to the workplace) dropped about 30% for males and almost 20% for females (Halperin, 2001).[7] Referring to this often overlooked aspect of the transition to adulthood, Morris and Western (1999) argued that "it should be kept in mind that the 'rise' in the college premium was almost entirely driven by the *collapse* in the earnings of high-school graduates and dropouts. . . . This is what caused the doubling of the college premium" (p. 633, emphasis in original; the *college premium* is the salary and employability advantage that a college degree has over a high school diploma).

In considering the nature of the identity moratorium, then, one must be concerned with the experiences of all emerging adults, not just the more fortunate ones. Noting a "generational divide in the labour market . . . with those [men] younger than 40 experiencing earnings losses, and those over 40, particularly over 50 experiencing gains" during the 1980s and 1990s, Statistics Canada (2003b, p. 11) interpreted the census results from 1981 through 2001 as follows:

> These results are consistent with earlier Statistics Canada research showing that the earnings path of young men [in particular] has veered downward. The generation of men who came of age during the late 1980s and 1990s started their careers making less than their counterparts who came of age in the 1970s, and made much slower progress for at least the first 10 years of their working lives. . . . A university education offers the young only a partial buffer to this tendency.[8]

Adding to difficulties in the education-to-work transition is the disjunctive nature of the link between the higher education sphere and the workplace. For example, many high school graduates have highly unstable work histories, including multiple, concurrent part-time jobs (Tannock, 2001), and up to one half of college graduates experience long periods of underemployment during which they are working at jobs that do not require their level of earned credential (e.g., Frenette, 2000; Nobert & McDowell, 1994).

The Contemporary Moratorium: A Normative Perspective

In addition to this education-to-work transition perspective, the characteristics of the current transition to adulthood can be viewed in terms of the normative

---

[7] This deteriorated economic situation is associated with the doubling of the incarceration rate of emerging adult males in the United States from the 1980s to the 1990s. Currently, 10% of American males in their 20s are involved in the criminal justice system, on probation, in jail, or on parole (Halperin, 2001).

[8] The experiences of young women were similar, except that a university education did not have the same buffering effect as it did for men, and the generational dividing line is put at age 30 for females by Statistics Canada.

structures (i.e., value-based patterns and standards of behavior) that might underpin an institutionalized moratorium, which for Erikson ostensibly guide young people during this transition. From the perspective of normative guidance, there is reason to believe that society has entered a late-modern (some prefer the term *postmodern*) period that is increasingly anomic (or less normed) in certain respects (see Côté, 2000, for a discussion of this and the distinctions between the concepts of late-modern and postmodern). This anomie seems to have affected the life courses of many people. In particular, it likely adversely affects those with little guidance from their families-of-origin or an organized religion, who are coping with decoupled and erratic life-transition options (such as from family-of-origin to family-of-orientation). Also, anomie can make self-development more difficult because it requires people to compensate for fragmented institutional contexts (such as education-to-work transitions; Côté, 2000). Faced with these challenges, adolescents and emerging adults more then ever need a repertoire of personal resources—some of which I call *identity capital* (Côté, 1996, 1997)[9]—to successfully integrate themselves into mainstream adult society, if they so wish.

At the same time, mainstream society is less insistent that everyone become an adult member (because their sustained economic participation is not as crucial as it was in industrial or preindustrial societies, except as a reserve of cheap labor). Thus there is little normative pressure for some people to grow up in terms of what most people in Western societies would consider a traditional adulthood defined in terms of commitments to lifelong roles and obligations based on identities embedded in community attachments. Under circumstances in which well-structured socialization practices have diminished, adolescents and emerging adults find that they must compensate by engaging in what Heinz (2002) refers to as *self-socialization*, an individualization process bound to be fraught with challenges requiring more time to enter even forms of post-traditional adulthood. Referring to the "loose coupling between social structure and the life course," Heinz (2002) proposed two principles for viewing development in terms of self-socialization:

> (1) Individuals construct their own life course by attempting to come to terms with opportunities and constraints concerning transition pathways and life stages.
>
> (2) Individuals select pathways, act and appraise the consequences of their actions in terms of their self-identity in reference to social contexts which are embedded in institutions and markets. (p. 58)

---

[9] Identity capital resources have been identified as being both tangible and intangible (Côté, 1996). Tangible resources include the possessions, social networks, and behaviors of individuals, whereas intangible resources constitute their personality attributes. Tangible attributes comprise financial resources, educational credentials, group memberships, and parental social status along with impression management skills and social skills. Intangible resources include psychological capacities such as ego strength, an internal locus of control, self-esteem, a sense of purpose in life, social perspective taking, critical thinking abilities, and moral reasoning abilities (Côté, 1997). The common feature of intangible attributes is that they can afford the person the cognitive and behavioral capacities with which to understand and negotiate the various obstacles and opportunities commonly encountered throughout the late-modern life course with its decoupled and multifaceted transitions.

This new self-socialization requirement presents both risks and benefits to adolescents and emerging adults. Although it provides greater freedom from traditional constraints, not all opportunities are the same, and not all choices made in the context of new freedoms are good ones or in one's best interest over the long term (cf. Schwartz, 2000, 2004). In the context of freedom without guidance, people can exercise the choice to pursue a life course totally devoid of traditional social markers, with or without exerting much mental effort, by simply selecting a number of default options now available in youth culture, by which they follow paths of least resistance and effort, as in the imitation of the latest fashion and music trends. This type of individualization is referred to as *default individualization* because it involves little agentic assertion on the part of the person (Côté, 2000). Or people can now pursue life courses based on extensive deliberations of the alternatives and opportunities now available—given the decline of (potentially stifling) social markers and fewer economic barriers involving gender, ethnicity, and social class—in pursuit of stimulating and liberating possibilities. I call this type of individualization *developmental individualization* because it involves a life course of continual and deliberate growth (Côté, 2000).

On the surface, then, emerging adulthood looks like a positive development, with late-modern societies giving adolescents and emerging adults a greater amount of choice and freedom. However, when the ideology of free choice is peeled away (cf. Furlong & Cartmel, 1997), an absence of guiding structures and norms is noticed—a situation of relative anomie that can present serious challenges to some people. Without guiding structures to give meaning to the potential choices people face, realistic and informed choices become burdensome for many young persons (cf. Côté, 2000). This situation may be especially critical for those in their teens who may not have the personal wherewithal to chart their own life courses, especially teens from disadvantaged backgrounds, those with psychiatric challenges, and so forth. Indeed, Schwartz (2000, 2004) argued that Western societies now present many people with a "tyranny of freedom and choice" that actually decreases their quality of life and, to some extent, diminishes their life chances.

The Contemporary Moratorium: A Life-Course Differentiation Perspective

In view of the two preceding sociological perspectives concerning the changing nature of the transition to adulthood, one needs to carefully consider the potential liabilities of the contemporary identity moratorium. For example, most of the youth population now seems to undertake a prolonged moratorium; in fact, far more do so now than when Erikson first identified the phenomenon 50 years ago, with about eight times as many now using the college route during their early 20s. His focus was on the moratorium as a context within which the identity crisis was resolved, especially as individuals needed it to rework unconscious conflicts. In other words, the pattern would have been for those who needed it for psychosocial reasons to be pulled into a prolonged moratorium.

If this was true, then those who took advantage of it likely had more severe and prolonged crises to resolve, and if they took advantage of the moratorium offered by college, would have been more likely to have come from more affluent backgrounds. Now, the reasons for undertaking a prolonged moratorium are probably much more varied, with only a minority using it to actively resolve an identity crisis that reworks internal conflicts. Most others are likely undertaking it for a variety of reasons, including being pushed into institutionalized settings such as college: Among the middle class, college attendance has become a sort of rite of passage into white collar and professional careers, and among the working class, there are fewer alternatives to college as a means of moving into the workforce. Thus, previous generations were more likely pulled into identity moratoria and responded to its intrinsic qualities. Now, emerging adults may be more likely to be pushed into it and therefore may be more extrinsically motivated in terms of responding to its structural qualities (i.e., more grade-oriented in school and more financially concerned in terms of career choices), which creates further problems in gaining a sense of intrinsic meaning in their life courses (e.g., Levine & Cureton, 1998).

In light of the previous discussion, the high degree of freedom and choice now granted in the identity moratoria of late-modern societies should have rather predictable positive and negative consequences. The benefits of a loosely structured, prolonged, choice-oriented moratorium should include accelerated cognitive, emotional, and ego development if an individual makes propitious decisions in relation to the opportunities available. My research on identity capital suggests that well-invested efforts can compound to launch people into satisfying and successful lives (Côté, 2002). However, the liabilities of loosely structured moratoria can also include living with the consequences of poor educational guidance, as in the case where emerging adults are encouraged to earn devalued or even useless educational credentials that can lead to dead-end jobs or no jobs at all.[10] But, even these misdirected emerging adults may be better off than many in the forgotten half who are falling further and further behind those with postsecondary educations in terms of job and earning prospects. The liabilities can also include having to make choices among what appear to be opportunities for growth and development, if the person is ill equipped to make such decisions. The poor preparation may be due to a lack of information or emotional immaturity—both of which can be paradoxically associated with the inexperience produced by the delay granted by the moratorium (i.e., some maturational tasks may now simply be postponed from the teen years to the 20s). At the same time, those with intellectual and psychiatric challenges face increasing difficulties in individualizing or self-socializing, because of their greater need for benign and caring settings without which even day-to-day functioning can be burdensome. Last, but not least, liabilities can include the squandering of prospects if the moratorium is devoted mainly to hedonistic activities and immediate gratifications not associated with

---

[10]For an analysis of this problem in Europe, see the report entitled *Misleading Trajectories? An Evaluation of the Unintended Effects of Labour Market Integration Policies for Young Adults in Europe* accessed February 16, 2004, from http://www.iris-egris.de/egris/tser/MisleadingSummary.PDF.

occupational identity development and important forms of developmental individualization (Côté, 2000).

The long-term consequence of these trends can only be speculated on at this time, but a case can be made that the life course differentiates beyond emerging adulthood to include an optional period that can be called *youthhood* (Côté, 2000; cf. Mørch, 1995). This new period of life can be a prolonged extension of emerging adulthood, or even a permanent lifestyle, which an increasing number of people seem to be undertaking.

I use the term *youthhood* to parallel the established English words *childhood* and *adulthood*, in which the suffix *hood* designates "a group sharing a specified state or quality" as in the word *sisterhood*, or "a condition, state, or quality" of the person as in the term *womanhood*. Youthhood designates both a quality of the individual's state of mind and the nature of a group within which the individual can self-define. Youthhood thus can have both a structural quality that is related to a delay of adulthood imposed on certain people and an individual quality undertaken on the basis of individual disposition and choice to take a delay. In either case, youthhood constitutes an indefinitely prolonged identity moratorium, in the sense that it is socially permissible to remain young for an indefinite period when in earlier societies social sanctions would have pushed the person to accept adult roles and adult self-definitions.

As a phenomenon experienced on a mass scale, the primary structural root of youthhood is most likely economic, beginning with either the exclusion from the labor force or the extended education necessary to now enter the labor force, but once a person is in this period, individual modes of coping may be evident in the differences in how youthhood is handled. Some may heavily invest their identity explorations in popular youth culture, others in higher educational systems, and yet others in the now disjunctive education-to-work cycles that often do not culminate in financial independence. For some, youthhood can be an extended period of relative playfulness, with little preparation for an adulthood that might follow, whereas others may mix work and play. In the latter case, the work experience may constitute a preparation for eventual adult independence, and the play experience is simply making the best of an imposed set of life circumstances (the delay in self-sufficiency).

Whatever the initial cause, those who delay occupational preparations for a transition to an economically independent adulthood too long (beyond the early-20s focal period of emerging adulthood) may find such a passage more difficult to the extent that they will have to relinquish some of their playful youth-culture activities yet not have a viable identity capital repertoire that would give them access to economic self-sufficiency. In these cases, youthhood could become a permanent state. Indeed, in the individualized societies of the contemporary West, pressures to relinquish youthhood are relatively weak compared with more traditional-collectivist societies in which normative pressure to adopt adult roles and responsibilities override desires to carry on in a carefree, noncommittal fashion (see Mead, 1928, for early observations of this difference for females, and Gilmore, 1990, for more contemporary examples for males).

What Identity Formation Takes Place in the Prolonged Identity Moratorium?

On the basis of the preceding Eriksonian analysis of the moratorium period and the sociological analyses of the economic opportunities and normative structures of the contemporary moratorium, identity formation would be expected to proceed at variable rates for people, depending on their circumstances, opportunities, and need for a context within which to deal with identity confusion and resolve their identity crisis. Indeed, identity would be the primary psychosocial attribute to change during this period—now stretching into the 20s—especially in reference to the primary task associated with the adoption of identities with which to function in the adult world. Following Erikson, Arnett (2000) identified three areas of identity exploration to be relevant during this period: worldview, work, and love. The literature on identity formation during the emerging adult period will help determine how these new identity formation tasks are handled by emerging adults.

A review of the first 25 years of identity research by Pascarella and Terenzini (1991) in their voluminous study *How College Affects Students* revealed that college attendance is reliably related to increases in variables such as political liberalism, various forms of self-concept, personal adjustment, and psychological well-being. However, there is little demonstrable effect of college attendance for variables such as identity formation, ego development, maturity, and other aspects of personality development, net of maturational effects (i.e., changes in these variables during emerging adulthood that might take place without someone attending college). Although one would think that college attendance should enhance or accelerate aspects of personality development, it may be expecting too much of colleges to have a direct impact on factors such as identity formation because these factors are not specifically targeted by the school curriculum. In the next section, however, I look more closely at the nature and quality of the identity literature.

Identity Status

The identity status literature is the most extensive in the identity field, and most of those working in the various human development and youth studies fields are familiar with the identity status paradigm, which operationalizes identity formation in terms of an exploration–commitment matrix, producing four identity statuses called diffusion, foreclosure, moratorium, and achievement (Marcia, 1966, 1980). The identity statuses were originally thought to represent a developmental sequence mapping the identity stage as laid out by Erikson, where explorations would be normative (i.e., typical) occurrences leading to commitments to an occupation, belief system, and lifestyle. If this were the normative course toward resolution of the identity stage, identity explorations would constitute a major transformative life event of which most adults would have explicit memories. However, 35 years of research suggests that far fewer exploration-based commitments can be found among those who could be said to have resolved the identity stage in purely Eriksonian terms (i.e., among those who are functioning adults with apparently low levels of identity confusion). As a result, conscious exploration as the best route to the formation of adult identities constituting resolution of the identity stage has not been empirically established. Indeed, the developmental sensitivity of the identity statuses themselves has been called into question (Côté & Levine, 1988; van Hoof, 1999), and it is apparent that the statuses do not represent a hard-structural sequence of identity formation (cf. Snarey & Bell, 2003). However, it is possible that the life course being studied is not what it originally seemed to be, especially now in late/postmodernity (Côté, 1996, 2000).

One problem with the identity status literature in general, as Meeus (1996) reported, is that only 49 out of 163 studies he reviewed actually address developmental concerns, and then mostly by inference; the rest focused on classification and correlates of the statuses themselves. And, although the identity status literature has established a fairly robust set of relationships between the identity statuses and correlates—especially with diffusion and achievement being most distinguishable in ways one would expect from a reading of Erikson (Côté & Schwartz, 2002)—these studies tend to use small, nonrandom samples with cross-sectional designs. Thus a clear picture of what takes place as part of identity formation is not readily apparent, and studies often contradict one another, although a number of helpful meta-analyses have been carried out (e.g., Meeus, 1996; Meeus, Iedema, Helsen, & Vollebergh, 1999; van Hoof, 1999).

Methodological concerns aside, surely exploration-based identity formation must be commonplace among those of emerging adult age—especially college students—and most students must graduate with a strong sense of themselves and where they are going in the world, especially occupationally. In fact, there is little evidence for this. Waterman (1999, p. 610) accepted that although this may be the case, more people make their way to the most differentiated identity status (achievement) than is the case in other developmental areas such as moral reasoning (postconventional stage) or ego development (integrated stage). Kroger (2000, p. 146) suggested that this lack of identity development during adolescence leaves considerable scope for later identity formation in adulthood. However, these explanations serve only to highlight how the logic of the identity status paradigm diverges from Erikson's normative approach, where he saw the bulk of the population as routinely resolving the identity stage even if some difficulties are experienced along the way.

What is more common from the literature is evidence that identity formation patterns beyond adolescence are rather erratic, with commitments showing instability and people regressing to less mature identity statuses, such as diffusion or foreclosure (e.g., Marcia, 1976; van Hoof, 1999). One explanation for the erratic findings of extensive regressions and progressions, rather than smooth and consistent movement toward mature forms of identity, is the anomic and fragmented developmental context that produces erratic trajectories in which integrated identity structures or identity configurations (Schachter, 2004) are formed by only a minority of people.

Supporting this possibility is a study conducted by Fadjukoff and Pulkkinen (2005), following over 200 Finnish adults from ages 27 to 36, and again to 42. They reported that because of the piecemeal approach to identity issues that most adults in their sample took, they had a difficult time determining an overall identity status for most adults, even when based on same-status classifications for only three or more domains out of five (politics, religion, occupation, relationships, and lifestyle). Fewer than 10% of those studied shared all five domains in the same status at any of the three data collection points. Overall, only one half of the sample had the same overall identity status at all three points, even with the three out of five criterion. Because diffusion was more common than achievement in the ideological areas and cohort diffusion level actually increased with age, Fadjukoff and Pulkkinen speculated that this finding may be a reflection of so-called postmodern trends. Occupational identity status was the most stable of the domains, showing the most progression toward achievement and the least regression to less mature statuses, especially between ages 36 and 42.

In sum, it is difficult to conclude that the identity statuses capture stage-progressive forms of psychosocial development during emerging adulthood, although occupational identity seems to show the most progressive development. It seems that identity status researchers were overly optimistic in terms of how well the identity statuses captured Erikson's concern about normative development, especially in the context of late-modern societies (cf. Côté, 1997, 2000). Moreover, what development does appear to take place among the statuses and their domains is not linear and orderly for most people. Although firm conclusions cannot be drawn regarding stage development in general, perhaps some can be drawn regarding how extensively the identity crisis is experienced, with its associated forms of development.

In contrast to identity stage resolution, identity status research has yielded results that are more consistent with respect to the more specific factor of the identity crisis as a transformative feature of the life course. It appears that some adolescents and emerging adults do experience a developmental shift toward more mature forms of identity status based on an identity crisis, defined in terms of an active consideration of options (i.e., through moratorium to achievement), especially during high school but also during college (Meeus, 1996). However, the active, self-conscious crisis that might be considered the stereotype of youth (i.e., the intensely curious young person determined to learn about and change the world) characterizes only a small minority of adolescents and emerging adults. Apparently, only between 10% and 30% of young (Western) people go through such a period for a discernible length of time, experiencing what Marcia termed the moratorium status, which in Eriksonian terms would signify that they take full advantage of any institutionalized moratoria in terms of resolving an identity crisis (e.g., van Hoof, 1999).

Most people studied thus far apparently do little active, conscious deliberation on a variety of alternative identities—instead taking a passive approach to just letting things happen for them, as is characteristic of diffusion (an estimated 25% of college students and 10%–20% of the adult population), or avoiding active deliberation and quietly taking the lead from their parents with little forethought, as is characteristic of foreclosure (estimated at 30%–40% of the adult population; cf. Kroger, 2000; Meeus et al., 1999; van Hoof, 1999; Waterman, 1999).

Those who do consciously consider options in relation to their self-attributes and then settle on a committed course of action (those 20%–30% who would be classed as achievement) generally do so over a long period, often dealing with only one or two identity domains at a time (e.g., Kroger, 1989; van Hoof, 1999). Others may only ever do this for one or two identity domains (especially occupation), which is perhaps one reason why it is difficult to identify identity achievement as a global, integrated developmental characteristic for most people.

Findings Using a New Measure of Identity Stage Resolution

Although the identity status paradigm has been the most popular approach adopted by the research community, other approaches are available. My own line of research is based on a different reading of Erikson[11] that led me to develop the Identity Stage Resolution Index (ISRI), which I have used to longitudinally monitor resolutions of the identity stage.[12] The ISRI is a six-item scale that taps identity-based markers representing the degree to which individuals feel they have (a) matured into adulthood (Adult Identity Resolution Scale; AIRS), and (b) found a permanent niche (lifestyle and community) in life (Societal Identity Resolution Scale; SIRS). High scores can be taken as an indicator that a person has settled key aspects of identity formation in the conventional or traditional sense of accepting mature and committed roles in an adult community. Low scores can be taken to mean that the person does not feel he or she has matured and does not have stable roles in an adult community. The actual items and their psychometric properties are presented in Table 4.1.

Erikson's historically informed, cross-cultural position accounts for the wording in two of the items tapping societal identity (Table 4.1), where the emphasis is on permanent and lifelong commitments, as was likely the case in most human societies for the total of human evolutionary history. I surmised that Erikson took his position from his anthropological studies of tribal and traditional cultures in which identity formation is highly structured and young people do not have the luxury of a prolonged identity crisis: Their community needs them to "get on with it" and accept an adult identity after a short identity moratorium. When the items were designed, considerations were made to make the items less stringent by removing the phrase "for the remainder of your life." However, removing it would potentially confound the items with tentative commitments a person holds as part of the identity experimentation associated with the moratorium period. In line with Erikson's cross-cultural, historical

---

[11] See Côté and Levine (1987) for a different interpretation of Erikson's writings, Côté and Levine (1988) for a critique of the identity status paradigm based on this reading, and Côté and Levine (2002) for a current neo-Eriksonian formulation of identity formation.

[12] This research involved some 600 respondents who were 17 to 20 years old first assessed in 1990 and 1991 (T1), with two follow-ups over a 10-year period, one in 1993 (T2) when respondents were in their early 20s, and another in 1999 through 2001 (T3) while they were in their late 20s. Two subsamples were followed: one first contacted during their first year of university and another first contacted during their last year of high school.

Table 4.1. The Identity Stage Resolution Index (ISRI) Item Analysis: Principal Components With Varimax Rotation

| | Factor loading | | | | | |
| | T1 | | T2 | | T3 | |
Item	F1 AIRS 2.6 EV 44% V	F2 SIRS 1.2 EV 20% V	F1 AIRS 2.8 EV 47% V	F2 SIRS 1.2 EV 19% V	F1 AIRS 2.8 EV 48% V	F2 SIRS 1.1 EV 18% V
Adult	0.85	0.10	0.85	0.19	0.86	0.03
Respected	0.74	0.19	0.75	0.10	0.70	0.20
Matured	0.84	0.20	0.80	0.21	0.74	0.32
Niche	0.29	0.64	0.34	0.68	0.18	0.79
Lifestyle	0.17	0.78	0.20	0.82	0.43	0.75
Community	0.00	0.80	0.03	0.82	0.06	0.79
Cronbach alpha for the 3 items of each scale	0.77	0.64	0.75	0.71	0.69	0.75

Note. The ISRI scale ranges from 0 to 24. T1 = Time 1; T2 = Time 2; T3 = Time 3; F1 = Factor 1; F2 = Factor 2; F3 = Factor 3; AIRS = Adult Identity Resolution Scale ranges from 0 to 12. EV = eigenvalue; V = variance; Adult = you consider yourself to be an adult; Respected = you feel respected by others as an adult; Matured = you feel that you have matured fully. The Societal Identity Resolution Scale (SIRS) ranges from 0 to 12. Niche = you have found your niche in life; Lifestyle = you have settled on a lifestyle that you are satisfied with for the remainder of your life; Community = you have found a community in which to live for the remainder of your life. Instructions: "Below are some statements about how people feel toward their life circumstances. Please use the scale provided to indicate how you feel in terms of each statement." 4 = *entirely true*; 3 = *true for the most part*; 2 = *somewhat true*; 1 = *a little true*; 0 = *not at all true*.

thinking, then, the more stringent wording was maintained. Doing so promises to facilitate cross-cultural comparisons in future research and does not gear the measure to the current late-modern societal climate in which tentative commitments are normalized. Although some may consider this strict wording a weakness of the items, I disagree, seeing it as a strength, firmly rooting the items in Eriksonian theory.[13]

Figure 4.1 and Table 4.2 show how each of the six items represent varying degrees of challenge for emerging adults. Finding a community is the most difficult task in all three of the age periods, whereas self-defining as an adult is the least difficult. Most striking is the fact that the overall sample mean of 1.8 at Time (T) 3 for the community item is significantly lower than the mean

---

[13] A seventh item, not used here, was worded "You know where you stand on world issues (political and economic)." It showed the same pattern of results as the other items, with its means falling between the items from the two subscales (T1 *M* = 2.33; T2 = 2.24; T3 = 2.85). It was dropped from the present analyses to make each subscale compatible in terms of the number of items in each for easier subscale comparisons.

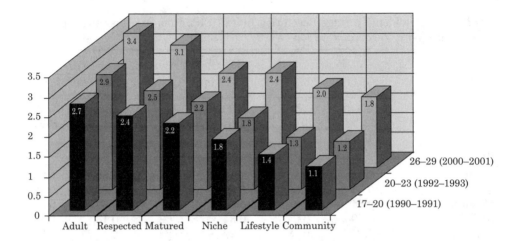

Figure 4.1. Means for individual items for the Identity Stage Resolution Index over the three age periods.

Table 4.2. Repeated Measures Multivariate Analyses of Variance F Values for Items by Panel and Sample

| Source | df | Items | | | | | |
		Adult	Respected	Matured	Niche	Lifestyle	Community
Time	2	36.7[***a]	40.3[***a]	4.4[**a]	22.9[***a]	20.9[***a]	20.9[***a]
Sample	2	0.0	0.2	0.0	0.6	0.0	0.1
Time × Sample	1	0.8	1.1	0.4	0.3	0.7	0.9

[a]Significant within-subject contrasts: Time 3 versus Time 1, Time 2.
*$p < .05$. **$p < .01$. ***$p < .001$.

of 2.7 for the adult item at T1, which supports the idea that the transition to adulthood is now more of a psychological than a sociological phenomenon, at least during the age ranges represented here (cf. Arnett, 2000). Moreover, no significant gains were made between the late teens and early 20s for any of the six individual items. It was only between the early and late 20s that gains show on item means.

Figure 4.2 and Table 4.3 show the pattern of results for the means of the two three-item subscales, along with the scale total, over the three data collection periods (the subscales correlate in the .40–.50 range). Significant, but small, progress is made on the AIRS from the late teens to the early 20s, in addition to slight progress made between the early 20s and late 20s. Consistent with the analysis of the individual items, the subscales show that more development takes place, and at an earlier age, for adult identity. However, societal identity develops at only about half the rate through to the late 20s. The slower passage for societal identity suggests that the cohort followed in this study was only about halfway to full resolution of this aspect of the identity stage even in their late 20s.

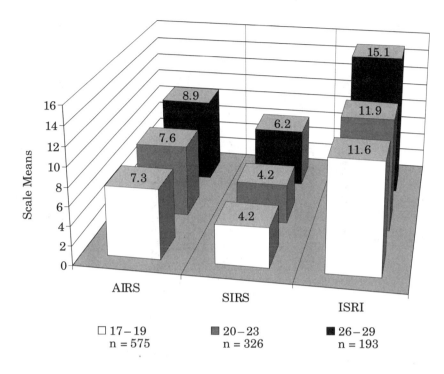

Figure 4.2. Means for the Identity Stage Resolution Index (ISRI) and its subscales over three age periods. AIRS = Adult Identity Resolution scale; SIRA = Societal Identity Resolution scale.

Table 4.3. Repeated Measures Multivariate Analyses of Variance F Values for Subscales by Panel, Sample, and Sex

Source		University		High school		Combined	
F tests	df	AIRS	SIRS	AIRS	SIRS	AIRS	SIRS
Within-subjects linear contrasts							
Time	2	40.3[***b]	31.6[***b]	18.6[***a,b]	13.7[***b]	52.2[***a,b]	54.8[***a,b]
Time × Sex	2	19.7[*a]	2.6	0.3	0.7	4.5[*]	3.1
Between-subjects effects							
Sex	1	0.9	0.5	0.7	1.6	0.5	1.2

Note. AIRS = Adult Identity Resolution scale; SIRS = Societal Identity Resolution scale.
[a]Significant within-subject contrast: Time 1 versus Time 2
[b]Significant within-subject contrast: Time 3 versus Time 2
*$p < .05$. **$p < .01$. ***$p < .001$.

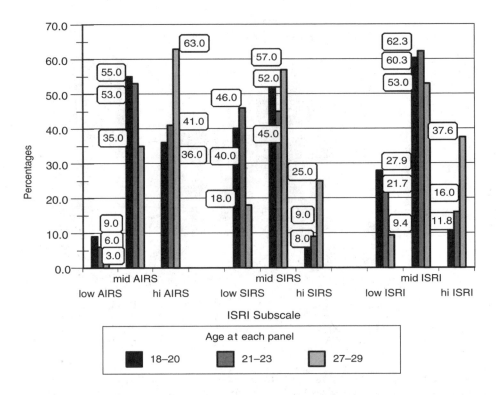

Figure 4.3. The Identity Stage Resolution Index (ISRI) and its subscales in tertiles for the three age periods. T1 = Time 1; T3 = Time 3; AIRS = Adult Identity Resolution Scale; SIRS = Societal Identity Resolution Scale.

Finally, when the scales are broken down into three equal categories (to represent the scale range rather than sample distribution), as shown in Figure 4.3, it is possible to estimate the proportions of the sample that could be said to have significantly resolved both of these aspects of the identity stage (high ISRI), those who are midway, and those who have made little progress (low ISRI) at each of the three age ranges. When overall stage resolution (total ISRI) is considered, only about one in three have significantly resolved the identity stage by their late 20s, 10% are seriously lagged, and about one half are midway. If the subscales are considered, far more could be said to have resolved the Adult Identity aspect of the identity stage than the Societal Identity aspect. On the basis of this breakdown, by their late 20s, 63% could be said to have significantly resolved the adult identity aspect of this stage (high AIRS), but only 25% have significantly resolved the societal identity aspect.

According to the crosstabulation of T1 and T3 overall ISRI categories (Table 4.4), being low on the ISRI at T1 made one less likely to be high at T3, which suggests a predisposition to a developmental arrest for a subsample of respondents. In contrast, being in the middle ISRI category at T1 made one more likely to move to the high ISRI category by T3. This finding demonstrates that the ISRI does indeed tap potentials for identity development during emerging adulthood. Scoring high at T1 did not predict future development, but self-

Table 4.4.   A Crosstabulation of T1 and T3 Identity Stage Resolution Index
Categories

Count/ adjusted residual	T3 ISRI tertile	T1 ISRI tertile			Total
		Low	Mid	High	
	Low	9	8	1	18
		1.9	−1.2	−0.8	
	Mid	35	52	13	100
		1.4	−1.7	0.6	
	High	14	49	8	71
		−2.5*	2.4*	−0.1	
Total		58	109	22	189

Note. * = significant using the 1.96 critical value.

designation of resolutions of the adult and societal aspects of the identity stage
is not expected to be stable, or particularly valid, in the late teens in late-
modern societies.

Identity Explorations During Emerging Adulthood

The longitudinal study using the ISRI also measured other aspects of identity
formation, some of which can be used as proxy measures of the three areas of
identity exploration identified by Arnett (2000): worldview, work, and love.
Some of these results have been presented elsewhere (Côté, 2002; Côté &
Roberts, 2003), whereas some are presented here for the first time.

Worldview

The short version of the Objective Measure–Ego Identity Status (Adams, Bennion, & Huh, 1987) has 16 items, with 4 items tapping each of the four identity
statuses in the domain of ideology (religion and politics), which can be considered a traditional pillar of a person's worldview (cf. Arnett, 2000). The moratorium scale most directly taps identity exploration with items such as "I'm not
sure what religion means to me. I'd like to make up my mind but I'm not done
looking yet" and "I'm not sure about my political beliefs, but I'm trying to figure
out what I can truly believe in." Results over the three data collection periods
suggest that only about one quarter of the sample was engaged in some form
of active exploration during the early emerging adulthood age ranges, whereas
virtually none doing so were in their late 20s. Results for the other three
identity status scales also reveal little ideological identity formation in terms
of politics and religion during emerging adulthood. There are no cohort-level
changes from T1 through T3 in endorsement of achievement items, although
it was the most widely endorsed status at all three age periods, with almost
three quarters indicating that they had settled these issues at each data point.
Foreclosure appears to be largely irrelevant, affecting few even in late

adolescence. Diffusion characterized about 25% of the sample throughout emerging adulthood.

This data set also allows the assessment of the relationship between the ISRI and identity status, which helps determine how useful the identity status measure might be in operationalizing the identity formation that might now be taking place during the 20s. For this analysis, the tertiles for the overall ISRI (combining the AIRS and SIRS) were used to simplify this presentation and to represent thresholds in the adulthood-transition aspect of identity stage resolution. In addition, only results for the Moratorium and Diffusion scales will be reported here to keep the focus on the issue of identity exploration and identity crisis. A series of one-way analyses of variance (ANOVAs) were separately conducted on each panel for identity Moratorium (active experimentation) and Diffusion (an apathetic noncommitment; Côté & Roberts, 2003).[14]

At T1, when respondents were in their late teens, those who were low and medium in terms of the ISRI were more engaged in identity explorations, as one would expect of those attempting to make progress in their identity formation. At T2, when respondents were in their early 20s, those in the low ISRI category showed greater diffusion, which indicates that those not making progress in their transition to adulthood were more noncommittal about their political and religious beliefs. Moratorium scores did not significantly differentiate the ISRI tertiles at T2. At T3, there was no significant differentiation in terms of moratorium or diffusion, which suggests that moratorium and diffusion are not relevant to circumstances differentiating late-20s cohort experiences.

These results suggest that what is measured by the ISRI means different things at different ages in terms of diffusion and moratorium. Most exploration and commitment activity regarding politics and religion apparently took place during the late teens. There was no significant change in the sample level of diffusion after the early 20s (i.e., levels of apathy are stable) and moratorium dropped off entirely (i.e., exploration ceases).

It appears, then, that at least for ideological identity formation among this sample, the most common position is for some emerging adults to make up their minds by their late teens and stick with those ideas; the second most common position was for other emerging adults to take an apathetic position and stick with it. Only about one third had engaged in active exploration of ideological identity issues in early emerging adulthood, with few doing so in their late 20s. There are several possible reasons for these findings. First, the identity statuses may be more appropriate for the ideological issues dealt with during adolescence than for those during emerging adulthood. Second, validity problems may make it difficult to draw any reliable nomothetic conclusions from the identity status operationalization, And, third, new issues may now be the object of exploration for emerging adults in late modernity, with its diminished normative structures making conventional religion and politics less relevant to their lives.

---

[14]Repeated measures multivariate analyses of variance (MANOVAs) were carried out, but the sample size loss is great when data from all three panels are included.

Work

Respondents were asked during the T3 data collection to indicate their current activity on a question providing the following alternatives: (a) working full-time with no specified termination date, (b) full-time work on a contract job, (c) part-time work with no specified termination date, (d) part-time temporary work, (e) education full time, and (f) other (e.g., homemaker). Although most were working full-time with no specified termination date (77% of the sample), those who were in the low ISRI category were significantly less likely to be in this activity (adjusted residual = −2.5) and significantly more likely to be in education full time (adjusted residual = +2.5). Although this question is admittedly a crude index of work exploration, one could surmise that those in permanent full-time jobs in the late 20s had completed this aspect of their work explorations, and those in full-time education (14% of the sample) were still in an institutionalized moratorium, and were yet to complete their work explorations. Those in the intermediate categories (9% of the sample) may have been having difficulties completing their work explorations perhaps because of economic conditions but were doing so outside of an institutionalized moratorium. A question tapping job satisfaction indicated that 48% were very satisfied with their jobs, 34% were satisfied, and the remainder endorsed responses ranging from having *mixed feelings* to being *not at all satisfied*. On an additional question, about two thirds expressed a satisfaction with their salaries. Thus, some 20% to 30% may be disposed to modify their occupational identity to find a more satisfactory job or one with a better salary.

What can be said with some confidence about these findings is that most of the sample had settled on some sort of occupational identity by the end of their 20s, and the majority of these were happy with those jobs and their salaries, so would be unlikely to be facing immediate changes and further exploration. However, that leaves about one quarter who may continue with occupational explorations and who would be considered prime candidates for involvement in youthhood as an alternative to adulthood.

Love

Respondents were also asked during the T3 data collection to indicate their current marital status and living arrangements. Forty-one percent indicated that they were currently married, and the remainder were single (including separated, divorced, or widowed). With respect to living arrangements, 22% were living alone, 14% were cohabiting with an unmarried spouse, 41% were residing with a married spouse, 14% were living with a friend, and 9% were co-residing with their parents. When cross-tabulated with the T3 ISRI categories, those in the low ISRI category were significantly more likely to be single (adjusted residual = +2.2) and significantly less likely to be married (adjusted residual = −2.2). The reverse was true for those in the high ISRI category: They were significantly more likely to be married (adjusted residual = +2.9) and significantly less likely to be single (adjusted residual = −2.9). Significance was found in the cross-tabulation between the ISRI categories and living arrangements only for "living with a married spouse," repeating the preceding findings for those in the high and low ISRI categories. However, those in the high ISRI category were underrepresented in every category except "living with a married spouse" and those in the low category were overrepresented in all but one of these other categories (cohabiting).

Again, this is a crude indicator, in this case of love explorations, but if "living with a married spouse" is used as an endpoint in love explorations, 41% of the sample can be counted as having completed their search. However, although those who were cohabiting may have completed their search, they had not made the traditional commitment signaling the end of the search. Those who were living alone, with friends, or with parents could be argued to be still searching or not interested in the search, but either way do not show signs of a completion of this aspect of their identity formation. This criterion would also make them prime candidates for inclusion in the growing number of people this age who appear to be undertaking a period of youthhood as an alternative to adulthood.

In sum, in reference to the identity explorations that might be taking place in emerging adulthood, it appears that the least activity is with the traditional religious and political worldviews, moderate levels of activity are evident in love explorations, and the most is accomplished in work explorations.

Identity Confusion

If the contemporary institutionalized moratorium provided a benign context for the resolution of the identity stage for all emerging adults, there would be little evidence of persistent identity problems, especially among those who had completed college and had steady employment, as in the samples I have studied. That assumption was put to the test when a portion of the sample (those contacted during the last year of high school, see footnote 11) was administered Steinberg and Schnall's (2000) Identity Confusion Scale, a 15-item 6-point scale with an alpha coefficient of .86 for this sample. This clinically derived questionnaire is used as part of a battery to detect dissociative identity disorder, with identity confusion constituting one of five possible symptom clusters.[15] Items forming this scale include statements such as "I feel that I need to find my true self," "There is a struggle inside me about who I really am," and "I feel confused as to who I really am." When the distribution of scores for this subsample was examined, 18.5% scored as having mild identity confusion, and 20% showed moderate identity confusion, the latter of which Steinberg suggests is indicative of an underlying clinical condition, perhaps related to earlier traumatic events.

Results indicate that identity confusion is implicated in low resolutions of the identity stage, with those in the "low" category of the AIRS, SIRS, and ISRI reporting significantly higher levels of identity confusion than do those

---

[15] This measure only became available in 2000, so was used only in the T3 questionnaire sent to the high school subsample in 2001.

in the other two categories (one-way ANOVAs for T3, F = 4.4, 3.3, 5.4, respectively, $p < .05$, Student-Newman-Keuls contrasts).

Analyses were conducted with the three categories of identity confusion previously identified (none, mild, moderate) to differentiate the ISRI scores from the three panels. These results show that those with "moderate" identity confusion in their late 20s had lower ISRI scores not only at that time but also at both T1 and T2 (repeated measures multivariate analysis of variance [MANOVA] F = 11.9, $p < .001$, with significant contrasts). This result suggests that identity confusion might have been a persistent condition for about 20% of the sample from their late teens that an identity crisis did not remedy. Also, it appears that higher levels of identity confusion make it difficult for some people, beginning in their late teens through their late 20s, to resolve the identity crisis and form an adult identity.

What Does the Empirical Research Show About Identity Formation During Emerging Adulthood?

On the basis of the preceding review of identity status literature, as well as findings from my own research focused on this issue, how can the now prolonged transition to adulthood be characterized in terms of identity formation? These sources of information constitute two different ways of approaching the problem, so I address them separately.

With respect to identity status research, the pattern of results seems to provide only rough estimates about identity formation and is of limited use in characterizing identity change during emerging adulthood and adulthood, particularly because of the instability of the status assignments. The identity statuses were developed to characterize adolescent development around expressions of present commitments and future courses of action. Although these results may provide gross estimates of identity activities, from an Eriksonian perspective, any commitments expressed during the identity moratorium should be viewed as experimental, and therefore unstable, unless there is evidence that the person has put them into concrete courses of action. For example, a 17-year-old stating that he or she is committed to becoming a lawyer needs to be taken lightly, because it is quite likely that those plans will change, perhaps to other careers, depending on ensuing circumstances, such as getting into a university, getting good grades there, getting into a law school, passing the bar exams, and so forth. A 27-year-old stating that he or she is a lawyer would be a much more convincing indicator of identity achievement in the area of occupation. With respect to ideological identity, my own research on religious and political identity formation during the 20s shows very little activity, which suggests that most emerging adults have already made their mind up or avoided the issue entirely and then stuck with that position.

My view has been that the identity statuses have a strong characterological component (e.g., Côté & Levine, 1988), such that some people have personality dispositions that may change during the identity stage but are likely to remain much the way they were before that stage. For example, a personality type that is conformist and deferent to authority, such as the prototypical foreclosure

(Marcia, 1980), is not likely to be radically affected by opportunities for noncon-formity and rejection of authority. In a similar manner, a diffuse–avoidant (Berzonsky, 1992) personality type is not likely to suddenly become focused and searching. Other personality or character types are more open to change and are most likely to be affected by opportunities to explore themselves and their world, as permitted by the institutionalized moratorium (I refer to two such types as searchers and resolvers; Côté & Levine, 2002). This character-type hypothesis helps explain why most adults score as foreclosure and diffu-sion, whereas only a minority has a history of engaging in in-depth exploration.

In light of my own research on identity formation during the 20s, it appears that for this sample, which largely undertook higher-education programs, the late teens to late 20s does indeed constitute a prolonged identity moratorium, which for many is apparently not over. With regard to the progress of the cohort in terms of fitting in as measured by the ISRI, some gains are made during the focal emerging adulthood period—the early 20s—for the formation of an Adult Identity, but none is evident for Societal Identity. In fact, most of the cohort progress measured by both ISRI subscales is made between the early and late 20s, not between the late teens and early 20s. This finding suggests that many important transitional events might be taking place in the mid-20s, so the original focus on the age period from 18 to 25 originally specified by Arnett (e.g., 2000, p. 469) should be expanded to explicitly include the full age period from 18 to 30, at least when college students are studied. Arnett does allow that the emerging adulthood period can constitute the entire 20s for some people, with ages 18 to 25 being the focal period of development. But the preceding results suggest that focusing on the early 20s may be too early for key features of identity formation to come to fruition for those who are taking the higher-education route to a career.

With respect to adult- and societal-identity formation, progress was made during the 20s, albeit at a slower pace than one might expect if the transition to adulthood were completed on a normative basis during the 20s. The results do support the notion that psychological progress to adulthood is more advanced than is the sociological progress during the age period previously discussed, which is consistent with the well-replicated findings that emerging adults identify psychological characteristics such as "accepting responsibility for the consequences of your actions" as being far more important in their minds than sociological characteristics such as being married or settled into a long-term career (see Arnett & Galambos, 2003, for cross-cultural replications of this).

Future Research: What Needs to Be Known About Identity Formation During Emerging Adulthood?

In contemplating an agenda for future research, emerging adulthood needs to be considered in an interdisciplinary fashion, taking the best of past theory while looking at contemporary circumstances with fresh eyes. What I mean by this is that both sociological and psychological aspects of emerging adulthood need to be considered from the insight provided by scholars such as Erikson who based his work on historical and cross-cultural observation of variation in the transition to adulthood. Armed with these scholarly perspectives, researchers need to examine the variety of experiences among emerging adults now facing the serious challenges and opportunities of the prolonged transition to adulthood.

For example, religion and politics may have an entirely different relevance for many emerging adults today. Current cohorts are at a historically low level of involvement in organized religion and the mainstream political process; among many of those who take an interest, involvements tend to be more individualized, based on a picking and choosing of various elements that they find personally appealing (Côté, 2000). Given the cohort-wide ambivalence and the consequent low level of pressure to explore these issues, researchers should not expect to find the type of crises that either Erikson or Marcia thought would be pivotal in terms of forging or adopting a worldview.

Therefore, with respect to the identity crisis and its relationship to the identity moratorium, I think there may be a new form of crisis focused on different issues, especially among college-attending youth. I call this the *post-modern identity crisis,* not because I think we are moving into a postmodern society (Côté, 2000), but because some people embrace and celebrate fluid identities associated with, among other things, superficial interpersonal displays of appearance, a lack of core character and consistency, and eschewing social commitments in favor of contextual allegiances (cf. Gergen, 1991). In Erikson's terms, some emerging adults can lack a sense of fidelity—something "larger than themselves" to have faith in—and will experience a sense of identity confusion as a result. Postmodern philosophy (e.g., Hollinger, 1994) currently provides a convenient but paradoxical solution to this dilemma—to have faith that there is nothing in which to have faith. This dilemma appears to be commonplace among college students in the arts and humanities, where their curriculum can teach them to think this way and where they may find inspiration from professors who have embraced postmodernism. These students may be able to explicitly articulate such a position, whereas other emerging adults may pick up a moral position akin to this from a culture that is itself normatively adrift in terms of core values and commitments to future courses of action tied to collective goals.

This is the type of dilemma that some academic postmodernists claim everyone is experiencing now, but I think it is less widespread than that and restricted more to the self-indulgent who have the luxury to play such youthful games because their parents are wealthy or they have ensconced themselves in higher-education settings that encourage such affectations. Certainly, it is easy to find this form of crisis—with an insistence that commitments are restrictive or dogmatic—among graduate students in the social sciences, arts, and humanities. These are bright emerging adults, but in celebrating extreme relativism and superficiality, they often think themselves out of an academic identity (i.e., they may be smart enough to get into postmodern thought, but not smart enough to get out of it). They are reminiscent of what Marcia (1980) once called "alienated Achievements," who were committed to a lack of commitment as a form of social protest in the 1960s and 1970s, but this new alienation seems more self-interested and narcissistic. In any event, a focused study on what a prolonged identity crisis does to those who stay in the educational system indefinitely would perhaps offer some idea of what the future holds if what I call *youthhood* continues to become more common. I have many personal anecdotes about the postmodern identity crisis flaunted by students I have encountered over the past decade or so, but I also think this development can be systematically studied. For example, 37% of those who were in the low ISRI category in their late 20s were still in educational institutions full-time, more than would be expected according to the distribution of observed frequencies (adjusted residual = +2.5, $p < .05$).

To take another step back, researchers can consider the postmodern identity crisis experienced by some academics who work in the field of identity studies. Academic postmodernism has grown to be a formidable force in many disciplines (see Gergen, 2001, for this force in psychology) and seems to draw membership from those disaffected with the conventional wisdom of those disciplines. Typically, postmodernists accuse the discipline of being centric in some way and they chide those afflicted with this centrism to relinquish their claims to generalizable knowledge (e.g., Payne, 2001).

This scenario applies to the postmodern critique of the so-called modernist perspectives such as developmental approaches to identity (e.g., Rattansi & Phoenix, 1997). On the one hand, although the normative transition to adulthood appears to be delayed because of structural (economically based) factors that are creating new identity problems, this situation does not appear to create universal identity fragmentation (here operationalized as identity stage resolution, diffusion, and identity confusion). Structural delays may be exacerbated by the challenges of integration into an atomized society where institutional routes to an economically self-sufficient adulthood are disjunctive and adulthood itself is vaguely defined and even hostile to new members (as in entering the workforce). On the other hand, it appears that more serious levels of identity confusion, which likely have roots in childhood and adolescent trauma, slow or arrest progress to adulthood. In short, identity confusion appears to be a significant impediment among a minority of those making the transition to adulthood, but it is not an inevitable disabling factor among the entire cohort, even as the cohort shows a historically delayed transition to adulthood. By their late 20s, over one third seem to have made significant progress in their transition to adulthood in terms of adult- and societal-identity factors, and an additional 50% have made moderate progress and will likely make more progress in their early 30s. Only 10% appear to be seriously lagged.

The concept of youthhood previously discussed is relevant in understanding responses to the postmodern claim of universal identity confusion and can be used to interpret the ISRI distributions over time and within cohort, adding to Arnett's propositions regarding emerging adulthood. Indeed, it is noteworthy that Arnett (2000) found that about 10% of those over 30 years of age answer "in some ways yes, in some ways no" to the question "Do you feel like you have reached adulthood?" These results suggest that there are cohort-wide structural delays in the progress to adulthood that last until the late 20s and that a sizable minority of the cohort shows signs of a more or less permanent condition associated with chronic identity problems. These problems may be manifestations of characterological identity diffusion or clinical identity confusion and become exacerbated by economic obstacles and reduced normative structures leading to adulthood. The possibility that chronic identity confusion is a problem for a significant minority is supported by the retrospective results showing that those who had moderate identity confusion (the highest level for this sample) had delayed identity formation progress dating back to their late teens. Thus, to the extent that identity formation is now individualized, personal characteristics can have an impact on the life circumstances now faced by the entire cohort. In the past, when identity was more ascribed, societies more collective, and personal characteristics less salient in adult roles, it is possible that identity confusion problems rooted in earlier stress and trauma would not have had the same impact on the transition to adulthood.

In other words, although the late teens and early 20s may be viewed as a prime transitory period of emerging adulthood, when the institutionalized moratorium is stretched to the late 20s, it may come to constitute a more permanent lifestyle—youthhood—for a smaller but significant proportion of contemporary cohorts. This would be expected to occur more often among those who do not use the institutionalized moratorium to deal with internal conflicts from previous psychosocial stages or to make preparations for external involvements in the adult world; either way, identity confusion may be exacerbated or engendered. For some of those experiencing this youthhood, the late 20s may now constitute an avoidance of traditional adulthood (low ISRI) whereas for others it may be a quasi adulthood (mid ISRI), with more subjective integration in terms of self-defining as an adult, but less of the objective integration into adult society (in reaction to structural barriers associated with economic exclusion from full participation). In the past, economic integration into adult society was not only earlier but also more directly monitored and normatively sanctioned by societies. Subjective, self-identification factors would likely have followed from community pressures to be a fully productive member, regardless of the psychological makeup of the person. Without societal monitoring and sanctioning, individual psychological differences may thus have become much more important in the progress a person makes toward adulthood. Therefore those with certain psychological characteristics may now be more likely to enter youthhood as a prolonged, even permanent, state. Those who treat this period as a temporary state may simply be patiently waiting longer for the economic opportunities that are now occurring later for current cohorts.

I close by providing an integration of Arnett's pioneering work on emerging adulthood with other recent work of my own pointing to a prolonged transition to adulthood, to begin the task of developing a more differentiated view of the life course for the scientific community to use. Accordingly, I offer the life-course option chart (Figure 4.4) as a starting point for discussion about the changing nature of the transition to adulthood. In this figure, I include adolescence, which is a normative period through which virtually everyone in Western societies now passes, if only in terms of a conferred age-based social status. Emerging adulthood designates a period that can be entered but that is not inevitable if the person elects to move into what would be considered traditional adulthood. Finally, youthhood is included as a state that people might enter after emerging adulthood if they take the conditions of emerging adulthood—their "youth"—as a more or less permanent alternative to adulthood. Finally,

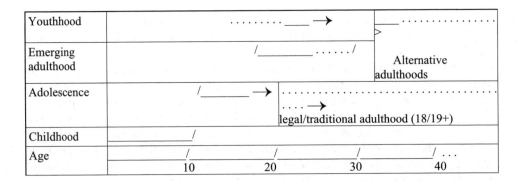

Figure 4.4. Potential life-course periods in the postindustrial, late-modern transition to adulthood.

the figure makes provisions for the development of new forms of adulthood that are just beginning to be recognized and understood (e.g., Côté, 2000).

The arrows show possible trajectories people can take in the transition to adulthood or youthhood, trajectories that can be based on choice or necessity. My hope is that this chart will further an understanding of the complexities emerging adults now face in contemporary society, whether in reaction to postindustrial economic or to late-modern anomic, influences with their myriad potentials and problems. And with this understanding, my hope is that the adult community will attend to those experiencing difficulties and lend them a hand in realizing their potentials as full, productive members of adult society.

Conclusions

On the basis of the available theory and empirical evidence, what can be said about the risks and benefits of identity formation during emerging adulthood in contemporary Western societies?

If it is assumed that a prolonged identity moratorium is now experienced by most emerging adults well into their 20s, sensitivity is needed to the fact that whereas it is voluntarily sought by some, it is also imposed on others because of economic circumstances (i.e., there may be no financial option but to delay the entry into adulthood). Among those for whom the delay is voluntary, we must also distinguish between those who are personally equipped and those who are not prepared to rise to the challenge of meeting the rigors for undertaking an individualized route to adulthood. Among the former are more likely to be found those whom (a) identity status researchers call Moratoriums and Achievements, (b) I suggest are undertaking developmental individualized routes armed with identity capital, and (c) Erikson would say use the period to resolve an identity crisis to manage and resolve identity confusion, and are therefore more likely to emerge from the identity moratorium with a viable resolution to the identity stage. Among those who are not equipped, one would expect to find extended periods of identity confusion that interfere with psychosocial task resolutions, such as undertaking productive forms of identity explorations in the areas of worldview, work, and love. These individuals would score low on Identity Stage Resolution even into the late 20s and beyond, and would be more likely to adopt youthhood as a permanent alternative to traditional forms of adulthood.

Among those on whom the identity moratorium is imposed, those who are prepared to benefit from it and those who are not need to be distinguished. According to what is known about identity formation, those who are prepared for an imposed moratorium would be more likely to be identified as foreclosure by identity status researchers (and therefore have the characterological basis for functional adaptation to emerging adulthood). They should also be more likely to take default individualized routes to adulthood armed with some forms of identity capital derived from their community integrations (Côté & Schwartz, 2002) and to experience a very muted form of identity crisis because of the high level of identification with their parents (Erikson, 1975). However, among those who are not equipped to deal with an imposed moratorium, those who are characterological diffusions as well as those who have low levels of identity capital (especially because of disadvantaged socioeconomic backgrounds) are of special concern. In addition, concern is needed for those who experience identity confusion (from the identity crisis, earlier traumatic events, or psychiatric or intellectual challenges) at levels that interfere with either an epigenetic (building the basis for the resolution of subsequent stages) or functional adaptation to the new requirements for an effective transition to adulthood.

In my view, keeping the potential risks and benefits of this period in full view when studying emerging adults will counteract the tendency to celebrate the period of emerging adulthood as something of an unmitigated advantage being granted to young people today. Certainly, for those who do benefit from it—whether it be because their parents are rich, they are smart, they are highly motivated, or they are lucky—it promises to be a wonderful privilege that extends their identity formation and enhances their identity options. But, not everyone has wealthy parents, is smart, has good emotional health, is bustling with enthusiasm, or is lucky. In fact, when the forgotten half (especially the 10% of American emerging adult males who are caught up in the justice system and the large numbers who are marginally employed; Halperin, 2001) is included, a sizable proportion of young people do not fit even one of these positive profiles. A theory of emerging adulthood must include everyone, not just those who are most easily contacted to fill out questionnaires.

In the future, my hope is that researchers in this area will carefully study the roots of emerging adulthood by laying out and empirically testing the various theories being generated about it (e.g., psychological, sociological, education-to-work, normative, as discussed earlier). As the roots of this new life-course phase are better understood, more should be learned about what can be done to ameliorate its negative consequences and enhance its positive consequences for all those passing through it, with special attention given to disadvantaged and disenfranchised groups, such as the forgotten half, minorities and immigrants, the disabled, the socially marginalized, and youth in developing countries who are finding that this period is becoming available to, or imposed on, them.

References

Adams, G. R., Bennion, L., & Huh, K. (1987). *Objective measure of ego identity status: A reference manual*. Unpublished manuscript, University of Guelph, Ontario, Canada.

Allen, M., Harris, S., & Butlin, G. (2001). *Finding their way: A profile of young Canadian graduates*. Ottawa, Ontario, Canada: Statistics Canada.

Arnett, J. J. (2000). Emerging adulthood: A theory of development from the late teens through the twenties. *American Psychologist, 55*, 469–480.

Arnett, J. J., & Galambos, N. (Eds.). (2003). *New directions for child and adolescent development: Vol. 100 Exploring cultural conceptions of the transition to adulthood*. San Francisco: Jossey-Bass.

Berzonsky, M. D. (1992). A process perspective on identity and stress management. In G. R. Adams, T. P. Gullotta, & R. Montemayor (Eds.), *Adolescent identity formation* (pp. 193–215). Newbury Park, CA: Sage.

Bowlby, G. (2000, Spring). The school-to-work transition. *Perspectives*, 43–48.

Bowlby, G., & Jennings, P. (1999). Youth employment: A lesson on its decline. *Education Quarterly Review, 5*(3), 36–42.

Butlin, G. (1999). Determinants of postsecondary participation. *Education Quarterly Review, 5*(3), 9–35.

Côté, J. E. (1996). Sociological perspectives on identity formation: The culture–identity link and identity capital. *Journal of Adolescence, 19*, 419–430.

Côté, J. E. (1997). An empirical test of the identity capital model. *Journal of Adolescence, 20*, 577–597.

Côté, J. E. (2000). *Arrested adulthood: The changing nature of maturity and identity*. New York: New York University Press.

Côté, J. E. (2002). The role of identity capital in the transition to adulthood: The individualization thesis examined. *Journal of Youth Studies, 5*(2), 117–134.

Côté, J. E., & Allahar, A. (1996). *Generation on hold: Coming of age in the late twentieth century*. New York: New York University Press.

Côté, J. E., & Levine, C. (1987). A formulation of Erikson's theory of ego identity formation. *Developmental Review, 7*, 273–325.

Côté, J. E., & Levine, C. (1988). A critical examination of the ego identity status paradigm. *Developmental Review, 8*, 147–184.

Côté, J. E., & Levine, C. (2002). *Identity formation, agency, and culture*. Hillsdale, NJ: Erlbaum.

Côté, J. E., & Roberts, S. (2003). *Monitoring the transition to adulthood: The identity stage resolution index*. Paper presented at the 10th annual meeting of the Society for Research on Identity Formation, Vancouver, British Columbia, Canada.

Côté, J. E., & Schwartz, S. (2002). Comparing psychological and sociological approaches to identity: Identity status, identity capital, and the individualization process. *Journal of Adolescence, 25*, 571–586.

Erikson, E. H. (1950). *Childhood and society*. New York: Norton.

Erikson, E. H. (1958). *Young man Luther*. New York: Norton.

Erikson, E. H. (1959). Late adolescence. In D. H. Funkenstein (Ed.), *The student and mental health: An international view* (pp. 66–106). Cambridge, MA: The Riverside Press.

Erikson, E. H. (1968). *Identity: Youth and crisis*. New York: Norton.

Erikson, E. H. (1975). *Life history and the historical moment*. New York: Norton.

Erikson, E. H. (1980). *Identity and the life cycle: A reissue*. New York: Norton.

Evans, R. I. (1969). *Dialogue with Erik Erikson*. New York: Dutton.

Fadjukoff, P., & Pulkkinen, L. (2005). Identity processes in adulthood: Diverging domains. *Identity: An International Journal of Theory and Research, 5*, 1–20.

Frenette, M. (2000). Overqualified? Recent graduates and the needs of their employers. *Education Quarterly Review, 7*(1), 6–20.

Furlong, A., & Cartmel, F. (1997). *Young people and social change: Individualization and risk in late modernity*. Buckingham, England: Open University Press.

Gergen, K. J. (1991). *The saturated self: Dilemmas of identity in contemporary life*. New York: Basic Books.

Gergen, K. J. (2001). Psychological science in a postmodern context. *American Psychologist, 56,* 803–813.

Gilmore, D. (1990). *Manhood in the making: Cultural concepts of masculinity.* New Haven, CT: Yale University Press.

Halperin, S. (Ed.). (2001). *The forgotten half revisited: American youth and young families, 1988–2008.* Washington, DC: American Youth Policy Forum.

Heinz, W. (2002). Self-socialization and post-traditional society. *Advances in Life Course Research, 7,* 41–64.

Hollinger, R. (1994). *Postmodernism and the social sciences: A thematic approach.* Thousand Oaks, CA: Sage.

Kroger, J. (1989). *Identity in adolescence: The balance between self and other.* London: Routledge.

Kroger, J. (2000). Ego identity status research in the new millennium. *International Journal of Behavioral Development, 24,* 145–148.

Lapsley, D., Enright, R. D., & Serlin, R. C. (1985). Toward a theoretical perspective on the legislation of adolescence. *Journal of Early Adolescence, 5,* 441–466.

Levine, A., & Cureton, J. S. (1998). *When hope and fear collide: A portrait of today's college student.* San Francisco: Jossey-Bass.

Marcia, J. E. (1976). *Studies in ego identity.* Unpublished manuscript, Simon Fraser University, Vancouver, Canada.

Marcia, J. E. (1966). Development and validation of ego identity status. *Journal of Personality and Social Psychology, 3,* 551–558.

Marcia, J. E. (1980). Identity in adolescence. In J. Adelson (Ed.), *Handbook of adolescent psychology* (pp. 159–187). New York: Wiley.

Mead, M. (1928). *Coming of age in Samoa.* New York: Morrow.

Meeus, W. (1996). Studies on identity development in adolescence: An overview of research and some new data. *Journal of Youth and Adolescence, 25,* 569–598.

Meeus, W., Iedema, J., Helsen, M., & Vollebergh, W. (1999). Patterns of adolescent identity development: Review of literature and longitudinal analysis. *Developmental Review, 19,* 419–461.

Montgomery, M., & Côté, J. E. (2003). The transition to university: Outcomes and adjustments. In G. Adams & M. Berzonsky (Eds.), *The Blackwell handbook of adolescence* (pp. 149–172). Oxford, England: Blackwell.

Mørch, S. (1995). Culture and the challenge of adaptation: Foreign youth in Denmark. *International Journal of Comparative Race and Ethnic Studies, 2,* 102–115.

Morris, M., & Western, B. (1999). Inequality in earnings at the close of the twentieth century. *Annual Review of Sociology, 25,* 623–657.

Nobert, L., & McDowell, R. (1994). *Profile of post-secondary education in Canada 1993 edition.* Ottawa, Ontario, Canada: Minister of Supply and Services.

Normand, J. (1995, Winter). Education of women in Canada. *Canadian Social Trends,* 17–21.

Pascarella, E. T., & Terenzini, P. T. (1991). *How college affects students: Findings and insights from twenty years of research.* San Francisco: Jossey Bass.

Payne, M. (2001). Limitations unlimited: Interrogating some finer points of the "scientific study" of adolescence. *Journal of Youth Studies, 4,* 175–193.

Psychoanalyst coined identity crisis. (1994, May 13). *The Globe and Mail,* p. E8.

Rattansi, A., & Phoenix, A. (1997). Rethinking youth identities: Modernist and postmodernist frameworks. In J. Bynner, L. Chisholm, & A. Furlong (Eds.), *Youth, citizenship and social change in a European* context (pp. 121–150). Aldershot, England: Ashgate.

Schachter, E. P. (2004). Identity configurations: A new perspective on identity formation in contemporary society. *Journal of Personality, 72,* 167–199.

Schwartz, B. (2000). Self-determination: The tyranny of freedom. *American Psychologist, 55,* 79–88.

Schwartz, B. (2004, January 23). The tyranny of choice. *The Chronicle of Higher Education, 50*(20), p. B6.

Snarey, J., & Bell, D. (2003). Distinguishing structural and functional models of human development: A response to "What transits in an identity status transition?" *Identity: An International Journal of Theory and Research, 3,* 221–230.

Snarey, J., Kohlberg, L., & Noam, G. (1983). Ego development in perspective: Structural stage, functional phase, and cultural age-period models. *Developmental Review, 3,* 303–338.

Statistics Canada. (2003a). *Education in Canada: Raising the standard. 2001 Census: Analysis series.* Ottawa, Ontario, Canada: Author.

Statistics Canada. (2003b). *2001 Census: Analysis series income of Canadian families. 2001 Census: Analysis series.* Ottawa, Ontario, Canada: Author.

Steinberg, M., & Schnall, M. (2000). *The stranger in the mirror: Dissociation—The hidden epidemic.* New York: Cliff Street Books.

Szasz, T. (1973). *The second sin.* Garden City, NY: Anchor Press.

Tannock, S. (2001). *Youth at work: The unionized fast-food and grocery workplace.* Philadelphia: Temple University Press.

van Hoof, A. (1999). The identity status field re-reviewed: An update of unresolved and neglected issues with a view on some alternative approaches. *Developmental Review, 19,* 497–556.

Waterman, A. (1999). Identity, the identity statuses, and identity status development: A contemporary statement. *Developmental Review, 19,* 591–647.

Weigert, A. J., Teitge, J. S., & Teitge, D. W. (1986). *Society and identity: Toward a sociological psychology.* Cambridge, England: Cambridge University Press.

5

Ethnic Identity Exploration in Emerging Adulthood

Jean S. Phinney

The concept of emerging adulthood refers to a period when young people are legally adult but do not yet see themselves as fully adult and have not taken on the range of responsibilities that are characteristic of adulthood in developed societies (Arnett, 2000). The challenges of this period have been defined largely in individualistic terms, such as forming a personal identity, attaining independence from one's parents, and assuming financial responsibility for oneself.

For members of ethnic minority groups in a society such as the United States, the criteria for reaching adulthood may be different for both demographic and cultural reasons. Specific experiences can either shorten or extend the period of emerging adulthood. Many factors, both individual and contextual, determine whether and to what extent young people experience a period when they are no longer adolescents but not yet adults. Young people from American ethnic minority backgrounds deal with many of the same issues as do their White peers, but they may have additional challenges and strengths that influence the point at which they attain adulthood (Arnett, 1998, 2003; Arnett & Galambos, 2003). Many minority youth are expected to take on adult responsibilities earlier than their peers from the mainstream culture (Cauce, Stewart, Roderguez, Cochran, & Ginzler, 2003). Minority young people, as part of their cultural heritage, typically value close and interdependent relationships with their family more strongly than do European American youth (Fuligni, Tseng, & Lam, 1999; Phinney, Ong, & Madden, 2000); as a result, they may feel obliged to assist the family with chores and to contribute financially to the family. For example, with socioeconomic status controlled, significantly more minority college students than European American students report that an important reason for attending college is to be able to help their family financially (Phinney, Dennis, & Osorio, in press). Young people from minority and immigrant backgrounds often provide support for their family when they are able (Fuligni & Witkow, 2004).

Because of their sense of interdependence and of responsibility to their families, minority young people may consider themselves as adults at an earlier age. Research with Canadian aboriginal college students has shown that they believe that they reach adulthood at a younger age than their European origin peers (Cheah & Nelson, 2004). Youth from some minority cultures also experience pressure to marry and have children at an early age (Phinney, 1999); if they become parents, these young people are likely to consider themselves adults. Although marriage is not always an indicator of adulthood in the majority culture (Arnett, 1998), it is seen as an important marker in many cultural contexts. Thus young people from minority and immigrant backgrounds may reach at least some of the markers of adulthood earlier than do their peers from the dominant culture and experience a shorter period of emerging adulthood.

However, in other respects, emerging adulthood may be extended for members of ethnic minority groups. Identity exploration in the areas of love, work, and worldviews has been cited as one of the defining characteristics of emerging adulthood (Arnett, 2000). In addition to identity exploration in those areas, ethnic group members must deal with identity issues in relation to their ethnic and racial heritage. These identity domains are far more central for minorities than for majority group members (Phinney & Alipuria, 1990). Their sense of membership in an ethnic, racial, or cultural group is an underlying issue that pervades and influences progress toward adulthood (Phinney, 1990). The need to explore the implications of their group membership may extend the identity exploration period throughout the 20s and often beyond. Minority young people may therefore experience a longer period of the fluidity that characterizes emerging adulthood. In fact, evidence of ethnic identity exploration well beyond adolescence provides the strongest argument for a distinct period of emerging adulthood for these young people. Fluidity in identity for minority persons may relate to the conflicting images of their ethnic group in American culture and the difficulty of finding a satisfactory identity option available to them. For European Americans, even if they do not buy into the stereotypical White image, the White image is generally positive and does not entail the more limited range of possibilities with which minority persons may be confronted.

The goals of this chapter are to examine the exploration of ethnic and racial identity issues beyond adolescence among minority group members. There is wide variation in the extent of ethnic identity exploration during the transition to adulthood, depending on aspects of both the individual and the context. Within the American context, ethnic identity exploration differs with individual characteristics such as ethnic background, racial heritage or phenotype, and generation of immigration, as well as with family and community context, socioeconomic status, and educational experience. There is even greater variability in ethnic identity meanings and processes across countries and cultures, but that topic is beyond the scope of the present chapter. Thus, this chapter focuses on ethnic identity exploration in the American context and specifically on ethnic and racial minorities within that context. I consider individual processes and characteristics that influence ethnic identity exploration and the contextual factors that shape the course of such exploration during emerging adulthood.

For convenience, I use the term *ethnic identity* to encompass three aspects of group identity processes: ethnic heritage, racial phenotype, and cultural background. Although these three aspects of group identity can be distinguished conceptually and have different implications for the individual (Alipuria, 2002), they often overlap as individuals strive to construct a coherent sense of self as group members. However, I use separate terms when discussing research that explicitly focuses on one or another aspect.

I begin with a summary of the development of ethnic identity before and during adolescence and then examine this process following adolescence in a variety of contexts and for individuals with a range of group identity challenges, such as being bicultural or being biracial.

Early Development of Ethnic Identity

Socialization within the family provides the initial foundation for ethnic identity (Bernal, Knight, Ocampo, Garza, & Cota, 1993). Children learn about their culture within the family, through daily activities, language, and traditions. For young children, whose family and community constitute their world, the customs and values in which they are immersed are seen as the way things are, the norm, rather than as group characteristics. Ethnic identity development begins with the awareness of distinctive characteristics that differentiate oneself from some people but that are shared with others. Children growing up in a modern society soon become aware of people who act and think differently, who may look different from them, and who differ in visibility and status in society.

The ways in which these differences are viewed vary with the context. Depending on the messages that children receive, differences may be seen as reflecting something bad or inferior; conversely, they may be seen as something to be valued and emulated. The task of ethnic identity formation involves sorting out and resolving positive and negative feelings and attitudes about one's own group and about other groups and identifying one's place in relation to both. One of the challenges for members of nondominant groups is that they must understand those of higher status. In contrast, dominant group members in the United States can live and work largely without having to understand other groups. Thus ethnic identity is far less salient for European Americans than it is for ethnic minority group members (Phinney, 1989).

The task of making sense of differences based on ethnicity and race begins in childhood and is highly salient during adolescence. It depends in part on developmental capacities. A cognitive–developmental perspective on awareness of ethnicity and ethnic differences has been described by Quintana and colleagues (Quintana, 1994; Quintana, Castaneda-English, & Ybarra, 1999). Ethnic differences are first understood by young children in concrete, physical terms, such as clothing and skin color, followed by literal features such as language and food preferences, and later by a nonliteral, social perspective of ethnicity, including an awareness of the social implications of ethnicity, such as prejudice. By adolescence, young people have the ability to understand an ethnic group as a communal whole, with a shared perspective; they can develop an ethnic group consciousness and explore the implications of their own ethnicity.

Quintana's model is consistent with research that has shown adolescence to be a critical period for ethnic identity development (Phinney, 1989, 1990). Before adolescence, children from minority backgrounds are aware of their group membership but they have little understanding of its meaning and implications for their lives. Adolescents move into a wider range of contexts, including ethnically diverse high schools and part-time jobs. Increased contact with people from backgrounds other than their own leads to greater awareness of differences and more questions about their own group membership. During the high school years, many young people explore their ethnicity through talking to people, reading, and learning about the history and customs of their group, thus laying the foundations for a secure ethnic identity. This exploration is assumed to lead eventually to a resolution in the form of a secure and stable sense of self as an ethnic group member.

However, the process of attaining a secure identity is not completed during adolescence. Phinney (1989) found that only about one quarter of 10th graders from ethnic minority backgrounds had explored and resolved ethnic identity issues and could be considered to have an achieved ethnic identity. This fact may be related in part to differing degrees of exposure to other groups. Research examining contextual effects on ethnic identity development (Umana-Taylor, 2003) showed that Latino adolescents in a high school that was predominantly non-Latino reported higher levels of ethnic identity than did those in schools with a larger proportion of Latinos. As a result of changing residential patterns, minority adolescents are increasingly likely to attend schools that are homogeneous rather than ethnically diverse. Many adolescents from ethnic minority backgrounds may thus have relatively little exposure to other ethnic groups during high school. Even in ethnically diverse high schools, there is considerable evidence of ethnic and racial self-segregation. Although adolescents may interact with students from a range of backgrounds in structured activities, they are likely to spend leisure time with same-group peers (Tatum, 1997). Research showing that three quarters of the high school students either had not examined ethnic issues at all or had explored but not resolved them (Phinney, 1989) suggests that ethnic identity formation often continues beyond adolescence.

Ethnic Identity Development Beyond Adolescence

Emerging adulthood implies a period during which identity issues continue to be explored and are not yet satisfactorily resolved. The years beyond high school lead to a variety of experiences that can enhance or reduce identity exploration. When young people leave high school, their pathways diverge, depending in part on the extent to which they pursue further education. Young people may attend any one of a range of institutions of higher learning, including elite research universities or private colleges, less selective public universities, community colleges, and trade schools, or they may not attend college but rather work, take time off, or stay at home to raise children. Ethnic identity in emerging adulthood cannot be considered apart from the contexts in which young people are living, studying, and working. The contexts they experience provide important settings for the exploration of ethnic identity. In addition to their immediate home and work contexts, they may be influenced by broader exposure, such as the media and national political movements.

If young people move directly from high school into stable jobs within their community, and also marry and settle down in the same setting, there may be no further pressure to examine their ethnicity. They can be considered identity foreclosed; they attain the markers of adulthood with little evidence of an extended exploration, and hence cannot be said to experience emerging adulthood.

However, with the transition into the wider world beyond high school, many emerging adults face situations in which their race, ethnicity, or culture is made salient. Research with adolescents has shown that issues of ethnic and racial identity are most salient in culturally diverse settings (Ogbu, 1987; Oyserman, Gant, & Ager, 1995; Phinney, 1989; Phinney & Rosenthal, 1992). Contrasts between their own background and those of others whom they encounter highlight cultural or ethnic differences and raise identity issues.

Even if a secure identity has been achieved during adolescence, it is likely to be reexamined as a result of changing contexts. Research on ego identity has established that individuals often reexamine identity issues after the initial resolution of the identity crisis (Stephen, Fraser, & Marcia, 1992). With regard to racial identity, Parham (1989) has similarly suggested that people return to racial identity issues as new situations arise. When lives are characterized by changing circumstances and new experiences, exploration is likely to continue.

Furthermore, developmental changes make ethnic identity increasingly important beyond adolescence. Increasing cognitive abilities can raise awareness of the implications of one's ethnic group membership. Quintana's (1994) model describes further progress beyond adolescence in the understanding of ethnicity. In their 20s, young people become capable of seeing ethnicity in a wider context. They can take the perspectives of other ethnic or racial minority groups and of the dominant ethnic group. They can thus develop a multicultural viewpoint that includes an increased understanding of both intergroup conflict and the possibility of intergroup acceptance and positive interaction. Furthermore, they have a greater awareness of the diversity within their own group and other groups that can lead to an increased appreciation for the complexity of experiences related to ethnicity. These broader perspectives are likely to contribute to continued exploration of the implications of ethnicity.

Ethnic Identity Development During the College Years

Most of the research on ethnic identity beyond adolescence has been with college students. College has been seen in the identity literature as a moratorium, a period when young people are allowed the opportunity to explore options before making commitments that will provide the basis for decisions regarding important identity domains.

Studies on ethnic and racial identity with college students have been carried out primarily at the prestigious universities where most researchers work. Research with students who attend major research universities has focused largely on discrimination and threats to one's ethnic identity that these students, typically a small minority of the student body, experience on predominantly White campuses (e.g., Mendoza-Denton, Downey, Purdie, Davis,

& Pietrzak, 2002). As college students attempt to understand and negotiate being a minority in a setting dominated by members of another group, ethnic identity is highly salient. Two pathways have been identified among minority students at largely White institutions (Ethier & Deaux, 1994); students with initially strong ethnic identities become more involved in cultural activities, which thus strengthens the identity, whereas those with a weaker initial ethnic identity perceive more threat and experience a further weakening of the identity. In either case, ethnicity is an issue that must be dealt with.

A narrative account by Ruben Navarrette (1993) of his experience as a minority student at an elite university provides a particularly vivid description of an extended ethnic identity exploration. Navarrette grew up in a small farming community in California and became one of the few Latino students at Harvard University. After arriving at Harvard, he became keenly aware of being different from the majority of students. Being Latino, which had not been salient in his hometown, became a focus of attention. He became deeply involved in programs and activities aimed at supporting Latino students and promoting ethnic awareness generally, but this did not resolve the conflicts he felt. He referred to himself and other members of the ethnic club that he was involved in the following:

> We were consumed with simply finding a precarious place to perch between two opposing worlds. . . . These were people poised to conquer the future, but who had not yet reconciled themselves with their past. We were torn, divided, conflicted. I loved and respected my parents and yet I wanted nothing as much as to live a life that was different, better, than theirs. I had avoided being part of a sorrowful statistic [of those who drop out of high school] . . . and yet instead of feeling lucky, I felt guilty, illegitimate, embarrassed. (pp. 135–136)

Navarrette (1993) described alternative ways of handling the feelings of difference. Some Latino students avoided involvement with ethnic activities and took an assimilationist position, attempting to become part of the larger campus community. However, they faced disapproval from the majority of Latinos for not being part of the Latino student groups. Usually they also lacked acceptance among students from the dominant White majority. Not only ethnic and cultural differences set Latino students apart: Skin color differences and the privilege that accompanied light skin were an ever-present aspect of the college experience of Navarrette and his Latino peers. An awareness of difference kept ethnic identity at the forefront of their developing sense of self. In accord with Quintana's model, Navarrette also became more aware of the experience of other minority groups on campus and developed a sense of solidarity with them. Eventually, over time, Navarrette also came to know and understand many White students and to develop a more nuanced appreciation of the diversity in their attitudes and experiences.

Although Navarrette's account provides a clear example of ethnic identity exploration, relatively few minority college students attend elite, selective institutions such as Harvard. Many more attend urban commuter universities in which a larger proportion of students are minorities and issues of discrimination are less salient. College freshman at an urban university in which 80% of the student body was from non-European backgrounds rated perceived discrimination very low, with a mean between *never* and *rarely* on a 5-point scale (Phinney & Tomiki, 2002). In such a setting, in which most other students were from similar backgrounds, there may be little pressure to examine ethnicity per se. A study of ethnic identity at the same institution (Romero, 2001) showed no change in ethnic identity exploration during the first 3 years in college. It seems likely, however, that once they leave the relatively homogeneous college atmosphere, they will face situations that provoke exploration.

Even if ethnic identity is not being actively explored, it remains an important concern. College students may study their ethnic language or take ethnic studies classes that allow them to learn more about the history and culture of their group. A study comparing the importance of five identity domains in college students from four ethnic groups attending the same urban university (Phinney & Alipuria, 1990) found that although occupation was rated as the most important identity issue for all ethnic groups, ethnic identity remained a significantly more important identity issue for ethnic minorities than for European American students. For the minority students, ethnic identity was rated equal in importance to two other identity domains, sex role and religious identity; for the European Americans, ethnic identity was rated as the least important domain. Continued uncertainty about ethnic identity is revealed in a statement by a 19-year-old Latino college student: "I consider myself Hispanic, but I'm not sure what ethnicity means" (Phinney, 2004). As long as underlying identity concerns about ethnicity remain unresolved, these students could be considered emerging adults.

Ethnic Identity Development Outside of Educational Settings

Although college has been described as a moratorium period that allows young people time to resolve identity issues, not all emerging adults attend 4-year colleges. There is little or no research on ethnic identity among minority youth who do not go to college. However, their experience outside educational settings may reflect to some extent that of their peers who attended college and are now working. A basic premise of identity theory is that new experiences can trigger identity exploration. The period of emerging adulthood is marked by a widening exposure to new situations, ideas, responsibilities, and persons. Whether they have attended college or not, emerging adults must make decisions about the kind of occupation to commit to, where to live, and the people they choose to associate with. They must also deal with the attitudes they encounter from others. In particular, as they enter the workplace and become more involved in the wider society, they are likely to face new challenges regarding the meaning and implications of their ethnicity. Such challenges typically provoke ethnic exploration.

Throughout development, but perhaps increasingly with age, as one has more contact with strangers, one's appearance provides others with the first evidence as to one's background. Being classified on the basis of appearance and treated differently, and negatively, because of it is a central issue of racial identity (Helms, 1990). For Black Americans especially, appearance, or phenotype, clearly identifies one's African origins. Asian Americans also are easily identifiable and often assumed to be immigrants or foreigners; for example, they report frequent comments such as how well they speak English. Latinos and members of other non-European groups are less easily identified by appearance alone, but they nevertheless are typically seen as non-White. The way in which one is seen by others is an important part of one's identity. A 26-year-old man with a Black father and White mother stated that he calls himself African American: "That's what everyone sees when they look at me, so that's what I am" (Phinney, 2004). A Mexican American emerging adult expressed a similar idea when she said, "I think it is ridiculous to say I am American when people see a Mexican-looking girl" (Phinney, 2004).

Although race has no biological reality, it is real in the way it is socially constructed and in the impact it has through racism. The pejorative implications resulting from society's need to classify people as *us* or *them* can result in internalized racism among minorities, leading to negative views of themselves. The task for visible minorities is to overcome such internalized negative images (Helms, 1990). The experience of being initially identified and categorized on the basis of appearance is universal, but there is wide variation in how individuals respond to the ways in which they are perceived. As an identity issue, responses to others' perceptions are as important as the perceptions themselves. An aspect of ethnic identity formation involves coming to understand others' perceptions but not allowing oneself to be defined by them.

A case study of an Asian American woman (Ho, 2004) illustrates the changes in the way the young woman's experience with racial categorization led to exploration. She reported experiencing hostility and feelings of noninclusion at her job and in the media, because of her Asian features. "I was raised American like everyone else, but I wasn't allowed to be American. And the media images! It was all White, sexy females, and that wasn't me." These feelings can result in internalized racism and self-hatred, as has been described in research with adolescents generally (Phinney, 1989) and with African Americans in particular (Cross & Fhagen-Smith, 2001). The Asian woman reported, "It got to a point where I hated myself because I was Asian. . . . My bad driving habits at that time were indicative of my self-hatred. If I was killed in an accident I wouldn't have to deal with being Asian." With support of her family and friends, this young woman engaged in a period of exploration or immersion (Cross & Fhagen-Smith, 2001), including the study of Asian culture, and was able to reclaim her Asian heritage. She stated, "I finally realized that it was all right for me to be an Asian American. . . . I am what I am." This woman's story provides a clear depiction of the resolution of an identity crisis, in which the process of exploration leads to a clear, secure sense of self in terms of one's race, that is, an achieved racial identity.

A study of Hispanics working in a European American business (Ferdman & Cortes, 1992) highlights the ways in which ethnic identity exploration may continue even with familiar colleagues in a work setting. Although it is not clear whether the participants in this study could be considered emerging adults on the basis of age, the experiences described are as likely to occur for employees in their 20s as for older ones. As minorities within the company, the Hispanic employees were aware of both differential treatment and cultural differences between themselves and their European American colleagues. To deal with these experiences, some employees Anglicized their names. Some tried to counteract stereotypes: "Too many people have a stereotypical view of what Hispanics are, and I, just through normal day-to-day activity . . . give them visible proof that . . . it's not necessarily true" (p. 269). Hispanic employees reported that their coworkers showed varying degree of awareness of their ethnic background, but most Hispanics felt that they were seen as being different. One stated, "Even though you consider yourself one of the guys, American, and a professional . . . people have subtle ways of letting you know that when they look at you they see . . . a Hispanic first" (p. 272).

These examples provide evidence about ethnic identity processes in emerging adulthood. Being seen as a minority and as different from the dominant group is a constant throughout life for many Americans from non-European backgrounds. What is important developmentally is the extent to which individuals have developed a confident sense of their own ethnicity. An achieved identity contributes to a positive sense of self and provides protection against those who are dismissive or demeaning toward one's group or see only a stereotype rather than the person (Phinney, Cantu, & Kurtz, 1997). One measure of reaching adulthood, in terms of ethnicity, might be the point at which individuals who have wrestled with negative feelings about their group membership no longer experience doubt or self-hatred based on their race or ethnicity. A 21-year-old Mexican American demonstrated his secure identity in stating "Even though a person may be racist—I don't think that's good obviously— but I'm not going to tell myself I shouldn't like myself because I'm Mexican" (Phinney, 2004).

Bicultural and Multicultural Identity

Any individuals living in settings that are different from their culture of origin are faced with questions regarding their bicultural or multicultural identity. They must determine how and to what extent to identify with the cultures they are exposed to: their native or parental cultural, the culture of the larger society in which they reside (LaFromboise, Coleman, & Gerton, 1993), and perhaps also other cultures with which they come in contact (Phinney & Alipuria, in press). Much of the research on this topic has been carried out with adolescents (Phinney, 2003). Ethnic minority adolescents in the United States are involved in exploring the meaning of being American as well as ethnic (Phinney & Devich-Navarro, 1997). They develop different approaches to this issue, such as keeping the ethnic and national identities separate, combining them in some way, or rejecting one of them.

Beyond high school, issues of bicultural and multicultural identity are likely to become more important as young people move away from their families and neighborhoods into the broader worlds of higher education and work. The widening experience of emerging adults from minority backgrounds can lead to a questioning of the traditional cultural values of their ethnic group. The mainstream cultural values of independence and self-assertion contrast with the family expectations for family closeness and interdependence (Phinney et al., 2000). Young people who live at home are expected to show deference to parents and to respond to the needs of the family find themselves in educational or work settings in which individual achievement is more valued and they are expected to be autonomous and assertive. Latino young people report family pressures to stay close to home that may restrict their options for job promotions that involve a move or graduate school in a distant city (Phinney, 2004).

The need for young Americans from non-European cultural backgrounds to make choices between contrasting values can result in the kind of identity crisis described by Erikson (1968). The crisis is assumed to provoke an exploration of the meaning of being members of both an ethnic group and the larger society. In interviews with college students regarding cultural identity issues (Phinney, 2004), an Asian American student stated, "I am attracted to the values of independence and doing my own thing, but it is also important for me to be close to my parents; it is sometimes hard to do both" (p. 11).

The differences in cultural values that are experienced by ethnic minorities can become sources of stress when young people are expected to put the needs of their family before their own needs. Tseng (2004) demonstrated the impact of cultural values and practices on academic achievement in a diverse sample of college students from immigrant backgrounds. A stronger endorsement of the cultural values of family interdependence was related to greater academic achievement. However, demands by the family for behavioral assistance, such as doing chores, detracted from academic achievement. In an interview, an Asian American college student reported that she had to "work to share the rent with my parents. Sometimes I am bothered because my parents ask me to help them out while I am studying" (Phinney, 2004, p. 12). Emerging adulthood for these young people includes efforts to understand and find a balance between the competing demands of their two cultural contexts.

Bicultural identity issues are framed in terms of the ways in which a person considers himself or herself to be both ethnic and part of the larger (e.g., American) society. A Latino college student identified differing sources of ethnic and American identity; she saw herself Latino on the basis of "the color of my skin, my language, the food, my place of birth." However, regarding her American identity, she stated, "the values and beliefs I hold come from American culture." A 21-year-old technical school graduate likewise endorsed American values of equality in a marriage, in contrast to what he saw as a Mexican tradition of men controlling their wives; but he also stated, "That doesn't mean that I'm going to close the door on Mexico and its traditions" (Phinney, 2004, p. 14).

Exploration of cultural identity issues is evident as well in a 24-year-old American from a Russian background, who reported learning about his culture of origin from stories by his grandfather. However, he also emphasized the importance of exploring other cultures. "To be a true American . . . you have to immerse yourself in the diversity that is around you" (Phinney, 2004, p. 16). The achievement of a secure ethnic identity requires coming to an understanding of oneself as part of an ethnic group and also of a larger, diverse national entity.

Biracial and Multiracial Identity

Young people who have parents from two or more different ethnic or racial backgrounds face particularly complex identity issues. Even the best way to describe these people is unclear; various terms are used, including biracial, multiracial, and multiethnic. The term *multiracial* is used here to encompass all those whose ancestors are from two or more ethnic or racial groups. These people must deal with the basic issues faced by all minorities, of developing a secure sense of who they are in ethnic terms. However, they develop their identity in the context of two (or more) families or groups, each of which they are part of to some extent but not exclusively (Phinney & Alipuria, in press). They must deal with, and explore, issues about both their racial identity, related to their appearance, and their ethnic identity, regarding a sense of group belonging. Because their appearance is often ambiguous, people cannot easily identify how to categorize them ethnically. They are therefore often faced with the question "What are you?" Depending on the background of their parents, the challenge of being biracial may overlap with that of being bicultural, that is, having different cultural traditions to choose from. In addition to having ties to at least two ethnic groups, they must also consider a third membership group, the larger society and the related national identity.

Because of the complexity of forming an identity as a multiracial person, the process appears to begin earlier and continue longer than for a mono-racial person. Multiracial children are typically aware at an early age that they are different from each of their parents (Kich, 1992). Depending on socialization within their family and contact with their parents' families of origin, they learn not only that they belong in some ways to both parental ethnic groups but also that they do not belong exclusively to either. From their awareness of difference, they struggle for acceptance as being biracial. In most cases they lack an existing biracial group with which to identify; identification with the group of one parent implies rejection of the other parent. Furthermore, they are unlikely to have peer groups of multiracial individuals to identify with. Kich (1992) suggested that self-acceptance of themselves as biracial, that is, an achieved biracial identity, is likely to occur during or after college or in the workplace; thus it extends into emerging adulthood.

A recent qualitative study of multiracial people in their 20s and early 30s from East Indian and European American backgrounds (Alipuria, 2002) provides strong evidence of continuing exploration of identity in these emerging adults. Virtually all areas of their lives are affected by their multiracial status as they seek to establish relationships and find communities that support their efforts to understand who they are. Perhaps no other group of young people is as strongly influenced by their context as are multiracial people. Because of their dual heritage, multiracial young people face continual challenges to find a place where they fit in. A 25-year-old graduate student in anthropology stated, "I have never had a comfort group. There just isn't one. Period. . . . I'm always a different person among different contexts" (Alipuria, 2002, p. 112). Another woman, at 31, continued to feel ambivalent about her dual heritage,

> My emotions are really mixed. . . . I sense on the one hand happiness that
> I . . . have seen so much of the world that I can appreciate . . . and feel like
> I am part of. But at the same time, I also have a sadness because I think
> it's harder, much harder, to grow up as a bicultural or multicultural person.
> . . . I never felt like I fit in totally in one place. (p. 133)

The feeling of not fitting in may be due in part to cultural differences, but
it is perhaps more strongly influenced by phenotypic ambiguity. The graduate
student previously quoted looked somewhat Indian but reported often being
taken for Middle Eastern,

> A large part of any sort of awareness of identity would be how others treat
> you. . . . I haven't formed my identity in a vacuum, thinking 'what do I want,
> what do I like?' I mean, that's been part of it, but it is also what others
> impose on you, for better or worse. (Alipuria, 2002, p. 109)

She noted, as well, that people who have not been challenged or stereotyped
because of their appearance have no idea of the problems faced by those who
have dealt with these experiences,

> I've had to have [racial consciousness]. . . . I have people constantly telling
> me, 'What's the big deal? Get over it.' Which is why I like to hang out with
> Black people. Because they never say, 'What's the big deal?' They know
> what the big deal is and talk about it explicitly. (p. 119)

For multiracial emerging adults, the search for supportive people to associate
with is an important aspect of their identity exploration.

The awareness of being different no doubt continues to some extent
throughout life. However, many multiracial people reach a resolution of their
status that leads to identity achievement. One woman in her early 30s reported
feeling like "a social misfit" (Alipuria, 2002, p. 137) when she was growing up.
Eventually she found a group of racially mixed friends with whom she could
discuss the reactions they got from other people. She stated, "I've gotten a lot
better as I've gotten older at not always wondering how people are perceiving
me" (p. 139). Another biracial woman in her early 30s, working in a nonprofit
organization dealing with immigrants' rights, appeared to have achieved a
secure sense of her dual heritage as East Indian and European American.
She stated,

> When I was younger I felt I didn't belong anywhere. But now I've just come
> to the conclusion that . . . that's just the way I am, . . . and my home is
> inside myself. . . . I no longer feel the compulsion to fit in 'cause if you're
> just trying to fit in you never do. (Alipuria, 2002, p. 143)

Other research suggests various ways in which multiracial people resolve
their ethnic identity (Root, 1996). Four alternatives have been described: One
can identify with just one of one's heritage groups; identify with both and
switch between them; claim membership in a new category as mixed; or choose
not to identify ethnically or racially but rather think of oneself in other terms

(Renn, 2000; Rockquemore & Brunsma, 2002). The setting is often a critical factor in the type of resolution chosen. In a study of multiracial university students on three different campuses, Renn (2000) found that the campus climate was a strong influence on identity processes. One campus, with a large group of multiracial students, provided a community in which being multiracial was accepted. In contrast, on a campus that had organized groups only for specific ethnic groups, multiracial students were less accepted. Experiences such as these can advance or delay the resolution of identity issues in multiracial emerging adults.

Clearly, exploration of ethnic identity continues for multiracial people throughout and beyond college and is common for people in their 20s and early 30s. Multiracial emerging adults who have attained many markers of adulthood, such as being settled into a career and fully responsible for themselves financially, may still be wrestling with fundamental identity questions. In that sense, they retain aspects of emerging adulthood.

Conclusions

It is evident that for members of ethnic minority groups within the United States, formation of a group identity relative to one's ethnic, racial, or cultural heritage is a salient, important, and extended process. Exploration and questioning about one's heritage and its implications continue well beyond adolescence, although the process varies widely across individuals and groups. Identity exploration has been seen as a characteristic of emerging adulthood (Arnett, 2000). Emerging adulthood is a period in which the identity issues encountered in adolescence are tested for fit with new experiences. New issues arise because of the unique experiences that may be encountered after schooling, involving financial responsibilities and decisions about life commitments in establishing a career and a home. However, several unresolved questions limit any conclusions about whether ethnic identity exploration is a defining characteristic of a distinct developmental period between adolescence and adulthood.

First, the environment is a critical determinant of the timing, duration, and nature of ethnic identity exploration, and the environments to which ethnic group members are exposed vary widely within the United States. Thus, there is necessarily variation in the identity formation process across groups and individuals. In largely homogeneous settings, ethnic exploration may be deferred indefinitely; it may occur in middle or later adulthood, or never take place. Individuals who have not explored but who have a committed sense of their ethnicity, that is, who have a foreclosed ethnic identity, can be fully functioning adults, comfortable with their ethnicity within their environment. From adolescence on, they have a clear and workable understanding of who they are, ethnically or racially, based on their early socialization in the family and community. If there are no striking changes in their environment, they may never initiate an exploration. For them, the concept of emerging adulthood in the domain of ethnicity does not seem to apply, although they may be exploring in other important domains, such as occupation and personal relationships.

For other individuals, typically those who live in a diverse setting or change their place of residence, ethnicity and the questions it raises are likely to be salient throughout life. Because members of ethnic and racial minority groups are frequently faced with discriminatory attitudes and evidence of their lower status and power in society, they may continually be negotiating their sense of self in relation to other groups; that is, they experience an extended moratorium in this domain. When this process of negotiation continues into the 30s, 40s, and beyond, it can hardly define emerging adulthood.

The concept of emerging adulthood is most relevant to those who, in whatever context, engage in exploration in their teens and 20s and then reach a relatively comfortable, stable understanding of their ethnicity that serves as a basis for dealing with ethnic and racial issues; that is, they have achieved an identity. The Asian American woman developing a confident sense of herself as Asian is a good example of this process.

However, context alone does not determine the extent or quality of exploration. Even within the same environment, individuals have varying degrees of need to confront and deal with ethnic issues. For example, the Asian woman described earlier developed self-hatred whereas other members of her family did not. One factor underlying individual differences in exploration stems from personality characteristics; some people may be more temperamentally inclined to explore. With regard to ethnic identity, some people feel a strong need to belong to a group; they may seek out people who share their ethnic background and obtain information about their ethnic heritage as a way of developing a place to belong. Others feel less need to belong or else fulfill the need within a different context, such as family or friends.

There are differences as well in sensitivity to discrimination. A study of perceived discrimination among a diverse group of adolescents attending ethnically mixed high schools (Phinney, Madden, & Santos, 1998) showed that some people were more likely to perceive discrimination than others; furthermore, individual differences in depression were a positive predictor, and intergroup competence a negative predictor, of perceived discrimination. People who perceive more discrimination are likely to engage in more exploration.

Another individual factor influencing exploration is phenotype. People whose appearance identifies them as members of a particular group are likely to be treated as members of that group. However, people whose appearance is ambiguous and does not allow easy categorization may be frequently asked to identify themselves ethnically. Experiences of being treated stereotypically or discriminated against, or being asked to label oneself ethnically, can be strong motivators of exploration, regardless of the larger context.

In addition to individual differences, group differences influence the extent of exploration. Both racism and cultural values may influence the course of exploration in emerging adults. In the United States, African Americans have experienced far more discrimination than have other groups. They consistently report stronger ethnic identity than do other groups (Phinney, 1992; Phinney et al., 1997) and may well face a more extended exploration period. The identity issues faced by other groups, such as Asians and Latinos, may focus more on cultural differences and stereotypes, although discrimination may also be involved. As discussed earlier, persons who have more than one cultural or ethnic heritage face other identity questions that influence their exploration. In addition, even for mono-ethnic members of the dominant culture, the exposure to a mix of cultural values and practices that results from the nation's growing diversity is likely to lead to exploration about how other cultures can impact one's own identity, even for the dominant group.

Level of education is also likely to influence ethnic identity exploration. Because of the lack of research with emerging adults who do not have a college education, there is little information about differences in exploration based on level of education. In addition to ethnic minorities, European Americans from noncollege backgrounds have been studied very little in terms of group identity formation. Although they typically face less discrimination, they have more limited options than do their peers with a college degree and may face ethnic identity issues related to being White but not fitting the images they see of prosperous Whites. There is clearly need for more research on the impact of education on emerging adulthood.

Because both environmental and individual characteristics influence exploration, conceptualization about a period of emerging adulthood needs to recognize the complexity of the topic. Researchers should consider and incorporate current views from developmental psychology regarding the interaction of the person and the environment. Depending on the interaction of both personal and contextual factors related to race and ethnicity, some people in some environments experience a distinct period of exploration between adolescence and adulthood, whereas others do not explore at all, or continue exploring throughout life. Little is known about factors that influence the initiation and duration of ethnic identity exploration. A task for future research is to identify more precisely which people in which circumstances are most likely to engage in, and complete, a period of exploration between adolescence and adulthood and thus fit the label of emerging adults.

An additional question is the importance of ethnic exploration as a marker of emerging adulthood. Cross and Fhagen-Smith (2001) suggested that for Black Americans the end product of racial identity exploration is a reference group orientation that, along with other key psychological characteristics, "undergirds the psychological platform upon which will be transacted certain adult challenges, tasks, and opportunities" (p. 258) that are encountered in the varied contexts of work, education, relationships, and family. From this perspective, resolving the question of who one is in ethnic or racial terms is critical to decisions in other areas of one's life. However, as has been noted, this identity domain is more important for some people than for others. For those who define themselves by their occupations or other salient identifications, ethnicity may never be a salient issue and hence have little or no role in defining emerging adulthood. Research on ethnic identity needs to take into account individual differences in both the extent of exploration and the importance of this group identity. Among those for whom ethnicity is highly important, an extended exploration beyond adolescence is most likely to indicate emerging adulthood, but not everyone has this experience. A more nuanced view of emerging adulthood should therefore include recognition that even among people from the same background in the same environment, there is wide variation in whether the concept of emerging adulthood applies.

In sum, a secure sense of oneself as a member of an ethnic or racial group is a defining attainment of adulthood for most people from minority backgrounds and is becoming important for nonminorities in many contexts. However, the completion of identity exploration and the achievement of a group identity cannot clearly be assigned to any given age range. Studying the interaction of personal and environmental factors that influence this process across a range of ethnic groups and contexts remains an important challenge for developmental researchers concerned with identity processes in emerging adulthood.

References

Alipuria, L. (2002). Ethnic, racial, and cultural identity/self: An integrated theory of identity/self in relation to large scale social cleavages. *Dissertation Abstracts International, 63B, 583*. (Doctoral dissertation, UMI No. 3039092)

Arnett, J. (1998). Learning to stand alone: The contemporary American transition to adulthood in cultural and historical context. *Human Development, 41, 295–315*.

Arnett, J. (2000). Emerging adulthood: A theory of development from late teens through the twenties. *American Psychologist, 55, 469–480*.

Arnett, J. (2003). Conceptions of the transition of adulthood among emerging adults in American ethnic groups. In J. Arnett & N. Galambos (Eds.), *Exploring cultural conceptions of the transition to adulthood* (pp. 63–75). San Francisco: Jossey-Bass.

Arnett, J., & Galambos, N. (2003). Culture and conceptions of adulthood. In J. Arnett & N. Galambos (Eds.), *Exploring cultural conceptions of the transition to adulthood* (pp. 91–98). San Francisco: Jossey-Bass.

Bernal, M., Knight, G., Ocampo, K., Garza, C., & Cota, M. (1993). Development of Mexican American identity. In M. Bernal & G. Knight (Eds.), *Ethnic identity: Formation and transmission among Hispanics and other minorities* (pp. 31–46). Albany: State University of New York Press.

Cauce, A., Stewart, A., Roderguez, M., Cochran, B., & Ginzler, J. (2003). Overcoming the odds? Adolescent development in the context of urban poverty. In S. Luthar (Ed.), *Resilience and vulnerability: Adaptation in the context of childhood adversities* (pp. 343–363). New York: Cambridge University Press.

Cheah, C. S. L., & Nelson, L. J. (2004). The role of acculturation in the emerging adulthood of aboriginal college students. *International Journal of Behavioral Development, 28, 495–507*.

Cross, W., & Fhagen-Smith, P. (2001). Patterns of African American identity development: A life span perspective. In C. Wijeyesinghe & B. Jackson III (Eds.), *New perspectives on racial identity development: A theoretical and practical anthology* (pp. 243–270). New York: New York University Press.

Erikson, E. (1968). *Identity: Youth and crisis*. New York: Norton.

Ethier, K., & Deaux, K. (1994). Negotiating social identity when contexts change: Maintaining and responding to threat. *Journal of Personality and Social Psychology, 67, 243–251*.

Ferdman, B., & Cortes, A. (1992). Culture and identity among Hispanic managers in an Anglo business. In S. Knouse, P. Rosenfield, & A. Culbertson (Eds.), *Hispanics in the workplace* (pp. 246–277). Thousand Oaks, CA: Sage.

Fuligni, A., Tseng, V., & Lam, M. (1999). Attitudes toward family obligations among American adolescents with Asian, Latin American, and European backgrounds. *Child Development, 70, 1030–1044*.

Fuligni, A., & Witkow, M. (2004). The postsecondary educational progress of youth from immigrant families. *Journal of Research on Adolescence, 14, 159–183*.

Helms, J. (1990). *Black and White racial identity: Theory, research, and practice*. New York: Greenwood Press.

Ho, M. (2004). *"I am what I am": A case study of ethnic identity development.* Unpublished manuscript, California State University, Los Angeles.

Kich, G. (1992). The developmental process of asserting a biracial, bicultural identity. In M. Root (Ed.), *Racially mixed people in America* (pp. 304–320). Newbury Park, CA: Sage.

LaFromboise, T., Coleman, H., & Gerton, J. (1993). Psychological impact of biculturalism: Evidence and theory. *Psychological Bulletin, 114,* 395–412.

Mendoza-Denton, R., Downey, G., Purdie, V., Davis, A., & Pietrzak, J. (2002). Sensitivity to status-based rejection: Implications for African American students' college experience. *Journal of Personality and Social Psychology, 83,* 896–918.

Navarrette, R., Jr. (1993). *A darker shade of crimson: Odyssey of a Harvard Chicano.* New York: Bantam Books.

Ogbu, J. (1987). Opportunity structure, cultural boundaries, and literacy. In J. Langer (Ed.), *Language, literacy, and culture: Issues of society and schooling* (pp. 149–177). Norwood, NJ: Ablex.

Oyserman, D., Gant, L., & Ager, J. (1995). A socially contextualized model of African American identity: Possible selves and school persistence. *Journal of Personality and Social Psychology, 69,* 1216–1232.

Parham, T. (1989). Cycles of psychological nigrescence. *The Counseling Psychologist, 17,* 187–226.

Phinney, J. (1989). Stages of ethnic identity development in minority group adolescents. *Journal of Early Adolescence, 9,* 34–49.

Phinney, J. (1990). Ethnic identity in adolescents and adults: A review of research. *Psychological Bulletin, 108,* 499–514.

Phinney, J. (1992). The Multigroup Ethnic Identity Measure: A new scale for use with diverse groups. *Journal of Adolescent Research, 7,* 156–176.

Phinney, J. (1999, May). Symposium. In J. Phinney (Chair), *Ethnic families in Southern California: Change and stability in multicultural settings.* Symposium conducted at the Western Psychological Association Annual Convention, Irvine, CA.

Phinney, J. (2003). Ethnic identity and acculturation. In K. Chun, P. Organista, & G. Marin (Eds.), *Acculturation: Advances in theory, measurement, and applied research* (pp. 63–81). Washington, DC: American Psychological Association.

Phinney, J. (2004). *Cultural identity in college students.* Unpublished manuscript, California State University, Los Angeles.

Phinney, J., & Alipuria, L. (1990). Ethnic identity in college students from four ethnic groups. *Journal of Adolescence, 13,* 171–184.

Phinney, J., & Alipuria, L. (in press). Multiple social categorization and identity among multiracial, multiethnic, and multicultural individuals: Processes and implications. In R. Crisp & M. Hewstone (Eds.), *Multiple social categorization: Processes, models, and applications.* Hove, Sussex, England: Psychology Press.

Phinney, J., Cantu, C., & Kurtz, D. (1997). Ethnic and American identity as predictors of self-esteem among African American, Latino, and White adolescents. *Journal of Youth and Adolescence, 26,* 165–185.

Phinney, J., Dennis, J., & Osorio, S. (in press). Motivations to attend college among college students from diverse ethnic and social class backgrounds. *Cultural Diversity and Ethnic Minority Psychology.*

Phinney, J., & Devich-Navarro, M. (1997). Variations in bicultural identification among African American and Mexican American adolescents. *Journal of Research on Adolescence, 7,* 3–32.

Phinney, J., Madden, T., & Santos, L. (1998). Psychological variables as predictors of perceived discrimination among minority and immigrant adolescents. *Journal of Applied Social Psychology, 28,* 937–993.

Phinney, J., Ong, A., & Madden, T. (2000). Cultural values and intergenerational value discrepancies in immigrant and non-immigrant families. *Child Development, 71,* 528–539.

Phinney, J., & Rosenthal, D. (1992). Ethnic identity formation in adolescence: Process, context, and outcome. In G. Adams, T. Gulotta, & R. Montemayor (Eds.), *Identity formation during adolescence* (pp. 145–172). Newbury Park, CA: Sage.

Phinney, J., & Tomiki, K. (2002). *Perceived discrimination among minority students at a predominantly minority institution.* Unpublished manuscript, California State University, Los Angeles.

Quintana, S. (1994). A model of ethnic perspective-taking ability applied to Mexican-American children and youth, *International Journal of Intercultural Relations, 18,* 419–118.

Quintana, S., Castaneda-English, P., & Ybarra, V. (1999). Role of perspective-taking abilities and ethnic socialization in development of adolescent ethnic identity. *Journal of Research on Adolescence, 9,* 161–184.

Renn, K. (2000). Patterns of situational identity among biracial and multiracial college students. *The Review of Higher Education, 23,* 399–420.

Rockquemore, K., & Brunsma, D. (2002). *Beyond Black: Biracial identity in America.* Thousand Oaks, CA: Sage.

Romero, I. (2001). *A longitudinal study of ethnic identity among college students.* Unpublished master's thesis, California State University, Los Angeles.

Root, M. (1996). The mulitracial experience: Racial borders as a significant frontier in race relations. In M. Root (Ed.), *The mulitracial experience: Racial borders as the new frontier* (pp. xiii–xxviii). Thousand Oaks, CA: Sage.

Stephen, J., Fraser, E., & Marcia, J. (1992). Moratorium-achievement (MAMA) cycles in lifespan identity development: Value orientations and reasoning system correlates. *Journal of Adolescence, 15,* 283–300.

Tatum, B. (1997). *"Why are all the Black kids sitting together in the cafeteria?" and other conversations about race.* New York: Basic Books.

Tseng, V. (2004). Family interdependence and academic adjustment in college: Youths from immigrant and US-born families. *Child Development, 75,* 966–983.

Umana-Taylor, A. (2003). Ethnic identity and self-esteem: Examining the role of social context. *Journal of Adolescence, 27,* 139–146.

6

Mental Health During Emerging Adulthood: Continuity and Discontinuity in Courses, Causes, and Functions

John E. Schulenberg and Nicole R. Zarrett

As one leaves high school and ventures into emerging adulthood, the new demands on one's inter- and intrapersonal resources may be extensive, testing and sometimes overwhelming one's coping capacity. In the United States, there is a deeply rooted norm that this is the time one needs to begin experiencing emotional, financial, and overall lifespace independence from one's family (Arnett, 2000, 2004). This transition may trigger some diverging courses of mental health: Some troubled adolescents, who perhaps experienced a mismatch between their needs and the affordances provided by their family, may find new life in this transition out of the family home; others doing well in adolescence, perhaps because of a good match with their primary contexts, may lose this match (and lose their way) as they enter the new contexts and social roles of emerging adulthood, which may result in brand new difficulties and emergent psychopathology. And still others may use this time of increased personal freedom, loose conventional bonds, and experimentation to get a little crazy on their journey to becoming well-adjusted adults.

In this chapter we embed considerations of mental health—particularly in terms of overall well-being, substance use, antisocial behavior, and depressive affect—within the experience of emerging adulthood. As a starting point, we offer the following general observations about the course of selected indices of mental health and maladaptation during emerging adulthood.

- In the general population, mental health improves and problem behaviors subside. Consider Figures 6.1–6.4, where, for example, during

I (Schulenberg) gratefully acknowledge grant support from the National Institute on Drug Abuse (DA01411) and the National Institute on Mental Health (MH59396). We appreciate the helpful comments of the editors and thank Ginny Laetz, Tanya Hart, and Patti Meyer for their assistance.

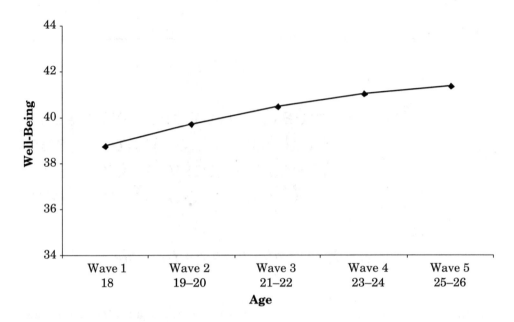

Figure 6.1. Well-being during emerging adulthood. Scale ranges from 1 (*disagree*) to 5 (*agree*).

emerging adulthood, well-being tends to increase (Figure 6.1); binge drinking (Figure 6.2) and marijuana use (Figure 6.3) increase during the first few years out of high school and then decrease; and risk taking, depressive affect, theft and property damage, and physical aggression decrease (Figure 6.4; based on nationally representative panel data from the Monitoring the Future study; Johnston, O'Malley, Bachman, & Schulenberg, 2004).[1]

---

[1]Data come from Monitoring the Future (MTF) nationally representative panel samples of high school seniors (cohorts 1989–1994). Constructs included here are based on previous MTF findings (Schulenberg et al., 2005; Schulenberg, O'Malley, Bachman, & Johnston, 2005). Well-being (Figure 6.1) was computed with a composite of three interrelated constructs including Self-Esteem (8 items), Self-Efficacy (5 items), and Social Support (6 items); possible responses ranged from *disagree* (1) to *agree* (5). Binge drinking (Figure 6.2) was measured by the frequency of having five or more drinks in a row in the past 2 weeks; possible responses ranged from *none* (1) to *10 or more times* (6). Marijuana use (Figure 6.3) was measured according to occasions of use in the past 12 months, with possible responses ranging from *none* (1) to *40 or more times* (7). Depressive affect (Figure 6.4) was an average of four items concerning feelings of sadness. Risk taking (Figure 6.4) was an average of two items concerning whether respondent got a kick out of doing things that are a little dangerous and enjoyed doing something a little risky (Schulenberg, Wadsworth, O'Malley, Bachman, & Johnston, 1996). For depressive affect and risk taking, possible responses ranged from *disagree* (1) to *agree* (5). Property damage (Figure 6.4) was an average of nine items measuring the 12-month frequency of stealing large and small amounts of money or property and trespassing or damaging property; interpersonal aggression (Figure 6.4) was an average of five items regarding behaviors such as hitting, fighting, or threatening someone with a weapon (Osgood, Johnston, O'Malley, & Bachman, 1988); for all items, possible responses ranged from *not at all* (1) to *five or more times* (5). In regard to age spans before (8th–12th grade) and after (ages 26–30) those illustrated in the figures, other cross-sectional and longitudinal data from MTF indicate age trend

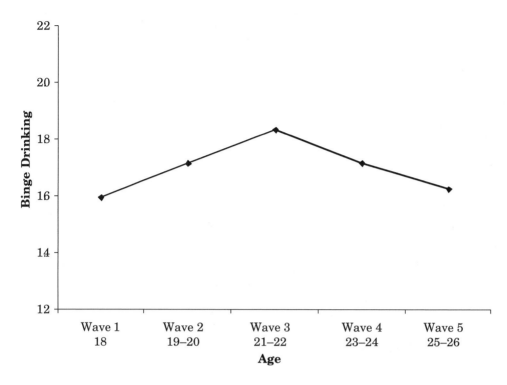

Figure 6.2. Two-week binge drinking during emerging adulthood. Scale ranges from 1 (*none*) to 6 (*10+ times*).

- The incidence of psychopathology increases. Major depressive disorders, schizophrenia, bipolar disorder, and borderline personality disorders, for example, typically manifest during late adolescence and early adulthood (American Psychiatric Association, 2000; Cicchetti & Rogosch, 2002; Grimes & Walker, 1994; Trull, 2001).
- Mental health and problem behaviors tend to be relatively stable between adolescence and adulthood. Stability, in terms of relative rank ordering of individuals over time, tends to be moderate to high for several of the relevant indices. For example, for constructs illustrated in Figures 6.1–6.4, wave-to-wave autocorrelations from ages 18 to 26 averaged .63 for well-being, .53 for binge drinking, .70 for marijuana use, .55 for depressive affect, .58 for risk taking, .42 for theft and property damage, and .25 for physical aggression.[2]

---

lines compatible with those shown in the figures; well-being, binge drinking, and marijuana use tend to peak during emerging adulthood, whereas risk taking, depressive affect, theft and property damage, and physical aggression peak prior to emerging adulthood.

[2] These average autocorrelations represent stability coefficients uncorrected for measurement error (and thus underestimate, to some extent, actual stability). As discussed in a later section of the chapter, autocorrelations tend to increase during emerging adulthood. According to some limited MTF longitudinal data from 8th graders on indices similar to those shown here, autocorrelations tend to be lower between 8th and 10th grade, but roughly equivalent to those shown here between

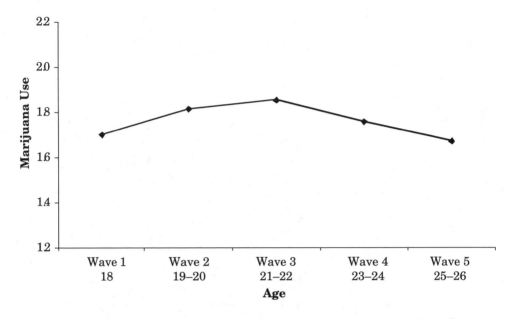

Figure 6.3. Annual marijuana use during emerging adulthood. Scale ranges from 1 (*none*) to 6 (*40 + times*).

Some obvious questions follow from these general observations: Why does mental health improve, problem behavior decrease, and the incidence of psychopathology increase in the general population during emerging adulthood? In particular, what accounts for the increase in both mental health and psychopathology? Then there are some less obvious but equally important questions: How well do these average trends reflect individual trajectories, particularly given the heterogeneity in life paths characteristic of emerging adulthood? Given that the moderate to high stability coefficients previously mentioned still leave room for some wide fluctuations in individual trajectories, to what extent are the many contextual and individual transitions characteristic of emerging adulthood sufficiently powerful to redirect individual trajectories of well-being and problem behaviors and to cause mental health difficulties to emerge or vanish during this period in life?

We pursue these and related questions in this chapter by considering a variety of conceptual and methodological issues relevant to the understanding of mental health during late adolescence, early adulthood, and the time between the two. We are interested in heterogeneity of developmental pathways, which likely corresponds with increased diversity in mental health during emerging adulthood. We are also interested in issues of continuity and discontinuity,

---

10th and 12th grade. The relatively low coefficients for theft and property damage and physical aggression are due in part to the low variance of these items; the large majority of young people do not engage in these activities, as suggested in Figure 6.4.

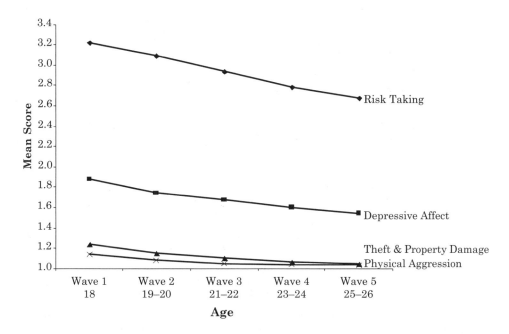

Figure 6.4. Risk taking, depressive affect, theft–property damage, and physical aggression during emerging adulthood. Risk Taking and Depressive Affect scales range from 1 (*disagree*) to 5 (*agree*). Theft and Property Damage and Physical Aggression scales range from 1 (*none*) to 5 (*5 or more times*).

which are at the core of developmental psychology and of developmental science more generally (Lerner, 2002; Sroufe & Jacobvitz, 1989; Werner, 1957). The relevant literatures hold a strong assumption that overall functioning and adjustment are continuous across life for the large majority of individuals— an assumption that is, on the face of it, quite reasonable. Theory and empirical work are, for the most part, consistent with this assumption, and indeed, without the existence of a fair amount of continuity within individuals over time, there would be little purpose in having a developmental perspective. Nonetheless, from a strong person–context interaction perspective on development—one that recognizes the potential power of life transitions to serve as turning points—it would be counterproductive to build an understanding of mental health from adolescence through adulthood entirely (or even mostly) on the assumption of continuity.

Our overview of the issues and literature is necessarily illustrative rather than comprehensive. In our examples, we focus in particular on overall well-being, substance use, antisocial behavior, and depressive affect. We begin with a conceptual overview and description of the challenges and opportunities for mental health during emerging adulthood. We then illustrate our key ideas by focusing on continuity and discontinuity, developmental transitions, and the potential functionality of deviance and difficulties. We conclude with a discussion of conceptual and methodological implications and challenges.

Emerging Adulthood: Opportunities and Challenges
for Mental Health

The perspective we offer is consistent with a broad interdisciplinary developmental science framework that emphasizes multidimensional and multidirectional developmental change across life, characterized by successive and
dynamic mutual selection and accommodation of individuals and their contexts
(Baltes, Lindenberger, & Staudinger, 1998; Cairns, 2000; Elder, 1998; Lerner,
2002; Sameroff, 2000). Through a process of niche selection, individuals select
available environments and activities on the basis of personal characteristics,
beliefs, interests, and competencies; selected ecological niches then provide
various opportunities for continued socialization and further selection. This
progressive accommodation suggests the qualities of coherence and continuity
in development. But consistent with an emphasis on dynamic person–context
interactions and multidirectional change, development does not necessarily
follow a smooth and progressive function, and early experiences do not always
have strong or lasting effects (e.g., Cairns, 2000; Laub & Sampson, 2003; Lewis,
1999; Loeber & Stouthamer-Loeber, 1998; Rutter, 1996). Thus, both continuity
and discontinuity are expected across the life span. A key question for us is
how continuity and discontinuity in mental health relate to the various transitions and experiences of emerging adulthood. In this section, we first consider
the transitions and experiences of emerging adulthood and then discuss mental
health and maladaptation during this time.

Transitions and Experiences of Emerging Adulthood

Between high school and whatever comes next in young people's lives, pervasive
and often simultaneous personal, contextual, and social role changes typically
occur. Indeed, the density of social role changes is greater in this period than
in any other period of life (Shanahan, 2000), and the same is true for geographic
mobility (Arnett, 2000, 2004). In the population, diversity in life paths increases
(Osgood, Ruth, Eccles, Jacobs, & Barber, 2005; Schulenberg, O'Malley, Bachman, & Johnston, 2005) and variability in the timing and content of developmental milestones expands (Cohen, Kasen, Chen, Hartmark, & Gordon, 2003;
Elder, 1998). For most, but not all, institutional structure tends to fall away
with the end of high school, and self-direction in life decisions, large and
small, increases (Aseltine & Gore, 1993; Shanahan, 2000). Some distinctive
and interrelated features of the transition to adulthood are pervasive personal
and social role changes, heterogeneity in life paths, and decreased institutional
structure coupled with increased agency for most.

Developmental transitions include major transformations in individuals,
their contexts, and the relations between individuals and their contexts across
life (e.g., Bronfenbrenner, 1979; Graber & Brooks-Gunn, 1996; Schulenberg &
Maggs, 2002). These transitions often are viewed globally as the connections
between major life periods, and include a series of specific interrelated developmental transitions that can be viewed as internally based (e.g., biological,
physical, cognitive, emotional, and identity-related changes) and externally

based (e.g., changes in social roles and contexts; Rutter, 1996; Susman & Rogol, 2004). Emerging adulthood occurs during the global transition from adolescence to adulthood, although as Arnett (2000, 2004) made clear, emerging adulthood as a total experience is more than a global transition. Embedded within this global transition are numerous changes involving perspective taking, emotional regulation, identity, independence, affiliation (e.g., transitions in parental, peer, and romantic involvements), and achievement (e.g., transitions from school to work; Keating, 2004; Masten et al., 1999; Schulenberg, Maggs, & O'Malley, 2003; Shiner & Masten, 2002). One particularly key transition is the movement toward self-reliance, including financial independence (Arnett, 2000, 2004). In addition, normal neurobiological changes take place during this time, involving, for example, transformations in the prefrontal cortex that relate to expanded executive functioning (Keating, 2004; Spear, 2000). It is clear that these various individual and social-role transitions are interrelated. As Cicchetti and Tucker (1994) indicated, often the individual's active strivings for self-organization provide the impetus for, and integration of, the many transitions ranging from brain growth to social-role changes. How well one can manage these many transitions is likely influenced by and, in turn, influences mental health.

Like all major life transitions, the transition to adulthood is set in a socio-cultural context and therefore may vary in timing, content, and meaning by such demographic characteristics as gender, socioeconomic background, ethnicity, culture, and historical period (Crockett, 1997; Elder, 1998; Fuligni & Pedersen, 2002). Culturally based age-related expectations and biological changes shape major life transitions by providing a normative timetable and agenda (Heckhausen, 1999; Neugarten, 1979). Nevertheless, as previously mentioned, a distinctive feature of this transition, particularly in the United States, is the often rapid decline in institutional structure and support (Hurrelmann, 1990). For example, the high school student role, occupied by roughly 90% of the middle adolescent population, is relatively structured and homogenous, imposing constraints on the range of interindividual variation in developmental pathways. In addition to this dynamic, living with one's parent(s) typically provides a fair amount of structure and support for, and constraints on, day-to-day-life. In contrast, post-high-school opportunities and role options are far more numerous and heterogeneous, and usually far less prescribed and structured.

Of course, some structure remains. For example, with regard to achievement-related transitions, postsecondary education provides some institutional structure during emerging adulthood, with roughly 60% of the graduating high school seniors in recent years going on to a 2- or 4-year college (Johnston et al., 2004). But it is clear that this transition does not represent a simple extension of the high school student role—there is much more variability and much less constraint in individual experiences. Furthermore, among those entering a 4-year college, most move out of the parental home, leaving behind (if only temporarily) a major source of support for, and constraint on, day-to-day life. Only about half of those who start a 4-year college complete their degree in 4 or 5 years (Schulenberg et al., 2005); among the others, some obviously drop out, some languish with indecision, and some change direction in their educational focus. For the roughly 40% who do not enter a 4-year college immediately following high school, there tends to be little institutional structure to facilitate their achievement-related transitions; because of necessity or preferences, regardless of any educational pursuits (e.g., 1- or 2-year colleges), most become engaged in temporary jobs with limited long-term career prospects.

The less defined and structured the transition to adulthood is, the more prominent individual characteristics will be in dictating the direction, timing, and duration of the transition. For most, this relative lack of structure can allow for greater self-selection of paths and activities. This greater capacity for self-selection of post-high-school contexts and roles is likely one reason for the increase in well-being that occurs at the population level during this transition (Aseltine & Gore, 1993; Schulenberg et al., 2005). However, for some young people, the relatively sudden drop in institutional structure can be debilitating: It can overwhelm one's coping capacities or create a mismatch between individual needs and contextual affordances. Such difficulties can contribute to a sense of floundering (Mortimer, Zimmer-Gembeck, Holmes, & Shanahan, 2002), which typically is not conducive to salutary trajectories of mental health. Furthermore, agency can happen only in a context in which viable options are available for selection, and thus when opportunities are limited, benefits associated with increased capacity for self-selection are unlikely to be realized.

Mental Health and Psychopathology During Emerging Adulthood

As we stated at the beginning of this chapter, during emerging adulthood well-being tends to increase, substance use tends to peak then subside, and problem behaviors tend to decrease; at the same time, psychopathology tends to increase. In this subsection, we first consider mental health as adaptation and then provide an illustrative overview of substance use, antisocial behavior, and depressive affect during emerging adulthood. These important but selective aspects of mental health are then used throughout the chapter to illustrate key conceptual and methodological issues. As we discuss in the concluding section, many of the issues we consider are relevant to other aspects of mental health and psychopathology during emerging adulthood.

MENTAL HEALTH AS ADAPTATION. Mental health can be viewed as successful psychosocial adaptation to changing contexts and life situations (Masten & Coatsworth, 1995). Psychopathology, then, reflects patterns of maladaptive behavior or psychological distress that interfere with some aspects of adaptation (Cicchetti, 1999; Masten & Coatsworth, 1995). Consistent with a strong person–context interaction perspective, the origins and course of adaptation and maladaptation are not understood by focusing solely on the individual or even his or her early adaptation, but rather by focusing on the ongoing interaction between the individual and the changing context (Sameroff, 2000; Sroufe & Rutter, 1984; Wills & Dishion, 2004). Challenges to a developmental system, such as changes in contexts that often come with major life transitions, result in reorganization, promoting either successful or maladaptive changes (Masten

& Coatsworth, 1995). Thus, early maladaptation may lead to a full range of adaptational outcomes in adulthood (reflecting multifinality). Likewise, maladaptation in emerging adulthood may stem from a full range of early adaptational experiences (reflecting equifinality; Cicchetti & Rogosch, 2002; Schulenberg & Maggs, 2002). Simply, early maladaptation is neither necessary nor sufficient for later maladaptation, and the same is true for successful adaptation; much depends on the ongoing interaction between individuals and their changing contexts.

The population-level increase in both successful adaptation (e.g., in terms of increased well-being) and maladaptation (e.g., in terms of increased incidence of major depression) during emerging adulthood is perplexing, but only momentarily so. Against the backdrop of multifinality and equifinality previously mentioned, the courses of various indices of mental health and maladaptation are given to increased heterogeneity across the life span, and the transitions and experiences of emerging adulthood contribute to this increased heterogeneity (Schulenberg, Sameroff, & Cicchetti, 2004). In the following section, we briefly illustrate these notions by focusing on substance use and abuse, antisociality, and depression.

SUBSTANCE USE AND ABUSE. By the end of high school, the use of alcohol and illicit drugs is normative: According to the 2003 Monitoring the Future (MTF) national survey of 12th graders, over half have used an illicit drug (typically marijuana) at least once in their lifetime, over three fourths have used alcohol, and nearly three fifths have been drunk (Johnston et al., 2004). The annual prevalence rate for marijuana use was 13% at 8th grade, peaked at 36% at age 20, and dropped to 18% by age 30; for illicit drug use other than marijuana (e.g., cocaine, amphetamines, LSD), the annual rate was 9% at 8th grade, peaked at 20% at age 20, and dropped to 11% by age 30; for alcohol use, the annual rate was 37% at 8th grade, peaked at 88% at age 24, and dropped to 84% by age 30. More telling of problematic substance use is current use: The 30-day prevalence rate for marijuana use was 8% at 8th grade, peaked at 22% at age 20, and dropped to 9% at age 30; the rate for binge drinking (five or more drinks in a row) in the past 2 weeks was 12% at Grade 8, peaked at 41% at age 22, and dropped to 26% at age 30. It is critical to note that these prevalence rates have shifted considerably over the past three decades (Johnston et al., 2004), although the relations between substance use and risk factors tend not to shift historically (Brown, Schulenberg, Bachman, O'Malley, & Johnston, 2001).

The correlates of and risk factors for substance use during adolescence and early adulthood have been studied extensively over the past few decades, yielding a long list of significant correlates and predictors. According to the MTF prevalence rates previously mentioned, substance use tends to be higher among males than females, higher among Whites than African Americans, and somewhat negatively related to family socioeconomic level (except for binge drinking, which is unrelated to family socioeconomic level; Johnston et al., 2004). Correlates and risk factors, which tend to be mostly similar for cigarette, alcohol, and illicit drug use, fall within many domains, including genetic (e.g., family history of alcohol and other drug use), biological (e.g., early pubertal timing), family (e.g., low parental monitoring), school (e.g., low grade point average), peers (e.g., peer substance use), personality (e.g., high sensation seeking, low conventionality), antisocial behavior (e.g., theft, property damage), and psychopathology (e.g., depression; see Cicchetti, 1999; Hawkins, Catalano, & Miller, 1992; Jessor, Donovan, & Costa, 1991). Often, especially during late adolescence and emerging adulthood when alcohol and illicit drug use is normative, such risk factors relate more to excessive use than to experimental use.

Of particular interest, changes in substance use are linked to the experiences and transitions of late adolescence and emerging adulthood (Schulenberg & Maggs, 2002). In general, the increase and subsequent decrease in substance use illustrated in Figures 6.2 and 6.3 are thought to be a function, in part, of the changes in freedoms and responsibilities (Bachman et al., 2002). Leaving home and attending college, for example, is associated with decreased constraints and increased opportunities for substance use. Likewise, through such transitions, one typically encounters more peers in a similar situation; although not ideal, substance use can serve important developmental task functions regarding peer bonding and identity exploration (Chassin, Pitts, & DeLucia, 1999; Maggs, 1997). An additional characteristic that may contribute to substance use during emerging adulthood is the role ambiguity and transience of this time (Arnett, 2000; Schulenberg & Maggs, 2002), which can work against commitments to social conventions (e.g., Sampson & Laub, 1990). With the onset of adulthood, however it may be defined, many freedoms recede and new responsibilities regarding family, work, and citizenship emerge (Masten et al., 1999; Schulenberg, Bryant, & O'Malley, 2004; Youniss & Yates, 1997). In particular, maturing out of substance use has been found to be a function of getting married (e.g., Bachman et al., 2002; Leonard & Rothbard, 1999).

Nonetheless, not all substance use follows this normative pattern during emerging adulthood. Indeed, a thrust of recent longitudinal research has been to identify and explain multiple trajectories of heavy alcohol use and of marijuana use during adolescence and emerging adulthood (e.g., Bates & Labouvie, 1997; Chassin, Pitts, & Prost, 2002; Ellickson, Martino, & Collins, 2004; Flory, Lynam, Milich, Leukefeld, & Clayton, 2004; Hill, White, Chung, Hawkins, & Catalano, 2000; Jackson, Sher, Cooper, & Wood, 2002; Kandel & Chen, 2000; Schulenberg, Wadsworth, O'Malley, Bachman, & Johnston, 1996; Windle & Wiesner, 2004), focusing on such longitudinal patterns as chronic use (early excessive use that continues across multiple waves), abstention, decreased use, increased use, and, of particular interest, fling use (use that peaks and declines across the waves). The various trajectories have different predictors and outcomes (for review see Maggs & Schulenberg, in press) as well as different configurations of time-varying covariates (Schulenberg, Merline, et al., 2005; Sher, Gotham, & Watson, 2004). For example, membership in chronic heavy-use trajectories during emerging adulthood is predicted by, for example, being male, parental substance use, early antisociality, school difficulties, and peer approval of substance use; in a similar manner, outcomes of chronic heavy-use trajectories in emerging adulthood include physical and mental health difficulties, criminal behavior, and antisocial personality disorders. In contrast, it is difficult to predict in advance membership in the fling trajectory groups (who have substance use levels nearly as high as that of the chronic group during emerging adulthood), and likewise, membership in this group appears to have few negative outcomes in adulthood.

These multiple trajectories, which underlie the population-based normative trajectories illustrated in Figures 6.2 and 6.3, represent distinct etiologies, signifying different types of substance use disorders, such as life course persistent and developmentally limited (Zucker, 1995). Attempting to distinguish substance use from substance abuse is difficult especially during late adolescence and emerging adulthood when some use is normative (Newcomb & Bentler, 1988). In some ways, this distinction depends on continued heavy use, as well as how maladaptive substance use may be in terms of normative developmental tasks (Cicchetti, 1999; Schulenberg et al., 2003). As we discuss later in this chapter, an emphasis on the multiple trajectories is key to understanding continuity and discontinuity in substance use during emerging adulthood.

ANTISOCIAL BEHAVIOR. At the population level, the prevalence of antisocial behavior is low during childhood, increases during adolescence, and then decreases rapidly during emerging adulthood (Elliott, Huizinga, & Menard, 1989). Antisociality is a broad term used to denote misconduct that is given to a typical developmental progression: for example, tantrums in early childhood; oppositional, defiant, and aggressive behaviors during middle childhood; shoplifting, lying, fighting, and involvement in more serious crimes during adolescence; and more serious and violent criminal activity in adulthood. Antisocial behaviors, often classified as conduct disorder, aggression, and delinquency, are logically and empirically related, such that both the risk factors and effective interventions are similar for each (Farrington, 2004; Hawkins et al., 1998; Patterson, Forgatch, Yoerger, & Stoolmiller, 1998). The prevalence rates for conduct disorder and delinquency are higher for boys than for girls at all ages. The incidence of conduct disorder, such as aggression toward people or animals, property destruction, stealing, running away, and violating rules, peaks at ages 15 to 17, with a rate of about 11% for boys and 4% for girls (Lahey et al., 2000). Delinquency, defined as acts prohibited by the criminal law, such as theft, burglary, violence, and drug use, follows similar trends. According to 2001 national U.S. statistics, the peak age for property offenses is 16 to 18 for males and 15 to 17 for females. For violence, male offenses peak at ages 18 to 19 and female offenses peak at ages 19 to 21 (Farrington, 2004).

The *Diagnostic and Statistical Manual of Mental Disorders* (4th ed., text rev.; *DSM–IV–TR;* American Psychiatric Association, 2000) recognizes two unique developmental routes to antisocial behavior—childhood-onset (before age 11) and postpubertal adolescent-onset (after age 11) antisociality—that vary in etiology, course, compounding features, prognosis, and treatment needs. Children with early-onset antisociality often exhibit neuropsychological deficits that affect the normal development of language, memory, and self-control (cognitive delays and a difficult, impulsive temperament); weak and disrupted parental relationships, harsh parenting, and parental antisociality and criminality appear to play a causative role. These neuropsychological deficits and family adversities not only are more likely to predispose early-onset delinquent youth to a life of antisocial behavior but also are linked with more physical aggression and more violent crime in adulthood than among late-onset delinquent youth (e.g., Aguilar, Sroufe, Egeland, & Carlson, 2000; Clarizio, 1997; Huesmann, Eron, & Dubrow, 2002). Patterson and his colleagues (1998) found that early-onset delinquent youth follow a trajectory of antisocial behavior that begins with child antisocial acts (such as tantrums and oppositional behavior), moves to early arrests, and then advances to chronic juvenile offending during adolescence. Dysfunctional parental discipline practices, parental antisociality, social disadvantage (low income and large family size), and multiple family changes (resulting from divorce, single-parent families, poverty, etc.) are contextual factors that have consistently been found to contribute to and maintain early-onset trajectories of offending (Dishion, Patterson, & Kavanagh, 1992; Farrington & Hawkins, 1991; Moffitt & Caspi, 2001; Patterson et al., 1998; Thornberry, Freeman-Gallant, Lizotte, Krohn, & Smith, 2003). The more dysfunctional the family (e.g., poor parent discipline and management strategies and multiple transitions) and the more involved the young person is with a deviant peer group, the greater the likelihood that he or she is on a life-persistent trajectory of antisociality.

In contrast, late-onset delinquent youth are often free from psychopathology and are more likely than early-onset delinquent youth to desist from antisociality by age 23 (Moffitt, 1993; Roisman, Aguilar, & Egeland, 2004). Overall, these youth come from normal family backgrounds (Moffitt & Caspi, 2001). Weak and disrupted parental relationships seem to be more a consequence of antisocial activity than a cause. At age 18, late-onset delinquent youth tend to be less aggressive than do early-onset delinquent youth and generally report greater attachments to parents and greater desires for close relationships with intimates. These youth are less likely to have come from single-parent homes or to have been maltreated, and overall they have experienced fewer psychosocial risk factors than have early-onset antisocial youth (Aguilar et al., 2000). Late-onset delinquency is relatively normative during adolescence. Several cultural and biological explanations for this normative behavior are possible, including a mismatch between biological and social maturity, a lack of adult supervision resulting in peer-motivated delinquency, and an increased desire for autonomy expression and risk taking. Previous findings suggest that during adolescence, some youth begin to admire aggressive peers (Bukowski, Sippola, & Newcomb, 2000). Whereas disruptive parenting and neuropsychological difficulties lead early-onset delinquent youth to affiliate with deviant peers, befriending deviant peers appears to be a primary factor promoting adolescent-onset delinquency (Moffitt & Caspi, 2001; Vitaro, Tremblay, Kerr, Pagani, & Bukowski, 1997). Recent evidence suggests that the negative consequences of adolescent-onset antisocial behavior are limited primarily to minor problem behaviors and not linked to more widespread failures of adaptive functioning in such domains as school and work (see Roisman et al., 2004); indeed, they are no more at risk for committing crimes or being arrested as adults than are non-antisocial youth (Moffitt & Caspi, 2001; Patterson et al., 1998).

Why does this group desist from lawbreaking and eventually leave behind antisocial behaviors? Part of the answer lies in individual characteristics and expectations: Earlier-mastered prosocial and cognitive skills favor such turn-arounds (Caspi & Moffitt, 1995; Moffitt, 1993; Nagin, Farrington, & Moffitt, 1995), and the expectations and experiences regarding antisocial behaviors during adolescence set the stage for desistance. And part of the answer lies in the experiences that characterize the end of adolescence and beginning of adulthood. The social role and context changes that occur during this time provide a rich set of opportunities for new experiences with work and romantic relationships and civic engagement that are related to desistance in antisocial behavior and offending (Uggen & Massoglia, 2003). But such experiences are likely to relate to desistance regardless of onset type. Indeed, Roisman, Aguilar, and Egeland (2004) found that the opportunity to engage in emerging adulthood tasks (e.g., establishing a stable career or serious romantic relationship) was most effective for desistance of delinquency among early-onset youth. These opportunities during emerging adulthood enable youth both to leave behind early contexts that helped create and sustain their difficulties and failures and to gain experience and competencies with adulthood tasks (Laub, Nagin, & Sampson, 1998; Roisman et al., 2004; Stouthamer-Loeber, Wei, Loeber, & Masten, 2004).

Consistent evidence suggests that early- and late-onset antisociality are two distinct paths to juvenile offending; the former is more likely to persist in offending into emerging adulthood and beyond, setting the stage for increased antisociality and psychopathy, whereas the latter is more likely to desist with the experiences and tasks of emerging adulthood. These two (and other) distinct pathways underlie the population-based age–crime curve illustrated in Figure 6.4, suggesting again the importance of considering the multiple trajectory groups that together form the population-based normative trajectory. Of course, not all child-onset offenders continue their antisocial behaviors into adulthood, and likewise, some adolescent-limited offenders do persist in antisocial behaviors well into adulthood (Farrington, 2004; Laub & Sampson, 2003; Petras et al., 2004), with much depending on their experiences during late adolescence and early adulthood (Moffitt, 1993; Sampson & Laub, 2003; Uggen & Massoglia, 2003).

DEPRESSION. Depressive disorders are classified in the *DSM IV* under the broad category of mood disorders. Depression is divided into two main categories: bipolar disorders and depressive disorders. The presence of manic or hypomanic symptoms that alternate with depression indicates a bipolar disorder. In this chapter, we are concerned with depressive disorders (without manic or hypomanic episodes), focusing specifically on major depressive disorder (MDD) as well as minor depression. MDD is characterized by at least a 2-week period of depressed mood that is accompanied by at least four additional symptoms, such as fatigue, insomnia, diminished ability to concentrate, or recurrent suicidal ideation. Minor depression involves depressed affect or low mood that does not meet the criteria for severity, duration, level of distress, or impairment as MDD (American Psychiatric Association, 2000).

According to recent evidence, approximately 18.8 million American adults (9.5% of the population) age 18 and older experience a depressive disorder in a given year, with the rate typically being twice as high among women (12%) as among men (6.6%; National Institute of Mental Health, 2001). Depression rates are lowest among prepubertal children (about 1%), and these rates are usually reported to be about equal in girls and boys (Fleming & Offord, 1990; Graber, 2004). Depression (usually in forms of general depressive affect, or minor depression) begins to manifest during early adolescence, as does the sex difference in depression (e.g., Galambos, 2004; Ge, Conger, & Elder, 2001; Graber, 2004; Leadbeater, Kuperminc, Blatt, & Hertzog, 1999). The average age of onset of MDD is about 15 (Graber, 2004), with the evidence generally suggesting the 2:1 ratio of prevalence between girls and boys (Culbertson, 1997; Nolen-Hoeksema, 1990; Reinherz, Giaconia, Carmola, Wasserman, & Silverman, 1999). According to the National Comorbidity Survey (Kessler & Walters, 1998), between the ages of 15 and 22, depression increases in a linear fashion. Lifetime prevalence of depression among 15- to 16-year-olds was 14.6% for MDD and 8.1% for minor depression; among young adults ages 21 to 22, lifetime prevalence was approximately 21.2% for MDD and 10.3% for minor depression (with the 2:1 ratio for girls and boys generally holding constant). Therefore, although the age of onset is quite variable, ranging from childhood into adulthood, adolescence and emerging adulthood appear to be sensitive periods for depressive disorders (Reinherz et al., 1999). It is interesting to juxtapose this increase in depressive disorders with the increase in well-being and decrease in depressive affect (see Figures 6.1 and 6.4) that occur at the population level during emerging adulthood. In all likelihood, as we discuss later in this chapter, these changes are a matter of increasing heterogeneity, inspired in part by the multiple transitions and social-role changes that occur during emerging adulthood.

Previous research has found strong continuity and recurrence of depression from childhood to adulthood (Fergusson & Woodward, 2002; Harrington, Fudge, Rutter, Pickles, & Hill, 1990). Early-onset mood disorders are considered a more severe and recurrent form of the disorder and are associated with increased familial loading of depression. In addition, early-onset depression is related to increased risk of later anxiety disorders, nicotine and alcohol abuse or dependence, eating disorders, suicide attempts, educational underachievement, unemployment, and early parenthood (Fergusson & Woodward, 2002; Graber, 2004; Johnson, Cohen, Kotler, Kasen, & Brook, 2002). These risk factors tend to be similar for girls and boys.

Similar to what has been found regarding substance use and antisociality, childhood-onset depression has been found to have different predictors than adult-onset depression, which suggests different etiologic processes depending on age of onset (e.g., Duggal, Carlson, Sroufe, & Egeland, 2001). Jaffee et al. (2002), using a longitudinal sample of 998 participants from the Dunedin Multidisciplinary Health and Development Study, found that child- and adult-onset MDD have distinct origins and thus reflect distinct subtypes. Mental health data were first collected when participants were 10 years of age, with multiple waves of follow-up data collected through age 26. Four groups were defined: (a) individuals diagnosed with MDD in adolescence (MDD diagnosis at age 11, 13, or 15) but not in early adulthood (ages 18, 21, 26; $n = 21$); (b) individuals first diagnosed with MDD in early adulthood (at 17 years or older; $n = 314$); (c) individuals diagnosed in both adolescence and early adulthood ($n = 34$); and (d) never-depressed individuals ($n = 629$). Although it appears that most depressed adolescents become depressed adults, reflecting continuity, most individuals who were diagnosed with depression in adulthood were not diagnosed with depression in adolescence. Findings based on these group distinctions suggest that, overall, the adult-depressed group resembled the never-depressed group in their experiences of low levels of early-childhood risk factors. The adolescence-depressed and adolescence-to-adult-depressed groups experienced similar significant childhood risk factors: neurodevelopmental problems, more family psychopathology and instability, and more behavioral disorders. In addition, children of depressed parents were at higher risk for adolescent-onset depression than those of nondepressed parents, but no relation between depressed parents and depressed offspring was found within the adult-onset depressed group. Therefore, although depression in adolescence tends to continue into adulthood (Birmaher et al., 1996; Rao et al., 1995), adult depression is typically not rooted in earlier experiences and risk factors. As we discuss later in this chapter, how the changes and experiences associated with emerging adulthood fit into desistence and emergence of depressive disorders is an important emphasis for future research.

As a major life transition, more individual and contextual change occurs during emerging adulthood than at any other time in life. And mental health, broadly defined, is best thought of in terms of moving targets, especially during late adolescence and emerging adulthood. It is not a coincidence that these changes in mental health and psychopathology occur during this major life transition. In the next section, we consider more systematically the range of connections between continuity and discontinuity in mental health and the transitions and experiences of emerging adulthood.

Continuity and Discontinuity in Mental Health: Transitions, Developmental Disturbances, Turning Points, and Functionality

Continuity and discontinuity are not easily defined. As concepts, they can be ambiguous and complex, often invoking systems-level and dynamic considerations (Kagan, 1980; Rutter, 1992; Sameroff, 2000; Werner, 1957). Stability and continuity are sometimes used interchangeably, but in general among developmental scientists the two are viewed as related but distinct; typically, the former pertains to the extent to which individuals maintain relative rank ordering over time, and the latter pertains to the course of intraindividual trajectories (e.g., Baltes, Reese, & Nesselroade, 1977; Lerner, 2002). Two uses of the concepts of continuity and discontinuity are common (Schulenberg et al., 2003), and both are highly relevant to understanding mental health during emerging adulthood. First, continuity and discontinuity can be considered in terms of connections and causative linkages across the life span (e.g., Lewis, 1999; Masten, 2001): Ontogenic continuity reflects strong developmentally distal effects, and ontogenic discontinuity reflects strong developmentally proximal effects (Masten, 2001; Schulenberg et al., 2003). The second use is consistent with an organismic developmental perspective in which discontinuity is viewed as reflecting qualitative or underlying structural-level change (e.g., the emergence of new structure or meaning; see Piaget, 1970; Werner, 1957): Continuity and discontinuity can be considered as having both descriptive components (pertaining to manifest behaviors) and explanatory components (pertaining to underlying purposes, functions, and meanings; e.g., Kagan, 1969; Lerner, 2002).

In this section, we first describe in more detail the two uses of continuity and discontinuity. We then focus on developmental transitions and how they can contribute to ontogenic continuity and discontinuity in mental health, highlighting discontinuity in the forms of turning points and developmental disturbances. We conclude this section by considering how descriptive and explanatory continuity and discontinuity can help in understanding shifts in the meaning and functionality of mental health during emerging adulthood.

Continuity and Discontinuity: Conceptual Considerations

When continuity and discontinuity across the life span is conceptualized, it must be acknowledged that continuity tends to prevail. This predominance of continuity makes it tempting to believe that continuity is the natural case that happens more or less automatically as life unfolds, with discontinuity being the special case thus provoking curiosity. But as developmental scientists, we should be as curious about why we see continuity as we are about why we see discontinuity.

ONTOGENIC CONTINUITY AND DISCONTINUITY. Development is a cumulative process. Ontogenic continuity reflects a progressive and individual coherence perspective, in which events and experiences of childhood and adolescence are viewed as formative and as causing future outcomes in adulthood (cf. Caspi, 2000; Roberts, Caspi, & Moffitt, 2001). This perspective is typically implied (and often explicit) in the literature that attempts to establish connections across different periods of life in general and to provide explanations of mental health and psychopathology in particular.

But it is not necessarily the case that early functioning determines later functioning (Cicchetti & Rogosch, 2002; Lewis, 1999; P. Martin & Martin, 2002). Indeed, from a developmental science perspective emphasizing plasticity and development across the life span, the effects of early experiences may be amplified, neutralized, or reversed by later experiences. This focus on more developmentally proximal influences reflects an ontogenic discontinuity perspective, whereby functioning is assumed to be due more to recent and current experiences than to early experiences (Lewis, 1999). This general theme of indeterminacy in developmental course and effects because of powerful proximal influences is consistent with the life-course literature suggesting the power of developmental transitions, such as the transition to marriage, in altering the course of substance use (Bachman et al., 2002; Schulenberg et al., 2005) and in reversing the effects of earlier violence and delinquency (Laub & Sampson, 2003; Uggen, 2000).

Ontogenic continuity and discontinuity are not necessarily mutually exclusive. Distal and proximal influences are often intertwined (Ge et al., 2001; P. Martin & Martin, 2002; Schulenberg et al., 2003): In terms of impact on adulthood functioning (e.g., substance abuse disorders), distal influences (e.g., poor early parent–child relations) may set the stage for proximal influences (e.g., difficulty with negotiating the transition from school to work). But proximal developmental influences in general, and developmental transitions in particular, may operate independently of distal influences or may even disrupt distal influences, thus setting the stage for discontinuity in mental health and psychopathology. As we discuss later in this section, an emphasis on how developmentally distal and proximal effects interrelate is especially useful in understanding how developmental transitions relate to the course of mental health.

DESCRIPTIVE AND EXPLANATORY CONTINUITY AND DISCONTINUITY. Continuity and discontinuity can be viewed at both the descriptive (manifest) level and the explanatory (underlying purpose, function, or meaning) level, allowing for four continuity–discontinuity categories. *Homotypic continuity* refers to the presence of both descriptive and explanatory continuity (Caspi & Roberts, 1999; Kagan, 1969). For example, a young adolescent who verbally bullies her peers on the playground to establish and maintain her place in the social hierarchy continues in emerging adulthood to order her peers around in the workplace to establish the same type of ranking in this new context. Often, however, behaviors vary across time while the underlying purpose or meaning of those varying behaviors remains invariant. For instance, the young adolescent who bullies her peers to maintain her place in the social hierarchy may find other more subtle interaction patterns that serve the same purpose in emerging adulthood. This is termed *heterotypic continuity* (descriptive discontinuity, explanatory continuity; Caspi & Roberts, 1999; Kagan, 1969). In general, adaptation to life's tasks may be continuous, but many of the activities and behaviors associated with adaptation tend to be discontinuous (Masten, 2001; Moffitt & Caspi, 2001; Rutter, 1996); thus, as we discuss in a later subsection, heterotypic continuity is especially useful in understanding how mental health may shift during emerging adulthood.

Functional discontinuity, which may be considered the opposite of heterotypic continuity, occurs when the manifest behavior appears unchanged yet the underlying function or meaning of that behavior changes over time (i.e., descriptive continuity, explanatory discontinuity). For example, a 14-year-old adolescent frequently uses marijuana primarily for the purposes of experimentation and sensation seeking; 10 years later, during emerging adulthood, he still uses marijuana frequently, but the main purpose is to attempt to cope with anxiety. Finally, shifts over time in both the manifest behaviors and underlying meanings and functions of those behaviors reflect *complete discontinuity*.

THE CONTEXT AND MEASUREMENT OF CONTINUITY AND DISCONTINUITY. The understanding of behaviors and their meanings across different points in time must be immersed in considerations of not just individual continuity and discontinuity but also the continuity or discontinuity of surrounding social context (Davis & Millon, 1994; Sameroff, Peck, & Eccles, 2004), along with considerations of the broader cultural context and historical time (Shanahan, 2000). For example, any distinction between ontogenic continuity and discontinuity might rest on the continuity of one's social contexts and person–context match. Likewise, emerging adulthood is accompanied by shifting role expectations, which in turn can reflect descriptive or explanatory discontinuity. Cultures vary in their support for and expectations regarding continuity and discontinuity across the life course (Furstenberg, 2002; Heckhausen, 1999; Shanahan, Mortimer, & Krueger, 2002), and the same holds true for varying historical periods marked by technological and political shifts.

Questions about continuity and discontinuity are necessarily methodologically bound (Lerner, 2002; Mortimer, Finch, & Kumka, 1982; Werner, 1957). All else being equal, there are distinct advantages to using longitudinal data spanning three or more waves when attempting to study continuity and discontinuity. Still, depending on the approach, one may find more or less continuity than is actually the case (McAdams, 1994; Parker & Asher, 1987); moreover, the timing of, and time between, measurement occasions can influence the extent to which one finds continuity or discontinuity. Finally, what is found for the general case in regard to continuity and discontinuity may have little to do with the given individuals when they are combined to make up the general case (Cairns, 2000). In our concluding comments in this chapter, we discuss some analytic strategies for studying continuity and discontinuity.

We now turn to considerations of developmental transitions and how they can serve as the mechanisms of ontogenetic continuity and discontinuity across emerging adulthood in particular and across the life span in general.

Developmental Transitions and Ontogenic Continuity and Discontinuity

Developmental transitions include major transformations in individuals, their contexts, and the relations between individuals and their contexts across the life span (e.g., Bronfenbrenner, 1979; Graber & Brooks-Gunn, 1996; Schulenberg & Maggs, 2002). As discussed previously, these transitions often are viewed globally as the connections between major life periods, such as the transition from adolescence to adulthood; these global transitions include other identifiable (and less global) internally based developmental transitions concerning biological, physical, cognitive, emotional, and identity-related change, and externally based developmental transitions concerning changes in social roles and contexts (Rutter, 1996; Susman & Rogol, 2004).

Issues of continuity and discontinuity are central to understanding the power of major developmental transitions on individuals' lives (Rutter, 1996). Although the power of transitions may be more obvious when there is discontinuity, transitions also contribute to continuity, with transitional experiences serving as proving grounds, which help consolidate ongoing trajectories of mental health and maladaptation. In regard to transition-induced discontinuity in ongoing trajectories of mental health and maladaptation, some discontinuity may best be viewed as a developmental disturbance, a short-term perturbation (e.g., temporary identity difficulties during the transition to college; temporary desistance of depressive affect with starting a new life), after which one's ongoing trajectory will resume (Schulenberg et al., 2003). Other discontinuity reflects a long-term change in course—a turning point—in mental health or maladaptation (Elder, 1998; Ronka, Oravala, & Pulkkinen, 2002; Rutter, 1996).

How can developmental transitions contribute to continuity and discontinuity in mental health? Schulenberg and Maggs (2002; see also Schulenberg et al., 2003) discussed five interrelated conceptual models concerning how developmental transitions relate to health risks in general and substance use in particular. Four of these models have implications for understanding how transitions relate to ontogenic continuity and discontinuity in mental health (the fifth model is discussed in a later subsection). In the overload model, major or multiple transitions overwhelm one's coping capacity, resulting in decrements in health and well-being. In the developmental match–mismatch model, transitions increase or decrease the match between the individual's developmental needs and contextual affordances, resulting in increases or decreases in health and well-being. In the increased heterogeneity model, developmental transitions exacerbate individual differences in ongoing well-being trajectories. In the heightened vulnerability to chance events model, the exploratory behavior engendered by major transitions can increase exposure and reactivity to positive and negative novel experiences. In the following sections, these models are used to help describe and explain continuity and discontinuity in mental health during emerging adulthood.

DEVELOPMENTAL TRANSITIONS DURING EMERGING ADULTHOOD AS CONDUITS OF CONTINUITY. According to Sroufe and Rutter (1984), continuity across the life span can be viewed in terms of causal processes represented by reactions built on one another over time, or chain reactions. For example, in the area the continuity of antisociality, one important causal stream involves peer interactions: Because antisocial children are often excluded from normal patterns of peer interaction (as a result of low acceptance among their peers), they are also excluded from normal socialization experiences and deprived of important sources of support, and these exclusions in turn serve to foster continued antisociality (Parker & Asher, 1987). In general, this approach, characteristic of the organizational developmental perspective, focuses on the progression of reorganizations within and among the biological, psychological, and social systems that account for continuities in and coherence of development despite shifts in context and maturational changes (Cicchetti & Rogosch, 2002; Sameroff, 2000). Major life transitions, many of which occur during emerging adulthood, can be important components of this progression.

In particular, young people with a history of difficulties (including intra- and interpersonal difficulties, along with difficulties in negotiating earlier transitions) may have trouble negotiating new transitions during emerging adulthood and thus fall further behind their well-functioning peers; in contrast, those with a history of doing well likely have more resources to deal with the stress of the multiple transitions and perhaps more resources to select those post-high-school contexts that best match their needs, which will increase positive adjustment during emerging adulthood (e.g., Compas, Wagner, Slavin, & Vannatta, 1986; Schulenberg, Bryant, & O'Malley, 2004). For example, Hussong and Chassin (2002) found that children of alcoholics (COAs), compared with matched controls, experienced more difficulties with leaving home during emerging adulthood, and these emerging adulthood difficulties were dependent to some extent on family disorganization and conflict during childhood. In turn, difficulty with this leaving-home transition may mediate or otherwise contribute to COA effects on subsequent adulthood functioning. This causal flow is consistent with the increased heterogeneity model, whereby challenging transitions can serve to magnify existing strengths and weaknesses, thus increasing interindividual differences in adjustment (e.g., Loukas, Zucker, Fitzgerald, & Krull, 2003).

Likewise, developmental transitions during emerging adulthood, such as from high school to college or from living with parents to living alone, often function as proving grounds. In general, individuals may rely on their intrinsic tendencies and behavioral repertoire in novel and ambiguous situations (e.g., Caspi, 2000; Dannefer, 1987), which suggests that transitions can serve to strengthen individual characteristics and coping styles (adaptive and maladaptive), thus becoming mechanisms for continuity across the life span. In this sense, again consistent with the increased heterogeneity model, developmental transitions (representing proximal effects) can serve to mediate, and perhaps amplify, the impact of earlier experiences (distal effects) on later adjustment. For example, Reinherz, Paradis, Gianconia, Stashwick, and Fitzmaurice (2003) found that some of the most salient predictors of depression during emerging adulthood (ages 18–26) were internalizing problems and anxiousness at age 9 (from participants' and their mothers' reports), which suggests not only ontogenic continuity, but also the way childhood behavioral–emotional characteristics may be amplified during emerging adulthood.

Consistent with the developmental match–mismatch model, ontogenic continuity in mental health and maladaptation across the transitions of emerging adulthood is likely to be dependent, to some extent, on the degree to which matches or mismatches between individual characteristics and contextual affordances are maintained (e.g., Eccles, Lord, Roeser, Barber, & Hernandez Jozefowicz, 1997). If such transitions—such as school to work—provide continued (or even a progressive increase in) developmentally appropriate challenges through which young people can experience competence, then those who were doing well prior to emerging adulthood likely will continue to do well during and after emerging adulthood. In contrast, if a transition—again, such as school to work—results in continued developmentally unstimulating opportunities for the young person, then difficulties will likely continue and become amplified.

Often, despite major life transitions, important contexts may change little. If one does not leave home during emerging adulthood and thus maintains similar relationships (good or bad) with parents, other family members, and peers, then the person–context match or mismatch may be maintained, contributing to some continuity in mental health or maladaptation. In addition, such continuity often occurs even if important relational contexts do change, as a result of geographical mobility, for instance, because one may still select into similar types of relational contexts (e.g., Furman, Simon, Shaffer, & Bouchey, 2002; Reis, Collins, & Berscheid, 2000; see also chap. 9, this volume). For example, Schulenberg and colleagues (Schulenberg et al., 1996, 2005) found that those who maintained either high or low levels of substance use from high school through emerging adulthood reported similar levels of peer substance use across this time regardless of whether their peer groups changed (e.g., because of leaving home for college), which suggests that continuity in substance use corresponds to continuity in peer contexts or person–context matches. And even when new peer contexts are not purposely selected, a continued person–context match is possible and consequential in ongoing trajectories of substance use. For example, in taking advantage of the natural experiment allowed by random roommate assignment among college freshman, Duncan, Boisjoly, Kremer, Levy, and Eccles (2005) found that for male college freshmen who engaged in binge drinking in high school (presumably with binge drinking peers), the drinking history of their new roommate was pivotal in their continued drinking: Binge drinkers randomly paired with other binge drinkers (reflecting a likely continued person–context match) continued and escalated their heavy drinking much more than did binge drinkers paired with nonbinge drinkers (reflecting a likely mismatch).

DEVELOPMENTAL TRANSITIONS DURING EMERGING ADULTHOOD AS CONTRIBUTORS TO DISCONTINUITY: TURNING POINTS AND DEVELOPMENTAL DISTURBANCES. Transitions during emerging adulthood can also contribute to developmental discontinuity. By providing shocks to the system, transitions can serve as proximal effects that counteract developmentally distal effects. Consistent with the overload model, these shocks can overwhelm one's coping capacity, setting the stage for maladaptation. The result of such shocks can range from long-term changes in course (reflecting turning points) to momentary perturbations yielding a jumbling of individual differences for a limited time (reflecting developmental disturbances). In many ways, the conditions of discontinuity are the opposite of those of continuity just discussed.

Regarding turning points, Rutter (1992) suggested that this type of discontinuity is most likely to occur when the transition events and experiences are drastically different from those prior to the transition. For example, consistent with the developmental match–mismatch model, if the transition from full-time school to full-time work results in a markedly better match between activities and challenges offered by the context and the young person's interests and life goals, then difficulties experienced during adolescence (e.g., use of illicit drugs to alleviate boredom and feelings of incompetence) may not continue into adulthood. Some of the decline in antisocial behavior from adolescence to emerging adulthood is consistent with this model: A major change in contexts and the opportunity to abandon past contexts that constrained these youth is believed to be the primary reason why some early-onset antisocial youth manage to move away from their disruptive pasts (e.g., Ronka et al., 2002; Rutter, 1996; Sampson & Laub, 1990). Evidence suggesting the positive effects of romantic and work arenas for derailing the progression of antisocial behaviors among early-onset youth supports the notion that this antisocial type may result from difficulties with developmental tasks of childhood and adolescence (e.g., Aguilar et al., 2000; Roisman et al., 2004). In a similar manner, the ending of college and entry into marriage and other adult roles relates to declines in substance use, including for those who were heavily involved in alcohol and other drug use (e.g., Bachman et al., 2002; Bartholow, Sher, & Krull, 2003).

As we previously discussed, emerging adulthood typically is accompanied by an increase in agency and decrease in institutional support, such that most individuals have more choice in their day-to-day activities and life decisions. This increase in choice may result in greater person–context match, which likely contributes to the population-level increase in well-being and decrease in depressive affect (Schulenberg, Bryant, & O'Malley, 2004). Likewise, increased agency and selection of new contexts and experiences increase the likelihood of chance encounters that can contribute to turning points (cf. Bandura, 1982). Consistent with the heightened vulnerability to chance events model, entering a brand new context can be associated with increases in the occurrence and effect of novel experiences as young people find their way in the new context, and these experiences can deflect ongoing trajectories of mental health for better or worse (Schulenberg & Maggs, 2002).

But with the decrease in structure, there might also be discontinuity in support, which may in turn result in a markedly worse person–context match contributing to negative turning points in mental health. For example, the transition to college may correspond with a drop in social support, resulting in the emergence of depressive affect and other adjustment difficulties (e.g., Compas et al., 1986). Similar effects might occur when transitions overwhelm coping capacities (the overload model). Late-onset depression during emerging adulthood may be partly a function of the relatively sudden and pervasive changes that occur, particularly when the changes reflect person–context mismatch (see Gutman & Sameroff, 2004).

With regard to distinguishing turning points and developmental disturbances, Cicchetti and Rogosch (2002) discussed how the increase in externalizing and internalizing forms of psychopathology during adolescence contributes to a blurring of the boundaries between normative struggles and psychopathology. They asked the following questions:

> When are irritability, dysphoria, and emotional lability part of normative adolescent self-searching versus symptoms of mood disorder? When does experimentation with alcohol and drugs lapse into substance abuse? Which adolescents are most vulnerable to moving into the psychopathological extremes? . . . What current and historical developmental factors influence

the trajectories engaged that involve normative struggles versus emerging disorder? (p. 7)

The same can be asked about emerging adulthood regarding the challenges of determining whether the observed behavior is a developmental disturbance or a turning point. Once individuals are given time to adjust and contexts and developmental tasks shift, it is likely that one's ongoing trajectory, prior to the developmental disruption, will resume. In this case, a major transition may result simply in momentary disturbances (e.g., temporary identity difficulties during the transition to college) and not have long-term effects on development or be predictive of later functioning.

The notion of developmental disturbances draws partly from Anna Freud's (1958) view about the lack of manifest continuity between childhood and adolescence and adolescence and adulthood. Although few current scholars adhere to her views on adolescence, the idea of developmental disturbances is compelling. A developmental disturbance has three operational features: (a) an instability of individual differences that is time-limited, (b) functioning during the disturbance period that is unpredictable in advance, and (c) functioning during the disturbance period that does not predict postdisturbance functioning. Continuity (as well as rank-order stability) may appear between the predisturbance and postdisturbance periods, suggesting that a turning point is not the appropriate conceptualization. For example, adolescent-onset antisociality can reflect a developmental disturbance: There is a relatively quick onset and decline antisociality for some between middle adolescence and emerging adulthood, and this antisociality has little connection to childhood risk factors or to negative adulthood outcomes (as previously discussed).

As an illustration of one way to consider developmental disturbances, Figure 6.5 shows imagined (but realistic) longitudinal data on marijuana use from characters in the movie *Animal House* before and after their transition to college. As shown, between age 18 (when individuals are in high school) and age 19 (when they are in college away from home), marijuana use increases for many and individual differences become jumbled, reflecting a developmental disturbance; by age 21, the age 18 levels and rank ordering of individuals resume. The stability coefficient between ages 18 and 19 might be quite low, as it would be from ages 20 to 21, but the coefficient from age 18 to 21 would be relatively high.

Of course, at the population level, continuity, turning points, and developmental disturbances occur together. In a series of studies based on national panel data from the Monitoring the Future study, Schulenberg and colleagues identified different trajectories groups of binge drinking (e.g., Schulenberg et al., 1996) and marijuana use (Schulenberg et al., 2005), reflecting continuity and discontinuity during emerging adulthood. The marijuana use trajectory groups are illustrated in Figure 6.6. Of particular interest are the increased, decreased, and fling trajectory groups (similar groups were found for binge drinking). Attempting to predict the fling group in advance on the basis of a wealth of demographic and psychosocial characteristics—distinguishing it from the rare or increased groups (both of which had similarly low substance use in

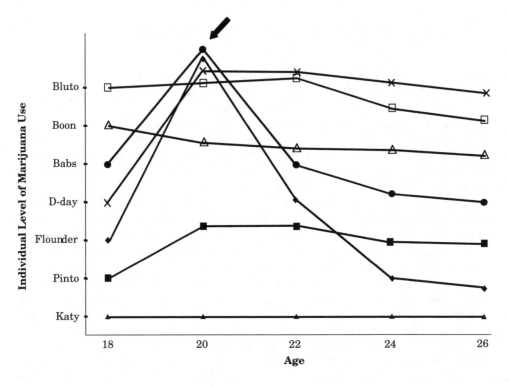

Figure 6.5. An illustration of individual data reflecting developmental disturbance.

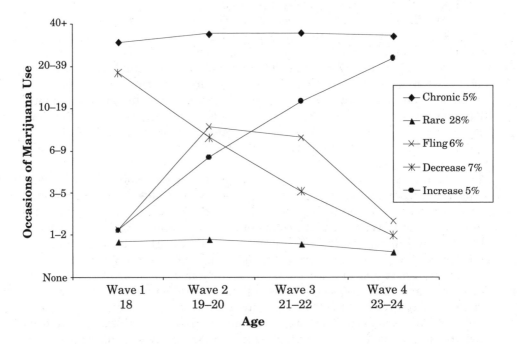

Figure 6.6. Marijuana use in the past 12 months by marijuana trajectory group.

late adolescence)—proved largely unsuccessful. During the few years following high school—during the developmental disturbance—the fling group was indistinguishable from the increased group but quite different from the rare group on the numerous psychosocial characteristics. In additional analyses considering outcomes at age 30, the fling group was found to be largely indistinguishable from the rare group on the basis of these measures, and both groups were quite different from the increased group. Together, the findings suggest that for the fling group (representing 7% of the population), emerging adulthood represents a developmental disturbance for substance use; it represents a turning point for the increased (5% of the population) and decreased (7%) groups; and for the majority of the population (chronic, rare, and abstainer, together accounting for over 75%), the level of marijuana use is continuous during emerging adulthood.

Functionality and Descriptive and Explanatory Continuity and Discontinuity

Is it reasonable to have one definition of mental health that applies equally well across the life span, or might the elements of mental health vary developmentally? In some cases, especially during emerging adulthood, what we usually label as maladaptive may in fact be a functional response in particular contexts for some individuals, facilitating rather than hindering successful development (Cicchetti & Rogosch, 2002; Spear, 2000). This paradox suggests the importance of focusing on the meaning, organization, and function of behaviors to understand continuity in adaptation and maladaptation (Sroufe & Jacobvitz, 1989). As summarized previously, in light of changes in social contexts and roles during emerging adulthood, behaviors may change considerably between adolescence and adulthood, but the underlying meaning or function of behaviors may remain the same (reflecting heterotypic continuity). And given the changing contexts that distinguish adolescence from adulthood, the meaning of the same behavior across time may also change (reflecting functional discontinuity). As we discuss in this subsection, these concepts of heterotypic continuity and functional discontinuity can be useful for understanding the adaptive and maladaptive functions of substance use, antisocial behavior, and depression during emerging adulthood.

Of the five models offered by Schulenberg and Maggs (2002) to consider how transitions relate to health risks, the transition catalyst–impediment model is most relevant to understanding the functions of apparent maladaptations: Risky and problem behaviors can sometimes be used for constructive purposes, such as to negotiate various social and identity transitions, and sometimes such behaviors and other maladaptations can impede successful negotiation of such transitions. Alcohol and other drug use, in particular, fit this model, especially during emerging adulthood: Substance use during early adolescence is typically more destructive than constructive in terms of developmental tasks (e.g., Brook, Adams, Balka, & Johnson, 2002), but during emerging adulthood, it may have several adaptive aspects related to social connections and identity exploration along with potentially destructive aspects (Chassin et al., 1999;

Cicchetti, 1999; Maggs, 1997; Schulenberg & Maggs, 2002). Thus, the same behavior (substance use) can have different meanings and functions between adolescence and emerging adulthood, reflecting functional discontinuity. Furthermore, the activities that represent successful adaptation (e.g., avoiding substance use in early adolescence vs. indulging in some substance use in emerging adulthood) can shift, reflecting heterotypic continuity.

With regard to antisocial behavior, it is likely that a host of related problem behaviors decline during late adolescence and emerging adulthood because such behaviors begin to mean something quite different after adolescence, reflecting functional discontinuity. For example, it is likely that any adaptive functions of antisociality tend to decrease and psychopathic and criminal functions tend to increase. Such behaviors simply become less developmentally normative and their psychosocial and legal consequences increase during emerging adulthood.

Although it seems evident that substance use, risk taking, and even antisocial behavior can, under certain circumstances, reflect adaptive behaviors, how can the same hold true for depression? Although all forms of depression typically have been perceived in the psychopathology literature as maladaptive or likely to interfere with the successful resolution of adaptational tasks of a given developmental period, depressive affect can sometimes be adaptational, a means to facilitate the achievement of particular developmental tasks (Nesse, 2000; Spear, 2000). Because pursuit of some goals can result in wasted effort or worse, low mood and minor depression can increase an individual's ability to, eventually, successfully cope with life's challenges (Nesse, 2000). A mismatch between achievements and expectations can be predictive of low mood and minor depression (Schwartz, 1990). Likewise, low mood can shift individuals' efforts toward more realistic goal pursuits (L. L. Martin & Tesser, 1996) and cognitions toward more systematic and realistic perceptions of self and others (Brunstein, 1993). Nesse (2000) discussed how this relationship at times might be functional: Individuals benefit from this regulation of investment strategies as a response to anticipated levels of payoff. Therefore, some emerging adults, in the midst of pervasive life changes, may be inclined to at least temporarily retreat inward and reflect on the self as a means to construct suitable aspirations for the future without expending too many resources and unnecessary energy on endeavors that lead to dead ends. Although depressive affect clearly has some maladaptive functions, it is useful to consider the potential long-term adaptive functions it may also have, particularly during major life transitions.

Conclusions and Implications

As Arnett (2000, 2004) has argued, the lengthening of the time between adolescence and adulthood makes it important to view this period as more than simply a staging ground for adulthood. Indeed, as a total experience, emerging adulthood is more than a major life transition. Still, like other major life transitions, this period is characterized by the potential for extensive changes in all aspects of life within a few years, coupled with increased heterogeneity in life paths. Consistent with the concept of emerging adulthood (Arnett, 2000,

2001), this period represents, for most, a time of increased personal freedoms, life-path options, and well-being. Perhaps it is no surprise that some troubled adolescents are able to gain more salutary trajectories of mental health during emerging adulthood—for them, this time constitutes a new start, a new set of social roles and contexts, and increased opportunities for person–context match. But for others, even some who appeared to be doing well during adolescence, the (often immediate) decline in structure and support that typically accompanies post-high-school life is debilitating, setting the stage for emerging or increased psychopathology. And for still others, because of limited resources and opportunities or because of relatively quick entry into adulthood responsibilities, post-high-school life is not associated with increased personal freedoms. This heterogeneity of life paths is associated with, and likely contributes to, diversity in trajectories of mental health and maladaptation (Schulenberg, Sameroff, & Cicchetti, 2004).

In this chapter, we use themes of continuity, turning points, developmental disturbances, and functionality to illustrate what may happen to mental health—broadly defined—during emerging adulthood, focusing on how developmental transitions can consolidate and deflect ongoing trajectories of mental health and maladaptation. Continuity, particularly in the forms of ontogenic continuity (reflecting childhood effects on adulthood adjustment) and heterotypic continuity (reflecting the continuity of adaptation despite changes in adaptive behavior), is the rule before, during, and after emerging adulthood, and we do not want to overstate the incidence or potential of discontinuity in mental health. Nonetheless, it would be unwise to simply assume such continuity or ignore the relatively few cases of discontinuity. In discussing the contribution of developmental psychopathology, Cicchetti and Rogosch (2002) drew a distinction between typical developmental psychology and typical developmental psychopathology perspectives:

> Developmental psychologists are primarily interested in understanding constancies in developmental processes as well as the typical, central tendencies in functioning and adaptation. . . . The extremes of the distribution in this context may be regarded as problematic outliers or cases that need to be transformed statistically to be more in line with the normal distribution. Developmental psychopathologists regard such extremes as of significance for study because of their potential to provide insight into the full range of developmental processes and functioning. (p. 8)

Although all might not agree with this distinction, it helps make the point that an emphasis on extreme or off-diagonal cases (e.g., in which we see discontinuity in overall adjustment between adolescence and adulthood) can serve an important purpose in our understanding of mental health during emerging adulthood. In addition to guiding us to find these off-diagonals in our data and offering an explanation of why relatively few change course, this emphasis can encourage us to examine the reasons that most follow a consistent course.

In this concluding section, we first briefly summarize some key themes, questions, and future directions regarding the study of mental health during emerging adulthood. We then consider broader conceptual and methodological implications and challenges.

Themes, Questions, and Future Directions

HISTORICAL, CULTURAL, AND SUBCULTURAL EMBEDDEDNESS. The experiences and meanings of emerging adulthood are historically and culturally bound (Arnett, 2000). The relationships between various transitions and trajectories of mental health may shift as the transitions shift. For example, marriage is a key transition that corresponds with a decrease in substance use and antisocial behavior (Bachman et al., 2002; Laub et al., 1998); the average age of marriage has increased considerably over the past few decades, suggesting the potential for this marriage effect to lose some of its salutary power on trajectories of substance use and antisociality. In terms of cultural embeddedness, it is essential to understand within-cultural meanings of various behaviors in terms of adaptation and maladaptation, as well as expectations and timetables for various normative transitions (Garcia Coll, Akerman, & Cicchetti, 2000; Shanahan et al., 2002). Indeed, all segments of societies have various strengths and vulnerabilities in terms of the intersection of mental health and developmental tasks (Luthar, 2003).

INCREASES IN BOTH WELL-BEING AND DEPRESSIVE DISORDERS. The seemingly incongruous population-based findings showing an increase in well-being and an increase in the incidence of depressive disorders during emerging adulthood likely reflect, in part, the multiple transitions, the increased individual agency, and the drop in institution structure that comes for most with emerging adulthood. The increase in well-being is likely due to the greater potential to select post-high-school contexts and activities that provide a better match with desires and goals; for most, this good match likely reflects a continuous salutary trajectory evident prior to emerging adulthood, and for others it reflects a positive turning point resulting in part from a greatly improved person–context match. The increase in depressive disorders is likely due in part to coping capacities being overwhelmed, to the drop in structure and support, or to a decline in person–context match; for most, this bad match reflects a continuous maladaptive trajectory evident prior to emerging adulthood and for others, it reflects a negative turning point. Greater understanding of the conditions of increased well-being and increased depressive disorders during emerging adulthood is needed.

MENTAL HEALTH INDICES. Substance use, antisociality, and depression are three important indices of mental health and psychopathology, broadly defined, and we focused purposely on them in part because they helped illustrate key conceptual issues. There is more to mental health and psychopathology than what we covered in this chapter, but the conceptual issues regarding continuity and discontinuity we illustrated likely apply to other indices, especially those that may involve a strong contextual component (e.g., eating disorders, anxiety). More serious forms of psychopathology, such as schizophrenia and other thought disorders, may be less given to transition-based variation, but even in these cases, the stress of multiple and simultaneous transitions likely exacerbates the condition (Spear, 2000).

Although we do not attend much to interrelationships among mental health indices, such interrelationships have been of central concern in relevant literatures (e.g., Elliot et al., 1989; Hawkins et al., 1992; Jessor et al., 1991). Especially at the more extreme ends of the continua of various maladaptations, there are extensive overlaps (Trull, Waudby, & Sher, 2004), and ongoing overlaps are likely indicative of difficulties with the tasks and transitions of early adulthood (Hussong, Curran, Moffitt, Caspi, & Carrig, 2004). In addition to concern with causal (or at least temporal) ordering among indices and associated correlates, recent efforts have focused on how trajectories of indices interrelate with each other (Jackson et al., 2002; Jackson, Sher, & Schulenberg, in press) and associated time-varying risk factors (Schulenberg et al., 2005; Sher et al., 2004).

TURNING POINTS, DEVELOPMENTAL DISTURBANCES, AND RESILIENCY. Positive turning points can be viewed as reflecting resiliency (Luthar, Cicchetti, & Becker, 2000; Masten, 2001), and more effort is needed to connect processes of resiliency and outcomes reflected in turning points. Turning points and developmental disturbances can be reflected in distinct changes in course, disconnection from early experiences, and instability of individual differences. The distinction between turning points and developmental disturbances may not always be clear. For example, a developmental disturbance reflects two noticeable changes in course—perhaps conceived as two turning points, albeit relatively close in time. One concern with the notion of developmental disturbance is that it suggests a predetermined peak or nadir in a trajectory, when in fact, the actual trajectory is more a function of ongoing person–context interactions. A developmental disturbance, in which one temporarily ventures into risky behaviors, may reflect more of a self-correcting course.

FUNCTIONALITY. The normative increases and subsequent decreases in substance use, risk taking, and antisocial behavior during adolescence and emerging adulthood suggest that these maladaptive behaviors may also involve some functionality for positive adaptation (Spear, 2000). Later onset difficulties, compared with earlier onset difficulties, may have more to do with transition-inspired positive adaptation, although it is clear that not all later onset difficulties are suggestive of functional adaptation. In particular, some serious depressive disorders and some forms of alcoholism do not manifest until later in adolescence or emerging adulthood (Cicchetti & Rogosch, 2002; Zucker, 1995). Given that all of these behaviors involve health and other risks, attending only to potential constructive aspects without recognizing destructive aspects would be unwise. Still, an emphasis on potentially constructive aspects is clearly needed. It is noteworthy that functionality may be tapping into similar themes as developmental disturbances, in which the former pertains to the underlying meaning (which does not shift) and the latter pertains to the behavior (which does shift)—that is, heterotypic continuity.

Conceptual and Methodological Implications and Challenges

Issues of intraindividual change and interindividual differences in such change have long been defining themes of life-course studies, life span development, developmental science, and developmental psychopathology (e.g., Baltes et al., 1998; Cairns, 2000; Cicchetti & Rogosch, 2002; Elder, 1998; Rutter & Sroufe, 2000; Settersten, 2003). Given dynamic person–context interactions and multidirectional change, we should expect individual differences in processes and effects of linkages across life. Explicit throughout this chapter has been the notion that there are wide individual differences in the course of mental health, partly as a function of differential experiences and multiple transitions during emerging adulthood. What is found to be true in our research regarding the elusive normative case may not be true for many or even most individuals. For many purposes, knowing the normative case or normative trajectory is essential. But often, it is equally if not more meaningful to identify developmental types according to how constructs are found to covary within individuals within and over time (Cairns, 2000; Magnusson & Bergman, 1988; Seidman & French, 2004). Recent advances in individual trajectory and growth mixture modeling (Curran & Willoughby, 2003; Muthén & Muthén, 2000; Nagin et al., 1995; Raudenbush, 2001) make the emphasis on developmental types an essential component of research programs examining adaptation and psychopathology across multiple waves.

Identification of continuity and discontinuity in mental health, broadly defined, is often an imprecise undertaking and constitutes a key challenge for research requiring richness and depth in measures. Particularly when the functionality of behaviors over time is explored, an emphasis on in-depth measures and more qualitative data is important. Likewise, developmental transitions are often difficult to define operationally, which is another key challenge. Furthermore, between-person differences in the content, timing, and sequence of transitional changes, such as the completion of full-time education or the transition to parenthood, are great. They may vary systematically by gender, cohort, social class, ethnicity, country, and other social contextual moderators. This potential variability highlights the importance of large-scale representative samples as well as in-depth assessments in our research.

Another key challenge for research is to determine when and how various developmental transitions can operate as a source of potentially long-term discontinuity, a cause of temporary fluctuations or disturbances in adjustment, or a possible conduit of continuity in adaptation. In particular, distinguishing between temporary perturbations and long-term cumulative change is essential (e.g., Nagin, Pagani, Tremblay, & Vitaro, 2003; Ronka et al., 2002). As we have discussed, adjustment difficulties during major life transitions may simply represent transitory states or behaviors, or they may be the first signs of continuing maladjustment that can be seen only in retrospect with multiwave longitudinal data. Drawing connections between earlier behaviors and events and later outcomes remains one of the fundamental challenges in our research; often such connections are circuitous and indirect (Rutter, 1996), and just as often, the connections that apply to some individuals in some contexts do not apply to all (Cairns, 2000).

In many ways, emerging adulthood represents an ideal time to examine issues of continuity and discontinuity in adaptation. The ending of high school brings a decline in institutional structure along with pervasive and sometimes simultaneous social role and context changes. There are also accompanying intra- and interpersonal transitions in biological, cognitive, identity, family, peer, and achievement domains. This rich matrix of life changes allows for consideration of how social and individual transitions relate to amplifications and deflections of ongoing trajectories of mental health. Although there are unique aspects of this period of life, the many transitions likely share similarities with major life transitions at other periods in life, such as into school or into retirement. Much of what we have examined about continuity, turning points, developmental disturbances, and functionality in mental health likely pertains to the study of mental health and psychopathology across other transitions.

References

Aguilar, B., Sroufe, L. A., Egeland, B., & Carlson, E. (2000). Distinguishing the early-onset/persistent and adolescence-limited antisocial behavior types: From birth to 16 years. *Development and Psychopathology, 12,* 109–132.

American Psychiatric Association. (2000). *Diagnostic and statistical manual of mental disorders* (4th ed., text revision). Washington, DC: Author.

Arnett, J. J. (2000). Emerging adulthood: A theory of development from the late teens through the twenties. *American Psychologist, 55,* 469–480.

Arnett, J. J. (2001). Conceptions of the transition to adulthood: Perspectives from adolescence through midlife. *Journal of Adult Development, 8,* 133–143.

Arnett, J. J. (2004). *Emerging adulthood: The winding road from the late teens through the twenties.* New York: Oxford University Press.

Aseltine, R. H., & Gore, S. (1993). Mental health and social adaptation following the transition from high school. *Journal of Research on Adolescence, 3,* 247–270.

Bachman, J. G., O'Malley, P. M., Schulenberg, J. E., Johnston, L. D., Bryant, A. L., & Merline, A. C. (2002). *The decline of substance use in young adulthood: Changes in social activities, roles, and beliefs.* Mahwah, NJ: Erlbaum.

Baltes, P. B., Lindenberger, U., & Staudinger, U. M. (1998). Life-span theory in developmental psychology. In R. M. Lerner (Ed.), *Handbook of child psychology: Vol. 1. Theoretical models of human development* (pp. 1029–1143). New York: Wiley.

Baltes, P. B., Reese, H. W., & Nesselroade, J. R. (1977). *Life-span developmental psychology: Introduction to research methods.* Mahwah, NJ: Erlbaum.

Bandura, A. (1982). The psychology of chance encounters and life paths. *American Psychologist, 37,* 747–755.

Bartholow, B. D., Sher, K. J., & Krull, J. L. (2003). Changes in heavy drinking over the third decade of life as a function of collegiate fraternity and sorority involvement: A prospective, multilevel analysis. *Health Psychology, 22,* 616–626.

Bates, M. E., & Labouvie, E. W. (1997). Adolescent risk factors and the prediction of persistent alcohol and drug use into adulthood. *Alcoholism: Clinical and Experimental Research, 21,* 944–950.

Birmaher, B., Ryan, N. D., Williamson, D. E., Brent, D. A., Kaufman, J., Dahl, R. E., et al. (1996). Childhood and adolescent depression: Part I. A review of the past 10 years. *Journal of American Academy of Child and Adolescent Psychiatry, 35,* 1427–1439.

Bronfenbrenner, U. (1979). *The ecology of human development: Experiments by nature and design.* Cambridge, MA: Harvard University Press.

Brook, J. S., Adams, R. E., Balka, E. B., & Johnson, E. (2002). Early adolescent marijuana use: Risks for the transition to adulthood. *Psychological Medicine, 32,* 79–91.

Brown, T. N., Schulenberg, J., Bachman, J. G., O'Malley, P. M., & Johnston, L. D. (2001). Are risk and protective factors for substance use consistent across historical time? National data from twenty-two consecutive cohorts of high school seniors. *Prevention Science, 2,* 29–43.

Brunstein, J. C. (1993). Personal goals and subjective well-being. *Journal of Personality and Social Psychology, 65,* 1061–1070.

Bukowski, W. M., Sippola, L. K., & Newcomb, A. F. (2000). Variations in patterns of attraction to same- and other-sex peers during early adolescence. *Developmental Psychology, 36,* 147–154.

Cairns, R. B. (2000). Developmental science: Three audacious implications. In L. R. Bergman, R. B. Cairns, L. G. Nilsson, & L. Nystedt (Eds.), *Developmental science and the holistic approach* (pp. 49–62). Mahwah, NJ: Erlbaum.

Caspi, A. (2000). The child is father of the man: Personality continuities from childhood to adulthood. *Journal of Personality and Social Psychology, 78,* 158–172.

Caspi, A., & Moffitt, T. (1995). The continuity of maladaptive behavior: From description to understanding in the study of antisocial behavior. In D. Cicchetti & D. Cohen (Eds.), *Developmental psychopathology: Vol. 2. Risk, disorder, and adaptation* (pp. 472–511). New York: Wiley.

Caspi, A., & Roberts, B. W. (1999). Personality change and continuity across the life course. In L. A. Pervin & O. P. John (Eds.), *Handbook of personality theory and research* (Vol. 2, pp. 300–326). New York: Guilford Press.

Chassin, L., Pitts, S. C., & DeLucia, C. (1999). The relation of adolescent substance use to young adult autonomy, positive activity involvement, and perceived competence. *Development and Psychopathology, 11,* 915–932.

Chassin, L., Pitts, S. C., & Prost, J. (2002). Binge drinking trajectories from adolescence to emerging adulthood in a high-risk sample: Predictors and substance abuse outcomes. *Journal of Consulting and Clinical Psychology, 70,* 67–78.

Cicchetti, D. (1999). A developmental psychopathology perspective on drug abuse. In M. D. Glantz & C. R. Hartel (Eds.), *Drug abuse: Origins and interventions* (pp. 97–117). Washington, DC: American Psychological Association.

Cicchetti, D., & Rogosch, F. A. (2002). A developmental psychopathology perspective on adolescence. *Journal of Consulting and Clinical Psychology, 70,* 6–20.

Cicchetti, D., & Tucker, D. (1994). Development and self-regulatory structures of the mind. *Development and Psychopathology, 6,* 533–549.

Clarizio, H. F. (1997). Conduct disorder: Developmental considerations. *Psychology in the Schools, 34,* 253–265.

Cohen, P., Kasen, S., Chen, H., Hartmark, C., & Gordon, K. (2003). Variations in patterns of developmental transitions in the emerging adulthood period. *Developmental Psychology, 39,* 657–669.

Compas, B. E., Wagner, B. M., Slavin, L. A., & Vannatta, K. (1986). A prospective study of life events, social support, and psychological symptomatology during the transition from high school to college. *American Journal of Community Psychology, 14,* 241–257.

Crockett, L. J. (1997). Cultural, historical, and subcultural contexts of adolescence: Implications for health and development. In J. Schulenberg, J. L. Maggs, & K. Hurrelmann (Eds.), *Health risks and developmental transitions during adolescence* (pp. 23–53). New York: Cambridge University Press.

Culbertson, F. M. (1997). Depression and gender: An international review. *American Psychologist, 52,* 25–31.

Curran, P. J., & Willoughby, M. T. (2003). Implications of latent trajectory models for the study of developmental psychopathology. *Development and Psychopathology, 15,* 581–612.

Dannefer, D. (1987). Aging as intracohort differentiation: Accentuation, the Matthew effect, and the life course. *Sociological Forum, 2,* 211–236.

Davis, R. D., & Millon, T. (1994). Personality change: Metatheories and alternatives. In T. F. Heatherton & J. L. Weinberger (Eds.), *Can personality change?* (pp. 85–119). Washington, DC: American Psychological Association.

Dishion, T. J., Patterson, G. R., & Kavanagh, K. A. (1992). An experimental test of the coercion model: Linking theory, measurement, and intervention. In J. McCord & R. Tremblay (Eds.), *The interaction of theory and practice: Experimental studies of intervention* (pp. 253–282). New York: Guilford Press.

Duggal, S., Carlson, E., Sroufe, L. A., & Egeland, B. (2001). Depressive symptomatology in children and adolescents. *Development and Psychopathology, 13,* 143–164.

Duncan, G. J., Boisjoly, J., Kremer, M., Levy, D. M., & Eccles, J. (2005). Peer effects in drug use and sex among college students. *Journal of Abnormal Child Psychology, 33,* 375–385.

Eccles, J. S., Lord, S. E., Roeser, R. W., Barber, B., & Hernandez Jozefowicz, D. M. (1997). The association of school transitions in early adolescence with developmental trajectories through high school. In J. Schulenberg, J. L. Maggs, & K. Hurrelmann (Eds.), *Health risks and developmental transitions during adolescence* (pp. 283–320). New York: Cambridge University Press.

Elder, G. H. (1998). The life course and human development. In W. Damon & R. M. Lerner (Eds.), *Handbook of child psychology: Vol. 1. Theoretical models of human development* (pp. 939–991). New York: Wiley.

Ellickson, P. L., Martino, S. C., & Collins, R. L. (2004). Marijuana use from adolescence to young adulthood: Multiple developmental trajectories and their associated outcomes. *Health Psychology, 23,* 299–307.

Elliott, D. S., Huizinga, D., & Menard, S. (1989). *Multiple problem youth: Delinquency, substance abuse, and mental health problems.* New York: Springer-Verlag.

Farrington, D. P. (2004). Conduct disorder, aggression and delinquency. In R. M. Lerner & L. Steinberg (Eds.), *Handbook of adolescent psychology* (pp. 627–664). New York: Wiley.

Farrington, D. P., & Hawkins, J. D. (1991). Predicting participation, early onset and later persistence in officially recorded offending. *Criminal Behaviour and Mental Health, 1,* 1–33.

Fergusson, D. M., & Woodward, L. J. (2002). Mental health, educational, and social role outcomes of adolescents with depression. *Archives of General Psychiatry, 59,* 225–231.

Fleming, J. E., & Offord, D. R. (1990). Epidemiology of childhood depressive disorders: A critical review. *Journal of American Academy of Child and Adolescent Psychiatry, 29,* 571–580.

Flory, K., Lynam, D., Milich, R., Leukefeld, C., & Clayton, R. (2004). Early adolescent through young adult alcohol and marijuana use trajectories: Early predictors, young adult outcomes, and predictive utility. *Development and Psychopathology, 16,* 193–213.

Freud, A. (1958). Adolescence. *Psychoanalytic Study of the Child, 13,* 255–278.

Fuligni, A. J., & Pedersen, S. (2002). Family obligation and the transition to young adulthood. *Developmental Psychology, 38,* 856–868.

Furman, W., Simon, V. A., Shaffer, L., & Bouchey, H. A. (2002). Adolescents' working models and styles for relationships with parents, friends, and romantic partners. *Child Development, 73,* 241–255.

Furstenberg, F. F., Jr. (Ed.). (2002). Early adulthood in cross-national perspectives. *The Annals of the American Academy of Political and Social Science Series, 580.*

Galambos, N. L. (2004). Gender and gender role development in adolescence. In R. M. Lerner & L. Steinberg (Eds.), *Handbook of adolescent psychology* (pp. 233–262). New York: Wiley.

Garcia Coll, C., Akerman, A., & Cicchetti, D. (2000). Cultural influences on developmental processes and outcomes: Implications for the study of development and psychopathology. *Development and Psychopathology, 12,* 333–356.

Ge, X., Conger, R. D., & Elder, G. H., Jr. (2001). Pubertal transition, stressful life events, and the emergence of gender differences in adolescent depressive symptoms. *Developmental Psychology, 37,* 404–417.

Graber, J. A. (2004). Internalizing problems during adolescence. In R. M. Lerner & L. Steinberg (Eds.), *Handbook of adolescent psychology* (pp. 587–626). New York: Wiley.

Graber, J. A., & Brooks-Gunn, J. (1996). Transitions and turning points: Navigating the passage from childhood through adolescence. *Developmental Psychology, 32,* 768–776.

Grimes, K., & Walker, E. (1994). Childhood emotional expressions, educational attainment, and age at onset of illness in schizophrenia. *Journal of Abnormal Psychology, 103,* 784–790.

Gutman, L. M., & Sameroff, A. J. (2004). Continuities in depression from adolescence to young adulthood: Contrasting ecological influences. *Development and Psychopathology, 16,* 967–984.

Harrington, R., Fudge, H., Rutter, M., Pickles, A., & Hill, J. (1990). Adult outcomes of childhood and adolescent depression. *Archives of General Psychiatry, 47,* 465–473.

Hawkins, J. D., Catalano, R. F., & Miller, J. Y. (1992). Risk and protective factors for alcohol and other drug problems in adolescence and early adulthood: Implications for substance use prevention. *Psychological Bulletin, 112,* 64–105.

Hawkins, J. D., Herrenkohl, T., Farrington, D. P., Brewer, D., Catalano, R. F., & Harachi, T. W. (1998). A review of predictors of youth violence. In R. Loeber & D. P. Farrington (Eds.), *Serious and violent juvenile offenders: Risk factors and successful interventions* (pp. 106–146). Thousand Oaks, CA: Sage.

Heckhausen, J. (1999). *Developmental regulation in adulthood.* Cambridge, England: Cambridge University Press.

Hill, K. G., White, H. R., Chung, I. J., Hawkins, J. D., & Catalano, R. F. (2000). Early adult outcomes of adolescent binge drinking: Person- and variable-centered analyses of binge drinking trajectories. *Alcoholism: Clinical and Experimental Research, 24,* 892–901.

Huesmann, L. R., Eron, L. D., & Dubrow, E. F. (2002). Childhood predictors of adult criminology: Are all risk factors reflected in childhood aggression? *Criminal Behavior and Mental Health, 12,* 185–208.

Hurrelmann, K. (1990). Health promotion for adolescents: Preventive and corrective strategies against problem behavior. *Journal of Adolescence, 13,* 231–250.

Hussong, A. M., & Chassin, L. (2002). Parent alcoholism and the leaving home transition. *Development and Psychopathology, 14,* 139–157.

Hussong, A. M., Curran, P. J., Moffitt, T. E., Caspi, A., & Carrig, M. H. (2004). Substance abuse hinders desistence in young adults' antisocial behavior. *Development and Psychopathology, 16,* 1071–1094.

Jackson, K. M., Sher, K. J., Cooper, M. L., & Wood, P. K. (2002). Adolescent alcohol and tobacco use: Onset, persistence and trajectories of use across two samples. *Addiction, 97,* 517–531.

Jackson, K. M., Sher, K. J., & Schulenberg, J. E. (in press). Conjoint developmental trajectories of young adult alcohol and tobacco use. *Journal of Abnormal Psychology.*

Jaffee, S. R., Moffitt, T. E., Caspi, A., Fombonne, E., Poulton, R., & Martin, J. (2002). Differences in early childhood risk factors for juvenile-onset and adult-onset depression. *Archives of General Psychiatry, 59,* 215–222.

Jessor, R., Donovan, J. E., & Costa, F. M. (1991). *Beyond adolescence: Problem behaviour and young adult development.* New York: Cambridge University Press.

Johnson, J. G., Cohen, P., Kotler, L., Kasen, S., & Brook, J. (2002). Psychiatric disorders associated with risk for development of eating disorders during adolescence and early adulthood. *Journal of Consulting and Clinical Psychology, 70,* 1119–1128.

Johnston, L. D., O'Malley, P. M., Bachman, J. G., & Schulenberg, J. E. (2004). *Monitoring the Future national survey results on drug use, 1975–2003: Volume II, College students and adults ages 19–45* (NIH Publication No. 04-5508). Bethesda, MD: National Institute on Drug Abuse.

Kagan, J. (1969). The three faces of continuity in human development. In D. A. Goslin (Ed.), *Handbook of socialization theory and research* (pp. 983–1002). Chicago: Rand McNally.

Kagan, J. (1980). Perspectives on continuity. In O. G. Brim Jr., & J. Kagan (Eds.), *Constancy and change in human development* (pp. 26–74). Cambridge, MA: Harvard University Press.

Kandel, D. B., & Chen, K. (2000). Types of marijuana users by longitudinal course. *Journal of Studies on Alcohol, 61,* 367–378.

Keating, D. P. (2004). Cognitive and brain development. In R. M. Lerner & L. Steinberg (Eds.), *Handbook of adolescent psychology* (pp. 45–84). New York: Wiley.

Kessler, R. C., & Walters, E. E. (1998). Epidemiology of *DSM–III–R* major depression and minor depression among adolescents and young adults in the National Comorbidity Survey. *Depression and Anxiety, 7,* 3–14.

Lahey, B. B., Schwab-Stone, M., Goodman, S. H., Waldman, I. D., Canino, G., Rathouz, P. J., et al. (2000). Age and gender differences in oppositional behavior and conduct problems: A cross-sectional household study of middle childhood and adolescence. *Journal of Abnormal Psychology, 109,* 488–503.

Laub, J. H., Nagin, D. S., & Sampson, R. J. (1998). Trajectories of change in criminal offending: Good marriages and the desistence process. *American Sociological Review, 63,* 225–238.

Laub, J. H., & Sampson, R. J. (2003). *Shared beginnings, divergent lives: Delinquent boys to age 70.* Cambridge, MA: Harvard University Press.

Leadbeater, B. J., Kuperminc, G. P., Blatt, S. J., & Hertzog, C. (1999). A multivariate model of gender differences in adolescents' internalizing and externalizing problems. *Developmental Psychology, 55,* 1268–1282.

Leonard, K. E., & Rothbard, J. C. (1999). Alcohol and the marriage effect. Alcohol and the family: Opportunities for prevention [Special Issue]. *Journal of Studies on Alcohol, 13,* 139–146.

Lerner, R. M. (2002). Concepts and theories of human development (3rd ed.). Mahwah, NJ: Erlbaum.

Lewis, M. (1999). Contextualism and the issue of continuity. *Infant Behavior & Development, 22,* 431–444.

Loeber, R., & Stouthamer-Loeber, M. (1998). Development of juvenile aggression and violence: Some common misconceptions and controversies. *American Psychologist, 53,* 242–259.

Loukas, A., Zucker, R. A., Fitzgerald, H. E., & Krull, J. L. (2003). Developmental trajectories of disruptive behavior problems among sons of alcoholics: Effects of parent psychopathology, family conflict, and child undercontrol. *Journal of Abnormal Psychology, 12,* 119–131.

Luthar, S. S. (2003). The culture of affluence: Psychological costs of material wealth. *Child Development, 74,* 1581–1593.

Luthar, S. S., Cicchetti, D., & Becker, B. (2000). The construct of resilience: A critical evaluation and guidelines for future work. *Child Development, 71,* 543–562.

Maggs, J. L. (1997). Alcohol use and binge drinking as goal-directed action during the transition to post-secondary education. In J. Schulenberg, J. L. Maggs, & K. Hurrelmann (Eds.), *Health risks and developmental transitions during adolescence* (pp. 345–371). New York: Cambridge University Press.

Maggs, J. L., & Schulenberg, J. E. (in press). Trajectories of alcohol use during the transition to adulthood. *Alcohol Research and Health.*

Magnusson, D., & Bergman, L. R. (1988). Individual and variable-based approaches to longitudinal research on early risk factors. In M. Rutter (Ed.), *Studies of psychosocial risk* (pp. 45–61). Cambridge, England: Cambridge University Press.

Martin, L. L., & Tesser, A. (1996). *Striving and feeling: Interactions among goals, affect, and self-regulation.* Hillsdale, NJ: Erlbaum.

Martin, P., & Martin, M. (2002). Proximal and distal influences on development: The model of developmental adaptation. *Developmental Review, 22,* 78–96.

Masten, A. S. (2001). Ordinary magic: Resilience processes in development. *American Psychologist, 56,* 227–238.

Masten, A. S., & Coatsworth, J. D. (1995). Competence, resilience, and psychopathology. In D. Cicchetti & D. Cohen (Eds.), *Developmental psychopathology: Vol. 2. Risk, disorder, and adaptation* (pp. 715–752). New York: Wiley.

Masten, A. S., Hubbard, J. J., Gest, S. D., Tellegen, A., Garmezy, N., & Ramirez, M. (1999). Competence in the context of adversity: Pathways to resilience and maladaptation from childhood to late adolescence. *Development and Psychopathology, 11,* 143–169.

McAdams, D. P. (1994). Can personality change? Levels of stability and growth in personality across the life span. In T. F. Heatherton & J. L. Weinberger (Eds.), *Can personality change?* (pp. 299–313). Washington, DC: American Psychological Association.

Moffitt, T. E. (1993). Adolescence-limited and life-course-persistent antisocial behavior: A developmental taxonomy. *Psychological Review, 100,* 674–701.

Moffitt, T. E., & Caspi, A. (2001). Childhood predictors differentiate life-course persistent and adolescence-limited antisocial pathways among males and females. *Development and Psychopathology, 13,* 355–375.

Mortimer, J. T., Finch, M. D., & Kumka, D. S. (1982). Persistence and change in development: The multi-dimensional self concept. In P. B. Baltes & O. G. Brim Jr. (Eds.), *Life span development and behavior* (Vol. 4, pp. 263–313). New York: Academic Press.

Mortimer, J. T., Zimmer-Gembeck, M. J., Holmes, M., & Shanahan, M. J. (2002). The process of occupational decision making: Patterns during the transition to adulthood. *Journal of Vocational Behavior, 61,* 439–465.

Muthén, B., & Muthén, L. K. (2000). Integrating person- and variable-centered analyses: Growth mixture modeling with latent trajectory classes. *Alcoholism Clinical and Experimental Research, 24,* 882–891.

Nagin, D., Farrington, D., & Moffitt, T. (1995). Life-course trajectories of different types of offenders. *Criminology, 33,* 111–140.

Nagin, D. S., Pagani, L., Tremblay, R. E., & Vitaro, F. (2003). Life course turning points: The effect of grade retention on physical aggression. *Development and Psychopathology, 15,* 343–361.

National Institute of Mental Health. (2001). *The numbers count: Mental disorders in America.* Retrieved October 3, 2004, from http://www.nimh.nih.gov/publicat/numbers.cfm

Nesse, R. M. (2000). Is depression an adaptation? *Archives of General Psychiatry, 57,* 14–20.

Neugarten, B. L. (1979). Time, age, and the life cycle. *American Journal of Psychiatry, 136,* 887–894.

Newcomb, M. D., & Bentler, P. M. (1988). *Consequences of adolescent drug use: Impact on the lives of young adults.* Newbury Park, CA: Sage.

Nolen-Hoeksema, S. (1990). *Sex differences in depression*. Stanford, CA: Stanford University Press.

Osgood, D. W., Johnston, L. D., O'Malley, P. M., & Bachman, J. G. (1988). The generality of deviance in late adolescence and early adulthood. *American Sociological Review, 53,* 81–93.

Osgood, D. W., Ruth, G., Eccles, J., Jacobs, J., & Barber, B. (2005). Six paths to adulthood: Fast starters, parents without careers, educated partners, educated singles, working singles, and slow starters. In R. Settersten, F. Furstenberg, & R. Rumbaut (Eds.), *On the frontier of adulthood: Theory, research, and public policy* (pp. 417–453). Chicago: University of Chicago Press.

Parker, J., & Asher, S. (1987). Peer relations and later personal adjustment: Are low-accepted children at risk? *Psychological Bulletin, 102,* 357–389.

Patterson, G. R., Forgatch, M. S., Yoerger, K. L., & Stoolmiller, M. (1998). Variables that initiate and maintain an early-onset trajectory for juvenile offending. *Developmental and Psychopathology, 10,* 531–547.

Petras, H., Schaeffer, C. M., Ialongo, N., Hubbard, S., Muthén, B., Lambert, S., et al. (2004). When the course of aggressive behavior in childhood does not predict antisocial outcomes in adolescence. *Development and Psychopathology, 16,* 919–942.

Piaget, J. (1970). Piaget's theory. In P. H. Mussen (Ed.), *Carmichael's manual of child psychology: Vol. 1.* (pp. 703–732). New York: Wiley.

Rao, U., Ryan, N. D., Birmaher, B., Dahl, R. E., Williamson, D. E., Kaufman, J., et al. (1995). Unipolar depression in adolescents: Clinical outcome in adulthood. *Psychiatry, 34,* 566–578.

Raudenbush, S. W. (2001). Comparing personal trajectories and drawing causal inferences from longitudinal data. *Annual Review of Psychology, 52,* 501–525.

Reinherz, H. Z., Giaconia, R. M., Carmola, A. M., Wasserman, M. S., & Silverman, A. B. (1999). Major depression in the transition to adulthood: Risks and impairments. *Journal of Abnormal Psychology, 108,* 500–510.

Reinherz, H. Z., Paradis, A. D., Gianconia, R. M., Stashwick, C. K., & Fitzmaurice, G. (2003). Childhood and adolescent predictors of major depression in the transition to adulthood. *American Journal of Psychiatry, 160,* 2141–2147.

Reis, H. T., Collins, W. A., & Berscheid, E. (2000). The relationship context of human behavior and development. *Psychological Bulletin, 126,* 844–872.

Roberts, B. W., Caspi, A., & Moffitt, T. E. (2001). The kids are alright: Growth and stability in personality development from adolescence to adulthood. *Journal of Personality and Social Psychology, 81,* 670–683.

Roisman, G. I., Aguilar, B., & Egeland, B. (2004). Antisocial behavior in the transition to adulthood: The independent and interactive roles of developmental history and emerging developmental tasks. *Development and Psychopathology, 16,* 857–872.

Ronka, A., Oravala, S., & Pulkkinen, L. (2002). "I met this wife of mine and things got on a better track": Turning points in risk development. *Journal of Adolescence, 25,* 47–63.

Rutter, M. (1992). Adolescence as a transition period: Continuities and discontinuities in conduct disorder. *Journal of Adolescent Health, 13,* 452–460.

Rutter, M. (1996). Transitions and turning points in developmental psychopathology: As applied to the age span between childhood and mid-adulthood. *International Journal of Behavioral Development, 19,* 603–626.

Rutter, M., & Sroufe, L. A. (2000). Developmental psychopathology: Concepts and challenges. *Development and Psychopathology, 12,* 265–296.

Sameroff, A. J. (2000). Developmental systems and psychopathology. *Development and Psychopathology, 12,* 297–312.

Sameroff, A. J., Peck, S., & Eccles, J. (2004). Changing ecological determination of conduct problems from early adolescence to early adulthood. *Development and Psychopathology, 16,* 873–896.

Sampson, R. J., & Laub, J. H. (1990). Crime and deviance over the life course: The salience of adult social bonds. *American Sociological Review, 55,* 609–627.

Sampson, R. J., & Laub, J. H. (2003). Desistence from crime over the life course. In J. T. Mortimer & M. J. Shanahan (Eds.), *Handbook of the life course* (pp. 295–309). New York: Plenum.

Schulenberg, J. E., Bryant, A. L., & O'Malley, P. M. (2004). Taking hold of some kind of life: How developmental tasks relate to trajectories of well-being during the transition to adulthood. *Development and Psychopathology, 16,* 1119–1140.

Schulenberg, J., & Maggs, J. L. (2002). A developmental perspective on alcohol use and heavy drinking during adolescence and the transition to young adulthood. *Journal of Studies on Alcohol* (Suppl. 14), 54–70.

Schulenberg, J. E., Maggs, J. L., & O'Malley, P. M. (2003). How and why the understanding of developmental continuity and discontinuity is important: The sample case of long-term consequences of adolescent substance use. In J. T. Mortimer & M. J. Shanahan (Eds.), *Handbook of the life course* (pp. 413–436). New York: Plenum.

Schulenberg, J. E., Merline, A. C., Johnston, L. D., O'Malley, P. M., Bachman, J. G., & Laetz, V. B. (2005). Trajectories of marijuana use during the transition to adulthood: The big picture based on national panel data. *Journal of Drug Issues, 35,* 255–279.

Schulenberg, J. E., O'Malley, P. M., Bachman, J. G., & Johnston, L. D. (2005). Early adult transitions and their relation to well-being and substance use. In R. Settersten, F. Furstenberg, & R. Rumbaut (Eds.), *On the frontier of adulthood: Theory, research, and public policy* (pp. 417–453). Chicago: University of Chicago Press.

Schulenberg, J. E., Sameroff, A. J., & Cicchetti, D. (2004). The transition to adulthood as a critical juncture in the course of psychopathology and mental health: Editors' introduction. *Development and Psychopathology, 16,* 799–806.

Schulenberg, J., Wadsworth, K. N., O'Malley, P. M., Bachman, J. G., & Johnston, L. D. (1996). Adolescent risk factors for binge drinking during the transition to young adulthood: Variable- and pattern-centered approaches to change. *Developmental Psychology, 32,* 659–674.

Schwartz, N. (1990). Feelings as information: Informational and motivational functions of affective states. In E. T. Higgins & R. Sorrentino (Eds.), *Handbook of motivation and cognition* (pp. 527–559). New York: Guilford Press.

Seidman, E., & French, S. E. (2004). Developmental trajectories and ecological transitions: A two-step procedure to aid in the choice of prevention and promotion interventions. *Development and Psychopathology, 16,* 1141–1159.

Settersten, R. A., Jr. (2003). *Invitation to the life course: Toward new understandings of later life.* Amityville, NY: Baywood Publishing.

Shanahan, M. (2000). Pathways to adulthood in changing societies: Variability and mechanisms in life course perspective. *Annual Review of Sociology, 26,* 667–692.

Shanahan, M. J., Mortimer, J. T., & Krueger, H. (2002). Adolescence and adult work in the twenty-first century. *Journal of Research on Adolescence, 12,* 99–120.

Sher, K. J., Gotham, H. J., & Watson, A. L. (2004). Trajectories of dynamic predictors of disorder: Their meanings and implications. *Development and Psychopathology, 16,* 825–856.

Shiner, R. L., & Masten, A. S. (2002). Transactional links between personality and adaptation from childhood through adulthood. *Journal of Research in Personality, 36,* 580–588.

Spear, L. P. (2000). The adolescent brain and age-related behavioral manifestations. *Neuroscience and Biobehavioral Reviews, 24,* 417–463.

Sroufe, L. A., & Jacobvitz, D. (1989). Diverging pathways, developmental transformations, multiple etiologies, and the problem of continuity in development. *Human Development, 32,* 196–203.

Sroufe, L. A., & Rutter, M. (1984). The domain of developmental psychopathology. *Child Development, 55,* 17–29.

Stouthamer-Loeber, M., Wei, E., Loeber, R., & Masten, A. (2004). Desistance from persistent serious delinquency in the transition to adulthood. *Development and Psychopathology, 16,* 897–918.

Susman, E. J., & Rogol, A. (2004). Puberty and psychological development. In R. M. Lerner & L. Steinberg (Eds.), *Handbook of adolescent psychology* (pp. 15–44). New York: Wiley.

Thornberry, T. P., Freeman-Gallant, A., Lizotte, A. J., Krohn, M. D., & Smith, C. A. (2003). Linked lives: The intergenerational transmission of antisocial behavior. *Journal of Abnormal Child Psychology, 31,* 171–184.

Trull, T. J. (2001). Structural relations between borderline personality disorder features and putative etiological correlates. *Journal of Abnormal Psychology, 110,* 471–481.

Trull, T. J., Waudby, C. J., & Sher, K. J. (2004). Alcohol, tobacco, and drug use disorders and personality disorder symptoms. *Experimental and Clinical Psychopharmacology, 12,* 65–75.

Uggen, C. (2000). Work as a turning point in the life course of criminals: A duration model of age, employment, and recidivism. *American Sociological Review, 67,* 529–546.

Uggen, C., & Massoglia, M. (2003). Desistance from crime and deviance as a turning point in the life course. In J. T. Mortimer & M. J. Shanahan (Eds.), *Handbook of the life course* (pp. 311–329). New York: Plenum.

Vitaro, F., Tremblay, R. E., Kerr, M., Pagani, L., & Bukowski, W. M. (1997). Disruptiveness, friends' characteristics, and delinquency in early adolescence: A test of two competing models of development. *Child Development, 68,* 676–689.

Werner, H. (1957). The concept of development from a comparative and organismic point of view. In D. B. Harris (Ed.), *The concept of development: An issue in the study of human behavior* (pp. 125–148). Minneapolis: University of Minnesota Press.

Wills, T. A., & Dishion, T. J. (2004). Temperament and adolescent substance use: A transactional analysis of emerging self-control. *Journal of Clinical, Child, and Adolescent Psychology, 33,* 69–81.

Windle, M., & Wiesner, M. (2004). Trajectories of marijuana use from adolescence to young adulthood: Predictors and outcomes. Development and Psychopathology, 16, 1007–1028.

Youniss, J., & Yates, M. (1997). *Community service and social responsibility in youth.* Chicago: University of Chicago Press.

Zucker, R. A. (1995). Pathways to alcohol problems and alcoholism: A developmental account of the evidence for multiple alcoholisms and for contextual contributions to risk. In R. A. Zucker, G. M. Boyd, & J. Howard (Eds.), *The development of alcohol problems: Exploring the biopsychosocial matrix of risk* (NIAAA Monograph 26, pp. 255–289). Rockville, MD: U.S. Department of Health and Human Services.

7

Resilience in Emerging Adulthood: Developmental Perspectives on Continuity and Transformation

Ann S. Masten, Jelena Obradović, and Keith B. Burt

Individuals, parents, communities, and societies all share a stake in successful transitions to adulthood, both for adolescents already doing well and for those in trouble. Like all developmental transitions, this one denotes a period of concentrated change in individuals, their contexts, and their interactions that may increase vulnerabilities and threats for the individual as well as opportunities for positive transformation. Emerging adulthood (EA) in contemporary societies holds new challenges and new opportunities for young people as they negotiate a complex array of choices during a prolonged period of exploration, challenge, and change, as they make their way toward adult roles and responsibilities (Arnett, 2000). Many young people will negotiate this transition successfully, but others will not. To improve the chances of young people succeeding in the early adult years, one needs to understand when and how successful transitions to adulthood occur, and particularly what may make a difference for adolescents in danger of floundering along the way.

In this chapter, we examine the meaning of resilience in relation to emerging adulthood, focusing on development of individuals growing up with the odds stacked against them because of psychosocial risk and adversity. Several questions capture the themes of this chapter: What does resilience mean in the context of EA? Does resilience among youth at high risk endure through the transition to adulthood? Does resilience emerge during EA? Is EA a window of change that offers opportunities to redirect the life course in more positive directions? In the first part of the chapter, we define resilience in the context

The authors are deeply grateful to Michael Maddaus and all the participants in Project Competence who have shared their life histories with others so that we might learn more about successful transitions to adulthood and how to foster resilience. Research described in this chapter was supported over the course of 20 years by the William T. Grant Foundation, the National Institute of Mental Health, the National Science Foundation, and the University of Minnesota, through grants to Norman Garmezy, Ann Masten, and Auke Tellegen.

of EA, beginning with a case illustration. In the second section, we review the longitudinal evidence on psychosocial adaptation that spans EA, with a particular focus on clues to successful transitions among individuals at risk for problems and psychopathology. The conclusion of the chapter discusses the implications of this evidence for research and applications and presents a model of positive change during emerging adulthood.

From Delinquent to Surgeon: A Case of Emerging Resilience in Emerging Adulthood

The captivating story of Michael Maddaus exemplifies the power of the single case to draw attention to the phenomenon of resilience, at the same time that it generates ideas about the causes of dramatic turnarounds in the lives of individuals. His story was recently chronicled in a University of Minnesota alumni magazine, which traced his life from early adversities through a delinquent adolescence to the Navy and then medical school (Broderick, 2003). Maddaus described the chaos of his early life with the instability of a mother who was frequently drunk and an abusive stepfather. He took to the streets at an early age, hanging around with a gang of friends, getting into many kinds of trouble. He was arrested two dozen times as a juvenile, spending time in various detention centers, barely attending school. Yet, when he was about 17, after contemplating his options and the meaning of prosecution as an adult, Maddaus joined the Navy. He described boot camp as a positive experience that got him "cleaned up and physically fit." Realizing there wasn't much future for a high school dropout, Maddaus began to take classes, and after he was discharged (honorably) he completed a GED and enrolled in community college. Although his prospects were improving, Maddaus reported that he continued to have periodic problems with drugs and alcohol during his military service and afterward when he returned to the Twin Cities. The final impetus for change came in the form of a negative epiphany, as Maddaus lay on a gurney in the county medical center after a drunk-driving accident. Realizing that his behavior was putting his life at risk, Maddaus decided to travel a new road. Soon afterward, his life turned toward medicine, with the support and encouragement of key mentoring figures.

Maddaus delivered furniture to the home of a pediatric surgeon who took an interest in his life, becoming an important mentor who encouraged him to continue his education. Maddaus took a vocational interest test that encouraged the pursuit of physical therapy or other occupations in the medical field. He volunteered at a children's rehabilitation center, which led to a job with a neurosurgeon on the medical school faculty. Eventually, he completed his bachelor's degree and was accepted to medical school. Along the way, he married and began a family. Today, Maddaus is a well-known thoracic surgeon using minimally invasive techniques, and he gets invited to tell his story to adolescents in trouble.

What stands out in this account of resilience emerging in the transition to adulthood are the individual attributes, relationships, and opportunities that came together at propitious times, along with catalysts for change in the form of motivating insights, experiences, and mentors. Maddaus, for his part, clearly had intellectual talents, energy, and appeal to other people, along with the ability to focus his talents on his goals—once he figured out what they were. He took advantage of opportunities to avoid prison, join the military, go back to school, and connect with effective mentors who facilitated additional opportunities. Finally, his story, like other stories of resilience that emerges during this developmental window, suggests that insight and the internal commitment to change precede the external manifestations of change in the life course.

Resilience in Emerging Adulthood Defined

The concept of human resilience refers broadly to patterns of positive adaptation in the context of significant threats to functioning or development. The term *resilience* has been used variously to refer to the outcome and processes of achieving positive adaptation in the presence of risk or adversity (see Luthar, in press; Masten, Best, & Garmezy, 1990). Two fundamental judgments must be made to determine resilience: first, that the individual is adapting adequately or doing OK by some criteria and second, that there is or has been a significant threat to good functioning (the risk, stressor, or trauma; Masten & Coatsworth, 1998). Identifying a group of individuals as showing resilience during EA requires operational definitions of (a) adapting well in EA and (b) significant risk or adversity experiences in the past or present.

In the Project Competence studies (see Masten & Powell, 2003), we have defined *doing OK* in terms of competence in age-salient developmental tasks: that is, whether an individual is meeting expectations for behavior in major domains of psychosocial functioning. These developmental task domains are grounded in historical and cultural context (Masten, Burt, & Coatsworth, in press). Moreover, during the course of development, the salience of any given domain waxes and wanes as a function of development and sociocultural context (Roisman, Masten, Coatsworth, & Tellegen, 2004). During developmental transitions, key competence domains include those still salient from the previous developmental period along with newly emerging competence domains that will become important in the future. During the transition to adulthood in contemporary U.S. society, the task domains of academic achievement, peer relationships, and rule-governed conduct, which have been prominent throughout the school years, remain salient; at the same time, work and romantic relationships, which are key developmental tasks of adulthood, are emerging.

Given the multiple tasks confronting individuals at any time in development, researchers formulating models of resilience need to decide whether to consider only one competence domain at a time or functioning in multiple domains simultaneously. This difference is highlighted in two distinct approaches to analyzing resilience, one focused on variables and the other focused on persons (Masten, 2001). Variable-focused approaches are well suited both to specific and to detailed analysis of underlying mechanisms that may lead to good or poor functioning in a particular domain and to how functioning in one domain may influence functioning in another domain over time. Yet the construct of resilience also carries the connotation that a person is doing generally well, at least in regard to the essential domains by which people of his or her age are judged in society. From this perspective, resilience is best conceptualized as a pattern of adaptive functioning across multiple domains occurring in the lives of individuals considered as whole people. Person-focused approaches are well suited to identifying who is OK and who is not faring well, what combinations of problems and achievements tend to co-occur in real people, how interactions between people and their contexts influence adaptation, and what may make a difference in turning the whole life of a person in a new direction. Given the advantages of each approach, a number of resilience investigators, including the Project Competence investigators (e.g., Masten et al., 1999), the Kauai investigators (e.g., Werner & Smith, 1992, 2001), and others (see Luthar, 2003, in press), have combined the two approaches in their studies.

In defining the criteria by which "doing OK" will be judged, some investigators have chosen to explore different criteria of adaptation rather than developmental task achievement. Some include internal adaptation criteria in their definitions of resilience, focusing for example on subjective well-being (with indicators such as happiness, life satisfaction, low distress) or self-concept or identity. In Project Competence, although we are keenly interested in the psychological functioning of individuals, such as their emotion, cognition, and motivation, we have defined resilience on the basis of how well a person is achieving tasks of adapting and achieving in the external world.

Finally, some investigators define resilience on the basis of an absence of psychopathology rather than the presence of positive behavior, though clearly this negative definition usually implies some degree of positive functioning and adequate psychosocial adjustment. This approach has been most common among investigators focused on the study of risk and resilience for specific kinds of psychopathology. From this perspective resilience refers either to individuals at risk for a mental illness or a particular problem who do not manifest the disorder or problem or to individuals who manifest difficulties and then recover. Among samples of children at high risk who develop delinquent behavior, for example, desistance could be viewed from this perspective as a form of resilience. We would argue that evidence of positive adaptation measured in terms of good functioning, however defined, is an essential component of resilience. Moreover, it is likely that implicit criteria for positive adjustment embedded in studies of psychopathology need to be made explicit.

Researchers have also approached the second judgment necessary to identify resilience—the presence of a significant threat to development or adaptation—from diverse perspectives (Masten & Coatsworth, 1998; Masten et al., 1990). Investigators have studied a wide range of potentially negative experiences in a variety of ways. Such events include divorce, war, earthquakes, orphanage rearing, child abuse, neighborhood violence, poverty, school transitions, interparental conflict, and many other potentially negative life experiences. Methods have varied from intensive, detailed interviews to life-event checklists. Some investigators have focused on one kind of event or experience, whereas others consider cumulative adversity. Experiences out of an individual's control (e.g., earthquake, parent's illness) are usually distinguished from the kind of life experiences that are stressful, but likely related to an individual's own behavior (e.g., breaking up with a significant other, getting expelled from school). In sum, all of these approaches attempt to assess the degree of adversity that has threatened the course of development or adaptation.

Normative experiences do not generally qualify an individual for resilience. Thus, simply making it successfully through the transition to adulthood would not constitute resilience, even if everyone agreed that the transition was stressful. However, we might infer resilience when a young person who comes from a background of severe deprivation or has endured a number of extremely challenging life experiences is doing well during and following the emerging adult years. We might also infer resilience if the challenge of the EA years was compounded by a host of additional stressors coming at the same time.

Once investigators define their basic parameters for judging resilience, they are in a position to begin considering the many processes that may play a role in naturally occurring resilience. Understanding how resilience is sustained across EA, as well as how it may emerge, requires careful attention to continuity and change during this unique window of development.

Vulnerabilities and Possibilities in Emerging Adulthood

Emerging adulthood holds particular interest for the study of risk and resilience because this period may afford important changes in functional capacity, vulnerabilities, and opportunities that may play an important role in altering the life course. Recent neuroscience research, for example, indicates that brain development (e.g., myelination, structural maturation of neural pathways) continues well into the second decade of life (Benes, Turtle, Khan, & Farol, 1994; Dahl & Spear, 2004; Nelson, Thomas, & de Haan, in press; Sowell, Trauner, Gamst, & Jernigan, 2002). These developments may herald growing capacity during adolescence for integrated coordination of cognition, emotion, and action, or strategic executive control (Luciana, Conklin, Hooper, & Yarger, 2005; Nelson et al., in press; Steinberg, Dahl, Keating, Kupfer, Masten, & Pine, in press), setting the stage for the advances in planfulness, goal-directedness, and future orientation that have been observed behaviorally during EA. In addition, societies convey a clear message that emerging adults are expected to take greater responsibility for their behavior by according young people legal status as adults for many purposes at the age of 18. Many American youth leave home for extended periods for the first time during EA and by the end of this age period, most Americans have established an adult life on their own or with a romantic partner. At the same time, there is recognition that scaffolding may be needed to help young people make this transition. This is the period when societies provide a variety of structured experiences outside the home that facilitate transitions to adult status, including military or community service, apprenticeships, and higher education.

Some young people have serious problems establishing themselves as adults for various reasons. For some individuals, development already is not going well, in that these individuals are failing in multiple competence task accomplishments articulated by their society. For others, difficulties arise as vulnerable youth struggle to meet the challenges of the transition. These youth may be vulnerable because of disabilities in domains of functioning that are critical to negotiating these challenges or because of inadequate social supports. Youth who are aging out of the foster care system, for example, may not have the ordinary scaffolding provided by typical families to help young people with the transition to adulthood. In still other cases, new difficulties may arise in the form of emergent mental disorders that begin to profoundly impair developmental task engagement, such as schizophrenia.

However, even among the individuals showing great difficulty during EA, paths will diverge in adulthood. Some individuals will continue to struggle, whereas others gain or regain good adaptive functioning. Understanding the processes by which good adaptation develops, before, during, or after EA, particularly among children and youth at risk for problems resulting from hazardous environments, prior maladaptation, or biological vulnerabilities, requires developmental perspectives and longitudinal research.

Longitudinal Evidence on Positive Adaptation and Resilience

Classic studies of adaptation over the transition to adulthood, as well as more recent longitudinal studies that span EA, underscore themes of both continuity and change. Broad longitudinal studies of adjustment and personality indicate considerable predictive validity from childhood adjustment to adulthood adjustment, particularly when the criteria for adjustment encompass age-salient developmental tasks (Masten, Burt, & Coatsworth, in press; Masten, Roisman, et al., in press; Roisman et al., 2004). Decades ago, when Kohlberg and colleagues reviewed the literature predicting adult mental health from childhood, they observed that academic achievement, antisocial behavior, and peer acceptance during childhood and adolescence were good global predictors of adult adjustment (Kohlberg, LaCrosse, & Ricks, 1972). In more recent years, longitudinal studies of cohorts followed into adulthood generally not only have corroborated early observations about continuity but also have uncovered patterns of growth and decline in cohorts that suggest important developmental processes at work.

Antisocial behavior, for example, has garnered a great deal of attention as investigators have attempted to elucidate patterns of continuity and change over the transition to adulthood (Broidy et al., 2003; Moffitt, Caspi, Harrington, & Milne, 2002; Stouthamer-Loeber, Wei, Loeber, & Masten, 2004; Thornberry & Krohn, 2003). Several striking patterns have emerged from these studies. The early observation that antisocial behavior has considerable continuity over time has been supported time and again. A subgroup of children termed *life-course-persistent* by Moffitt (1993) appears to account for a substantial proportion of the continuity from childhood to adulthood. However, there is marked desistance from antisocial behavior during EA because of large numbers of individuals whose antisocial behavior, especially as defined by delinquent behavior, appears to increase during adolescence and wane during the transition to adulthood. Late-onset involvement in offending also occurs, with escalation during the EA period (Thornberry & Krohn, 2003).

As one might expect, given the burden of crime on society and the individual costs of antisocial behavior for adult success in society, there is great interest in understanding the processes that account for the general decline in aggression as well as specific turning points in the lives of individuals. To date, more research has been focused on identifying these processes in childhood and adolescence than during EA, though ongoing longitudinal studies will eventually provide a good database for examination of the change processes operating during EA (Krohn & Thornberry, 2003). Nonetheless, the longitudinal evidence does suggest that developmental changes and opportunities that society presents during the transition to adulthood may play a role.

Investigators have suggested from diverse longitudinal studies that military service, marriage and romantic relationships, higher education, religious affiliations, and work opportunities may provide turning-point opportunities for changing the life course during emerging adulthood (Elder, 1986, 1974/ 1999; Laub, Nagin, & Sampson, 1998; Masten & Powell, 2003; Rutter, 1990, 1996, 2000; Sampson & Laub, 1993; Werner & Smith, 1992). Both Elder and his colleagues, as well as Clausen, on the basis of their secondary analyses of data from the classic Berkeley and Oakland longitudinal studies, concluded that good marriages, military service, or higher education, particularly when the timing was right, could positively influence life trajectories during this age period (Clausen, 1991, 1993; Elder, 1974/1999, 2002; Elder, Liker, & Cross, 1984).

In the classic study of resilience among a birth cohort of children born on the island of Kauai, Werner and Smith (1992, 2001) observed positive changes in the life course among a subset of maladaptive adolescents at high risk as they moved into adulthood. These investigators also credited what they termed *second chance opportunities* in the form of marriages, military service, work, education, and religious engagement. Yet, it is clear that only some individuals take advantage of such opportunities; thus, the question remains as to what spurs the development of resilience during the EA period.

Scholars have focused on identifying individual qualities that may help explain who changes and elucidating the role of relationships in the transition to adulthood. The individual qualities that have received considerable attention include a wide variety of attributes related to motivation and planfulness about the future, whereas the relationships attracting particular attention include adult support and mentorship in addition to supportive romantic relationships.

Clausen (1991), for example, focused on the construct of planful competence in the Berkeley cohort, a composite score based on multiple indicators of adaptive behavior, including realistic goal setting, dependability, and self-control. Clausen found that adolescents from lower class backgrounds were less likely to score high on this variable, but if they did show planful competence, they were more socioeconomically successful as adults. He also noted a general upward trend among the cohort on planful competence as they took on the roles of worker, spouse, and parent (p. 831).

Studies focused on successful outcomes among high-risk samples also point to the role of agency on the part of the young people who turn in more positive directions during EA. Long and Vaillant (1984) noted that the disadvantaged boys from the Glueck and Glueck study (1950) who became successful adults seemed to have a "knack for finding a niche" (p. 221). The studies of Quinton, Rutter, and their colleagues implicated positive marriages and school experiences as well as planfulness in the positive trajectories of institutionally reared women and conduct-disordered youth (Quinton, Pickles, Maughan, & Rutter, 1993; Rutter, 1996; Rutter & Quinton, 1984).

As a whole, this set of longitudinal studies points to continuity and change in resilience in relation to EA. Good adaptation that is well established in adolescence tends to persist through the transition to adulthood in many of these studies. Moreover, whereas there appear to be subgroups of persistently maladaptive individuals, there also appears to be a general trend of improving socialization during EA, as observed in the form of desistance from antisocial behavior. This general positive trend also has been observed in studies of adolescents believed to be at risk for lingering problems because of adolescent troubles, such as teen pregnancy. In their studies of low-income teen mothers in Baltimore, for example, Furstenberg and colleagues have found reasonably positive outcomes in adulthood for many of these young women (Furstenberg, 2002; Furstenberg, Brooks-Gunn, & Morgan, 1987). Finally, these studies also point to instances of dramatic change in a small number of individuals whose lives take a sharp turn for the better as they make their way through EA. Understanding the processes that account for such continuity and change during EA holds the promise of informing those stakeholders who seek to facilitate successful transitions to adulthood.

Longitudinal Evidence on Continuity and Change in Adaptation From Project Competence

Findings from the Project Competence longitudinal study of a school-based cohort of children followed into adulthood also tell a story of both continuity and change during EA (Masten & Powell, 2003; Masten et al., 2004; Masten, Roisman, et al., in press). This study was initiated by Norman Garmezy in the late 1970s during the first wave of research on resilience (Masten & Powell, 2003). It was launched as a cross-sectional study of competence in the context of stressful life experiences, in an early effort to identify risk and protective factors for adaptation among school-age children. A normative sample of 205 children who were initially 8 to 12 years old, along with their parents, participated in the initial intensive study of competence and its correlates. These children were followed up after 7, 10, and 20 years, with 90% of the original living cohort continuing to participate in the 20-year follow-up. The original cohort attended two elementary schools from the same catchment area of Minneapolis, selected to represent a good cross-section of the urban school population in terms of ethnicity and socioeconomic status (SES). At the time, the schools were estimated to have 27% minority students and were diverse in SES. The longitudinal cohort of 205 children (29% minority, 114 girls, 91 boys) was also diverse in SES, with a predominance of lower to middle working class families, but also included families living in poverty on welfare and well-off professional families. Over the years, test scores for the cohort on standardized tests have corroborated the normative nature of the sample, with IQ scores and achievement test scores, for example, close to population mean scores. The sample retained over time also has proven to be quite representative of the original cohort, with the participants at all four time points or those still participating at Time (T) 4 not differing from the missing cases on key childhood competence, resources, and adversity scores.

The timing of the assessments in this longitudinal study, which occurred before, during, and after the EA years, has allowed us to examine several perspectives on continuity and change in relation to this developmental window. Highlights of the findings will be presented here. First, we highlight results pertaining to competence and resilience defined in terms of adaptive functioning during the EA years, at T3 of this study, when the sample was 17 to 23 years old. In particular, we focus on the antecedent predictors of doing well in EA, particularly for individuals who grew up in a context of significant adversity. Second, we highlight results on the predictive validity of competence during EA for the future, as assessed 10 years down the road (T4), when the cohort was around the age of 30. Third, we present findings more specifically focused on resilience: whether resilience endures the transition to adulthood among the young people already manifesting it by the time they entered the EA period, and also whether resilience emerges after EA among young people who were maladaptive during EA.

From the outset, the goals of this study required operationalizing the construct of resilience, which meant focusing on the assessment of competence and adversity. For each of the major assessments of this study, multiple-method and multiple-informant strategies were used to assess multiple domains of competence, defined as manifesting effectiveness in major developmental tasks, as previously noted. We have tried to assess success in the core developmental tasks and also the emerging and waning domains that we expect to be important later or were important in earlier years as standards by which society judges whether a young person is doing well (see Masten et al., 1995, 1999, 2004; Roisman et al., 2004). Our analytic approach included both variable- and person-focused components. For variable-focused analyses predicting competence, we used composite scores of effective performance within a particular domain, such as academic achievement or work competence, averaging z-scores across multiple indicators. For person-focused analyses, we wanted to classify young people as doing OK (or not) across all the major designated domains of developmental tasks for their age. Therefore, we identified the age-salient domains and then defined an individual as OK on competence if they were in the average range (within a 1/2 SD of the mean on that variable for the cohort) or better on multiple domains. Thus, an individual could be defined as doing OK even if that person was slightly below average on all domains. Resilience, in our view, does not require outstanding achievement in any domain, but rather, it means that a person is manifesting effectiveness at least in the acceptable normal range (or better) with respect to key developmental task domains of competence.

In regard to adversity, the data presented here draw on our most comprehensive assessment of adversity (see Gest, Reed, & Masten, 1999). Drawing on all the information we had collected through life event scales, interviews, and other questionnaires during the course of each assessment, we created a database of negative life events outside the control of the individual, including chronic conditions and acute events, as well as experiences arising from within the family and community. Clinical judges used individual life charts spanning time periods before the first competence assessment and between subsequent assessments to rate participants' adversity exposure during particular windows of time. These judgments were made independent of any other time window, without knowledge of an individual's resources or competence. The scale we used was based on the 7-point stressor rating scale (where 1 means *little or no adversity* and 7 means *catastrophic levels of adversity*) of the *Diagnostic and Statistical Manual of Mental Disorders* (3rd ed., rev.; *DSM–III–R;* American Psychiatric Association, 1987). Agreement across judges was excellent for these adversity ratings (see Gest et al., 1999). For variable-focused analyses of resilience, we averaged adversity scores across childhood (prior to the first competence assessment) and during adolescence (between the first and second assessments of competence). For person-focused analyses, a strict definition of high adversity was used to classify individuals as resilient during EA: Their adversity ratings had to exceed a rating of 5 (*severe*) on the 7-point scale across both childhood and adolescence. In contrast to the competence criteria, which were designed to identify those who were doing OK across life domains, this stricter adversity cutoff was intended to identify those individuals who had experienced significant challenges to development or adaptation.

With strategies for defining how well individuals were doing on developmental tasks and judging whether they had experienced substantial adversity growing up, we were in a position not only to consider continuity and change in competence in relation to adversity background but also to look for predictors of competence, resilience, and change in classification. For example, key suspects for a central role in the development of competence and resilience were the quality of resources available to individuals, in the form of cognitive development or intellectual capacity, parenting quality, and SES; which are widely corroborated correlates and predictors of adaptation (poor and good; Masten & Coatsworth, 1998). However, beyond these global markers of developmental resources, we were keenly interested in more specific qualities of the person or environment that might make a difference in a particular window of development. For EA, on the basis of the literature described earlier, we were particularly interested in the role of adaptive resources related to this transition, such as future aspirations, planfulness, autonomy, and adult support.

Following the 10-year follow-up at T3, we considered the question of resilience in this cohort, based on how they were doing during the EA years, which we labeled *late adolescence* at the time (Masten et al., 1999). Core competence domains for these analyses were academic achievement, conduct (following the rules and laws of society vs. breaking them), and social competence (having close, reciprocal friendships and an active social life). Variable-focused analyses indicated that IQ, parenting quality, and SES were related to doing well in both childhood and EA. Considerable continuity in competence was observed over the 10-year interval from T1 to T3 in the study, particularly for the conduct domain. In short, doing well in EA was predictable from doing well 10 years earlier. Nonetheless, there was evidence of predictable rank-order change among individuals over time. Childhood IQ, for example, predicted changes in academic achievement and childhood parenting quality predicted changes in social competence. When there was a history of very high adversity, childhood IQ was particularly important for predicting changes in conduct, suggesting that intellectual skills might function as a moderator of adversity. In other words, low intellectual skills in some individuals may increase susceptibility to worsening conduct over time in the face of high adversity, or better intellectual skills in other individuals may function protectively for adapting to adversity, or both.

Person-focused analyses provided in many ways a more dramatic picture of the similarities and differences among groups of individuals we had classified as doing OK or not, and underscored the similarity of the participants who were doing well, regardless of their adversity background, in contrast to their maladaptive peers. Four categories of people held particular interest: competent-low adversity, competent-high adversity (this is the resilient group), maladaptive-high adversity, and maladaptive-low adversity. The first two groups met our classification criteria for competence (doing OK in all three major domains of academic, conduct, and social competence) and differed in adversity. The second two groups were doing poorly (below the competence cutoff for OK on at least two domains of competence) but differed in adversity background. We found only three people who met the criteria for maladaptive-low adversity, which suggests that this pattern is not common in a normative sample; most maladaptive individuals in EA in our study had a history of adversity as well as poor resources. In group comparisons, therefore, we compared the other three groups, which we labeled *competent* (low adversity), *resilient* (high adversity), and *maladaptive* (high adversity).

Results were striking in showing many similarities among the two groups who were doing well (regardless of adversity) and many differences between these two groups and the maladaptive individuals. During EA, the individuals who were doing well from high-adversity backgrounds had similar resources of intellect, personality, and family as their competent-with-low-adversity peers, despite the differences in adversity. Maladaptive young people during EA not only had a history of adversity but also appeared to be markedly disadvantaged on assets and protective resources for development, including parenting quality and intellectual skills. In addition, they also appeared to be stress-reactive.

When we relocated this cohort 10 years later, we again assessed their competence in age-relevant developmental task domains (see Roisman et al., 2004). By young adulthood, the domains of work and romantic relationships had become salient. We expected and found considerable continuity in competence from EA to young adulthood. On the basis of a refinement of developmental task theory, we expected that success manifested by EA in three core domains of adaptation—academic, conduct, and social—would forecast success 10 years later in adulthood in the newly salient tasks of work competence and the quality of romantic relationships, as well as predicting continuing success in each of these domains over time. This is what we found. In contrast, how well an individual was doing during EA with respect to still-emerging domains of work and romantic relationships had little unique predictive significance for future competence. In other words, work and romantic competence domains were undergoing much change over the 10-year interval from EA to young adulthood in this study. This is consistent with our developmental task theory, in that these tasks would be considered to be in an exploratory phase during EA. It is performance in the well-established, core tasks of a developmental era in a given historical and cultural context that would be expected to carry the most long-term predictive significance.

Next, we examined the possible role of resource differences among the individuals in the study, to see whether changes in competence from EA to adulthood were predictable either from the core resource markers of IQ, parenting, and SES differences associated with competence in childhood and changes in competence from childhood to EA or from a set of what we termed *EA adaptive resources* (Masten et al., 2004). On the basis of the sparse but intriguing literature on the qualities associated with positive change during EA (previously described), we developed a set of scores during EA that focused on future orientation and planfulness, autonomy, adult support, and coping skills. These composites were drawn from multiple measures available from interviews of the participant and parent, questionnaires completed by the parent and target, and clinical judgments of interviewers and raters. Someone high on the composite index of achievement motivation/future orientation was rated as "concerned with who or what they will become . . . have put some thought into their future and there is a high degree of planfulness." Autonomy included indicators of both behavioral autonomy (*self-reliant*) and emotional autonomy (*absence of childish dependencies*). Adult support included ratings of connectedness to adults in and beyond the family (e.g., having a "close, warm relationship with an adult other than mother or father" or "have adults they can turn to when they're in trouble"). Coping-with-stress scores were based on self and clinical ratings of doing well even under a lot of stress.

It is not surprising that we found that core resources predicted change from EA to adulthood in several of the five competence domains that we examined in variable-focused analyses. For example, academic attainment in adulthood was predicted strongly by achievement already evident in EA, indicating continuity, but also by IQ assessed during EA.

Of particular interest, however, was the unique contribution of the set of EA adaptive resource variables for predicting change within competence domains, over and above the core resource measures. For academic attainment in young adulthood, the EA adaptive resource predictors added substantially to the prediction of change, with the most unique prediction provided by the measure of future orientation/achievement motivation. The set of EA resources also added to the prediction of success in the work and romantic domains in young adulthood. In the case of work competence, this effect was mediated largely by EA competence in the core domains of academic and conduct. However, for romantic relationships, there was a substantial overall predictive effect with all predictors considered, and the measure of autonomy appeared to be most unique as a predictor of growth or change in this domain.

To address the question of change more specifically in terms of resilience, we reconsidered the original groups of competent, resilient, and maladaptive individuals with respect to concurrent resources during EA and future outcome in young adulthood. Thus, we compared the same three groups previously described, on their EA adaptive resources (concurrently measured) and also on competence assessed 10 years later. Once again, a remarkably consistent pattern emerged. The competent and resilient groups had far better outcomes in adulthood than did their maladaptive peers, indicating that resilience endures and that competence has considerable continuity over this developmental window. It is not surprising that those who were competent or resilient in EA also had better adaptive resources associated with this period. However, the question of late-blooming resilience remained: that is, whether individuals could be identified whose classification changed from maladaptive in EA to resilient in young adulthood.

To see whether resilience could emerge in adulthood among those who were following a maladaptive life course in EA, we formed new groups on the basis of competence in adulthood, using the same adversity scores but new criteria for doing OK in young adulthood. In young adulthood, given that life patterns tend to differentiate, we modified our strategy of diagnosing resilience. We wanted to allow for the possibility that a young parent might step back from the work domain for a time or that an individual might focus on work rather than romantic relationships as a young adult. Young adults were considered to be doing OK if they scored average (again defined by a score within 1/2 *SD* of the sample mean) or better on at least four competence domains, including academic, friendship, conduct, work, romantic, and (for those with children) parenting domains of competence. If an individual was a parent, then diagnosis as doing OK required adequate parenting. Those who were doing poorly in three or more domains were classified as maladaptive. Reclassifying the cohort in young adulthood made it possible to examine continuity and change in status and what might account for those changes. Both continuity and change were evident in classification, as one would expect. Given the potential for small variations on indicators to move an individual in or out of a category, we focused our attention on young people who changed from maladaptive to resilient, representing a large shift in overall functioning. This group was small, with only seven of the longitudinal participants changing category from maladaptive to resilient between EA and the young adult assessment. Nonetheless, this subgroup differed in interesting ways from those who remained maladaptive and also from those who were already resilient during EA. In comparison to the continuing resilient group, this turnaround group had fewer core and EA resources; however, compared with their maladaptive peers who would remain maladaptive, this group had significantly better adaptive resources associated in the literature with positive change during these transition years, including planfulness, adult support, and autonomy.

In summary, results from the Project Competence longitudinal study suggest that the course of competence leading to, during, and following the developmental period of emerging adulthood has predictable continuity and change. There is considerable continuity in how well people do in the salient tasks they are expected to master at different ages in society and, as developmentalists have long posited (e.g., Sroufe, 1979), doing well in these tasks in one period sets the stage for success in the next. Thus, a track record of success in age-salient developmental tasks bodes well for the future. Developmental task theory has been refined and supported, in that the future predictors of success, even in newly emerging task domains, appears to be forecasted best by how well one has done on the core tasks in preceding developmental periods.

Competence in age-salient tasks also appears to reflect in profound ways the capacity for adaptation as well. Not only is competence during EA associated with past and present resources, but adversity experiences in childhood do not in and of themselves typically undermine the development of competence; rather, it is the combination of poor psychosocial resources and high and chronic adversity that appears to threaten development.

Change also can be predicted, at least to some degree. Not only data from our study but also results from other longitudinal studies of resilience, as well as captivating individual life stories, indicate that positive changes do occur. Most intriguing is the observation that some of the young people who appear to be floundering in adolescence or EA manage to get their lives together and back on track in adulthood. Adult support, individual agency, and opportunities appear to play a role. Our analyses did not focus on the opportunities available to individuals, but we found positive changes related to adaptive resources often associated with development in late adolescence and the transition to adulthood, such as future orientation, planfulness, adult support outside the family, and the capacity for autonomy. Such resources were associated broadly with positive changes in competence, but also with emerging resilience over the transition to adulthood among individuals coming from high-adversity backgrounds.

Conclusions and Implications

Longitudinal research on competence and resilience through the emerging adulthood years converges on several conclusions:

- Achievements in the developmental tasks of adolescence provide a strong foundation for successful transitions to adulthood.
- Resilience already evident in adolescence holds up well during EA.
- Resilience can emerge during and following EA.
- Conjunctions of individual motivation for change, growth in thinking and planning capacity, adult support, and contextual opportunities may create the conditions for changing the life course.
- EA may provide a unique window of opportunity for strategic intervention to promote positive change.
- Research on the timing, prediction, and processes of change during EA is needed.

It is also clear that developmental research and thinking has focused more on continuity than change over the transition to adulthood, such that we know little about the conditions and mediators of change during EA. Yet clues in this literature do raise the exciting possibility that EA is a transformational window during which multiple systems are in flux and the potential for reorganization and redirection is increased. The scaffolding that families and cultures

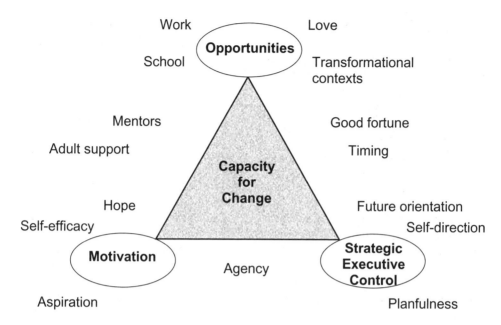

Figure 7.1. Moving toward resilience: A model of positive change in emerging adulthood.

have provided for this transition long has implicitly suggested that this time window is assumed to be an impressionable period when guidance and structure may be needed to influence the life course in the desired direction. The recent attention to EA as a unique developmental period, evidenced by this volume and the conference on which it is based, may signal that the time has come for a systematic examination of the conditions and processes that influence development during EA to inform deliberate efforts to promote positive transitions among youth at risk of maladaptation.

Figure 7.1 provides a schematic model for positive change during EA that reflects the longitudinal data to date on positive adaptation and resilience in this developmental window. The model illustrates how the conjunction of changing capacity, adult support, and opportunities can set the stage for movement toward positive adaptation. Capacity for change increases in this model as a result of brain development, changes in executive functioning, experience directing the self in planful ways, motivation for adult success arising from perceptions of the self as effective and hope for the future, and opportunities provided in the environment to realize plans for future success in the worlds of work and relationships. Catalysts for change may vary, in some cases arising from internal motivation, epiphanies, or conversion experiences, and in other cases engendered by mentors who offer a helping hand along with hope, as they open doors to the future. In the case story of Michael Maddaus, both kinds of catalysts for change were evident. A romantic relationship or birth of a child also may serve as a catalyst for change, as an individual gains a stake in the future and has more to lose by failing to engage the developmental tasks of adulthood. Of course, this model is merely an illustrative sketch of how change may occur during EA; the developmental science of this period requires more detailed and deeper analysis of the processes involved to reach the goal of effectively shifting conditions in favor of positive change.

In naturally occurring resilience, luck may play a significant role in the conjunction of a ready-to-change individual and transformational opportunities. For stakeholders in the successful transitions of young people to adulthood, it would be desirable to rely less on lucky conjunctions and more on thoughtful scaffolding of this transition. Societies, of course, already offer structured contexts for this transition, in the form of higher education, military service, public service, or apprenticeships. Many young people at risk, however, may not have access to these opportunities, either because of their psychosocial disadvantage or their mental health vulnerabilities or as a consequence of earlier troubles with authority, school, or interpersonal relationships. Children in foster care systems, for example, may age out of qualification for the kind of help that most young people in modern societies require to establish themselves as independent young adults. More opportunities and support may be required for youth at high risk to negotiate this transition successfully and for maladaptive youth to turn their lives around. As research begins to provide a better understanding of the processes that influence planful competence, future orientation, motivation to change, successful mentoring, and positive engagement in age-salient developmental tasks, it will become possible to design more strategic interventions to deliberately mobilize positive forces for transformation. What is gleaned from the study of resilience before, during, and after emerging adulthood has the potential to guide efforts to promote the conditions that in turn promote positive change.

References

American Psychiatric Association. (1987). *Diagnostic and statistical manual of mental disorders* (3rd ed., rev.). Washington, DC: Author.

Arnett, J. J. (2000). Emerging adulthood: A theory of development from the late teens through the twenties. *American Psychologist, 55,* 469–480.

Benes, F. M., Turtle, M., Khan, Y., & Farol, P. (1994). Myelination of a key relay zone in the hippocampal formation occurs in the human brain during childhood, adolescence, and adulthood. *Archives of General Psychiatry, 51,* 477–484.

Broderick, R. (2003, July/August). A surgeon's saga. *Minnesota: The magazine of the University of Minnesota Alumni Association,* 26–31.

Broidy, L. M., Nagin, D. S., Tremblay, R. E., Bates, J. E., Brame, B., Dodge, K. A., et al. (2003). Developmental trajectories of childhood disruptive behaviors and adolescent delinquency: A six-site, cross-national study. *Developmental Psychology, 39,* 222–245.

Clausen, J. S. (1991). Adolescent competence and the shaping of the life course. *American Journal of Sociology, 96,* 805–842.

Clausen, J. S. (1993). *American lives: Looking back at the children of the Great Depression.* New York: Free Press.

Dahl, R. E., & Spear, L. P. (Eds.). (2004). Adolescent brain development: Vulnerabilities and opportunities. *Annals of the New York Academy of Sciences, 1021.*

Elder, G. H., Jr. (1986). Military times and turning points in men's lives. *Developmental Psychology, 22,* 233–245.

Elder, G. H., Jr. (1999). *Children of the Great Depression: Social change in life experience.* Boulder, CO: Westview Press. (Original work published 1974)

Elder, G. H., Jr. (2002). Historical times and lives: A journey through time and space. In E. Phelps, F. F. Furstenberg, & A. Colby (Eds.), *Looking at lives: American longitudinal studies of the twentieth century* (pp. 194–218). New York: Russell Sage Foundation.

Elder, G. H. J., Liker, J. K., & Cross, C. E. (1984). Parent-child behavior in the Great Depression: Life course and intergenerational influences. In P. B. Baltes & O. G. J. Brim (Eds.), *Life-span development and behavior* (pp. 109–158). New York: Academic Press.

Furstenberg, F. F., Jr. (2002). How it takes thirty years to do a study. In E. Phelps, F. F. Furstenberg, & A. Colby (Eds.), *Looking at lives: American longitudinal studies of the twentieth century* (pp. 37–57). New York: Russell Sage Foundation.

Furstenberg, F. F., Jr., Brooks-Gunn, J., & Morgan, S. P. (1987). *Adolescent mothers in later life.* New York: Cambridge University Press.

Gest, S. D., Reed, M.-G. J., & Masten, A. S. (1999). Measuring developmental changes in exposure to adversity: A life chart and rating scale approach. *Development and Psychopathology, 11,* 171–192.

Glueck, S., & Glueck, E. (1950). *Unraveling juvenile delinquency.* New York: Commonwealth Fund.

Kohlberg, L., LaCrosse, J., & Ricks, D. (1972). The predictability of adult mental health from childhood behavior. In B. B. Wolman (Ed.), *Manual of child psychopathology* (pp. 1217–1284). New York: McGraw-Hill.

Krohn, M. D., & Thornberry, T. P. (2003). Common themes, future directions. In T. P. Thornberry & M. D. Krohn (Eds.), *Taking stock of delinquency* (pp. 313–326). New York: Academic/Plenum Publishers.

Laub, J. H., Nagin, D. S., & Sampson, R. J. (1998). Trajectories of change in criminal offending: Good marriages and the desistance process. *American Sociological Review, 63,* 225–238.

Long, J. V. F., & Vaillant, G. E. (1984). Natural history of male psychological health, XI: Escape from the underclass. *American Journal of Psychiatry, 141,* 341–346.

Luciana, M., Conklin, H. M., Hooper, C. J., & Yarger, R. S. (2005). The development of nonverbal working memory and executive control processes in adolescents. *Child Development, 76,* 697–712.

Luthar, S. S. (Ed.). (2003). *Resilience and vulnerability: Adaptation in the context of childhood adversities.* New York: Cambridge University Press.

Luthar, S. S. (in press). Resilience in development: A synthesis of research across five decades. In D. Cicchetti & D. J. Cohen (Eds.), *Developmental psychopathology: Vol. 3. Risk, disorder, and adaptation* (2nd ed.). New York: Wiley.

Masten, A. S. (2001). Ordinary magic: Resilience processes in development. *American Psychologist, 56,* 227–238.

Masten, A. S., Best, K. M., & Garmezy, N. (1990). Resilience and development: Contributions from the study of children who overcome adversity. *Development and Psychopathology, 2,* 425–444.

Masten, A. S., Burt, K., & Coatsworth, J. D. (in press). Competence and psychopathology in development. In D. Cicchetti & D. J. Cohen (Eds.), *Developmental psychopathology: Vol. 3* (2nd ed.). New York: Wiley.

Masten, A. S., Burt, K., Roisman, G. I., Obradović, J., Long, J. D., & Tellegen, A. (2004). Resources and resilience in the transition to adulthood: Continuity and change. *Development and Psychopathology, 16,* 1071–1094.

Masten, A. S., & Coatsworth, J. D. (1998). The development of competence in favorable and unfavorable environments: Lessons from successful children. *American Psychologist, 53,* 205–220.

Masten, A. S., Coatsworth, J. D., Neemann, J., Gest, S. D., Tellegen, A., & Garmezy, N. (1995). The structure and coherence of competence from childhood through adolescence. *Child Development, 66,* 1635–1659.

Masten, A. S., Hubbard, J. J., Gest, S. D., Tellegen, A., Garmezy, N., & Ramirez, M. L. (1999). Competence in the context of adversity: Pathways to resilience and maladaptation from childhood to late adolescence. *Development and Psychopathology, 11,* 143–169.

Masten, A. S., & Powell, J. L. (2003). A resilience framework for research, policy, and practice. In S. S. Luthar (Ed.), *Resilience and vulnerability: Adaptation in the context of childhood adversities* (pp. 1–25). New York: Cambridge University Press.

Masten, A. S., Roisman, G. I., Long, J. D., Burt, K. B., Obradović, J., Riley, J. R., et al. (in press). Developmental cascades: Linking academic achievement, externalizing and internalizing symptoms over 20 years. *Developmental Psychology.*

Moffit, T. E. (1993). "Life-course-persistent" and "adolescence-limited" antisocial behavior: A developmental taxonomy. *Psychological Review, 100,* 674–701.

Moffitt, T. E., Caspi, A., Harrington, H., & Milne, B. J. (2002). Males on the life-course-persistent and adolescence-limited antisocial pathways: Follow-up at age 26 years. *Development and Psychopathology, 14,* 179–207.

Nelson, C. A., Thomas, K. M., & de Haan, M. (in press). Neural bases of cognitive development. In W. Damon, R. Lerner, D. Kuhn, & R. Siegler (Eds.), *Handbook of child psychology: Vol. 2. Cognition, perception and language* (6th ed.). New York: Wiley.

Quinton, D., Pickles, A., Maughan, B., & Rutter, M. (1993). Partners, peers, and pathways: Assortive pairing and continuities in conduct disorder. *Development and Psychopathology, 5,* 763–783.

Roisman, G. I., Masten, A. S., Coatsworth, J. D., & Tellegen, A. (2004). Salient and emerging developmental tasks in the transition to adulthood. *Child Development, 75,* 1–11.

Rutter, M. (1990). Psychosocial resilience and protective mechanisms. In J. Rolf, A. S. Masten, D. Cicchetti, K. H. Nuechterlein, & S. Weintraub (Eds.), *Risk and protective factors in the development of psychopathology* (pp. 181–214). New York: Cambridge University Press.

Rutter, M. (1996). Transitions and turning points in developmental psychopathology: As applied to the age span between childhood and mid-adulthood. *International Journal of Behavioral Development, 19,* 603–626.

Rutter, M. (2000). Resilience reconsidered: Conceptual considerations, empirical findings, and policy implications. In J. P. Shonkoff & S. J. Meisels (Eds.), *Handbook of early childhood intervention* (2nd ed., pp. 651–682). New York: Cambridge University Press.

Rutter, M., & Quinton, D. (1984). Long-term follow-up of women institutionalized in childhood: Factors promoting good functioning in adult life. *British Journal of Developmental Psychology, 18,* 225–234.

Sampson, R. J., & Laub, J. H. (1993). *Crime in the making: Pathways and turning points through life.* Cambridge, MA: Harvard University Press.

Sowell, E. R., Trauner, D. A., Gamst, A., & Jernigan, T. L. (2002). Development of cortical and subcortical brain structures in childhood and adolescence: A structural MRI study. *Developmental Medicine and Child Neurology, 44,* 4–16.

Sroufe, L. A. (1979). The coherence of individual development: Early care, attachment, and subsequent developmental issues. *American Psychologist, 34,* 834–841.

Steinberg, L., Dahl, R. E., Keating, D., Kupfer, D. J., Masten, A. S., & Pine, D. (in press). The study of developmental psychopathology in adolescence: Integrating affective neuroscience with the study of context. In D. Cicchetti & D. J. Cohen (Eds.), *Developmental psychopathology: Vol. 3* (2nd ed.). New York: Wiley.

Stouthamer-Loeber, M., Wei, E., Loeber, R., & Masten, A. S. (2004). Desistance from persistent serious delinquency in the transition to adulthood. *Development and Psychopathology, 16,* 897–918.

Thornberry, T. P., & Krohn, M. D. (2003). *Taking stock of delinquency: An overview of findings from contemporary longitudinal studies.* New York: Kluwer Academic/Plenum Publishers.

Werner, E. E., & Smith, R. S. (1992). *Overcoming the odds: High risk children from birth to adulthood.* Ithaca, NY: Cornell University Press.

Werner, E., & Smith, R. S. (2001). *Journeys from childhood to midlife: Risk, resilience, and recovery.* Ithaca, NY: Cornell University Press.

Part III

Contexts

8

Family Relationships and Support Systems in Emerging Adulthood

William S. Aquilino

Development over the years of emerging adulthood is linked inextricably to relationships in the family of origin. Emerging adults' new interests, abilities, transitions, and behaviors shake up the family system, leading to new styles of relating to parents, siblings, and relatives. At the same time, the network of family relationships in which emerging adults are embedded continues to influence their developmental trajectories and life chances. This dual dynamic (Elder, 1984) of individual and family change creates some of the unique challenges that differentiate emerging adulthood from other phases of development.

Emerging adulthood, the age range from 18 to 25, is a developmental period distinct from adolescence and the later phases of young adulthood (Arnett, 2004). There is tremendous diversity across individuals in this age range in the occurrence, timing, and sequencing of life-course transitions, and often great volatility within individual life trajectories. Emerging adults may be living with parents or living independently. They move into and out of dating, cohabiting, and marital relationships; enter the labor force and change jobs; and transition into and out of college, military service, and vocational schools. The distinguishing characteristic of the period is that most emerging adults are not settled down. Their capacity for exploration and experimentation in new roles results in frequent and fast-paced life-course changes.

My goals in this chapter are to describe the unique characteristics of family relationships during emerging adulthood, the factors that bring about change in family relationships during this time, and the influence of family relationships and family support on the developmental trajectories of emerging adults. The chapter concentrates mostly on parent–child relationships (where the bulk of research has been done) but also explores the less visible areas of emerging adults' sibling relationships and their relationships with grandparents and other extended kin.

Distinguishing Characteristics of Family Relationships in Emerging Adulthood

What are some of the unique dynamics and processes in family relationships during emerging adulthood that distinguish it both from adolescence and from later adulthood? The 18- to 25-year-old is physically mature, legally an adult in most respects, and is likely on the road to self-sufficiency and independence from parents (Dubas & Petersen, 1996). The parent–child relationship is moving toward a relationship between two adults, rather than between parent and dependent child. This new reality requires a reappraisal of many aspects of family relationships, which leads to new expectations and patterns of interaction. The challenges unique to the parent–child relationship at this stage of life include parental acknowledgment of the child's emerging adult status, the development of filial and parental maturity; and the interplay of emerging adults' autonomy and dependency needs.

Acknowledging the Child's Emerging Adult Status

One of the challenges to parents during this stage is coming to terms with the adult status of their children. Blos (1985) theorized that parents' acknowledgment and acceptance of their offspring's adult status ("the blessing") is a critical aspect of the maturation process that needs to be settled before childhood can come to a natural termination. Bjornsen (2000) found that about 70% of college students reported experiencing a blessing, that is, a parent did something or said something that implied that they were grown up or had reached maturity. Parents who are unable or reluctant to make this acknowledgment may slow their children's development. Parents' anxiety about their emerging adult child's separation and distancing from the family has been shown to hinder identity achievement, whereas parental comfort in the role of providing a secure base during emerging adulthood facilitates identity exploration and commitment (Bartle-Haring, Brucker, & Hock, 2002).

Difficulties in acknowledging emerging adult status may be especially prevalent when children continue to co-reside with parents. A qualitative study of Australian adults aged 18 to 25 living with parents found that the co-resident sons and daughters felt they were treated as both children and not-children (almost adults) at the same time (White, 2002). They valued parental nurture and care but simultaneously felt the need to be recognized as independent adults. Although still needing to live in the parental home, they prized having a room of their own, a space that parents respected. Emotional boundaries, physical privacy, and parental intrusiveness remained critical issues in their relationships with parents. In contrast, the act of home-leaving itself may promote individuation, psychological growth, and the opportunity for emerging adults to interact with parents in more satisfying ways, as adult-to-adult rather than adult-to-dependent-child (Arnett, 2004; Dubas & Petersen, 1996).

Development of Filial and Parental Maturity

The ability of adult children to become a source of support for parents and the ability of parents to seek and accept support from their grown children are critical aspects of filial and parental maturity (Nydegger, 1991). Filial maturity also involves the child's ability to see the parent as an individual (apart from the parent role) and to understand a parent's life history, experiences, needs, and point of view (Arnett, 2004). Filial and parental maturity are precursors to increasing reciprocity in parent–child exchange over the life course.

Filial maturity is one of the key developmental tasks of emerging adulthood and sets the stage for later caregiving and mutual support as parents move from midlife to old age and their offspring into middle adulthood. Fuligni and Pedersen (2002) found that young people's sense of obligation to support, assist, and respect their families increased significantly in the 3 years after high school graduation. The sense of obligation increased even as youth were entering a period typically thought to focus on individuation, autonomy, and independence from parents. Adults in their 20s and 30s who act as caregivers to parents or grandparents cite filial responsibility as the strongest impetus for taking on the caregiver role (Dellmann-Jenkins, Blankemeyer, & Pinkard, 2001).

The Interplay of Autonomy and Dependency Needs

Tensions and contradictions in the parent–emerging adult relationship result from the child's having adult status in many domains while still dependent on parents in some ways. Emerging adults can legally drive, vote, drink alcohol (at 21), and make their own decisions about where to live, when to quit school, which job to take, and whether to marry or join the military. At the same time, most still need some measure of parental support to thrive, which thus creates a contradiction between society's granting of (legal) adult status and autonomy while economic realities often necessitate a lingering dependency on parents.

The emerging adult's achievement of financial self-sufficiency and residential independence may proceed in fits and starts and span many years (Goldscheider & Goldscheider, 1999). Changes in the U.S. economy and labor market have made it advantageous for emerging adults to delay moving into adult roles. Workers with fewer skills and educational credentials have increasingly unfavorable career prospects (Hill & Yeung, 1999). Thus emerging adults have become more willing to put off the role transitions that have traditionally defined adulthood (marriage, parenthood, full-time work) to increase their education and training and gain more labor-market experience (Furstenberg, 2000). It is parents' economic support, including coresidence, that enables emerging adults to increase their education and explore career possibilities (Semyonov & Lewin-Epstein, 2001). The contradictions between the emerging adult's autonomy and dependency needs will have an impact on family dynamics, requiring parents and children to reassess the nature of their interaction, what they want or need from the relationship, and their mutual responsibilities.

In sum, the tasks that face both emerging adults and their parents often involve reconciling contradictory impulses. Parents need to acknowledge the adult status of their sons and daughters, relinquish control, and, at the same time, remain ready to provide the care and material support their offspring need to thrive. A developmental challenge for parents is to begin to see their adult children as sources of support. Emerging adults need to pursue independence from the family of origin while still relying on support from parents or other kin to enhance their development and capacity for autonomy. Maturity for emerging adults also means coming to understand their parents as individuals in their own right. Parents and offspring need to negotiate their expectations about family obligations as emerging adults move toward financial and residential independence and establish their own families and households. Grappling with these tasks will lead to fundamental change in the nature of parent–child interaction.

The Quality of Emerging Adults' Family Relationships

In this section I review what is known about the antecedents and consequences of emerging adults' family relationships, applying the family life-course theoretical framework to organize the findings from this literature. The family life-course framework emphasizes the interdependence of family members' life paths and the constant interplay between individual development and family development (Bengtson & Allen, 1993). The individual life course can be viewed as a sequence of interlocking life trajectories (or careers) in education, work, intimate relationships, parenthood, and social networks. Family systems are shaped by the various career lines of the individual members (Elder, 1984). Events and transitions occurring in one generation have consequences for the lives of older and younger generations in the family (Hagestad, 1984). Elder's dual dynamic of family interaction holds that two processes of change occur simultaneously: (a) Family relationships change in response to the individual developmental paths of family members and (b) the life trajectories of individual family members change in response to transformations in family relationships. Life-course research has revealed the potential for continuity over time and over generations in family processes, but has also shown how the life-course transitions of individual family members transform patterns of family interaction (Aquilino, 1997; Caspi & Elder, 1988). In this chapter I examine continuity and change in parent–child relationships over time, the influence of parent–child relationships on emerging adults' development, and the importance of family support in the transition to adulthood.

Continuity and Change in Emerging Adults' Relationships With Parents

What factors predict the quality of parent–child relations as sons and daughters move into the emerging adult years? Extent research suggests that three sets of factors influence relationship quality during this phase: earlier patterns of parent–child interaction, the history of family composition and transitions, and the individual development and life-course transitions of family members.

THE INFLUENCE OF EARLIER PATTERNS OF INTERACTION. Parent–child relationships during emerging adulthood are in part a function of the history of family relationships. Social learning theory suggests that styles of family interaction learned in earlier childhood continue to be played out in adulthood (Whitbeck, Hoyt, & Huck, 1994). The repetition of patterns of family communication, negotiation, and conflict resolution over the years of childhood and adolescence causes these styles to persist as children become adults. Familiar patterns of interaction help family members deal with new or ambiguous situations as families cope with life-course changes and the new roles of individual members (Caspi & Elder, 1988). Attachment theory also supports the prediction of continuity over time in parent–child relations. The attachment relationship formed in early childhood may become a relatively stable aspect of personality through internal working models and the generalized expectations of the self, others, and the world that influence later attachment relationships (Waters, Hamilton, & Weinfield, 2000).

Studies consistently have found a small to moderate degree of continuity between earlier patterns of parent–child interaction and parent–child relationships in the emerging adult phase, but the lingering effects of earlier patterns appear to weaken as children move further into adulthood. Research based on adults' retrospective reports of parental behavior has found evidence of continuity. Recalled parental rejection leads to more relationship strain, less affection, and less concern for parents' well-being among adults (Whitbeck et al., 1994; Whitbeck, Simons, & Conger, 1991). Emerging adults who reported higher levels of family cohesion, parental affection, and emotional closeness when they were adolescents felt closer to their parents in adulthood (Rossi & Rossi, 1990).

Although evidence based on retrospective accounts is questionable because of recall bias, prospective and longitudinal studies have yielded similar results. Thornton, Orbuch, and Axinn (1995) found strong continuity in parents' and children's reports of relationship quality from age 18 to age 23. Longitudinal studies by Tubman and Lerner (1994a, 1994b) reported moderate stability in affective relations with parents from middle childhood into emerging adulthood. However, the associations between past and present parent–child relationships weakened gradually over time. From adolescence to the late 20s, there was increasing divergence between parents' and children's perceptions of the relationship, reflecting increasing separation.

National survey data from the parent's perspective showed that parent–adolescent relationships influenced emotional closeness and conflict between parents and emerging adult children measured 6 years later (Aquilino, 1997). The parent–adolescent measures accounted for about 9% of the variance in these two indicators. Parents who reported warm, involved, and helping relationships with adolescent children also reported higher levels of emotional closeness, shared activities, and support from children when their sons and daughters were entering adulthood. Parents who reported higher levels of yelling, arguing, shouting, and disagreement with their adolescents reported lower levels of emotional closeness, lower levels of support exchange, and higher levels of conflict with emerging adult children.

Belsky and his colleagues explored the antecedents of intergenerational relationship quality in a New Zealand sample followed from age 3 to age 26 (Belsky, Jaffee, Hsieh, & Silva, 2001). They found little evidence that parenting in early childhood or middle childhood was related to intergenerational relations at age 26. The strongest evidence of continuity was from adolescence. Parent–child relationship quality in early adolescence predicted higher affection, support, and contact with mothers and higher affection with fathers. But the effects were weak. Earlier family patterns accounted for about 4% of the variance in affection with mothers and father, and about 1% of the variance in support exchange and contact with mothers.

Studies exploring whether attachment security forged with parents in infancy and early childhood has a lasting influence on attachment to parents in emerging adulthood have produced mixed results. Waters, Weinfield, and Hamilton (2000) reported that 72% of the children in their sample received the same attachment classification at age 21 as they did at age 1. In contrast, two similar studies found little evidence of continuity in attachment classification from infancy to age 18 or 19 (Lewis, Feiring, & Rosenthal, 2000; Weinfield, Sroufe, & Egeland, 2000). Change in attachment classification is linked to the experience of negative life events, such as parental divorce or severe illness, maternal depression, or child maltreatment.

In sum, most prospective and retrospective studies support the contention that the history of the parent–child relationship affects its future. Patterns of interaction from an earlier stage have a small but persistent influence in emerging adulthood. Evidence of continuity is most likely to be found between parent–adolescent relations and emerging adulthood. The further back into childhood one looks, the less the likelihood of detecting continuity.

FAMILY DISRUPTION AND PARENT–ADULT CHILD RELATIONSHIPS. Parental divorce, custody arrangements, and remarriage have lasting effects on emerging adults' relationships with parents. National survey data from respondents aged 19 to 34 have shown that divorce results in weaker relationships with parents (Aquilino, 1994a). The negative effects were especially strong for relations with noncustodial parents. The remarriage of the custodial parent also resulted in weaker parent–adult child relationships. The experience of being separated from both biological parents, that is, being raised for a time by relatives or foster parents, had severe negative effects on relationship quality with both mothers and fathers.

Emerging adults report many painful memories of their parents' divorce (Laumann-Billings & Emery, 2000). Their distress about family experiences appears to depend on the level of interparental conflict and the quality of relations with parents after the divorce. Continuing interparental conflict after the divorce leads to reduced intimacy with parents, whereas maintaining good parent–child relationships buffers the effects of divorce on emerging adults (Richardson & McCabe, 2001). The level of contact with noncustodial fathers may be particularly important (Laumann-Billings & Emery, 2000). When a strong relationship with the father is maintained throughout childhood, there tends to be less anger and sense of loss in emerging adulthood and a fuller understanding of the divorce (Shulman, Scharf, Lumer, & Maurer, 2001).

Children raised in intact families may also experience parental divorce as adults. Cooney (1994) analyzed a sample of emerging adults aged 18 to 23 raised in intact families but whose parents recently divorced. The divorce led to reduced contact between emerging adults and their fathers and lower intimacy in the father–daughter relationship, but had no effect on mother–child relations. The National Survey of Families and Households (NSFH) data also showed that parental divorce after the children were grown had particularly strong, negative effects on the father–child relationship (Aquilino, 1994b). Pryor (1999) conducted a qualitative study in New Zealand of emerging adults whose parents stayed together throughout childhood but divorced after the child was age 18. The participants had many complaints, including not having grown up in a well-functioning family, poorer parent–child relationships in emerging adulthood, a sense that their family was falling apart, lack of parental support, and being called on to care for one or both of their parents.

INDIVIDUAL DEVELOPMENT AND PARENT–CHILD RELATIONSHIP CHANGE. The weak effects of earlier relationship patterns suggest that parents and emerging adult children are not locked into the styles of interaction that characterized previous stages. What forces break up old patterns of relating and push for a reconfiguration of the emerging adult's family relationships? Research suggests that intraindividual change in the lives of parents and children provides the impetus for a reappraisal and renegotiation of the parent–child relationship (Aquilino, 1997; Kaufman & Uhlenberg, 1998). Intraindividual change includes both the psychological development of each family member and life transitions and changes in roles and statuses. As noted in the previous section, parental divorce and remarriage after the children are grown have the potential to reshape family relationships at any point in the life course. The empty nest transition may lead midlife parents into new assessments of family relationships and an increased focus on their own individual needs and opportunities (Schnaiberg & Goldenberg, 1989). The child's movement into adult roles also furnishes an opportunity for parent and offspring to forge new patterns of interaction.

The emerging adult's home-leaving and other transitions to adult roles are major sources of discontinuity and change in the parent–child relationship. In a study of Israeli men who enter compulsory military service at age 18, Mayseless and Hai (1998) measured relationships with parents 3 months prior to and 3 months after conscription. They found that the home-leaving transition led to heightened feelings of autonomy and better relations with parents (more warmth, less confrontation). Sullivan and Sullivan (1980) explored change in parent–child relations during the transition to college among commuter students and students who moved away from home. Students boarding at school reported more affection, communication, satisfaction, and independence in relation to parents after moving away from home. These changes did not happen for commuter students. Dubas and Petersen (1996) similarly found that 21-year-olds living at home or close to home reported higher depression and poorer relationships with parents than did those who had moved farther away. They concluded that leaving home—ending the daily contact with and supervision by parents—pushes both child and parent toward an understanding that their relationship has changed.

Longitudinal data from the NSFH have shown that the influence of parent–child relationship dimensions measured in adolescence on parent–adult child relations diminishes after children leave home (Aquilino, 1997). Emerging adults' entry into adult roles, including marriage, cohabitation, labor force entry, and college enrollment, promoted positive changes in their relationships with parents. Conflict with parents declined when sons and daughters left home, married, worked full-time, or attended college. Not all transitions bring about positive change. When emerging adults have their own children, there tends to be less affectional solidarity with their parents and more conflict (Aquilino, 1997; Belsky et al., 2001). Adult children's divorce and negative changes in marital quality also lead to more strained relations with parents (Kaufman & Uhlenberg, 1998).

In sum, research has demonstrated the capacity for both continuity and change in parent–child relations during the emerging adulthood period. Effects of earlier interaction patterns weaken over time. Parental divorce, custody arrangements, and remarriage continue to shape parent–adult child relations. Parents' transition to an empty nest and emerging adults' home-leaving and other role transitions transform family relationships as each member of the parent–child dyad adapts to changes in the behaviors, status, and goals of the other (Maccoby, 1999). Emerging adults' increasing ability to live independently and be self-sufficient leads to a lessening of control issues with parents and encourages interaction based on affection, mutual respect, and voluntary association.

Impact of Parent–Child Relationships on Emerging Adults' Development and Outcomes

The well-being of emerging adults is closely tied to their ongoing relationships with parents (Cooney & Kurz, 1996; Umberson, 1992), whether they still live with parents or have left home. Research suggests that family relationships influence emerging adults' psychosocial development, including psychological well-being and adjustment to new roles, health and risk-taking behavior, capacity for intimacy, and identity. Family experiences and support also influence the life-course transitions of emerging adults, including the likelihood of home-leaving and returning home, forming and dissolving unions, childbearing, and educational attainment. The mechanisms of influence can be grouped in two categories: patterns of family interaction and the strength of emotional bonds, and the long-term effects of family composition and transitions.

FAMILY INTERACTION AND EMOTIONAL BONDS. Levels of involvement, warmth, support, and acceptance in the parent–child relationship influence the emerging adult's individuation, psychological adjustment, and the capacity for healthy interpersonal relationships (Tubman & Lerner, 1994a). From adolescence into emerging adulthood, the parent–child relationship needs to evolve into one supportive of independence and autonomy while maintaining strong attachment and emotional support from parents (Hill & Holmbeck, 1986; Ryan & Lynch, 1989). In an ideal situation, parents are partners with their offspring in the quest for independence.

A study of undergraduate women (Perosa, Perosa, & Tam, 2002) showed the benefits of the family system characteristics of open communication, conflict expression and resolution, clear boundaries, and the absence of alliances. Identity achievement was facilitated when women reported feeling close to their parents yet also feeling independent and competent, that is, experiencing a balance of separateness and connectedness. Parental acceptance and support for independence have been linked to higher self-esteem, individuation, and feelings of love, and worthiness among college students (Ryan & Lynch, 1989) whereas parental denial of autonomy contributes to hostility and impaired social functioning in emerging adulthood (Allen, Hauser, O'Connor, & Bell, 2002). A study of university students in Greece found that secure attachment leads to healthy separation from parents that leads in turn to adaptive psychological functioning (Leondari & Kiosseoglou, 2000). Securely attached students scored higher on self-esteem and lower on anxiety and loneliness. What seems advantageous for emerging adults' achievement of independence is feeling connected, secure, understood, and loved in their families, and having the willingness to call on parental resources. These findings support the view that continued connectedness to parents, rather than a repudiation of parental ties, facilitates individuation (Grotevant & Cooper, 1986; Hill & Holmbeck, 1986; Ryan & Lynch, 1989).

Parental acceptance, empathy, and support remain essential for children's healthy adjustment during the transition to emerging adulthood (Powers, Hauser, & Kilner, 1989). Most studies in this area have focused on the adjustment of college students. Mutuality and reciprocity in parent–child relationships (linked to an authoritative parenting style) bolster students' adjustment to college life and foster higher academic achievement (Wintre & Yaffe, 2000). A 2-year longitudinal study of college students found that parental support and low marital conflict led to higher well-being and social integration (Holahan, Valentiner, & Moos, 1994). Having disengaged parents leads to more stress among college students (Nicholson, Phillips, Peterson, & Battistutta, 2002), whereas parental acceptance is related to higher well-being and a lower likelihood of drug abuse (Campo & Rohner, 1992; Turner, Sarason, & Sarason, 2001). Intimacy with mother and intimacy with father were found to be the most important predictors of psychosocial adjustment in an Australian college student sample (Richardson & McCabe, 2001). Low intimacy with parents was associated with higher levels of depression and stress.

Attachment to parents influences the emotional well-being of emerging adults (McCarthy, Moller, & Fouladi, 2001). Among female undergraduates insecure attachment was associated with elevated levels of anger and hostility (Meesters & Muris, 2002). Longitudinal research in the Netherlands (van Wel, Linssen, & Ruud, 2000; van Wel, ter Bogt, & Raaijmakers, 2002) followed a national sample for 6 years, from ages 12 through 24 to 18 through 30, and found that the association between the strength of the bond with parents and psychological well-being did not diminish over time. The parent–child relationship remained an integral component of psychological well-being, on par with relationships with romantic partners and friends. Parent–child attachment may be transmitted across generations. New parents who have close relationships with their mothers tend to form more secure attachment relationships with their own children (Brook, Richter, & Whiteman, 2000).

The achievement of interpersonal intimacy is widely regarded as one of the central developmental tasks of emerging adulthood. Research suggests that parent–child experiences are carried forward into adults' intimate relationships. Family interaction processes affect the development of interpersonal skills, which in turn affect the capacity for intimacy in adult romantic relationships (Conger & Conger, 2002). Data from a longitudinal study of rural youth followed from age 12 to age 21 showed that nurturing, involved parenting (high in warmth, support, and monitoring, and low on hostility and harsh, inconsistent parenting) predicted behavior toward romantic partners that was warm, supportive, and low in hostility (Conger, Cui, Bryant, & Elder, 2000). Similar findings were reported by Feldman, Gowen, and Fisher (1998) in a sample interviewed first at ages 13 to 18 and followed up 6 years later at ages 19 to 25. Family cohesion and a flexible style of family control predicted higher self-reported happiness in romantic relationships, with results stronger for women than for men. Attachment security with parents at age 19 predicted more positive relational processes in romantic relationships at age 20 to 21 (Roisman, Madsen, Hennighausen, Sroufe, & Collins, 2001). Robinson (2000), with a sample of university students, showed that positive relations with mother and greater adaptability in the family system in adolescence predicted more positive intimate relationships in emerging adulthood.

A neglected aspect in research on family relationships and emerging adult adjustment is the possibility of bidirectional effects. The emerging adult's level of psychological adjustment and emotional maturity will likely affect parents' well-being and will set the stage for closer and more satisfying parent–child relationships. A next step for research in this area is to explore the reciprocal influences between parents' and emerging adults' psychological adjustment and family relationships.

LONG-TERM EFFECTS OF FAMILY COMPOSITION AND TRANSITIONS. Several longitudinal studies have reported that depression and other mental health problems are common symptoms among emerging adults who experienced parental divorce in childhood (Aro & Palosaari, 1992; Wallerstein & Blakeslee, 1989; Wallerstein & Corbin, 1989; Zill, Morrison, & Coiro, 1993). Wallerstein (1991) concluded that emerging adults whose parents divorced tended to become underachieving, anxious, and sometimes angry men and women who married impulsively and were prone to early divorce. Data from a large national sample in Great Britain showed that the effects of divorce on mental health outcomes became greater as children moved through emerging adulthood and into their 30s (Cherlin, Chase-Lansdale, & McRae, 1998). Parental divorce may influence the emerging adult life course even if strong effects are not evident during childhood.

The marital difficulties and conflict that children are exposed to prior to parental divorce account, at least in part, for effects on children after family disruption (Sun, 2001). An analysis of longitudinal data from Great Britain and the United States showed that a substantial portion of the effects attributed to divorce were evident before the parents' marital breakup and could be attributed to exposure to marital conflict and dysfunctional family relationships (Cherlin et al., 1991). But there is also evidence that family disruption has long-term effects on children beyond the circumstances that existed prior to the divorce. Furstenberg and Kiernan (2001) analyzed data from the British National Child Development Study on children born in 1958 and followed until age 33. Controlling for predivorce measures of family relationships and child adjustment accounted for only a small portion of divorce effects on adult children's mental health outcomes, educational attainment, and income. Both predivorce and postdivorce factors influenced offspring into adulthood.

Several studies suggest that experiencing parental divorce and family conflict negatively affects emerging adults' capacity for intimacy and security in romantic relationships (Summers, Forehand, Armistead, & Tannenbaum, 1998; Toomey & Nelson, 2001; Wallerstein, 1991). Jacquet and Surra (2001) interviewed a random sample of 404 single, never-married adults aged 19 to 35, divided between parents-still-married and parents-divorced. The effects of parental divorce on romantic relationships were stronger for women than for men. Compared with women from intact families, women with divorced parents reported less trust and satisfaction in relationships, and more ambivalence and conflict. The effects of parental divorce on romantic relationships in emerging adulthood may be mediated by paternal involvement. College students whose parents were divorced reported less father involvement than those whose parents were still married (van Schaick & Stolberg, 2001). Paternal involvement was positively related to commitment, intimacy, and trust in romantic relationships and was negatively related to insecurity, avoidance, and anxiety.

The impact of parental divorce on emerging adults' romantic relationships is not always negative. Effects may depend in part on sons' and daughters' understanding of the divorce. In a study of Israeli college students, those who had a more integrative understanding of the divorce, including awareness of complexity and appreciation of their mother's and father's viewpoints, had higher levels of intimacy and more enjoyment in romantic relationships (Shulman et al., 2001). A qualitative study of 28 college students showed that some were able to view their parents' divorce as a learning experience, and these students had more successful relationships than did others who dwelled on the negative aspects of the divorce (Mahl, 2001). Australian adults aged 18 to 26 who had been subjects of contested custody cases as children seemed highly aware of the risks of marriage, felt they needed to work harder to develop relationship skills, and were determined not to repeat their parents' mistakes (Darlington, 2001).

The Family Support System in Emerging Adulthood

The family of origin functions as a base of operations for the explorations of emerging adulthood, both literally through coresidence in a parental household, parental financial subsidies, and other material support, and figuratively through the availability of parents and kin as sources of wisdom and guidance in making one's way in the world.

FAMILY FINANCIAL SUPPORT. Economic support from parents may include paying for college and other postsecondary education; financial subsidies that enable the emerging adult to live independently; coresidence in the parental household; and the provision of health insurance, transportation, and other necessities to children regardless of where they live. Parents and grandparents also function as teachers of life skills and practical knowledge and as sounding boards when emerging adults face major decisions. The family plays a role in the formation of career goals in emerging adulthood, most importantly through reinforcement of children's achievement-oriented activities (Hargrove, Creagh, & Burgess, 2002).

Financial support from parents improves emerging adults' chances of success in the transition to adult roles. Subsidies for education, buying a house, and paying bills raise the living standards of adult children (Semyonov & Lewin-Epstein, 2001). Despite the apparent benefits of parental subsidies, there is a great deal of diversity among American parents in their attitudes toward the economic support of adult children and little national consensus across families concerning the situations that merit support (Goldscheider, Thornton, & Yang, 2001). Parents' opinions vary about whether married or unmarried children deserve more support, or whether children living at home or those living away merit more support. The divisions are deepest among the families with children not attending college. Adult children may overestimate the likelihood of financial subsidies. Goldscheider et al. (2001) found that the proportion of emerging adults expecting financial help was greater than the proportion of mothers willing to give it.

The type of economic support that has the highest degree of agreement across parents is support for education. National survey data have shown that about three quarters of parents with children entering adulthood agree that parents should help pay for college expenses (Aquilino, 2005). Parents appear motivated to invest in children's human capital (Lee & Aytac, 1998), and the investment in education pays off in better labor market outcomes for their children (Semyonov & Lewin-Epstein, 2001).

There is considerably more disagreement among parents concerning their obligation to give economic support to adult children who are struggling financially. Fewer than half of American parents with emerging adult children agreed that they were obligated to provide this type of support (Aquilino, 2005). There is evidence that parents respond to need, even if reluctantly. A qualitative study by Hamon (1995) found that parents provided a great deal of support to adult children in the midst of a divorce. In addition to advice and emotional support, parents provided money for a variety of needs, including day-to-day living expenses, property taxes, automobiles, attorney fees, mortgage payments, and paying off debts.

Research has shown that parents may use economic subsidies to influence the behavior of their emerging adult children, moving them out of the household faster or undercutting their ability to live independently (Avery, Goldscheider,

& Speare, 1992; Goldscheider & Goldscheider, 1993). Parents' willingness to help pay for daily living expenses makes it easier for children to leave home and establish their own household. By withholding this type of support, parents can make it harder for children to leave home or can encourage their return, especially if parents are unhappy with a child's lifestyle or decisions.

What predicts the extent of parental financial support? Parental resources play a large role in determining the amount of financial support available to children. The higher the parents' income and the fewer siblings among whom resources are divided, the more responsibility parents take in paying for college (Steelman & Powell, 1991). As the number of siblings increases, parents tend to deflect this responsibility onto their children. Among Israeli families, parental economic support of adult children was more prevalent among higher socioeconomic status (SES) families and families with fewer siblings (Semyonov & Lewin-Epstein, 2001). Parents with greater educational aspirations for their children are more likely to believe that they should bear the financial responsibility for college expenses (Steelman & Powell, 1991). Divorced parents provide less financial support for children in part because of the decline in parental assets following divorce (Cooney & Uhlenberg, 1992; Eggebeen, 1992; White, 1992). Remarriage and the transition to a stepfamily also weaken parental feelings of obligation to support children economically (Aquilino, 2005), and research has shown that stepchildren receive less parental support for higher education compared with children from two-genetic-parent households (Zvoch, 1999).

CORESIDENCE AS A FORM OF FAMILY SUPPORT. Over the past several decades there has been a shift toward later home-leaving and an increased likelihood of adult children returning home. Although the median age at first home-leaving is about age 19, 40% of those who leave home for the first time at ages 17 to 20 return to live in the parental household, and about a quarter of emerging adults do not leave for the first time until age 22 or later (Goldscheider & Goldscheider, 1999). As a result, the proportion of adults aged 18 to 24 living with parents has increased steadily since 1970. Year 2000 Census data show that 56% of men and 43% of women in this age range lived at home with one or both of their parents (Fields & Casper, 2001). Emerging adults who return home after living independently tend to stay for a limited time. NSFH data show that about two thirds of returning adults stay in the parental home for less than 2 years (Aquilino, 1996).

The continued residence of adult children in the parental home has been termed a failure of socialization and the sign of an incomplete transition to adulthood (Schnaiberg & Goldenberg, 1989). Although there has been an increasing trend among modern parents to value self-direction and independence in children (Alwin, 1988; Phillips & Sandstrom, 1990), parents do not necessarily view coresidence as a violation of these values or as a failure of any sort (Aquilino & Supple, 1991). As noted earlier, the labor market increasingly favors job seekers with more education and skills (Hill & Yeung, 1999). Parents appear to recognize that their emerging adult children may legitimately need the secure base of the parental home for a period during the emerging adult years to prepare themselves for adult roles (DaVanzo & Goldscheider, 1990).

For many emerging adults, the economic benefits of coresidence make attend-ing college or acquiring other postsecondary training more feasible. Periods of coresidence may also facilitate a fuller exploration of career options. Without the pressure of paying rent and other daily living expenses, emerging adults can more readily leave a dead-end job and return to school, or take a lower paid position that offers greater opportunities for training and long-term advancement.

My earlier research on coresidence showed that American parents appear quite willing to provide room and board to their emerging adult chil-dren so long as they perceive that their sons and daughters are making prog-ress in the movement toward autonomy through education or employment (Aquilino, 1991, 1996). Parent–child conflict and parental dissatisfaction with coresidence increase when children are neither working nor in school, and when adult children return home after separation or divorce, especially if they bring grandchildren into the household; parents' responses to coresidence are more positive when children contribute to their own upkeep by paying for their own transportation, clothing, and entertainment (Aquilino & Supple, 1991). Graber and Brooks-Gunn (1996) similarly reported that women who returned to live with parents after finishing college enjoyed good relationships with parents and that the daughters and parents were able to live together while respecting each other's independence (sons were not included in this research). The returning daughters primarily needed the financial advantages offered by a temporary sojourn in the parental home; it allowed them to save enough so they could be more confident in their ability to meet the financial demands of independent living.

Although leaving home appears to boost emerging adults' self-confidence and capacity for autonomy (Dubas & Petersen, 1996; Mayseless & Hai, 1998), it is unrealistic to expect that all emerging adults are ready for independent living at age 18 or 19. Children develop at different rates, and the psychosocial maturity needed for successful entry into adult roles comes at later ages for some. To the extent that coresidence provides structural support and more time to acquire confidence and life skills, it may enhance rather than detract from emerging adults' development. Coresidence with parents may be the best option, or only option, for emerging adults from poor or lower SES families. With parents unable to afford room and board, commuting to a local college may be the only option for postsecondary education. For emerging adults not attending college, coresidence provides basic needs and a measure of security as they try to make their way in a difficult job market. Lower SES families may also rely on the economic contributions of their emerging adult offspring. Becoming a source of support for the family of origin may bolster emerging adults' psychosocial maturity in a way comparable to home-leaving.

In sum, parent–child interaction characterized by strong connections (affection, open communication, mutual respect and acceptance), acknowledg-ment of separateness, and support for autonomy enhances emerging adults' psychosocial development and capacity for intimacy. A growing body of research shows that changes in family composition and custody arrangements during childhood continue to influence the quality of parent–child relations in emerg-ing adulthood. Strained relationships are especially likely with noncustodial parents and remarried parents. Material support from parents is critical in enhancing emerging adults' education and training and improving their prospects for successful transitions to adult roles. In addition to financial transfers, coresidence in the parental household is a common form of material support that may facilitate the transition to self-sufficiency.

Emerging Adults' Relationships With Siblings and Grandparents

Research on the family relationships of emerging adults has centered almost exclusively on the parent–child relationship. This singular focus overlooks the possibility that relationships with other family members may have a substantial and long-lasting influence on emerging adults' development. Recent studies suggest that relations with siblings and with grandparents may be important factors in the life course of emerging adults.

Sibling Relationships

The sibling bond is one of the most long-lasting relationships in people's lives. Siblings not only are genetically similar but share a long history of family experiences (Cicirelli, 1991) and often function as a source of support during stressful times. Despite its potential importance, the sibling relationship in emerging adulthood is the least studied relationship in the family (Shortt & Gottman, 1997). The few studies of emerging adults' sibling relationships have focused almost exclusively on college students.

How does the sibling relationship change as children move into adulthood? Sibling relationships in childhood are often quite intense, with a great deal of conflict. Bedford, Volling, and Avioli (2000) speculated that this intensity derives from unique aspects of the relationship. Compared with other relationships, such as with peers, siblings have greater familiarity and access, parents often consider sibling conflict normal, there is an unequal distribution of power and dominance (based on age), and there is forced contact in a complex, long-term relationship. As siblings move from childhood into adulthood, they have a choice about whether to remain involved in each other's lives. The relationship is no longer inescapable, as it may have been during childhood.

There is conflicting evidence about how important sibling relationships are to emerging adults' social networks and well-being. Cicirelli (1980) found that, in terms of seeking emotional support and someone to confide in, college women's ties to siblings were as strong or stronger than their ties to mothers. However, there is evidence that college students feel closer to friends than to their closest sibling and have more joint activities and discussions with friends than with siblings (Pulakos, 1989). Closeness and contact with siblings decrease during the early adult years (White, 2001), then increase later in adulthood (Cicirelli, 1991). Siblings become more important sources of help as adults get older, and sibling support appears to be especially important in old age (Cicirelli, 1991). Thus the task for emerging adults may be to maintain relations with siblings that are strong enough to form the basis of a long-term relationship, even if these relationships are not of primary importance compared with peers, romantic partners, and parents.

An observational study by Shortt and Gottman (1997) identified the processes underlying the quality of college students' sibling relationships. Sibling pairs were videotaped in a lab setting having two conversations, one on an enjoyable topic and one on a topic of disagreement or differences. Results showed that siblings who were not close struggled to resolve power issues in their relationship. Earlier in life, older siblings naturally had more power. Shortt and Gottman concluded that eliminating these power imbalances is one of the central tasks for siblings during emerging adulthood. To remain close, siblings need to move from the asymmetrical relationship characteristic of childhood to a more symmetrical relationship between equals. Research on college students' defensiveness in response to help from siblings supports this conclusion. Searcy and Eisenberg (1992) found that defensive reactions to help were more likely when there was conflict between siblings and when the power differential between siblings remained an issue.

Grandparent Relationships

There are relatively few studies of emerging adults' relationships with their grandparents. Most research in this area has also relied on college student samples. Students tend to express strong emotional bonds to grandparents (Kennedy, 1992; Mills, Wakeman, & Fea, 2001) and value the attention, support, and appreciation they receive from them (Kennedy, 1991). Gender of the child, parent, and grandparent plays an important role in shaping this relationship. Emerging adult women have more contact with grandparents than do men (Dubas, 2001). College students report feeling closer to grandmothers than to grandfathers (Kennedy, 1991; Mills et al., 2001). Thus the granddaughter–grandmother relationship tends to be the closest compared with other gender pairings (Dubas, 2001). Affection for grandfathers grows as grandchildren move into adult roles such as employment, marriage, and parenthood (Mills, 1999).

Emerging adults feel closer to maternal than to paternal grandparents (Mills et al., 2001). Women often function as "kin-keepers" in the family, maintaining stronger ties to their extended families than do men (Chan & Elder, 2000). Mothers' stronger connection to the matrilineal line (compared with fathers' connection to the patrilineal line) facilitates children's relationships with the maternal grandparents. Mills and colleagues (2001) found evidence that parents mediate the relationship between emerging adult children and grandparents. There is less closeness to grandparents when the biological parent has died. Parental divorce strengthens relationships to the maternal grandparents, most likely because children are in the mother's custody after divorce. In a similar manner, grandparents who are divorced tend to have more distant relationships with their adult children, which leads to less closeness with their grandchildren (King, 2003). Among immigrants to the United States, acculturation tends to weaken the bonds between grandchildren and grandparents. Mexican American grandchildren who were more acculturated than their grandparents expressed less affection and had less frequent interaction with grandparents (Silverstein & Chen, 1999).

In sum, there has been relatively little research on emerging adults' sibling relationships and connections to grandparents, despite the potential importance of these relationships for adult well-being. The role of grandparents and siblings in providing instrumental and expressive support to emerging adults has gone largely unexamined.

Unanswered (and Unasked) Questions: Directions for Future Research

Qualitative and quantitative research is needed to fill a number of gaps in our knowledge of emerging adults' family relationships. Areas that need a great deal more research include family communication patterns; racial, ethnic, and socioeconomic diversity; the role of extended kin; stepfamily relationships; and the sources of variability in emerging adults' family relationships.

Parent–Child Communication

Do emerging adult children and their parents talk to each other about the changes that are occurring in their lives and in their relationship? The extent and nature of such communication is one of the least understood areas of emerging adults' family relationships. There is little research on how parents acknowledge the adult status of their sons and daughters or how emerging adults solicit that acknowledgment. Communication is essential in creating mutual expectations about family obligations, control issues, and the level of involvement parents and children will have in each other's lives. The life-course decisions of emerging adults will depend on whether parents and children communicate openly about financial support. To what extent do parents make clear to their offspring the amount of financial support they can expect, and for what purposes? How much influence do children have in eliciting economic transfers from parents? The parameters of these negotiations will have major implications for how the lives of emerging adults unfold.

Racial, Ethnic, and Socioeconomic Diversity

The empirical literature on emerging adults' family relationships has paid insufficient attention to racial, ethnic, and socioeconomic diversity partly because of the overreliance on college student samples, which tend to be primarily White and middle class. Although a great deal has been learned from university students, these samples are not representative of the emerging adult population. The overreliance on undergraduate samples ignores the considerable number of emerging adults who do not enroll in college or who drop out of college before completing a degree. In October 2000, according to U.S. Census data, about 54% of 18- and 19-year-old adults were enrolled in college (excluding those who were still in high school). Among adults aged 20 and 21, only 43% were enrolled in any type of college. Thus about half of the college-age emerging adult population is not enrolled in postsecondary education. The family relationships and family support systems of this forgotten half (Halperin, 1998) of the emerging adult population are not well understood. There likely are substantial differences between the college and noncollege populations on questions such as how decisions are made about home-leaving and coresidence in the parental household; the types of family support emerging adults can rely on as they seek additional training or enter the labor market; and the ways in which emerging adults contribute to their families of origin. The family support systems and exchange relationships of emerging adults cannot be fully understood with samples that exclude less affluent and non-White groups.

The student samples drawn in most studies of emerging adults also do not provide an adequate representation of the college student population. Most researchers in psychology, sociology, and related disciplines work at the more prestigious universities, those in which research is integral to the institution's mission. Thus the undergraduate samples inevitably overrepresent students from middle- and upper-middle-class families who attend the more research-oriented universities. In the emerging adult literature there is almost no sampling of community colleges, 2-year vocational or technical colleges, smaller 4-year colleges, or branch campuses of state universities in which research is not high on the agenda. This practice excludes a large proportion of lower SES and minority students from studies of emerging adulthood. Results found with middle- and upper-middle-class samples cannot be generalized to lower SES college students or to the noncollege population.

Researchers who initiate studies of emerging adulthood with an undergraduate sample should be encouraged to expand their research by adding a community-based sample that taps the non-college-attending population of the same age and, if possible, a sample of students drawn from community colleges or technical schools. This would enable researchers to test whether the family dynamics and relationship processes that affect emerging adults vary across social class levels.

Extended Family Relationships

Little is known about emerging adults' extended family relationships. This is an especially critical area for understanding racial ethnic diversity in emerging adulthood. Studies that rely on White, middle-class samples may underestimate the importance of the extended kin network and the role of grandparents in particular.

Most American grandparents describe a companionate style of relationship with their grandchildren, emphasizing affection and the sharing of recreational activities while avoiding direct involvement in raising their grandchildren (Cherlin & Furstenberg, 1986). Nonetheless, over recent decades grandparents have been increasingly called on for help in rearing grandchildren. The proportion of children under age 18 living in a grandparent's household increased by 76% from 1970 to 1997 (Casper & Bryson, 1998) and about one third of those children were being raised solely by grandparents. The latest Census data show that 10% of American children under 6 years old live with a grandparent (Fields, 2003). Very little is known about the extent to which grandparents (and other relatives) who are involved in rearing children remain involved in children's lives as they move into emerging adulthood. To what extent do these family members continue to be sources of emotional and instrumental support?

Grandparents may be especially important sources of support in African American and other minority families (Burton & Jayakody, 2001). African American college students report more exchange of services with grandparents than do White students and are more likely to view a grandparent as a surrogate parent (Kennedy, 1991, 1992). To understand the resources available to emerging adults, researchers need to examine the resources of the grandparents and other extended kin who may have participated in their upbringing (Burton & Jayakody, 2001). Important areas for research include the extent and purpose of grandparents' economic support, the impact of such support on emerging adults' life-course decisions, and the factors that affect the likelihood of support. Support from grandparents may be especially critical in families in which parents are struggling financially.

More research is needed on transformations in sibling relationships over the years of emerging adulthood and the individual, familial, and contextual factors that shape the nature of sibling interaction. The importance of sibling relationships relative to other family and peer relationships is not well understood. A critical question is the degree to which changes in the sibling relationship during emerging adulthood predict closeness and mutual support in later years.

Relationships in Stepfamilies

The number of children who make the transition to a stepfamily during childhood continues to increase (Simmons & O'Neill, 2001). Very little is known about what happens to stepparent–stepchild relationships as stepchildren move into emerging adulthood. Parental remarriage brings not only a stepparent into children's lives but the possibility of stepgrandparents and stepsiblings as well. More research is needed on the factors that lead to stronger or weaker long-term bonds and that support exchange between emerging adults and these potential kin. The few studies in this area suggest that college students' relations with stepgrandparents are weaker than their relations with biological grandparents (Christensen & Smith, 2002) and that grandparents' perceived obligations to stepgrandchildren are weaker than their obligations to biological grandchildren (Coleman, Ganong, & Cable, 1997).

Variability in Emerging Adults' Family Relationships

The transformations in family relationships that take place across emerging adulthood may not be tightly controlled by cultural norms. Because emerging adulthood is a relatively new phenomenon (Arnett, 2004) brought about by economic and social trends (the need for more education and training to succeed economically; later ages at marriage and parenthood), the situation may be similar to the "incomplete institution" of remarriage described by Cherlin (1978). There are strong normative expectations (and legal requirements) for parents' responsibilities to minor children, and fairly clear expectations about contact and exchange between aging parents and their older adult offspring (Rossi & Rossi, 1990). In contrast, emerging adulthood is an in-between period that lacks a well-defined set of expectations. The lack of strong cultural expectations and societal norms for how parents and emerging adults should negotiate relationship changes opens the door to great variability across families. Research is needed to explore this variability both at the individual level (individual differences within any subgroup of society) and also across the cultural landscape defined by gender, race, ethnicity, region, socioeconomic status, and combinations of these social addresses.

Conclusion

Emerging adulthood is a unique and fascinating phase of development. The individual transformations of this period play out within a network of family relationships. Emerging adults pursue physical and psychological autonomy from the family of origin while simultaneously seeking to maintain strong emotional bonds to parents and other kin. Parents and kin provide the emotional and material support needed to enhance the emerging adult's life chances and well-being. In turn, the new behaviors, roles, and transitions of the emerging adult transform family relationships. An expanded scope of research on family dynamics in emerging adulthood is needed, with an agenda that includes closer examination of interaction and communication processes, the role of extended kin, and samples that capture the racial, ethnic, and socioeconomic diversity of the emerging adult population.

References

Allen, J., Hauser, S., O'Connor, T., & Bell, K. (2002). Prediction of peer-rated adult hostility from autonomy struggles in adolescent–family interactions. *Development and Psychopathology, 14*, 123–137.

Alwin, D. F. (1988). From obedience to autonomy: Changes in traits desired in children, 1924–1978. *Public Opinion Quarterly, 52*, 33–52.

Aquilino, W. (1991). Predicting parents' experiences with coresident adult children. *Journal of Family Issues 12*, 323–342.

Aquilino, W. (1994a). Impact of childhood family structure on young adults' relationships with parents. *Journal of Marriage and the Family, 56*, 295–313.

Aquilino, W. (1994b). Later-life parental divorce and widow-hood: Impact on young adults' assessment of parent–child relations. *Journal of Marriage and the Family, 56*, 908–922.

Aquilino, W. (1996). The returning adult child and parental experience at midlife. In C. Ryff & M. Seltzer (Eds.), *The parental experience in midlife* (pp. 423–458). Chicago: University of Chicago Press.

Aquilino, W. (1997). From adolescent to young adult: A prospective study of parent–child relations during the transition to adulthood. *Journal of Marriage and the Family, 59*, 670–686.

Aquilino, W. (2005). Impact of family structure on parental attitudes toward the economic support of adult children over the transition to adulthood. *Journal of Family Issues, 26*, 143–167.

Aquilino, W., & Supple, K. (1991). Parent–child relations and parental satisfaction with living arrangements when adult children live at home. *Journal of Marriage and the Family, 53,* 13–27.

Arnett, J. J. (2004). *Emerging adulthood: The winding road from the late teens through the twenties.* New York: Oxford University Press.

Aro, H. M., & Palosaari, U. (1992). Parental divorce, adolescence, and the transition to young adulthood: A follow-up study. *American Journal of Orthopsychiatry, 62,* 421–429.

Avery, R., Goldscheider, F., & Speare, A., Jr. (1992). Feathered nest/gilded cage: The effects of parental income on young adults' leaving home. *Demography, 29,* 375–388.

Bartle-Haring, S., Brucker, P., & Hock, E. (2002). The impact of parental separation anxiety on identity development in late adolescence and early adulthood. *Journal of Adolescent Research, 17,* 439–450.

Bedford, V. H., Volling, B. L., & Avioli, P. S. (2000). Positive consequences of sibling conflict in childhood and adulthood. *International Journal of Aging and Human Development, 51,* 53–69.

Belsky, J., Jaffee, S., Hsieh, K., & Silva, P. (2001). Child-rearing antecedents of intergenerational relations in young adulthood: A prospective study. *Developmental Psychology, 37,* 801–813.

Bengtson, V., & Allen, K. (1993). The life-course perspective applied to families over time. In P. Boss, W. Doherty, R. LaRossa, W. Schumm, & S. Steinmetz (Eds.), *Sourcebook of family theories and methods: A contextual approach* (pp. 469–499). New York: Plenum Press.

Bjornsen, C. (2000). The blessing as a rite of passage in adolescence. *Adolescence, 35,* 357–363.

Blos, P. (1985). *Son and father: Before and beyond the Oedipus complex.* New York: Free Press.

Brook, J., Richter, L., & Whiteman, M. (2000). Effects of parent personality, upbringing, and marijuana use on the parent–child attachment relationship. *Journal of the American Academy of Child and Adolescent Psychiatry, 39,* 240–248.

Burton, L. M., & Jayakody, R. (2001). Rethinking family structure and single parenthood: Implications for future studies of African American families and children. In A. Thornton (Ed.), *The well-being of children and families: Research and data needs* (pp. 127–153). Ann Arbor: University of Michigan Press.

Campo, A., & Rohner, R. (1992). Relationships between perceived parental acceptance-rejection, psychological adjustment, and substance use among young adults. *Child Abuse & Neglect, 16,* 429–440.

Casper, L. M., & Bryson, K. R. (1998). *Co-resident grandparents and their grandchildren: Grandparent maintained families* (Population Division Working Paper No. 26). Washington, DC: U.S. Bureau of the Census.

Caspi, A., & Elder, G. (1988). Emergent family patterns: The intergenerational construction of problem behavior and relationships. In R. Hinde & J. Steven-son-Hinde (Eds.), *Relationships within families* (pp. 218–240). Oxford, England: Clarendon Press.

Chan, C. G., & Elder, G. H. (2000). Matrilineal advantage in grandchild–grandparent relations. *The Gerontologist, 40,* 179–190.

Cherlin, A. (1978). Remarriage as an incomplete institution. *American Journal of Sociology, 84,* 634-650.

Cherlin, A. J., Chase-Lansdale, P. L., & McRae, C. (1998). Effects of parental divorce on mental health throughout the life course. *American Sociological Review, 63,* 239–249.

Cherlin, A., & Furstenberg, F. (1986). *The new American grandparent: A place in the family, a life apart.* New York: Basic Books.

Cherlin, A., Furstenberg, F., Chase-Lansdale, P., Kiernan, K., Robins, P., Morrison, D., & Teitler, J. (1991, June 7). Longitudinal studies of effects of divorce on children in Great Britain and the United States. *Science, 252,* 1386–1389.

Christensen, F. B., & Smith, T. A. (2002). What is happening to satisfaction and quality of relationships between step/grandparents and step/grandchildren? *Journal of Divorce and Remarriage, 37,* 117–133.

Cicirelli, V. G. (1980). A comparison of college women's feelings toward their siblings and parents. *Journal of Marriage and the Family, 42,* 111–118.

Cicirelli, V. G. (1991). Sibling relationships in adulthood. *Marriage and Family Review, 16,* 291–310.

Coleman, M., Ganong, L. H., & Cable, S. M. (1997). Beliefs about women's intergenerational family obligations to provide support before and after divorce and remarriage. *Journal of Marriage and the Family, 59,* 165–176.

Conger, R., & Conger, K. (2002). Resilience in Midwestern families: Selected findings from the first decade of a prospective, longitudinal study. *Journal of Marriage and the Family, 64*, 361–373.

Conger, R., Cui, M., Bryant, C., & Elder, G. (2000). Competence in early adult romantic relationships: A developmental perspective on family influences. *Journal of Personality and Social Psychology, 79*, 224–237.

Cooney, T. M. (1994). Young adults' relations with parents: The influence of recent parental divorce. *Journal of Marriage and the* Family, *56*, 45–56.

Cooney, T. M., & Kurz, J. (1996). Mental health outcomes following recent parental divorce: The case of young adult offspring. *Journal of Family Issues, 17*, 495–513.

Cooney, T., & Uhlenberg, P. (1992). Support from parents over the life course: The adult child's perspective. *Social Forces, 71*, 63–84.

Darlington, Y. (2001). "When all is said and done": The impact of parental divorce and contested custody in childhood on young adults' relationships with their parents and their attitudes to relationships and marriage. *Journal of Divorce and Remarriage, 35*, 23–42.

DaVanzo, J., & Goldscheider, F. K. (1990). Coming home again: Returns to the parental home of young adults. *Population Studies, 44*, 241–255.

Dellmann-Jenkins, M., Blankemeyer, M., & Pinkard, O. (2001). Incorporating the elder caregiving role into the developmental tasks of young adulthood. *International Journal of Aging and Human Development, 52*, 1–18.

Dubas, J. S. (2001). How gender moderates the grandparent-grandchild relationship: A comparison of kin-keeper and kin-selector theories. *Journal of Family Issues, 22*, 478–492.

Dubas, J. S., & Petersen, A. C. (1996). Geographical distance from parents and adjustment during adolescence and young adulthood. In J. Graber & J. Dubas (Eds.), *New directions for child development: Vol. 71. Leaving home: Understanding the transition to adulthood* (pp. 3–20). San Francisco: Jossey-Bass.

Eggebeen, D. (1992). Family structure and intergenerational exchanges. *Research on Aging, 14*, 427–447.

Elder, G. H. (1984). Families, kin, and the life course: A sociological perspective. In R. Park (Ed.), *Advances in child development research: The family* (pp. 80–135). Chicago: University of Chicago Press.

Feldman, S., Gowen, L., & Fisher, L. (1998). Family relationships and gender as predictors of romantic intimacy in young adults: A longitudinal study. *Journal of Research on Adolescence, 8*, 263–286.

Fields, J. (2003). *Children's living arrangements and characteristics: March 2002* (Current Population Reports, P20-547). Washington, DC: U.S. Census Bureau.

Fields, J., & Casper, L. (2001). *America's families and living arrangements: Population characteristics* (Current Population Reports, P20-537). Washington, DC: U.S. Census Bureau.

Fuligni, A., & Pedersen, S. (2002). Family obligation and the transition to young adulthood. *Developmental Psychology, 38*, 856–868.

Furstenberg, F. F. (2000). The sociology of adolescence and youth in the 1990s: A critical commentary. *Journal of Marriage and the Family, 62*, 896–910.

Furstenberg, F., & Kiernan, K. (2001). Delayed parental divorce: How much do children benefit? *Journal of Marriage and the Family, 63*, 446–457.

Goldscheider, F., & Goldscheider, C. (1993). Whose nest? A two-generational view of leaving home during the 1980s. *Journal of Marriage and the Family, 55*, 851–862.

Goldscheider, F., & Goldscheider, C. (1999). *The changing transition to adulthood: Leaving and returning home*. Thousand Oaks, CA: Sage.

Goldscheider, F. K., Thornton, A., & Yang, S. (2001). Helping out the kids: Expectations about parental support in young adulthood. *Journal of Marriage and the Family, 63*, 727–740.

Graber, J. A., & Brooks-Gunn, J. (1996). Expectations for and precursors to leaving home in young women. In J. A. Graber & J. S. Dubas (Eds.), *New directions for child development: Vol. 71. Leaving home: Understanding the transition to adulthood* (pp. 21–38). San Francisco: Jossey-Bass.

Grotevant, H., & Cooper, C. (1986). Individuation in family relationships: A perspective on individual differences in the development of identity and role-taking skill in adolescence. *Human Development, 29*, 82–100.

Hagestad, G. (1984). The continuous bond: A dynamic, multigenerational perspective on parent–child relations. In M. Perlmutter (Ed.), *Minnesota Symposia on Child Psychology: Vol. 17. Parent–child interaction and parent–child relations in child development* (pp. 129–158). Hillsdale, NJ: Erlbaum.

Halperin, S. (1998). *The forgotten half revisited: American youth and young families, 1988–2008.* Washington, DC: American Youth Policy Forum.

Hamon, R. (1995). Parents as resources when adult children divorce. *Journal of Divorce and Remarriage, 23,* 171–183.

Hargrove, B., Creagh, M., & Burgess, B. (2002). Family interaction patterns as predictors of vocational identity and career decision-making self-efficacy. *Journal of Vocational Behavior, 61,* 185–201.

Hill, J. P., & Holmbeck, G. N. (1986). Attachment and autonomy during adolescence. *Annals of Child Development, 3,* 145–189.

Hill, M., & Yeung, W. (1999). How has the changing structure of opportunities affected transitions to adulthood? In A. Booth, A. Crouter, & M. Shanahan (Eds.), *Transitions to adulthood in a changing economy: No work, no family, no future?* (pp. 3–39). Westport, CT: Praeger Publishers.

Holahan, C., Valentiner, D., & Moos, R. (1994). Parental support and psychological adjustment during the transition to young adulthood in a college sample. *Journal of Family Psychology, 8,* 215–223.

Jacquet, S., & Surra, C. (2001). Parental divorce and premarital couples: Commitment and other relationship characteristics. *Journal of Marriage and the Family, 63,* 627–638.

Kaufman, G., & Uhlenberg, P. (1998). Effects of life course transitions on the quality of relationships between adult children and their parents. *Journal of Marriage and the Family, 60,* 924–938.

Kennedy, G. E. (1991). Grandchildren's reasons for closeness with grandparents. *Journal of Social Behavior and Personality, 6,* 697–712.

Kennedy, G. E. (1992). Shared activities of grandparents and grandchildren. *Psychological Reports, 70,* 211–227.

King, V. (2003). The legacy of a grandparent's divorce: Consequences for ties between grandparents and grandchildren. *Journal of Marriage and Family, 65,* 170–183.

Laumann-Billings, L., & Emery, R. (2000). Distress among young adults from divorced families. *Journal of Family Psychology, 14,* 671–687.

Lee, Y., & Aytac, I. (1998). Intergenerational financial support among Whites, African Americans, and Latinos. *Journal of Marriage and the Family, 60,* 426–441.

Leondari, A., & Kiosseoglou, G. (2000). The relationship of parental attachment and psychological separation to the psychological functioning of young adults. *Journal of Social Psychology, 140,* 451–464.

Lewis, M., Feiring, C., & Rosenthal, S. (2000). Attachment over time. *Child Development, 71,* 707–720.

Maccoby, E. (1999). The uniqueness of the parent–child relationship. In W. A. Collins & B. Laursen (Eds.), *Minnesota Symposium on Child Psychology: Vol. 30. Relationships as developmental contexts* (pp. 157–175). Mahwah, NJ: Erlbaum.

Mahl, D. (2001). The influence of parental divorce on the romantic relationship beliefs of young adults. *Journal of Divorce and Remarriage, 34,* 89–118.

Mayseless, O., & Hai, I. (1998). Leaving home transition in Israel: Changes in parent–adolescent relationships and adolescents' adaptation to military service. *International Journal of Behavioral Development, 22,* 589–609.

McCarthy, C., Moller, N., & Fouladi, R. (2001). Continued attachment to parents: Its relationship to affect regulation and perceived stress among college students. *Measurement and Evaluation in Counseling and Development, 33,* 198–213.

Meesters, C., & Muris, P. (2002). Attachment style and self-reported aggression. *Psychological Reports, 90,* 231–235.

Mills, T. L. (1999). When grandchildren grow up: Role transition and family solidarity among baby boomer grandchildren and their grandparents. *Journal of Aging Studies, 13,* 219–239.

Mills, T. L., Wakeman, M. A., & Fea, C. B. (2001). Adult grandchildren's perceptions of emotional closeness and consensus with their maternal and paternal grandparents. *Journal of Family Issues, 22,* 427–455.

Nicholson, J., Phillips, M., Peterson, C., & Battistutta, D. (2002). Relationship between the parenting styles of biological parents and stepparents and the adjustment of young adult stepchildren. *Journal of Divorce and Remarriage, 36,* 57–76.

Nydegger, C. (1991). The development of paternal and filial maturity. In K. Pillemer & K. McCartney (Eds.), *Parent–child relations throughout life* (pp. 93–112). Hillsdale, NJ: Erlbaum.

Perosa, L., Perosa, S., & Tam, H. (2002). Intergenerational systems theory and identity development in young adult women. *Journal of Adolescent Research, 17,* 235–259.

Phillips, S., & Sandstrom, K. L. (1990). Parental attitudes toward youth work. *Youth & Society, 22,* 160–183.

Powers, S. I., Hauser, S. T., & Kilner, L. A. (1989). Adolescent mental health. *American Psychologist, 44,* 200–208.

Pryor, J. (1999). Waiting until they leave home: The experiences of young adults whose parents separate. *Journal of Divorce & Remarriage, 32,* 47–61.

Pulakos, J. (1989). Young adult relationships: Siblings and friends. *Journal of Psychology, 123,* 237–244.

Richardson, S., & McCabe, M. (2001). Parental divorce during adolescence and adjustment in early adulthood. *Adolescence, 36,* 467–489.

Robinson, L. C. (2000). Interpersonal relationship quality in young adulthood: A gender analysis. *Adolescence, 35,* 775–784.

Roisman, G., Madsen, S., Hennighausen, K., Sroufe, L. A., & Collins, W. A. (2001). The coherence of dyadic behavior across parent–child and romantic relationships as mediated by the internalized representation of experience. *Attachment and Human Development, 3,* 156–172.

Rossi, A., & Rossi, P. (1990). *Of human bonding: Parent–child relations across the life course.* New York: Aldine de Gruyter.

Ryan, R. M., & Lynch, J. H. (1989). Emotional autonomy versus detachment: Revisiting the vicissitudes of adolescence and young adulthood. *Child Development, 60,* 340–356.

Schnaiberg, A., & Goldenberg, S. (1989). From empty nest to crowded nest: The dynamics of incompletely launched young adults. *Social Problems, 36,* 251–269.

Searcy, E., & Eisenberg, N. (1992). Defensiveness in response to aid from a sibling. *Journal of Personality and Social Psychology, 62,* 422–433.

Semyonov, M., & Lewin-Epstein, N. (2001). The impact of parental transfers on living standards of married children. *Social Indicators Research, 54,* 115–137.

Shortt, J. W., & Gottman, J. M. (1997). Closeness in young adult sibling relationships: Affective and physiological processes. *Social Development, 6,* 142–164.

Shulman, S., Scharf, M., Lumer, D., & Maurer, O. (2001). How young adults perceive parental divorce: The role of their relationships with their fathers and mothers. *Journal of Divorce and Remarriage, 34,* 3–17.

Silverstein, M., & Chen, X. (1999). The impact of acculturation in Mexican American families on the quality of adult grandchild–grandparent relationships. *Journal of Marriage and the Family, 61,* 188–198.

Simmons, T., & O'Neill, G. (2001). *Households and families, 2000* (Census 2000 Brief C2KBR/01-8). Washington, DC: U.S. Census Bureau.

Steelman, L. C., & Powell, B. (1991). Sponsoring the next generation: Parental willingness to pay for higher education. *American Journal of Sociology, 96,* 1505–1529.

Sullivan, K., & Sullivan, A. (1980). Adolescent–parent separation. *Developmental Psychology, 16,* 93–99.

Summers, P., Forehand, R., Armistead, L., & Tannenbaum, L. (1998). Parental divorce during early adolescence in Caucasian families: The role of family process variables in predicting the long-term consequences for early adult psychosocial adjustment. *Journal of Consulting and Clinical Psychology, 66,* 327–336.

Sun, Y. (2001). Family environment and adolescents' well-being before and after parents' marital disruption: A longitudinal analysis. *Journal of Marriage and the Family, 63,* 697–713.

Thornton, A., Orbuch, T., & Axinn, W. (1995). Parent–child relationships during the transition to adulthood. *Journal of Family Issues, 16,* 538–564.

Toomey, E., & Nelson, E. (2001). Family conflict and young adults' attitudes toward intimacy. *Journal of Divorce and Remarriage, 34,* 49–69.

Tubman, J., & Lerner, R. (1994a). Affective experiences of parents and their children from adolescence to young adulthood: Stability of affective experiences. *Journal of Adolescence, 17,* 81–98.

Tubman, J., & Lerner, R. (1994b). Continuity and discontinuity in the affective experiences of parents and children: Evidence from the New York Longitudinal Study. *American Journal of Orthopsychiatry, 64,* 112–125.

Turner, A., Sarason, I., & Sarason, B. (2001). Exploring the link between parental acceptance and young adult adjustment. *Cognitive Therapy and Research, 25,* 185–199.

Umberson, D. (1992). Relationships between adult children and their parents: Psychological consequences for both generations. *Journal of Marriage and the Family, 54,* 664–674.

van Schaick, K., & Stolberg, A. (2001). The impact of paternal involvement and parental divorce on young adults' intimate relationships. *Journal of Divorce and Remarriage, 36,* 99–122.

van Wel, F., Linssen, H., & Ruud, A. (2000). The parental bond and the well-being of adolescents and young adults. *Journal of Youth and Adolescence, 29,* 307–318.

van Wel, F., ter Bogt, T., & Raaijmakers, Q. (2002). Changes in the parental bond and the well-being of adolescents and young adults. *Adolescence, 37,* 317–333.

Wallerstein, J. (1991). Long-term effects of divorce on children: A review. *Journal of the Academy of Child & Adolescent Psychiatry, 30,* 349–360.

Wallerstein, J., & Blakeslee, S. (1989). *Second chances: Men, women and children a decade after divorce, who wins, who loses—and why.* New York: Ticnor & Fields.

Wallerstein, J., & Corbin, S. B. (1989). Daughters of divorce: Report from a ten-year follow-up. *American Journal of Orthopsychiatry, 59,* 593–604.

Waters, E., Hamilton, C. E., & Weinfield, N. S. (2000). The stability of attachment security from infancy to adolescence and early adulthood: General introduction. *Child Development, 71,* 678–683.

Waters, E., Weinfield, N. S., & Hamilton, C. E. (2000). The stability of attachment security from infancy to adolescence and early adulthood: General discussion. *Child Development, 71,* 703–706.

Weinfield, N. S., Sroufe, L. A., & Egeland, B. (2000). Attachment from infancy to early adulthood in a high-risk sample: Continuity, discontinuity, and their correlates. *Child Development, 71,* 695–702.

Whitbeck, L., Hoyt, D., & Huck, S. (1994). Early family relationships, intergenerational solidarity, and support provided to parents by adult children. *Journals of Gerontology: Social Sciences, 49,* S85–S94.

Whitbeck, L., Simons, R., & Conger, R. (1991). The effects of early family relationships on contemporary relationships and assistance patterns between adult children and their parents. *Journal of Gerontology: Social Sciences, 46,* S330–S337.

White, L. (1992). The effect of parental divorce and remarriage on parental support for adult children. *Journal of Family Issues, 13,* 234–250.

White, L. (2001). Sibling relationships over the life course: A panel analysis. *Journal of Marriage and the Family, 63,* 555–568.

White, N. R. (2002). "Not under my roof!" Young people's experience of home. *Youth & Society, 34,* 214–231.

Wintre, M., & Yaffe, M. (2000). First-year students' adjustment to university life as a function of relationships with parents. *Journal of Adolescent Research, 15,* 9–37.

Zill, N., Morrison, R. D., & Coiro, M. (1993). Long-term effects of parental divorce on parent–child relationships, adjustment, and achievement in young adulthood. *Journal of Family Psychology, 7,* 91–103.

Zvoch, K. (1999). Family type and investment in education: A comparison of genetic and stepparent families. *Evolution and Human Behavior, 20,* 453–464.

9

Friendships and Romance in Emerging Adulthood: Assessing Distinctiveness in Close Relationships

W. Andrew Collins and Manfred van Dulmen

Arnett's (2000) proposal that the years from the late teens to the late 20s constitute a distinctive period of experiences in social relationships stems partly from readily apparent social and demographic changes. The implicit hypothesis that this demographic and behavioral distinctiveness also involves discernible psychological differences between 18- and 28-year-olds and both younger and older groups, however, requires evidence of a more challenging kind. A rigorous appraisal of this latter contention requires not only evidence of age-group differences but also additional evidence of a developmental progression and an associated set of processes for changing from one period to another.

This chapter examines the implications of the distinctiveness hypothesis for the voluntary close relationships of 18- to 28-year-olds. Whereas parent–child and sibling relationships are involuntary, circumscribed by biological kinship, emerging adults voluntarily form relationships with friends and romantic partners (Laursen & Collins, 1994; Reis, Collins, & Berscheid, 2000). Voluntary relationships depend more heavily than do involuntary ones on the motivation of the partners to maintain connections over time. Because emerging adults as a group often are characterized as preferring transitory to sustained involvements, a key question is whether their friendships and romantic relationships are somehow distinctive from those of younger and older groups. Of particular interest, then, are comparisons of this age group with mid- to late adolescents and with 28- to 35-year-olds.

The chapter is divided into three major sections. The first section outlines findings from research relevant to the distinctiveness proposal. The second section assesses evidence that bears on two specific contentions regarding the sources of distinctiveness in close relationships: (a) continued identity exploration in the realm of close relationships, along with signs that possible

Preparation of the chapter was supported partly by the Minnesota Longitudinal Study of Parents and Children under a National Institute of Mental Health grant to Byron Egeland, L. Alan Sroufe, and W. Andrew Collins.

alternative partners and arrangements are highly salient and self-focus is intense in close relationships, and (b) that behaviors regarding close relationships are unstable and feelings of uncertainty are pronounced. The third section addresses implications of research findings for both the conceptual and the empirical status of Arnett's proposal. The section also advances a possible framework for the further study of the distinctive characteristics of close relationships among 18- to 28-year-olds.

Research on Close Relationships During Emerging Adulthood

In the emerging science of relationships (Laursen & Bukowski, 1997; Reis et al., 2000), the term *relationship* refers to a pair of persons who are interdependent with each other, that is, each person affects and is affected by the behavior of the other person over time. Interdependence in relationships can vary in degree. Some pairs manifest a high degree of mutual impact over a period of years; the involvement and impact of other pairs may be more transitory. Longer term, more salient, and more mutually influential relationships correspond to the commonly used term *close*. For convenience, in this chapter the term *close relationships* will be used to refer explicitly to the two most salient types of interdependent relationships outside of the family, friendships, and romantic relationships. This section briefly characterizes current research approaches to studying close relationships among emerging adults.

Friendships and romantic couples alike vary in content or kinds of interactions; the patterning, or distribution of positive and negative exchanges; quality, or the degree of responsiveness that each shows to the other; and the cognitive and emotional responses of each individual to events in the relationship (Collins, 2003; Hinde, 1979). With respect to the latter, pairs who consider themselves close also report mostly positive thoughts and feelings (Berscheid, Snyder, & Omoto, 1989; Laursen & Williams, 1997), although a minority appear to have highly interdependent and mutually influential relationships composed predominantly of negative interactions in which one person feels neither positive toward nor close to the other person (Huston, Niehuis, & Smith, 2001). This negative pattern may be somewhat more likely in romantic relationships than in friendships, although no explicit comparisons have been reported.

Evidence regarding differing developmental patterns of friendships and romantic relationships has come from highly varied methods. Sociologists have relied almost exclusively on self-report methods, most often using them in cross-sectional surveys (e.g., Sprecher & Felmlee, 1992; Surra, 1990). Social psychologists, too, have relied heavily on self-report methods but have reported some findings from experimental manipulations (e.g., Regan, Kocan, & Whitlock, 1998). The well-known PAIRS (Processes of Adaptation in Intimate Relationships) Project (e.g., Huston, Niehuis, & Smith, 2001) is an example of research tracking romantic partnerships from emerging adulthood to later life. Developmental psychologists have relied more extensively on longitudinal studies. In most cases, the methods of choice involve self-report from interviews and questionnaires; in some studies, the reports of other individuals (e.g., teachers, observers) sometimes have been included (e.g., Collins & Sroufe, 1999; Furman, Simon, Shaffer, & Bouchey, 2002; Neeman, Hubbard, & Masten, 1995; Shulman & Levan, 2002). Some work consists primarily of informants' open-ended accounts (e.g., Arnett, 2004). Only a minority of studies have included formal observational methods (see Roisman, Madsen, Hennighausen, Sroufe, & Collins, 2001, for an exception).

Voluntary close relationships are tightly interwoven in adolescence and in emerging adulthood. In both periods, friendships are the most prominent feature of peer society. Friends are perceived as the most important source of support during adolescence, and intimacy, mutuality, and self-disclosure with friends peak during this period (Furman & Buhrmester, 1992). Same-sex friends in adolescence, as the first intimate, voluntary relationship, may provide critical interpersonal experiences that establish a template for all subsequent close peer affiliations (Sullivan, 1953). Romantic relationships begin as an informal extension of friendship groups. Indeed, for contemporary adolescents, unsupervised mixed-sex groups have rendered obsolete the dating patterns of their parents. Today, observers (and participants) may have difficulty distinguishing between opposite-sex friends and romantic partners (Connolly & Goldberg, 1999). Developmentally speaking, close friendships eventually may undercut their own long-term significance, for successful adolescent friendships enable emerging adults to turn their full attention to romantic relationships and pair bonding, sometimes at the expense of time spent with friends (Collins & Laursen, 2000, 2004; Surra, 1990).

Still, some things remain constant across generations. The high-status members of a social crowd are the first to initiate heterosexual contact. These nascent romances inevitably involve participants who lack intimate experience with the opposite sex (Maccoby, 1998). Socialized in same-sex cliques, males and females bring vastly different expectations and interpersonal styles to romantic relationships. By age 15, most individuals have been involved in at least one romantic relationship and, by the early years of emerging adulthood, most are currently participating in an ongoing romantic relationship (Brown, 2004). Although romantic interconnections initially are predicated on principles of social exchange, commitment drives participants to transform this voluntary relationship into one that is more obligatory and permanent (Laursen & Jensen-Campbell, 1999). Eventually, most emerging adults marry and reproduce, further transforming the relationship and marginalizing remaining friendships, thus effectively ending the peer group's dominance of relationship experiences (Collins & Laursen, 2000, 2004).

The social worlds of those involved in romantic relationships differ from those who are not, as romantic partners quickly become dominant in the relationship hierarchy. For example, adolescents (ages 12–18) who were not involved in romantic relationships reported more daily social interaction in most family and friend relationships than did adolescents who had romantic partners. Moreover, those with romantic partners, especially males and older adolescents, interacted more with romantic partners than with others, whereas females and younger adolescents' interactions were more equally distributed across family members, friends, and romantic partners (Laursen & Williams, 1997). At the same time, extensive evidence showing the interrelations of family, peer, and romantic relationships is consistent with the view that these relative changes in interaction frequency represent a transformation, but not a displacement, of family and peer relationships in favor of romantic ones (Collins & Laursen, 2000, 2004; Furman et al., 2002).

Few longitudinal studies have assessed their respondents on these topics with sufficient frequency to permit a stringent test of distinctiveness predictions. Even in the few longitudinal investigations that are available, the close relationships of 18- to 28-year-olds so often have been elided with those in either earlier or later periods that it is difficult to specify how distinctive emerging adult relationships are, or in what ways. Nevertheless, because comparisons of the same individuals' relationships in multiple developmental periods so clearly pertain to Arnett's distinctiveness hypothesis, the remainder of this chapter emphasizes longitudinal evidence.

Are Close Relationships in Emerging Adulthood Distinctive?

Does the evidence from such studies support the distinctiveness hypothesis? At first glance, the characteristics of adolescent close relationships seem closely related to the attributes from which Arnett (2000) infers the distinctiveness of the later period. A number of findings—perhaps most—portray the emerging adulthood years as part of a continuous progression toward the close relationships of adulthood (e.g., Hartup & Stevens, 1999). Collins (2003) argued that existing findings point to a shift in the qualitative characteristics of dating relationships between the ages of 15 and 17 years and that dating among emerging adults seems similar in key ways to dating among late adolescents. Except for the larger proportions of persons in committed relationships (including cohabitation) after age 28, however, there is presently little compelling evidence that either expectancies or behavior patterns differ between this older group and 18- to 28-year-olds (see Surra, 1990, for a review of findings on mate selection and premarital relationships).

A few findings, however, raise the possibility of distinctiveness in behavior, cognition, and emotions regarding relationships. The most compelling example is the finding that everyday social interaction patterns change from the beginning to the end of the emerging adulthood period. This finding comes from a longitudinal study using the Rochester Interaction Record, a well regarded event-recording method, to study the behavior of the same individuals at 18 and again at ages 26 to 31 (Reis, Lin, Bennet, & Nezlek, 1993). The authors documented three differences between the beginning and end of the hypothesized range that encompasses emerging adulthood. Compared with their younger selves, the 26- to 31-year-olds engaged in more opposite-sex socializing and correspondingly less same-sex, mixed-sex, and group interaction. Moreover, more intimacy occurred in all types of interactions reported at the older age, compared with the younger. It is striking that these age-related contrasts emerged despite considerable stability in the rank-ordering of individuals' scores over time. These differences undoubtedly reflect a changing potential for the formation of close relationships and, perhaps, also the contributions of close relationship partners to the overall social experiences of individuals as they near the end of emerging adulthood.

Oswald and Clark (2003) recently discovered signs of an earlier shift in friendships, as well. They found that best friendships from high school typically decline in satisfaction, commitment, rewards, and investments during the first year in college. Deterioration was less when friends maintained high levels of communication. When best friendships were maintained across this transition, the negative impact of loneliness was mitigated, relative to situations in which individuals did not retain their best friendships.

Other research implies the increased intertwining of closer relationships of different types during adolescence and emerging adulthood. In two recent essays, Collins and Laursen (2000, 2004) argued that "Affiliations with friends, romantic partners, siblings, and parents unfold along varied and somewhat discrete trajectories for most of the second decade of life, then coalesce during the early twenties into an integrated interpersonal structure" (Collins & Laursen, 2000, p. 59). Relationships with parents, friends, and romantic partners increasingly overlap and complement each other as emerging adulthood approaches (Ainsworth, 1989). Representations of romantic relationships are linked to representations of other close relationships, especially relationships with friends, and these interrelated expectancies parallel interrelations in features such as support and control (Furman et al., 2002). Friends and romantic partners typically are the individuals with whom emerging adults most like to spend time (proximity-seeking) and with whom they most want to be when feeling down (safe-haven function). Parents, however, are just as likely to be the primary people from whom emerging adults seek advice and on whom they depend (Fraley & Davis, 1997).

In general, evidence of differences between 14- to 17-year-olds and 25-year-olds is consistent with the impression of increasing differentiation and complexity of thoughts about relationships, but continuity in relationship motives, concerns, and expectations. For example, in a longitudinal analysis of relationship narratives (Waldinger et al., 2002), the structure and complexity of narratives increased between ages 14 to 17 and age 25, whereas the themes mentioned in the narratives were surprisingly similar across this age gap. A desire for closeness was the dominant theme in the narratives of adolescents and those of 25-year-olds. Themes of distance also were present at both ages. Among 14- to 17-year-olds this theme was characterized by separateness, whereas at age 25 the emphasis was on independence. As U.S. respondents are highly likely to reflect the wish for independence throughout adulthood, these findings imply greater continuity than discontinuity between emerging adults and both foregoing and succeeding periods (e.g., Zimmer-Gembeck & Collins, 2003).

Coexisting with these normative transformations within and between relationships are important signs of convergence across relationships before, during, and after the years referred to as emerging adulthood. Qualities of friendships in middle and late adolescence are associated with concurrent qualities of romantic relationship (Collins, 2003; Furman et al., 2002). Representations of friendships and romantic relationships are interrelated as well (Treboux, Crowell, Owens, & Pan, 1994). Displaying safe-haven and secure base behaviors with best friends is associated positively with displaying these behaviors with dating partners. Perhaps the growing importance of romantic relationships makes the common relationship properties across types of relationships more apparent than before. It is equally likely, however, that the parallels between early adults' friendships and romantic relationships reflect their common similarity to prior relationships with parents and peers (Owens, Crowell, Pan, Treboux, O'Connor, & Waters, 1995; Waters, Merrick, Albersheim, Treboux, & Crowell, 2000). The nature and processes of these developmentally significant interrelations of relationships promise to become an increasingly prominent focus of future research.

Moreover, continuity in social networks from the teen years may set the stage for considerable influence from contexts of close dyadic relationships among 18- to 28-year-olds. Pertinent evidence comes from research in which the networks of parents and friends significantly influence continuation or dissolution of a romantic relationship. For example, Sprecher and Felmlee (1992) showed that network support for a relationship was associated positively with the quality of the relationship. Numerous other studies have shown that although couples vary in the degree to which they remain integrally involved with their former networks of kin and friends, those who do continue close involvements show effects of the support or interference they receive.

Distinctiveness and Similarity Across Developmental Periods in a Longitudinal Sample

In addition to influence from preexisting social networks, romantic relationships also are embedded deeply in relationship experiences prior to emerging adulthood. In the Minnesota Longitudinal Study of Parents and Children (Sroufe, Egeland, Carlson, & Collins, 2005), the hypothesis, derived from an attachment model of development, is that salient relationships throughout development contribute to the quality of relationships in emerging adulthood. Research findings repeatedly show that parents and peers each play direct and indirect roles in this developmental process. Data showing this developmental embedding come from the 162 individuals followed from birth to age 23. This diverse sample was initially recruited from among women who were pregnant with their first child and who were obtaining prenatal services from the Minneapolis Public Health Clinics. Today the sample is statistically ideal: About half of the participants are doing well; the other half manifest moderate to severe dysfunction.

We saw these participants seven times in the child's first year, twice in each of the next 3 years, yearly through Grade 4, and at ages 12, 13, 16, 17½, 19, and 23. The assessments have included both individual and dyadic measures of both child and parents. With respect to romantic relationships, we conducted extensive interviews when participants were ages 16, 19, and 23, asking them detailed questions about current friendships and romantic relationships. We asked participants to describe their dating histories; and we also asked them a series of specific questions about the activities shared with dating partners and feelings about the partner and the relationship. For example, we asked them to describe "a time when you felt especially close to your partner" and we also asked for a description of "the biggest fight or argument you had with your partner in the past month." For those in dating relationships of 2 months or more (at ages 16 and 19) and 4 months or more (at age 23), we rated responses on 5-point scales of overall quality. It is not surprising that relationships receiving the highest ratings were characterized by mutual caring, trust, support, and emotional closeness. Intraclass correlations for these ratings ranged from .85 to .93.

At ages 20 and 21, each participant who had been in a self-defined romantic relationship for 4 months or longer and his or her partner separately completed interviews about their relationship. In addition, the couple participated jointly in two collaborative problem-solving tasks. The intraclass correlation reliability for ratings of overall quality was .95.

Predictors of longitudinal patterns of close relationships were theoretically chosen measures of relationship functioning in earlier age periods. From early life, we took the composite of caregiving scores from ages 12 to 42 months. These ratings encompass assessments of attachment at 12 and 18 months with Ainsworth's Strange Situation procedure and also measures of the child's experience in a problem-solving task with tools at 24 months and mother's supportive presence in a teaching task at 42 months. From adolescence, we used ratings of collaborative problem solving and emotional support in videotaped parent–child interactions at age 13. We also used ratings of adolescents' friendship security from interviews with participants at age 16. These ratings picked up participants' sense that they can be wholly themselves in their friendships and be accepted by their friends. The intraclass correlation reliability coefficients ranged from .69 to .78.

The findings to date pertain most closely to the degree to which familial and peer-group experiences in childhood and adolescence accord with later romantic ones at each age: 16, 19, and 23. We first investigated whether mean levels of relationship processes changed from age 16 through age 23 (Collins & Madsen, 2002). When levels of romantic relationship quality at ages 19, 21, and 23 were compared, analysis of variance did not reveal any statistically significant differences between these three ages. We also analyzed whether there were significant differences in romantic relationship security from age 16 through age 23. These scales were coded on the basis of the participant's interviews at the various assessment points. Analysis of variance results showed no significant differences in relationship security from adolescence through emerging adulthood. In addition to these indicators of romantic relationship quality, we also investigated whether average levels of friendship security changed from age 16 to age 19. Analysis of variance yielded significant differences on friendship security between age 16 and age 19, $F(1, 321) = 27.82$, $p < .001$. Friendship security was significantly higher at age 19 compared with age 16 (Collins & Madsen, 2002).

Many analyses addressing the relations between close relationships at each of these ages and predictors from earlier life consistently have shown that qualities of familial interactions and degree of peer competence in middle childhood significantly predicted involvement in romantic relationships at each of the four data-collection waves. By *involvement* we mean whether adolescents are dating at ages 16 and 19 and whether they are in relationships they define as romantic at ages 21 and 23. In other words, earlier relationships reliably forecasted whether these participants would have an actual or potential romantic partner in adolescent and emerging adulthood.

The same predictors accounted for variations in quality of romantic relationships, but—unlike the prediction of romantic involvement—parent–child relationships prior to adolescence also contributed over and above the other predictors. This finding is evident from the combination of two different hierarchical regressions, one in which the predictors are added in chronological order and also one in which they are added in reverse chronological order. Early caregiving was a significant contributor of relationship quality at all four ages in both types of regressions, which implies that the variance contributed by chronologically later measures does not overlap entirely with the variance accounted for by early measures. The apparently differing significance of early care vis-à-vis later parent–child and peer relationships for different aspects of romantic relationships implies that understanding the forerunners of adolescent romance requires a more differentiated framework—including careful attention to indicators of timing—than has guided most of the work in the field up to this point (Collins & Madsen, 2002).

Identity Exploration and Uncertainty in Emerging Adults' Close Relationships

Although distinctiveness vis-à-vis other age periods is at the heart of Arnett's (2000) emerging adulthood proposal, several corollary propositions flesh out key sources of this distinctiveness. To emphasize the transitional nature of emerging adulthood, Arnett identified five key markers that distinguish 18- to 28-year-olds as a group from adults beyond the age of 28. These five markers imply two superordinate factors. The more dominant of the two appears to be a continuation of the identity exploration that has been virtually synonymous with psychosocial development in adolescence. Corollaries of this focus are a high degree of self-focus, marked feelings of being in-between, and awareness of multiple possibilities. A second, closely related implicit factor has to do with characteristics of instability and uncertainty in the relationships of 18- to 28-year-olds. In this section we summarize and evaluate the meager evidence pertaining to Arnett's contention that these two factors motivate distinctive behaviors and attitudes regarding close relationships in this period.

Identity and Exploration

Although identity exploration is typically viewed as an issue of adolescent development, 18- to 28-year-olds frequently report that they feel they need to experience a wide variety of personal relationships and don't feel ready to make a commitment. Arnett (2004) has viewed this as evidence that emerging adulthood is a period of exploration with the goal of determining a good fit between self and significant others. Following Erikson's (e.g., 1968) propensity for distilling the quandaries of a developmental issue into a single question, his view might be phrased as serving the implicit question "Given the kind of person I am, what kind of person do I wish to have as a partner through life?" In the friendship arena, the question might well be modified to "Given the kind of person I am, what kinds of persons do I wish to affiliate with, and what do I expect from those affiliations?" Because emerging adults ordinarily experience less parental surveillance than they did as adolescents, Arnett considers ages 18 to 28 an ideal time to address these questions.

Identity concerns accompanied by lack of commitments to close relationships also may underlie the self-focus attributed to emerging adults. Arnett's point is reminiscent of Erikson's (1968) contention that resolving identity issues is prerequisite for true intimacy with others. When identity issues pervade, individuals feel in-between adult and nonadult status with respect to relationship commitment. Further, not having arrived at a satisfactory vision of who they are and whom they wish to be with, emerging adults may continually perceive—or imagine—new opportunities. With respect to close relationships, the possibilities would typically involve forming new relationships—either with romantic partners or with friends—that carry with them new options for the future. (This prospective view is familiar in adulthood as networking.)

Few researchers have reported findings that bear directly on exploration in the close relationship domain. Two lines of work make somewhat relevant points, however. One line of work examines more specific processes that are implicit in ideas about the explorations of emerging adults. Reasoning that exploration might well imply that emerging adults seek casual relationships more extensively than do younger or older individuals, we asked participants in the Minnesota Longitudinal Study of Parents and Children to report the number of dating partners in the past 2 years at both age 19 and age 23. Analysis of variance revealed no significant difference between the number of dating partners at age 19 versus age 23, although the average number was slightly higher ($p = .075$) at age 19 ($M = 4.05$) as compared with age 23 ($M = 2.84$).

We next investigated whether a similar trend was apparent for the number of sexual partners from adolescence to emerging adulthood, comparing the lifetime number of sexual partners reported at age 16, age 19, and age 23. Analysis of variance results indicated that the number of sexual partners significantly increased from age 16 to age 23, $F(2, 495) = 78.27$, $p < .001$. All post hoc comparisons (age 16 vs. age 19, age 16 vs. age 23, age 19 vs. age 23) were statistically significant, indicating a consistent linear increase for the number of sexual partners to increase from age 16 to age 23. On a 5-point scale, the average level increased from $M = 1.07$ (1 = 1 partner) at age 16 to $M = 2.69$ at age 23 (3 = 6 to 10 partners). Increased sexual activity is normative during these years, and both exploratory motives and the greater social acceptability of sexual involvement by individuals over age 18 may well be implicated in this pattern. Neither this latter explanation, nor Arnett's exploration thesis, has been confirmed as the sole reason for increased sexual activity.

As an additional step in testing the predictions regarding exploration in dating and sexual relationships, we studied changes in friendship relationships during emerging adulthood. At age 23, participants were asked whether they were spending the same amount of time with their friends as 3 to 4 years ago. Sixty-nine percent of the participants indicated at age 23 that they were spending less time with their friends than they were 3 to 4 years ago. Nineteen percent indicated spending the same amount of time, and 12% reported spending more time than 3 to 4 years ago.

Next, we conducted several analyses to address Arnett's (2004) suggestion that exploration of close relationships between ages 18 and 28 serves as preparation for later close relationships. We analyzed whether the exploration we found at ages 19 and 23 would predict romantic relationship commitment and romantic relationship quality at age 23. Correlational analyses indicated that the average number of dating partners (age 19 and age 23) and the average number of sexual partners (age 16, age 19, and age 23) were not significantly associated with age 23 relationship quality and age 23 relationship commitment. The correlations were generally small ($r < -.15$) and negative in direction. One correlation approached significance: A larger number of sexual partners during adolescence or emerging adulthood was associated with a lower level of relationship quality at age 23 ($r = -.20$, $p = .055$).

We then turned to the interrelations of the impact of distinctive exploration in the area of romantic relationships and the size of friendship networks at age 23. To learn about social networks at age 23, we administered a form with three concentric circles with the word *you* in the middle. In the inner circle, they were to write the names of all the people "to whom you feel so close that it is hard to imagine life without them." In the middle circle, participants were to name "people to whom you might not feel quite that close, but who are still important to you." In the outer circle, participants were to include people "who are close enough and important enough in your life that they should be included in this circle." The total number of nonromantic friends indicated in the inner, middle, and outer network circle was calculated for each individual. Correlational analyses showed that the relation between friendship network size at age 23 and the number of dating partners during adolescence or emerging adulthood was nonsignificant. Nor was there a significant association between friendship network size at age 23 and the number of sexual partners during adolescence or emerging adulthood.

A second line of studies addresses the question of whether success in the salient developmental tasks of emerging adulthood is related to more successful functioning in adulthood. The prime example is work by Roisman, Masten, Coatsworth, and Tellegen (2004), which considers both predictors relevant to the developmental tasks of adolescence and those relevant to the developmental tasks of emerging adulthood in connection with adult adaptation (age 30). The authors conclude that "Work and romantic competence, reflecting successful engagement in emerging tasks during adolescence and the transition to adulthood, showed little prediction to adult outcomes as compared to the long-established salient developmental tasks of adolescence, including friendship, academic, and conduct-related competencies" (p. 18). Although noting that experiences in romantic relationships and work may have significant ramifications for psychosocial status during emerging adulthood, Roisman and colleagues believe that compared with adolescent developmental challenges, exploration and its associated states may not add significantly to predicting competence in adulthood, over and above indicators of exploration in adolescence.

These findings, like most of the evidence regarding the general question of distinctiveness, provide some evidence of exploration in the friendships and romantic relationships of 18- to 28-year-olds. The "phase two" evidence (Collins, 1993) is yet to come, however. What is needed now are studies examining exploration and the associated psychosocial phenomena suggested by Arnett (2000, 2004)—self-focus, feelings of being in-between, and continually imagining new possibilities—along with the duration, content, quality, and subjective experiences of close relationships involving emerging adults.

Instability and Uncertainty

In his second cluster of markers of emerging adulthood. Arnett (2000, 2004) viewed 18- to 28-year-olds as distinctive in their instability and in their feelings of uncertainty about both their present lives and their likely future pathways. In close relationships, especially romantic ones, instability is evident from frequent changes in living arrangements, including terminating cohabiting arrangements with romantic partners and with friends who may have become roommates. Frequent moves may disrupt contacts with friends, as well.

This contention, although plausible on demographic grounds if nothing else, is almost completely unstudied. The one exception appears to be Arnett's own interview study. The next step in research should be the development of appropriate instruments for assessing instability and uncertainty, followed by systematic studies in which representative samples of 18- to 28-year-olds, as well as both younger and older individuals, are included. A difficulty in making this step may well be transcending the distinctive demographics of emerging adults (living on one's own in a series of rooms or apartments, perhaps shared with a number of unrelated individuals). Nevertheless, if the goal is to examine the psychosocial distinctiveness of emerging adults, some standardization of measurement—or at least, carefully established functional equivalencies—across age groups is necessary.

Continuities and Discontinuities in Adolescence and Emerging Adulthood

An evaluation of the distinctiveness hypothesis is clearly premature, given the obvious gaps in research findings on close relationships. Nevertheless, several findings are suggestive. The most compelling evidence comes from the few explicit comparisons of individuals in the 18- to 28-year-old age range with other age groups (typically, adolescents). These comparisons constitute "phase one" (Collins, 1993) confirmation of Arnett's theorizing about distinctiveness. *Phase one* refers to findings that show some age-related differences clearly exist but that provide no evidence as to whether the differences can be attributed to the psychological and developmental processes suggested in Arnett's formulation. It is important to note, though, that the fragmentary evidence on these latter points falls short of the specificity that the hypotheses imply. In this case, resorting to the familiar bromide that "further research is needed" is not only justified, but responsible.

The existing age-group comparisons, on balance, reveal greater continuity than discontinuity between close relationships in adolescence and in emerging adulthood. The apparent contrasts imply a process of refinement, rather than of disjunction or redirection, of social and psychological functioning. Especially powerful is the consistent finding that the markers and the predictors of functioning in the close relationships of emerging adulthood are essentially the same as predictors of relationship competence in adolescence—and, for that matter, in childhood. Although less is known about the predictors of competent adult functioning, suggestive findings imply that similar predictors will be relevant (Reis et al., 2000).

Together, the longitudinal data encompassing emerging adulthood reiterate a key principle: Development in each new phase of life builds on development in previous phases (Collins & Sroufe, 1999). In light of the focus of this chapter, the issue is how extensive the observed similarities between emerging adults and younger and older adults must be before the hypothesis of distinctiveness is no longer viable. Some formulations contend that, far from being disjunctive from the teen years, the early and middle 20s represent a prolonged time for resolving the interpersonal issues and emphases that are typical of teens. For example, White, Speisman, and Costos (1983) found that relationships between parents and their 28-year-old children were just beginning to show a degree of equanimity following a period of disruption during adolescence (for reviews, see Collins, 1995; Grotevant, 1998). White and colleagues interpreted this finding as evidence that the realignments of adolescence are resolved only gradually and do not automatically cease when young people age beyond the years traditionally assigned to adolescence in a highly age-graded social system like that in the United States. A slightly different view emphasizes the nature of the transition from adolescent–parent relationships to relationships between parents and their emerging adult children. Ten- to 16-year-olds, for example, typically turn first to parents under highly stressful conditions, and even 18- to 22-year-olds often look to parents for emotional support when experiencing difficulties (Allen & Land, 1999; Fraley & Davis, 1997). These views, although differing in emphases, argue for functional transformations, rather than disjunctions, in the close relationships of individuals between the ages of 18 and 28. Finally, Ainsworth (1989) has argued that nonfamilial close relationships in emerging adulthood parallel the functional significance and general patterns of relationships at younger ages.

Evidence based on data collected from early adults, though useful sources of "phase one" information (Collins, 1993) generally, cannot address the foregoing predictions. Arnett's (2004) own reports of interviews with emerging adults provide invaluable windows into the subjective states of these young people. At the same time, the findings underscore the need for research that attends not only to an analysis of the themes of self-perceived distinctiveness of emerging adults but also to similar analyses of the themes in the discourse of middle and late adolescents, on the one hand, and those of 30-somethings, on the other. The most compelling accounts would come from longitudinal data sets in which repeated accounts are sought from the same individuals in, for example, their early teen years, early 20s, and early 30s. Whether the studies are cross-sectional or longitudinal, however, there is a pressing need for carefully developed measures that will be appropriate for all three age groups and thus will allow for comparisons across standard reporting devices and using standard metrics.

In addition, further research on the nature and significance of emerging adults' close relationships can be pursued most beneficially within the theoretical framework of the rapidly growing science of relationships (Reis et al., 2000). As an example, findings on interactions in close relationships imply that one aspect of the distinctiveness of emerging adults' close relationships may be the relative balance between closeness and conflict, compared with close relationships in adolescence. A focus on the impact of the unique joint patterns of interaction, emotion, and cognition between the two persons, rather than the actions, emotions, and thoughts of either one alone, requires attention to properties of both conflict and closeness. These terms refer to distinct but overlapping properties of relationships. *Closeness* is an umbrella term for the degree to which individuals affect and are affected by each other across time. Commonly invoked indicators include interdependence, intimacy, closeness, trust, and communication (Collins, 1995; Collins & Repinski, 1994). There is considerable continuity, however, between positive features of relationships during adolescence and those in earlier life, despite the altered patterns of interaction, emotion, and cognition (Allen & Land, 1999; Collins, 1995). Conflict, which is ubiquitous in close relationships, is best defined as disagreement and overt behavioral opposition, to distinguish it from other negative interactions (Laursen & Collins, 1994). A key implication of research findings is that indicators of the quality of conflict resolution (the degree to which conflicts are worked out to the satisfaction of both persons) rather than the incidence of conflict per se are important in assessing close relationships. Moreover, the content of, and balance between, expressions of closeness and disagreement substantially determines the impact of close relationships on individual development and functioning.

Theories of adolescent development give a central role to increasing conflict in relationships with parents and to increasing closeness with peers and extrafamilial adults (for a review, see Laursen & Collins, 1994). Surveys of adolescents indicate that disagreements are most common with mothers, followed by siblings, friends, and romantic partners, then fathers; angry disputes arise more frequently with family members than with close peers (Laursen, 1996). These findings underscore the fact that, as voluntary relationships, friendships and romantic partners provide more options for responses to conflict, including leaving the relationship, than do involuntary relationships with parents and siblings. As a consequence, friends and romantic partners are more highly motivated to reach mutually acceptable resolutions of conflict to preserve their connection. It may be that as 18- to 28-year-olds interact with family members less often and are less answerable to parents for their actions, they experience less conflict in relationships than in earlier periods. Living outside regular partnerships may be a factor in this possible decline, as well.

These and other examples underscore a key point: the scientific and, ultimately, the practical significance of the psychological distinctiveness of emerging adulthood rests on its usefulness in illuminating the nature and course of human development. Arnett's (2000, 2004) proposals are providing a stimulant to reconsider both the theoretical and the empirical foundations of developmentalists' views of the years just after adolescence. The manifestations of distinctiveness in the close relationships of 18- to 28-year-olds provide a compelling arena in which to undertake that reconsideration.

References

Ainsworth, M. D. S. (1989). Attachments beyond infancy. *American Psychologist, 44,* 709–716.

Allen, J. P., & Land, D. (1999). Attachment in adolescence. In J. Cassidy & P. R. Shaver (Eds.), *Handbook of attachment: Theory, research, and clinical applications* (pp. 319–335). New York: Guilford Press.

Arnett, J. J. (2000). Emerging adulthood: A theory of development from the late teens through the twenties. *American Psychologist, 54,* 317–326.

Arnett, J. J. (2004). *Emerging adulthood: The winding road from the late teens through the twenties.* New York: Oxford University Press.

Berscheid, E., Snyder, M., & Omoto, A. (1989). The Relationships Closeness Inventory: Assessing the closeness of interpersonal relationships. *Journal of Personality and Social Psychology, 57,* 792–807.

Brown, B. B. (2004). Adolescents' relationships with peers. In R. Lerner & L. Steinberg (Eds.), *Handbook of adolescent psychology* (pp. 363–394). New York: Wiley.

Collins, W. A. (1993). From phase 1 findings to phase 2 questions: New directions in research on fathers' roles in adolescent development. In S. Shulman & W. A. Collins (Eds.), *New directions for child development: Vol. 62. Father–adolescent relationships and their developmental significance* (pp. 91–96). San Francisco: Jossey-Bass.

Collins, W. A. (1995). Relationships and development: Family adaptation to individual change. In S. Shulman (Ed.), *Close relationships and socioemotional development* (pp. 128–154). New York: Ablex Publishing.

Collins, W. A. (2003). More than myth: The developmental significance of romantic relationships during adolescence. *Journal of Research on Adolescence, 13,* 1–24.

Collins, W. A., & Laursen, B. (2000). Adolescent relationships: The art of fugue. In C. Hendrick & S. Hendrick (Eds.), *Close relationships: A sourcebook* (pp. 59–70). Thousand Oaks, CA: Sage.

Collins, W. A., & Laursen, B. (2004). Parent–adolescent relationships and influence. In R. Lerner & L. Steinberg (Eds.), *Handbook of adolescent psychology* (pp. 331–362). New York: Wiley.

Collins, W. A., & Madsen, S. D. (2002, August). Relational histories and trajectories of later romantic experiences. In W. A. Collins & S. Shulman (Chairs), *Trajectories in the development of romantic relationships: Childhood and adolescent precursors of interpersonal transitions.* Symposium conducted at the conference of the International Society for the Study of Behavioral Development, Ottawa, Ontario, Canada.

Collins, W. A., & Repinski, D. J. (1994). Relationships during adolescence: Continuity and change in interpersonal perspective. In R. Montemayor, G. Adams, & T. Gullotta (Eds.), *Advances in adolescent development: Vol. 5. Personal relationships during adolescence* (pp. 7–36). Beverly Hills, CA: Sage.

Collins, W. A., & Sroufe, L. A. (1999). Capacity for intimate relationships: A developmental construction. In W. Furman, B. B. Brown, & C. Feiring (Eds.), *Contemporary perspectives on adolescent romantic relationships* (pp. 123–147). New York: Cambridge University Press.

Connolly, J., & Goldberg, A. (1999). Romantic relationships in adolescence: The role of friends and peers in their emergence and development. In W. Furman, B. B. Brown, & C. Feiring (Eds.), *Contemporary perspectives on adolescent romantic relationships* (pp. 266–290). New York: Cambridge University Press.

Erikson, E. H. (1968). *Identity: Youth and crisis*. New York: Norton.

Fraley, R. C., & Davis, K. E. (1997). Attachment formation and transfer in young adults' close friendships and romantic relationships. *Personal Relationships, 4,* 131–144.

Furman, W., & Buhrmester, D. (1992). Age and sex differences in perceptions of networks and personal relationships. *Child Development, 63,* 103–115.

Furman, W., Simon, V. A., Shaffer, L., & Bouchey, H. A. (2002). Adolescents' working models and styles for relationships with parents, friends, and romantic partners. *Child Development, 73,* 241–255.

Grotevant, H. D. (1998). Adolescent development in family contexts. In W. Damon & N. Eisenberg (Eds.), *Handbook of child psychology: Vol. 3. Social, emotional, and personality development* (5th ed., pp. 1097–1150). New York: Wiley.

Hartup, W. W., & Stevens, N. (1999). Friendships and adaptation across the life span. *Current Issues in Psychological Science, 8,* 76–79.

Hinde, R. (1979). *Towards understanding relationships*. London: Academic Press.

Huston, T., Niehuis, S., & Smith, S. (2001). The early marital roots of conjugal distress and divorce. *Current Directions in Psychological Science, 10,* 116–119.

Laursen, B. (1996). Closeness and conflict in adolescent peer relationships: Interdependence with friends and romantic partners. In W. M. Bukowski, A. F. Newcomb, & W. W. Hartup (Eds.), *The company they keep: Friendship in childhood and adolescence* (pp. 186–210). New York: Cambridge University Press.

Laursen, B., & Bukowski, W. M. (1997). A developmental guide to the organisation of close relationships. *International Journal of Behavioral Development, 21,* 747–770.

Laursen, B., & Collins, W. A. (1994). Interpersonal conflict during adolescence. *Psychological Bulletin, 115,* 197–209.

Laursen, B., & Jensen-Campbell, L. A. (1999). The nature and functions of social exchange in adolescent romantic relationships. In W. Furman, B. B. Brown, & C. Feiring (Eds.), *Contemporary perspectives on adolescent romantic relationships* (pp. 50–74). New York: Cambridge University Press.

Laursen, B., & Williams, V. (1997). Perceptions of interdependence and closeness in family and peer relationships among adolescents with and without romantic partners. In S. Shulman & W. A. Collins (Eds.), *New directions for child development: Vol. 78. Romantic relationships in adolescence: Developmental perspectives* (pp. 3–20). San Francisco: Jossey-Bass.

Maccoby, E. E. (1998). *The two sexes: Growing up apart, coming together*. Cambridge, MA: Harvard University Press.

Neeman, J., Hubbard, J., & Masten, A. S. (1995). The changing importance of romantic relationship involvement to competence from late childhood to adolescence. *Development and Psychopathology, 7,* 727–750.

Oswald, D. L., & Clark, E. M. (2003). Best friends forever? High school best friendships and the transition to college. *Personal Relationships, 10,* 187–196.

Owens, G., Crowell, J., Pan, H., Treboux, D., O'Connor, E., & Waters, E. (1995). The prototype hypothesis and the origins of attachment working models: Adult relationships with parents and romantic partners. *Monographs of the Society for Research in Child Development, 60*(2–3, Serial No. 244), 216–233.

Regan, P. C., Kocan, E. R., & Whitlock, T. (1998). Ain't love grand! A prototype analysis of romantic love. *Journal of Social and Personal Relationships, 15,* 411–420.

Reis, H., Collins, W. A., & Berscheid, E. (2000). The relationship context of human behavior and development. *Psychological Bulletin, 126,* 844–872.

Reis, H. T., Lin, Y.-C., Bennett, M. E., & Nezlek, J. B. (1993). Change and consistency in social participation during early adulthood. *Developmental Psychology, 29,* 633–645.

Roisman, G. I., Madsen, S. D., Hennighausen, K. H., Sroufe, L. A., & Collins, W. A. (2001). The coherence of dyadic behavior across parent-child and romantic relationships as mediated by the internalized representation of experience. *Attachment and Human Development, 3,* 156–172.

Roisman, G., Masten, A., Coatsworth, J. D., & Tellegen, A. (2004). Salient and emerging developmental tasks in the transition to adulthood. *Child Development, 75,* 123–133.

Shulman, S., & Levan, E. (2002, April). Predicting longevity of adolescent romantic relationships: Individual and dyadic attributes. In S. Shulman & I. Seiffge-Krenke (Co-chairs), *Antecedents of the quality and stability of adolescent romantic relationships.* Symposium conducted at the conference of the Society for Research on Adolescence, New Orleans, LA.

Sprecher, S., & Felmlee, D. (1992). The influence of parents and friends on the quality and stability of romantic relationships: A three-wave longitudinal investigation. *Journal of Marriage and the Family, 54,* 888–900.

Sroufe, L. A., Egeland, B., Carlson, E. A., & Collins, W. A. (2005). *The development of the person.* New York: Guilford Press.

Sullivan, H. S. (1953). *The interpersonal theory of psychiatry.* New York: Norton.

Surra, C. (1990). Research and theory on mate selection and premarital relationships in the 1980s. *Journal of Marriage and the Family, 52,* 844–865.

Treboux, D., Crowell, J. A., Owens, G., & Pan, H. S. (1994, February). *Attachment behaviors and working models: Relations to best friendship and romantic relationships.* Paper presented at the Society for Research on Adolescence, San Diego, CA.

Waldinger, R. J., Diguer, L, Guastella, F., Lefebvre, R., Allen, J. P., Luborsky, L., et al. (2002). The same old song? Stability and change in relationship schemas from adolescence to young adulthood. *Journal of Youth and Adolescence, 31,* 17–44.

Waters, E., Merrick, S., Albersheim, L., Treboux, D., & Crowell, J. (2000). Attachment from infancy to early adulthood: A 20-year longitudinal study of relations between infant Strange Situation classifications and attachment representations in adulthood. *Child Development, 71,* 684–689.

White, K. M., Speisman, J. C., & Costos, D. (1983). Young adults and their parents: Individuation to mutuality. In H. Grotevant & C. Cooper (Eds.), *New directions for child development: Vol. 22. Adolescent development in the family* (pp. 61–76). San Francisco: Jossey-Bass.

Zimmer-Gembeck, M. J., & Collins, W. A. (2003). Autonomy development during adolescence. In G. R. Adams & M. D. Berzonsky (Eds.), *Blackwell handbook of adolescence* (pp. 175–204). Malden, MA: Blackwell Publishing.

10

"Sex Is Just a Normal Part of Life": Sexuality in Emerging Adulthood

Eva S. Lefkowitz and Meghan M. Gillen

When we asked college students how their views about sex changed since they began college (Lefkowitz, 2005), a 23-year-old female wrote, "I didn't start having sex until I came to college. So everything I know about sex has evolved since freshman days. My views have changed from curiosity about sex to knowing myself and enjoying sex." A 19-year-old female provided a more succinct response: "Sex can be fun and not as scary as your parents think it is." As expressed by these young women, one of the major tasks of emerging adulthood is the establishment of intimacy, which often includes sexual intimacy (Erikson, 1950; Sullivan, 1953). The average age at first sexual intercourse is 16 or 17 (Alan Guttmacher Institute [AGI], 1994); the average age at first marriage is almost 27 for males, and 25 for females (U.S. Census Bureau, 2001). Thus, emerging adulthood corresponds to the years that the majority of individuals are both sexually active and unmarried.

Many of the reasons for becoming sexually active, particularly love and exploration, appear to be similar during adolescence and emerging adulthood. During emerging adulthood, sexuality may be influenced by the various changes that occur in the areas of identity, residence, and relationships (Arnett, 2000). Identity exploration during emerging adulthood may include exploration of sexual orientation, and sexual beliefs regarding abstinence, premarital sex, monogamy, contraception, and sexual behaviors. Moving away from the parents' home may result in increased freedom and, as a consequence, exploration and experimentation with sexual behaviors. Involvement in intimate and romantic relationships may situate sexual behaviors within the context of emotional connections.

To date, no theories of sexuality adequately address the development of sexual behavior and beliefs in emerging adulthood. Biological theories focus on pubertal development and hormonal activation, making these theories more

Support for the preparation of this chapter was provided by the National Institute of Child Health and Human Development (R-01 HD 41720). Conversations and collaborations with the following colleagues have contributed to the ideas presented in this chapter: Tanya Boone, Graciela Espinosa-Hernandez, Shelley Hosterman, Eric Loken, Jennifer Maggs, Susan McHale, and Cindy Shearer.

235

relevant for adolescents than for emerging adults (Rodgers & Rowe, 1993; Udry, Billy, Morris, Gruff, & Raj, 1985). Problem behavior theories posit that adolescent sexual behaviors exist within a constellation of other problem behaviors and share their antecedents (e.g., Jessor & Jessor, 1975; Newcomb, Huba, & Bentler, 1986). Although we acknowledge that certain sexual behaviors may pose risks for a number of emerging adults, we do not take a strict problem behavior perspective on sexuality in emerging adulthood. Responsible sexual behaviors between two consenting emerging adults is not necessarily linked with negative psychological or physical consequences (Bingham & Crockett, 1996; Ensminger, 1990). Theories focusing on attitudes and beliefs that predict sexual behavior include the theory of planned behavior (Ajzen, 1985) and the health belief model (Maiman & Becker, 1974; Rosenstock, 1974). Although these theories have resulted in understanding important links between beliefs, attitudes, and subjective norms and sexual and contraceptive behavior, they assume a rational being and ignore contextual factors such as the sexual partner and the individual's relationship with him or her (Brown, DiClemente, & Reynolds, 1991) as well as personal attitudes about topics other than HIV and sex, such as gender role beliefs or ethnic identity. Finally, social influence theories (Fisher, 1988; Sutherland, 1947) address how the social influence of parents and peers affects adolescents' sexual behavior. Although evidence suggests that parent and peer influence may be important in adolescence and even into emerging adulthood, it is important also to recognize both more context-specific and broader influences. At the context-specific level, one's relationship with one's partner is likely to influence one's sexual behaviors. At the broader institutional level, religious institutions, college and work environments, and societal mores are likely to influence one's own sexual beliefs and behaviors.

Thus, no single existing theory adequately addresses sexual behavior in emerging adults. Sociosexual behavior is by nature interactive, and attitude models ignore social context. Most models are universalistic, assuming that attitudes and social influences will relate to behaviors similarly across gender and ethnic groups. Yet, empirical evidence suggests differential risks of HIV-related behavior between these groups (Costa, Jessor, Donovan, & Fortenberry, 1995; Perkins, Luster, Villarruel, & Small, 1998). Most models also fail to account for development beyond puberty or first sexual intercourse because they focus mainly on the transition from virginity to nonvirginity.

Research on emerging adulthood mirrors some of the limitations of the theoretical perspectives. The majority of research relies on White, convenience samples of college students, thus limiting researchers' ability to understand sexuality among noncollege or minority individuals. Most research on sexuality in emerging adulthood takes a risk-focused approach, examining the factors that predict safer sex or risky sexual behaviors. However, sexual behavior in emerging adulthood is normative, and therefore a strict risk focus does not capture the range of behaviors and beliefs in this period of development. For a true understanding of sexuality in emerging adulthood to develop, an understanding of the context of normative behaviors between two individuals needs to be incorporated. Not only their behaviors but also the desires, emotions, decision processes, and motivations surrounding these behaviors need to be understood.

Next we summarize what is known about sexual behaviors and beliefs in emerging adulthood. Although, as previously described, we do not take a strict risk focus on sexuality in emerging adulthood, much of our review focuses on risk because of the focus of prior empirical work. We then provide suggestions for future directions on examining sexuality in emerging adulthood.

Sexual Behavior

At the start of emerging adulthood (age 18), approximately half of individuals are sexually active (Siegel, Klein, & Roghmann, 1999). By the end of emerging adulthood (age 25), almost all have become sexually active (Michael, Gagnon, Laumann, & Kolata, 1994). These rates may differ by gender. Males become sexually active earlier than do females and therefore are more likely to be sexually active at the beginning of emerging adulthood. However, for both males and females, first intercourse is more likely to happen in adolescence than in emerging adulthood. By emerging adulthood, males report on average more lifetime partners than do females (MacNair-Semands & Simono, 1996; Poppen, 1995). Males also report having had more casual partners (Poppen, 1995). It is not surprising, then, that females report being more selective about their partners than do males (Hawkins, Gray, & Hawkins, 1995). Gender differences in sexual behavior, however, should be interpreted with caution. Because males and females are predominantly reporting on heterosexual behavior, gender differences in number of lifetime partners may reflect differences in reporting rather than differences in actual behavior.

There are also ethnic group differences in sexual behavior. Research suggests that African Americans are more likely to have multiple partners than are European Americans or Latino Americans (Centers for Disease Control [CDC], 2000a; Samuels, 1997). Asian Americans tend to become sexually active at later ages than do European Americans or African Americans and are less likely to engage in vaginal or oral sex (Baldwin, Whiteley, & Baldwin, 1992). In addition, Asian Americans tend to have had fewer lifetime partners than have European Americans (McLaughlin, Chen, Greenberger, & Biermeier, 1997). The extent to which ethnic differences are explained by socioeconomic status remains unclear, though, given that individuals from lower socioeconomic status backgrounds tend to become sexually active at earlier ages (Baldwin et al., 1992; Samuels, 1997). It is important to note that by the middle to the end of emerging adulthood, gender and ethnic differences appear to taper off, and similar proportions of these groups are sexually active, although there may still be differences in lifetime partners and other behaviors among those who are sexually active.

For the average emerging adult, it is common to have had only one sexual partner in the past year; this is true for close to 60% of individuals aged 18 to 24 (Critelli & Suire, 1998; Michael et al., 1994). Still, compared with older individuals, emerging adults are more likely to have had two or more partners.

At least one third of 18- to 24-year-olds have had two or more partners in the past year (including 9% who have had five or more partners; Civic, 1999; Critelli & Suire, 1998; Michael et al., 1994). In contrast, about a quarter of individuals aged 25 to 29 have had two or more partners. In addition, about a quarter of college students have had six or more lifetime partners (Douglas et al., 1997).

Although emerging adults are more likely to have more partners than are older individuals, they tend to have sex less frequently (Michael et al., 1994). For instance, 36% of emerging adult males have had sex only a few times or not at all in the past year; this figure contrasts with 22% to 27% of men aged 25 to 49 and is slightly higher than the rate for men aged 50 to 59. Twenty-seven percent of emerging adult women report no or infrequent sex in the past year; this figure is higher than it is for individuals aged 25 to 39, although rates of infrequent sex are higher among women age 40 and older.

The experience of casual sex may be relatively common in emerging adulthood. In one study, 30% of emerging adults reported at least one experience of hooking up and having sexual intercourse during college, with an additional 48% reporting one or more hookups that did not involve intercourse (Paul, McManus, & Hayes, 2000). Hooking up may be more common for males than for females and very infrequently leads to a future relationship (12% of the time). These numbers appear to be higher than at other ages (Michael et al., 1994), perhaps because of the exploration and freedom associated with this developmental period.

Sexual Attitudes

Less is known about how the sexual attitudes of emerging adults differ from younger or older individuals. Some evidence does suggest that college students feel more accepting of casual sex and feel less guilt about sex than do younger individuals (Chara & Kuennen, 1994; Miller & Moore, 1990). In terms of attitudes toward sexual intimacy, males tend to be more likely than females to engage in sexual behaviors with nonromantic partners: Males more than females report willingness to have intercourse with someone they had known for only 3 hours, to have sex with two different partners within the same day, and to have sex with someone they did not love or someone with whom they did not have a good relationship (Knox, Sturdivant, & Zusman, 2001). There is also evidence that both male and female emerging adults continue to endorse a sexual double standard that allows men more sexual freedom than women (Crawford & Popp, 2003).

In a study of college students' own perceptions of changes in their views about sex since beginning college, 46% of participants described changes in their attitudes (Lefkowitz, 2005). The most common attitudinal changes were becoming less judging and more open-minded (although no particular type of attitudinal change was described by more than 10% of the sample). Participants described these changes in predominantly positive ways. There was some difference depending on year in college, with students who had been at school longer more likely to report attitudinal changes and to describe changes in more positive ways.

Predictors of Sexual Behavior

Age of onset of sexual behavior is associated with level of risk. In particular, individuals who become sexually active during emerging adulthood tend to engage in fewer risky behaviors than do those who began in adolescence (Capaldi, Stoolmiller, Clark, & Owen, 2002; Langer, Warheit, & McDonald, 2001). In addition, older college students tend to engage in riskier sexual behaviors than do younger students (Langer et al., 2001). Males are more likely than females to engage in risky sexual behaviors (Langer et al., 2001).

Emerging adults who perceive themselves as more attractive tend to have more sexual partners than do those who perceive themselves as less attractive (McLaughlin et al., 1997). Other researchers have found that the association between body image and risky sexual behavior differs for males and females (Gillen & Lefkowitz, 2005). As in McLaughlin et al.'s work, males' more positive body image was associated with riskier sexual behavior. The finding was different for females, however, for whom having a more positive body image was associated with less risky sexual behaviors. Traditional attitudes about gender also appear to be associated with risky sexual behavior. For instance, males (but not females) with more traditional views of masculinity tend to engage in riskier sexual behaviors and have riskier condom-related attitudes than do less traditional males. In addition, for both males and females, more traditional attitudes about family roles and endorsement of the sexual double standard are associated with riskier condom-related attitudes (Shearer, Hosterman, Gillen, & Lefkowitz, 2005). Risky sexual behaviors are associated with level of functioning in other areas. For instance, emerging adults who engage in antisocial behaviors are more likely than others to engage in risky sexual behaviors and to get sexually transmitted infections (STIs; Capaldi et al., 2002).

Religiosity is associated with sexual behaviors and attitudes. Sexually abstinent emerging adults attend religious services more frequently and feel religion has a more important role in their daily lives than do sexually active individuals (Jessor & Jessor, 1975; Lefkowitz, Gillen, Shearer, & Boone, 2004). Among those who are sexually active, more religious emerging adults tend to have had fewer lifetime partners and engage in fewer risky behaviors (Langer et al., 2001; Lefkowitz et al., 2004). Religiosity is also associated with sexual attitudes. More religious individuals tend to hold more conservative attitudes about sex, have more negative beliefs about condoms' preventive abilities, and tend to perceive more barriers to condom use (Lefkowitz et al., 2004).

A number of sex-specific attitudinal and personal concept measures are associated with sexual risk taking. Individuals who engage in riskier sex tend to have more positive and fewer negative expectancies of the outcomes of sexual behavior, higher perceived vulnerability to HIV, more positive condom attitudes, and lower sexual self-efficacy (Boone & Lefkowitz, 2004; Langer et al., 2001).

It may be difficult for emerging adults to correctly estimate their risks with a current partner given the partner's potential motivation to lie. Although almost half of individuals in one study reported almost always asking their new partner about previous sexual partners (Moore & Davidson, 2000), as many as half of males and about 10% of females admitted to lying to their partners or failing to disclose STI status or past risky sexual behaviors (Cochran & Mays, 1990; Desiderato & Crawford, 1995). In addition, 36% of males and 21% of females have reported being unfaithful to a partner (Stebleton & Rothenberger, 1993). Therefore, many emerging adults do engage in sexual behaviors that are known to be associated with dangerous or unwanted outcomes, such as STIs or unplanned pregnancy.

Virginity

By the time they reach emerging adulthood, the majority of individuals have been presented with opportunities for sexual intercourse (Sprecher & Regan, 1996). Therefore, individuals who remain abstinent into emerging adulthood are likely to be active abstainers, rather than accidental abstainers. Although little research has examined correlates of virginity in emerging adulthood per se, some important correlates are religious involvement and being Asian or Asian American (Feldman et al., 1997; McLaughlin et al., 1997).

In addition to correlates of virginity (i.e., differences between virgins and nonvirgins), it is important to consider individuals' stated reasons for remaining virgins in emerging adulthood. Research by Sprecher and Regan (1996) suggests that the most common reasons to be a virgin in emerging adulthood are fear of negative outcomes such as pregnancy, AIDS, STIs, and feeling as though one has not been in a relationship long enough or has not yet met the right person. Less common reasons, which are still used somewhat frequently, involve a set of personal beliefs that includes religion, morality, and fear of parental disapproval. The least commonly reported reason for remaining a virgin is feeling inadequate or insecure, including feelings of embarrassment, unattractiveness, lack of desire, and an unwilling partner. Women are more likely than men to report fear, personal beliefs, and relationship commitment, whereas men are more likely than women to report inadequacy as a reason not to be sexually active. Both male and female virgins tend to report a mixture of pride and anxiety about their virginity status, although women tend to report more positive and fewer negative feelings than do men. Also, men are more likely than women to plan to become sexually active in the near future, whereas women are more likely than men to feel pressure to remain a virgin. Thus, individuals who remain virgins through all or most of emerging adulthood tend to have strong motivations to do so.

Sexual Minority Emerging Adults

Most lesbian, gay, bisexual, and transgendered (LGBT) individuals experience their first same-sex sexual attraction, same-sex sexual behavior, and self-labeling as LGBT during adolescence (Savin-Williams & Diamond, 2000). Therefore, by emerging adulthood, the majority of LGBT individuals already consider themselves to be LGBT. Of course, these data are based on means, and the range of these experiences is certainly inclusive of emerging adulthood. In fact, Lindley, Nicholson, Kerby, and Lu (2003) found that 10% to 11% of

LGBT college students reported their first same-sex attraction at age 19 or older, and 16% of males and 23% of females first acknowledged their sexual orientation at age 19 or older. Thus, some individuals experience first same-sex attraction, behavior, or labeling as LGBT during emerging adulthood. For many LGBT individuals, their first same-sex relationship, unlike their first same-sex sexual experience, happens during emerging adulthood; for instance, on average, sexual minority males have their first relationship between ages 17 and 19 (Dubé & Savin-Williams, 1999).

There are somewhat more mixed findings about first disclosure of sexual orientation or coming out. Some research suggests that average disclosure happens around age 16 or 17 (e.g., D'Augelli & Hershberger, 1993; Rosario, Rotheram-Borus, & Reid, 1996) or age 17 or 18 (Dubé & Savin-Williams, 1999). However, Savin-Williams and Diamond (2000) found that first sexual disclosure happened on average around age 18, which suggests that many individuals first come out to others during emerging adulthood. They suggest that their findings differ from others because their sample was college students and not recruited through community support groups. Whatever the reason, it is clear that although most LGBT individuals identify and engage in same-sex behaviors in adolescence, many do not talk about it with family or friends until emerging adulthood.

The period of emerging adulthood involves identity exploration in many domains, and sexual orientation and behavior are no different. There is some evidence that a minority of women—about one quarter—who identify as lesbian or bisexual during emerging adulthood relinquish this identity during emerging adulthood as well (Diamond, 2003). It is important to note that only half of these women begin to label themselves as heterosexual; the other half no longer label themselves as lesbian, bisexual, or heterosexual. It is also important to note that these women tend to have fewer same-sex attractions and engage in fewer same-sex behaviors before relinquishing their identity than do their nonrelinquishing peers. However, none of these women fully relinquish same-sex attraction. Therefore, although their self-labels and often their behaviors change, their attraction to women remains. These findings demonstrate the importance of distinguishing identity or self-labels from attraction and recognizing that like many other aspects of identity development, there is fluidity in one's sexual identity (Diamond, 2000; Diamond & Savin-Williams, 2000).

Condom and Contraceptive Use

Rates of condom use decline with age, with adolescents more likely than emerging adults to use condoms (Capaldi et al., 2002). These decreases are most likely due to the fact that condom use is less common with close relationship partners than with casual sexual partners (Misovich, Fisher, & Fisher, 1997; Oncale & King, 2001). When rates of condom use are examined, three of the most important rates to consider are those who consistently use condoms, those who infrequently or never use condoms, and whether a condom was used at most recent intercourse. Although data on consistent use vary dramatically across studies and depend on definitions, evidence suggests that 17% to 43%

of emerging adults use condoms consistently (Desiderato & Crawford, 1995; Eisenberg, 2001; Hogben & Williams, 2001; Oncale & King, 2001). At the other end of the spectrum, 10% to 25% of emerging adults never or infrequently use condoms (Eisenberg, 2001; MacNair-Semands & Simono, 1996). According to one study, at their most recent sexual intercourse, 43% of emerging adults used condoms (Freimuth, Hammond, Edgar, McDonald, & Fink, 1992). Condoms do appear to be the most commonly used contraceptive choice for emerging adults, with more than 50% reporting condoms as their primary contraceptive method in the past month (Civic, 1999; Siegel et al., 1999). However, they are clearly used in inconsistent ways, and few emerging adults are using them in the majority of their sexual encounters. Condoms may not always be used correctly, either. Evidence suggests that applying a condom after initial penetration is relatively common among college students, particularly with regular partners (de Visser & Smith, 2000).

Sex with a new partner is more likely to involve condom use than is sex with a regular partner, with as many as 50% of emerging adults reporting condom use their first time with a new partner, and 81% reporting using condoms during a hookup (Cooper, Agocha, & Powers, 1999; Corbin & Fromme, 2002; Oncale & King, 2001; Paul et al., 2000). It is interesting to note that when individuals do not use another form of contraception, condoms are used approximately 60% of the time, whether with a casual or monogamous partner (Critelli & Suire, 1998). However, when another method of contraception is used, condoms are much more likely to be used in casual (58%) than in monogamous (28%) relationships. In fact, when asked why they use condoms, 41% of emerging adults said to prevent pregnancy, 11% said to prevent STIs, and 48% said to prevent both (Cooper et al., 1999). Thus, a substantial proportion of emerging adults are viewing condoms' role in their own sexual behaviors as protection against pregnancy more than as STI prevention.

Slightly less than 40% of emerging adults report using the birth control pill with their current partner (Civic, 1999; Hogben & Williams, 2001; Siegel et al., 1999). One possible reason for using oral contraception rather than condoms is that it may involve less hassle and is actually more effective at preventing pregnancy. However, there are emotional reasons for emerging adults to transition to oral contraception, particularly in committed relationships. There is evidence that emerging adults perceive the change from condoms to birth control pills as a significant transition in a relationship, signifying more trust and commitment (Hammer, Fisher, Fitzgerald, & Fisher, 1996).

Few (6%) emerging adults report never using a contraceptive method, although more than a quarter report inconsistent use of contraception (Civic, 1999; Hogben & Williams, 2001). However, some emerging adults report using less effective contraception, such as withdrawal (9%) or the rhythm method (4%; Hogben & Williams, 2001).

Condom use, like sexual behaviors, is predicted by both demographic and individual factors. Males report more consistent condom use than do females (Brown, DiClemente, & Park, 1992; Leigh, Morrison, Trocki, & Temple, 1994). As with general sexual behaviors, gender differences in condom use should be interpreted with caution, as they may reflect reporting differences more than behavioral differences. It is possible that the questions themselves are ambiguous (e.g., females may interpret questions such as "Did you use a condom?" to be asking whether they actively used one rather than did their partner use one), or that males feel more comfortable reporting condom use.

Another important factor is attitudes about condoms. Individuals who believe that condoms interfere with pleasure or are embarrassed about buying condoms are less likely to use condoms (Lewis, Malow, & Ireland, 1997). In addition, more general positive attitudes about sex and communicating with one's partner are associated with a greater likelihood of condom use (Boone & Lefkowitz, 2004; Lefkowitz, Boone, & Shearer, 2004). African Americans may be more positive than college students from other ethnic groups about condoms and may be more likely to use them (Beckman & Harvey, 1996).

Although many emerging adults recognize the protective value of using condoms, many also admit to having attempted to convince a partner not to use condoms (Oncale & King, 2001). In one study, 14% of females and 17% of males described having tried to dissuade a partner from using condoms, and 30% of males and 41% of females reported having had a partner attempt to dissuade them from using condoms. The reasons they provided to the partner were relatively similar for males and females and included that sex feels better without a condom, that the female would not get pregnant or that the partner would not get an STI, or that not using one would emphasize love and intimacy in the relationship. In summary, although most emerging adults use some form of contraception the majority of the time, usage is inconsistent and thus may put individuals at risk. Individual differences in demographic characteristics and attitudes help to explain much of the variation in rates of contraceptive behavior.

Pregnancy and Parenthood

For many emerging adults, the potential consequences of sexual behavior—pregnancy and parenthood—are important considerations. During adolescence, pregnancy may pose risks to both young mothers and their children. Female adolescents who give birth are more likely to come from families with lower levels of education and income (Singh, Darroch, & Frost, 2001). Because of living in more disadvantaged environments, these adolescents may have less access to health care and fewer opportunities to pursue higher education and to obtain good-paying jobs. As a consequence, adolescent mothers and their children are at increased risk for various physical and emotional health problems.

Less attention has been devoted to pregnancy during emerging adulthood. National data on college students suggest that 15% of college students have experienced their own or a partner's pregnancy (Douglas et al., 1997). The pregnancy rate is higher in emerging adulthood than it is in adolescence. Specifically, among adolescents aged 15 to 17, the rate is 59 pregnancies per 1,000 women per year; among those 18 or 19 years old, the rate is 140 per 1,000; and among those aged 20 to 24, it is 164 per 1,000 (Henshaw, 1998). There are also differences in pregnancy intent between adolescents and emerging adults. Whereas 83% of adolescents (ages 15–17) report that their pregnancies were unintended, 75% of 18- to 19-year-olds and 59% of 20- to 24-year-olds report unplanned pregnancies (Henshaw, 1998). The higher pregnancy rates and lower rates of unintended pregnancies among emerging adults relative to adolescents may be due to their increased likelihood of cohabiting with a partner or being married (AGI, 2002). Thus, becoming pregnant during emerging adulthood in comparison to adolescence may be somewhat less risky for mothers and their children because the mothers may be in more committed relationships from which they can garner physical, emotional, and financial support.

Although pregnancy might pose less of a risk in the context of a committed relationship, it may limit women's exploration in multiple domains, an experience that is salient for many individuals during emerging adulthood (Arnett, 2000). For example, raising a child during emerging adulthood may limit women's opportunities for exploring educational and career options. In the United States, women aged 20 to 24 with the lowest levels of education are more likely than their better educated peers to have had a child before age 20 (Singh et al., 2001). It is possible that early childbearing, through the financial and time constraints it may impose, may interfere with the opportunity to pursue higher education and preclude individuals from being exposed to various career options and different views of the world. Research shows that although most adolescent mothers complete high school, they are less likely than their peers who have not had children to enter college (AGI, 1999). Besides education, early childbearing may also limit exploration of romantic relationships with individuals other than the child's father, and for women who are single, it may also leave little time for dating. Thus, pregnancy and childrearing in emerging adulthood may pose fewer risks to mothers and their children than in adolescence, but it may nonetheless limit their ability to engage in exploration during this developmental period.

Abortion

Women who become pregnant and feel that giving birth is not an option may elect to have an abortion. Torres and Forrest (1988) found that the three most important reasons women give for choosing an abortion are not being able to afford a baby, being unready for the responsibility, and feeling that one's life would change too much after the birth of the child. Nearly all women (95%) provided at least one reason for choosing abortion; the mean number of reasons offered was 3.7.

How common is it for emerging adults to have an abortion? The likelihood of obtaining an abortion is measured by the abortion ratio, or the percentage of pregnancies that end in abortion (excluding miscarriages; Darroch, Singh, Frost, & Study Team, 2001). For women aged 18 to 19 who become pregnant, 35% elect to have an abortion; the ratio is similar among women aged 20 to 24 (32%), but it drops through the late 30s, and then begins to rise (Henshaw, 1998). Data collected in the 1980s also demonstrate this pattern (Henshaw, Koonin, & Smith, 1991). These changes may reflect the fact that beyond emerging adulthood women are more likely to become pregnant in the context of marriage but that beginning in the late 30s when fertility begins to decline, more women may be concerned about health complications associated with later childbearing.

The decision to have an abortion differs by various demographic characteristics. Abortion statistics for different demographic groups are typically presented in two ways: the abortion ratio, as previously described, and the abortion rate (percentage of women in a subgroup who have an abortion in a given year; Henshaw et al., 1991). The abortion rate is higher during emerging adulthood than in any other period of life. In 1987, among women aged 18 to 19, the rate was 62 per 1,000 women and among those aged 20 to 24 it was 52 per 1,000 women. The rate decreases steadily for women in their middle 20s and beyond— ages 25 to 29 (30), ages 30 to 34 (18), ages 35 to 39 (10), and ages 40 and older (3; Henshaw et al., 1991).

Other work has examined the characteristics of women who have abortions and found that most women who do so are in their 20s (54%–56%). Adolescents account for relatively fewer of the women having abortions (12%–19%), as do women in their 30s (18%–22%). In terms of marital status, women who are unmarried (82%–83%) account for the majority of abortions (Henshaw et al., 1991; Jones, Darroch, & Henshaw, 2002). Although Henshaw et al.'s data from the 1980s show that White women represent the majority of individuals who have abortions, Jones et al.'s more recent data indicate that minority women make up more than half of women having abortions. Black women in particular report significantly higher rates of unintended pregnancy compared with White women. Their greater need for abortion services, along with a possible increase in access to these services, may be at least partially responsible for their increased presence among women having abortions (Henshaw, 1998).

Emotional Consequences

In contrast to earlier work, which drew on psychoanalytic theory and thereby emphasized psychopathological responses to abortion, current work typically examines abortion from a stress and coping perspective (Adler et al., 1992; Bradshaw & Slade, 2003). According to this perspective, women perceive unwanted pregnancy and abortion as stressful events. Their responses to these events can range from positive to negative and can be influenced by various factors, such as social support and personal coping strategies.

In line with the stress and coping perspective, research demonstrates that women's responses to abortion are not overwhelmingly negative. Studies of adolescents and emerging adults demonstrate that most women do not suffer from psychological and emotional trauma following an abortion (Pope, Adler, & Tschann, 2001; Russo & Dabul, 1997). Women's distress levels are often high right before an abortion but tend to drop immediately following the procedure and for some time after (Pope et al., 2001). Furthermore, Zabin, Hirsch, and Emerson (1989) found that women who have abortions as adolescents tend to fare better in emerging adulthood in terms of economic situations and effective contraception than their peers who had not been pregnant or who gave birth. Women who had abortions were also no more likely than these peers to have psychological problems as emerging adults. Thus, emerging adults who had an abortion fare similarly and, in some areas, show more positive outcomes than do women who chose to give birth or who had never been pregnant.

There is of course some variability in women's responses to abortion. Adolescent and emerging adult women who have lower emotional and psychological well-being prior to abortion, as well as perceived pressure from a partner, are more likely than others to experience postabortion distress (Pope et al., 2001; Russo & Dabul, 1997). In other words, circumstances or factors that existed before an abortion demonstrate stronger associations with postabortion outcomes than with the abortion experience itself (Pope et al., 2001).

STIs and HIV/AIDS

One half of all Americans have had an STI by age 24 (Cates, Herndon, Schulz, & Darroch, 2004). Research from health clinics reports similar findings, with more than 40% of adolescents and emerging adults attending such clinics testing positive for an STI (Banikarim, Chacko, Wiemann, & Smith, 2003). Chlamydia is the most frequently reported bacterial STI in the United States, and girls aged 15 to 19 represent 46% of these infections (Banikarim et al., 2003; CDC, 2000b). Therefore, STIs are not unique to emerging adults, but are also quite prevalent in adolescence.

Human papillomavirus (HPV) is a less familiar but perhaps riskier STI than chlamydia for emerging adults. In recent studies, 24% to 32% of college women tested positive for HPV (Burk et al., 1996; Cothran & White, 2002; Winer et al., 2003). HPV is an STI that can cause genital warts and cervical cancer, but like many STIs, can also be symptomless for long periods. It may be highly risky because only 37% of university students surveyed in 1996 had even heard of HPV, and students did very poorly on a measure of HPV-related knowledge (Baer, Allen, & Braun, 2000; Yacobi, Tennant, Ferrante, Pal, & Roetzheim, 1999). This number is somewhat surprising given that when asked about genital warts, more than 90% of college students reported that they had heard of them (Baer et al., 2000). Only 12% of women and 4% of men in this study thought that HPV was the cause of genital warts. Second, students knew less about HPV than about six other STIs, few considered HPV to be a common STI, and males knew less than females did (Baer et al., 2000; Yacobi et al., 1999). In addition, those who were at most risk tended to have the most inaccurate knowledge. Third, in contrast to other common STIs such as chlamydia, HPV cannot be treated with antibiotics (Workosi, Lampe, Wong, Watts, & Stamm, 1993). For many women infected with HPV, the virus goes away on its own, but in others it is more persistent. Treatments have been developed for genital warts and for precancerous cells, but there is no known treatment for HPV per se. HPV, as the major cause of cervical cancer, is therefore a risk for emerging adults' current and future health. HPV is clearly a disease for which awareness among emerging adults needs to be increased, and more research needs to be done to understand HPV prevention.

Risks of HIV increase between adolescence and emerging adulthood (CDC, 2000a). Emerging adults tend to have very good knowledge of HIV, its transmission, and condoms' preventive abilities (DiIorio, Parsons, Lehr, Adame, & Carlone, 1993; Lance, 2001). Research on perceptions of risk are mixed. Some data suggest that emerging adults may actually overestimate their risk of HIV infection. For instance, Cohen and Bruce (1997) reported that college students are accurate in their perceived risk of chlamydia but that they overestimate their risk of HIV infection. First-year college students tend to be more concerned about HIV than they are about any other STI (Baer et al., 2000). In contrast, other research suggests that emerging adults do not perceive themselves to be at high risk. An optimistic bias appears to exist in which individuals believe that others are more likely to be infected than themselves. For instance, about three quarters of emerging adults believe that their friends are more at risk for HIV infection than they are (Lewis et al., 1997). Ku et al. (2002) found that only about 40% of emerging adults thought that they were at some risk for an STI, even though the majority of their participants had engaged in unprotected sex. Evidence also suggests that there is not necessarily a link between perceived risk and the risk reduction behaviors that individuals engage in (Cohen & Bruce, 1997).

There is evidence that many emerging adults do not use medical care to diagnose STIs. Ku et al. (2002) found that only one in six emerging adults reported ever having been tested for an STI. Even among those who reported having some STI-like symptoms, only between one third and one fourth had been tested for it. In Ku et al.'s work, about 3% to 4% tested positive for an STI at the time of the study, and the majority of these individuals did not report any symptoms at that time. In summary, high rates of STIs are not surprising given what is known about risky behavior among emerging adults, but they do suggest that intervention and prevention are needed.

Alcohol Use and Sexual Behavior

Estimates vary, but during their most recent sexual encounter, from one quarter to more than one half of emerging adults report having consumed alcohol beforehand (Desiderato & Crawford, 1995; MacNair-Semands & Simono, 1996). Emerging adults who are heavy drinkers are more likely than nonheavy drinkers to have had multiple sexual partners recently (Santelli, Brener, Lowry, Bhatt, & Zabin, 1998; Wechsler, Davenport, Dowdall, Moeykens, & Castillo, 1994). This area in particular is one in which rates may vary for noncollege youth, although there are no known data to make this comparison. The college environment may be particularly conducive to drinking and hooking up. Many college students live independently for the first time and therefore have new freedoms for coming home intoxicated, coming home with someone else, or not coming home at all. Attitudes on many college campuses may encourage or endorse both heavy drinking and sexual experiences with casual partners (Sperber, 2001). Thus, the availability of both alcohol and prospective sexual partners at Greek parties and other social events may lead to the linking of drinking and hooking up.

There is evidence that mixing alcohol with sex is associated with more risky sexual behaviors (MacNair-Semands & Simono, 1996; McNair, Carter, & Williams, 1998). Sex with a new partner is also more likely to involve alcohol use than is sex with a regular partner (Corbin & Fromme, 2002). In addition, individuals who use drugs are more likely to engage in risky sexual behaviors (Capaldi et al., 2002). What no one has really examined, however, is the direction of these associations. Does frequent alcohol use cause individuals to behave in less protective ways, or are certain types of individuals more likely to engage in both risky substance use and risky sexual behaviors?

There is less evidence for links between heavy drinking and condom use in particular. Data suggest that heavy and nonheavy drinkers do not differ in their use of condoms (Wechsler et al., 1994). However, Graves (1995) did find links between heavy drinking behaviors and unprotected sexual behavior. In a review, Cooper (2002) suggested that there is little evidence of a link between drinking and condom use.

The previously referenced studies address links between drinking and sex across individuals. However, within individuals, links between alcohol and sexual behavior are less clear (Cooper, 2002). For instance, using within-subject comparisons, Bon, Hittner, and Lawandales (2001) found that individuals tended to engage in more unprotected sex and more oral sex when they were not drunk or high than when they were. This is not to say that mixing alcohol and sex is without risk. When individuals drink, they are more likely to have sex with a casual partner and are less likely to discuss potential risks with their partner (see Cooper, 2002, for a review). Thus, alcohol and drugs may be associated with certain risky behaviors more than with others.

Sexual Assault

The experience of sexual assault is not uncommon for emerging adults, and evidence suggests that women on college campuses are likely to experience some form of sexual assault. Although rates vary across studies and depend on definitions, evidence suggests that many emerging adults are involved in sexual assault experiences in one way or another. One national survey reported that 54% of women had been the recipients of sexual assault since age 14, with 27% experiencing rape. In contrast, 25% of men reported initiating sexual assault, and 8% rape (Koss, Gidycz, & Wisniewski, 1987; Ullman, Karabatsos, & Koss, 1999). More specific to experiences during emerging adulthood, Ward, Chapman, Cohn, White, and Williams (1991) surveyed college women about their experiences during the current academic year, and only as part of the college setting. Findings suggested that one third of these college women had been the recipients of unwanted sexual contact in the prior 6 months, 20% had experienced unwanted intercourse attempts, and 10% had experienced unwanted completed intercourse. Muehlenhard and Linton (1987) reported that rates of unwanted sexual contact were already high in the first year of college, so the experiences appear to happen early in emerging adulthood for many individuals. Unwanted sexual contact has been associated with drinking by both the women and the men involved, and individuals who drink before a sexual assault incident tend to be involved in more severe incidents (Abbey, McAuslan, & Ross, 1998; Larimer, Lydum, Anderson, & Turner, 1999; Ullman et al., 1999; Ward et al., 1991). The most common locations for sexual assault to occur are dorms, fraternity houses, and apartments (Abbey et al., 1998; Ward et al., 1991), and most were party-related incidents. The initiator of the unwanted sexual contact was most likely to be an acquaintance or friend; strangers and boyfriends were less common (Ward et al., 1991). Other researchers have examined the methods used to coerce sexual behaviors (Waldner-Haugrud & Magruder, 1995). The most commonly used methods, each experienced by more than half of the sample, were having the partner get the respondent drunk or stoned, and persistent touching. Also relatively frequently reported were the use of lies and guilt. Females were more likely to report being coerced than were males. Males did report being the recipient of coercion as well, though their experiences were more likely to be coerced kissing or fondling than coerced intercourse.

Suggestions for Future Directions

As our review demonstrates, much is known about sexuality in emerging adulthood. However, this evidence focuses on a risk perspective and relies primarily on White college samples. To further an understanding of the range of sexual beliefs and behaviors in emerging adulthood, we need more studies that include individuals from ethnic minority backgrounds. In addition, it is critical to develop research regarding sexual beliefs and behaviors in noncollege students. To date, the extent to which aspects of sexuality in emerging adults are specific to the experience of attending college, or to the developmental stage more broadly, is unclear.

Almost all research on sexuality in emerging adulthood has relied on standard survey methodology. However, to gain a more complete understanding of the phenomenon, we need to incorporate other methodologies into this research. In particular, work on sexuality in emerging adulthood would benefit from the use of open-ended questions and interviewing to conceptualize a more complete picture of sexuality in emerging adulthood (see Diamond, 2003; Lefkowitz, 2005). Second, there are virtually no longitudinal studies of sexuality in emerging adulthood. One-time studies of convenience samples of college sophomores do not provide information about how sexuality changes over the course of emerging adulthood. In addition, many studies ask about lifetime experiences, which makes it difficult to determine whether events (e.g., sexual assault) occurred during emerging adulthood or earlier. Studies that follow individuals across the transition from adolescence to emerging adulthood, and from emerging adulthood to young adulthood, would help to illuminate both the continuous and the unique qualities of sexuality in each period. In a similar manner, it is important to understand how transitions during emerging adulthood are associated with sexuality. Does transitioning to college affect sexual behaviors and beliefs? Do transitions to work, cohabitation, marriage, and parenting affect sexuality? It would also be useful and informative to develop a large-scale national survey that examines not only the negative aspects of sexuality in emerging adulthood but also the positive aspects.

Although sociosexual behavior is by nature a couple-level behavior, most research in this area has examined the individual as the unit of analysis. Research that uses couple-level analyses—interviewing or providing surveys to both members of a partnership—would provide critical information about the dynamic nature of sexual relationships. Research to date has generally examined either sexuality or romantic relationships and intimacy. More often than not, however, these partnerings are intertwined. Thus, a more complete understanding of sexuality would include an examination of sexuality in the context of romantic relationships. As one example, a number of researchers have presented gender differences in reports of condom use (Brown et al., 1992; Johnson et al., 1994; Leigh et al., 1994). However, in heterosexual relationships, there should not be any gender differences in condom use. Thus, methods need to be developed to help improve the accuracy of self-report.

One technique being used is diary methodology (de Visser & Smith, 2000; Jaccard, McDonald, Wan, Dittus, & Quinlan, 2002). These types of measures are useful in that individuals can report on recent (e.g., daily, weekly) behaviors rather than having to recall behaviors over long periods. In addition, diary measures allow researchers to examine within-person variability in addition to between-person, which can illuminate the pairing of behaviors (e.g., alcohol and condom use). In one study, Jaccard et al. (2002) used sexual behavior diaries weekly for 1 year with female emerging and young adults. Comparisons of standard self-report measures with the diary measures indicated that standard measures in which individuals report on moderate intervals (e.g., behavior over past 3 or 6 months) were more accurate than short (1 month) or long (1 year) intervals.

Little is known about how attitudes about sexuality develop over time; therefore, it is difficult to know whether adolescents and emerging adults share attitudes. In addition, little is known about nonpenetrative sexual behaviors. However, many emerging adults consider behaviors such as making out and oral sex an important component of their sexual activity and self. Therefore, longitudinal studies that focus not only on penetrative sexual behavior but also on nonpenetrative behaviors and the formation of attitudes and beliefs would provide critical information for understanding emerging adults' sexuality.

Part of identity formation is the understanding of a sexual self. This sexual self includes sexual orientation. One's identity as a sexual being also includes other aspects of one's sexuality and may be referred to as a sexual self-schema (Andersen, Cyranowski, & Espindle, 1999). For instance, does the individual believe in, and practice, premarital sex? Does the individual believe that condoms or abortions are wrong? What is the individual's perspective on male–female power within relationships? These aspects of sexual self-schema probably begin in adolescence. However, because emerging adulthood is a period during which exploration of sexuality is particularly salient, it is expected that emerging adulthood is more formative for these constructs. It is likely that by the end of emerging adulthood, many individuals have incorporated sexuality into their self-concept. As stated by one female student when asked how her views about sex had changed since she started college: "It's not such a bad thing to do, now. Sex is just a normal part of life and no one flips about you having it."

References

Abbey, A., McAuslan, P., & Ross, L. T. (1998). Sexual assault perpetration by college men: The role of alcohol, misperception of sexual intent, and sexual beliefs and experiences. *Journal of Social and Clinical Psychology, 17,* 167–195.

Adler, N. E., David, H. P., Major, B. N., Roth, S. H., Russo, N. F., & Wyatt, G. E. (1992). Psychological factors in abortion: A review. *American Psychologist, 47,* 1194–1204.

Ajzen, I. (1985). From decisions to actions: A theory of planned behavior. In J. Kuhl & J. Beckmann (Eds.), *Action-control: From cognition to behavior* (pp. 11–39). New York: Springer.

Alan Guttmacher Institute. (1994). *Sex and America's teenagers.* New York: Author.

Alan Guttmacher Institute. (1999). Teen sex and pregnancy. *Facts in Brief sheets from the Alan Guttmacher Institute.* New York: Author.

Alan Guttmacher Institute. (2002). Teenagers' sexual and reproductive health. *Facts in Brief sheets from the Alan Guttmacher Institute.* New York: Author.

Andersen, B. L., Cyranowski, J. M., & Espindle, D. (1999). Men's sexual self-schema. *Journal of Personality and Social Psychology, 76,* 645–661.

Arnett, J. J. (2000). Emerging adulthood: A theory of development from the late teens through the twenties. *American Psychologist, 55,* 469–480.

Baer, H., Allen, S., & Braun, L. (2000). Knowledge of human papillomavirus infection among young adult men and women. *Journal of Community Health, 25,* 67–78.

Baldwin, J. D., Whiteley, S., & Baldwin, J. I. (1992). The effect of ethnic group on sexual activities related to contraception and STDs. *Journal of Sex Research, 29,* 189–205.

Banikarim, C., Chacko, M. R., Wiemann, C. M., & Smith, P. B. (2003). Gonorrhea and chlamydia screening among young women: Stage of change, decisional balance, and self-efficacy. *Journal of Adolescent Health, 32,* 288–295.

Beckman, L. J., & Harvey, M. (1996). Attitudes about condoms and condom use among college students. *Journal of American College Health, 44,* 243–255.

Bingham, C. R., & Crockett, L. J. (1996). Longitudinal adjustment patterns of boys and girls experiencing early, middle, and late sexual intercourse. *Developmental Psychology, 32,* 647–658.

Bon, S. R., Hittner, J. B., & Lawandales, J. P. (2001). Normative perceptions in relation to substance use and HIV-risky sexual behaviors of college students. *The Journal of Psychology, 135,* 165–178.

Boone, T. L., & Lefkowitz, E. S. (2004). Safer sex and the health belief model: Considering the contributions. *Journal of Psychology and Human Sexuality, 16,* 51–68.

Bradshaw, Z., & Slade, P. (2003). The effects of induced abortion on emotional experiences and relationships: A critical review of the literature. *Clinical Psychology Review, 23,* 929–958.

Brown, L. K., DiClemente, R. J., & Park, T. (1992). Predictors of condom use in sexually active adolescents. *Journal of Adolescent Health, 13,* 651–657.

Brown, L. K., DiClemente, R. J., & Reynolds, L. A. (1991). HIV prevention for adolescents: Utility of the Health Belief Model. *AIDS Education and Prevention, 3,* 50–59.

Burk, R. D., Ho, G. Y., Beardsley, L., Lempa, M., Peters, M., & Bierman, R. (1996). Sexual behavior and partner characteristics are the predominant risk factors for genital human papillomavirus infection in young women. *Journal of Infectious Diseases, 174,* 679–689.

Capaldi, D. M., Stoolmiller, M., Clark, S., & Owen, L. D. (2002). Heterosexual risk behaviors in at-risk young men from early adolescence to young adulthood: Prevalence, prediction, and association with STD contraction. *Developmental Psychology, 38,* 394–406.

Cates, J. R., Herndon, N. L., Schulz, S. L., & Darroch, J. E. (2004). *Our voices, our lives, our futures: Youth and sexually transmitted diseases.* Chapel Hill: School of Journalism and Mass Communication, University of North Carolina, Chapel Hill.

Centers for Disease Control and Prevention. (2000a). *Health, United States, 2000*. Washington, DC: U.S. Government Printing Office.

Centers for Disease Control and Prevention. (2000b). *Tracking the hidden epidemic: Trends in sexually transmitted diseases in the US—2000*. Atlanta, GA: Department of Health and Human Services, Division of Sexually Transmitted Disease Prevention.

Chara, P. J., & Kuennen, L. M. (1994). Diverging gender attitudes regarding casual sex: A cross-sectional study. *Psychological Reports, 74*, 57–58.

Civic, D. (1999). The association between characteristics of dating relationships and condom use among heterosexual young adults. *AIDS Education and Prevention, 11*, 343–352.

Cochran, S. D., & Mays, V. M. (1990). Women and AIDS-related concerns: Roles for psychologists in helping the worried well. *American Psychologist, 44*, 529–535.

Cohen, D. J., & Bruce, K. E. (1997). Sex and mortality: Real risk and perceived vulnerability. *Journal of Sex Research, 34*, 279–291.

Cooper, M. L. (2002). Alcohol use and risky sexual behavior among college students and youth: Evaluating the evidence. *Journal of Studies on Alcohol, 14*, 101–117.

Cooper, M. L., Agocha, V. B., & Powers, A. M. (1999). Motivations for condom use: Do pregnancy prevention goals undermine disease prevention among heterosexual young adults? *Health Psychology, 18*, 464–474.

Corbin, W. R., & Fromme, K. (2002). Alcohol use and serial monogamy as risks for sexually transmitted diseases in young adults. *Health Psychology, 21*, 229–236.

Costa, F. M., Jessor, R., Donovan, J. E., & Fortenberry, J. D. (1995). Early initiation of sexual intercourse: The influence of psychosocial unconventionality. *Journal of Research on Adolescence, 5*, 93–121.

Cothran, M. M., & White, J. P. (2002). Adolescent behavior and sexually transmitted diseases: The dilemma of human papillomavirus. *Health Care for Women International, 23*, 306–319.

Crawford, M., & Popp, D. (2003). Sexual double standards: A review and methodological critique of two decades of research. *The Journal of Sex Research, 40*, 13–26.

Critelli, J. W., & Suire, D. M. (1998). Obstacles to condom use: The combination of other forms of birth control and short-term monogamy. *Journal of American College Health, 46*, 215–222.

Darroch, J. E., Singh, S., Frost, J. J., & Study Team. (2001). Differences in teenage pregnancy rates among five developed countries: the roles of sexual activity and contraceptive use. *Perspectives on Sexual and Reproductive Health, 33*, 244–250, 281.

D'Augelli, A. R., & Hershberger, S. L. (1993). Lesbian, gay, and bisexual youth in community settings: Personal challenges and mental health problems. *American Journal of Community Psychology, 21*, 421–448.

Desiderato, L. L., & Crawford, H. J. (1995). Risky sexual behavior in college students: Relationships between number of sexual partners, disclosure of previous risky behavior, and alcohol use. *Journal of Youth and Adolescence, 24*, 55–68.

de Visser, R. O., & Smith, A. M. A. (2000). When always isn't enough: Implications of the late application of condoms for the validity and reliability of self-reported condom use. *AIDS Care, 12*, 221–224.

Diamond, L. M. (2000). Sexual identity, attractions, and behavior among young sexual-minority women over a 2-year period. *Developmental Psychology, 36*, 241–250.

Diamond, L. M. (2003). Was it a phase? Young women's relinquishment of lesbian/bisexual identities over a 5-year period. *Journal of Personality and Social Psychology, 84*, 352–364.

Diamond, L. M., & Savin-Williams, R. C. (2000). Explaining diversity in the development of same-sex sexuality among young women. *Journal of Social Issues, 56*, 297–313.

DiIorio, C., Parsons, M., Lehr, S., Adame, D., & Carlone, J. (1993). Knowledge of AIDS and safer sex practices among college freshmen. *Public Health Nursing, 10*, 159–165.

Douglas, K. A., Collins, J. L., Warren, C., Kann, L., Gold, R., Clayton, S., et al. (1997). Results from the 1995 national college health risk behavior survey. *Journal of American College Health, 46*, 55–66.

Dubé, E. M., & Savin-Williams, R. C. (1999). Sexual identity development among ethnic sexual-minority male youths. *Developmental Psychology, 35*, 1389–1398.

Eisenberg, M. (2001). Differences in sexual risk behaviors between college students with same-sex and opposite-sex experience: Results from a national study. *Archives of Sexual Behavior, 30*, 575–589.

Ensminger, M. E. (1990). Sexual activity and problem behaviors among Black, urban adolescents. *Child Development, 61,* 2032–2046.

Erikson, E. H. (1950). *Childhood and society.* New York: Norton.

Feldman, L., Holoway, P., Harvey, B., Rannie, K., Shortt, L., & Jamal, A. (1997). A comparison of the demographic, lifestyle, and sexual behaviour characteristics of virgin and non-virgin adolescents. *Canadian Journal of Human Sexuality, 6,* 197–209.

Fisher, J. D. (1988). Possible effects of reference group-based social influence on AIDS-risk behavior and AIDS-prevention. *American Psychologist, 43,* 914–920.

Freimuth, V. S., Hammond, S. L., Edgar, T., McDonald, D. A., & Fink, E. L. (1992). Factors explaining intent, discussion and use of condoms in first-time sexual encounters. *Health Education Research, 7,* 203–215.

Gillen, M. M., & Lefkowitz, E. S. (2005). *Is body image associated with risky sexual behavior?* Manuscript submitted for publication.

Graves, K. L. (1995). Risky sexual behavior and alcohol use among young adults: Results from a national survey. *American Journal of Health Promotion, 10,* 27–36.

Hammer, J. C., Fisher, J. D., Fitzgerald, P., & Fisher, W. A. (1996). When two heads aren't better than one: AIDS risk behavior in college-age couples. *Journal of Applied Social Psychology, 26,* 375–397.

Hawkins, M. J., Gray, C., & Hawkins, W. E. (1995). Gender differences of reported safer sex behaviors within a random sample of college students. *Psychological Reports, 77,* 963–968.

Henshaw, S. K. (1998). Unintended pregnancy in the United States. *Family Planning Perspectives, 30,* 24–29, 46.

Henshaw, S. K., Koonin, L. M., & Smith, J. C. (1991). Characteristics of U.S. women having abortions, 1987. *Family Planning Perspectives, 23,* 75–81.

Hogben, M., & Williams, S. P. (2001). Exploring the context of women's relationship perceptions, sexual behavior, and contraceptive strategies. *Journal of Psychology and Human Sexuality, 13,* 1–19.

Jaccard, J., McDonald, R., Wan, C. K., Dittus, P. J., & Quinlan, S. (2002). The accuracy of self-reports of condom use and sexual behavior. *Journal of Applied Social Psychology, 32,* 1863–1905.

Jessor, S. J., & Jessor, R. (1975). Transition from virginity to nonvirginity among youth: A social-psychological study over time. *Developmental Psychology, 11,* 473–484.

Johnson, E. H., Jackson, L. A., Hinkle, Y., Gilbert, D., Hoopwood, T., Lollis, C. M., et al. (1994). What is the significance of black-white differences in risky sexual behavior? *Journal of the National Medical Association, 86,* 745–759.

Jones, R. K., Darroch, J. E., & Henshaw, S. K. (2002). Contraceptive use among U.S. women having abortions in 2000–2001. *Perspectives on Sexual and Reproductive Health, 34,* 294–303.

Knox, D., Sturdivant, L., Zusman, M. E. (2001). College student attitudes toward sexual intimacy. *College Student Journal, 35,* 241–243.

Koss, M. P., Gidycz, C. A., & Wisniewski, N. (1987). The scope of rape: Incidence and prevalence of sexual aggression and victimization in a national sample of higher education students. *Journal of Consulting and Clinical Psychology, 55,* 162–170.

Ku, L., St. Louis, M., Farshy, C., Aral, S., Turner, C. F., Lindberg, L. D., & Sonenstein, F. (2002). Risk behaviors, medical care, and chlamydial infection among young men in the United States. *American Journal of Public Health, 92,* 1140–1143.

Lance, L. M. (2001). HIV/AIDS perceptions and knowledge heterosexual college student within the context of sexual activity: Suggestions for the future. *College Student Journal, 35,* 401–409.

Langer, L. M., Warheit, G. J., & McDonald, L. P. (2001). Correlates and predictors of risky sexual practices among a multi-racial/ethnic sample of university students. *Social Behavior and Personality, 29,* 133–144.

Larimer, M. E., Lydum, A. R., Anderson, B. K., & Turner, A. P. (1999). Male and female recipients of unwanted sexual contact in a college student sample: Prevalence rates, alcohol use, and depression symptoms. *Sex Roles, 40,* 295–308.

Lefkowitz, E. S. (2005). "Things have gotten better": Developmental changes among emerging adults after the transition to university. *Journal of Adolescent Research, 20,* 40–63.

Lefkowitz, E. S., Boone, T. L., & Shearer, C. L. (2004). Communication with best friends about sex-related topics during emerging adulthood. *Journal of Youth and Adolescence, 33,* 339–351.

Lefkowitz, E. S., Gillen, M. M., Shearer, C. L., & Boone, T. L. (2004). Religiosity, sexual behaviors, and sexual attitudes during emerging adulthood. *Journal of Sex Research, 41,* 150–159.

Leigh, B. C., Morrison, D. M., Trocki, K., & Temple, M. T. (1994). Sexual behavior of American adolescents: Results from a U. S. national study. *Journal of Adolescent Health, 15,* 117–125.

Lewis, J. E., Malow, R. M., & Ireland, S. J. (1997). HIV/AIDS risk in heterosexual college students: A review of a decade of literature. *Journal of American College Health, 45,* 147–158.

Lindley, L. L., Nicholson, T. J., Kerby, M. B., & Lu, N. (2003). HIV/STI associated risk behaviors among self-identified lesbian, gay, bisexual, and transgender college students in the United States. *AIDS Education and Prevention, 15,* 413–429.

MacNair-Semands, R. R., & Simono, R. B. (1996). College student risk behaviors: Implications for the HIV-AIDS pandemic. *Journal of College Student Development, 37,* 574–583.

Maiman, L. A., & Becker, M. H. (1974). The Health Belief Model: Origins and correlates in psychological theory. In M. H. Becker (Ed.), *The Health Belief Model and personal health behavior.* Thorofare, NJ: Charles B. Slack.

McLaughlin, C. S., Chen, C., Greenberger, E., & Biermeier, C. (1997). Family, peer, and individual correlates of sexual experience among Caucasian and Asian American late adolescents. *Journal of Research on Adolescence, 7,* 33–53.

McNair, L. D., Carter, J. A., & Williams, M. K. (1998). Self-esteem, gender, and alcohol use: Relationships with HIV risk perception and behaviors in college students. *Journal of Sex and Marital Therapy, 24,* 29–36.

Michael, R. T., Gagnon, J. H., Laumann, E. O., & Kolata, G. (1994). *Sex in America: A definitive survey.* New York: Warner Books.

Miller, B., & Moore, K. (1990). Adolescent sexual behavior, pregnancy, and parenting: Research through the late 1980s. *Journal of Marriage and the Family, 52,* 1025–1044.

Misovich, S. J., Fisher, J. D., & Fisher, W. A. (1997). Close relationships and elevated HIV risk behavior: Evidence and possible underlying psychological processes. *Review of General Psychology, 1,* 72–107.

Moore, N. B., & Davidson, J. K., Sr. (2000). Communicating with new sex partners: College women and questions that make a difference. *Journal of Sex and Marital Therapy, 26,* 215–230.

Muehlenhard, C. L., & Linton, M. A. (1987). Date rape and sexual aggression in dating situations: Incidence and risk factors. *Journal of Counseling Psychology, 34,* 186–196.

Newcomb, M. D., Huba, G. J., & Bentler, P. M. (1986). Desirability of various life change events among adolescents: Effects of exposure, sex, age, and ethnicity. *Journal of Research in Personality, 20,* 207–227.

Oncale, R. M., & King, B. M. (2001). Comparison of men's and women's attempts to dissuade sexual partners from the couple using condoms. *Archives of Sexual Behavior, 30,* 379–391.

Paul, E. L., McManus, B., & Hayes, A. (2000). "Hookups": Characteristics and correlates of college students' spontaneous and anonymous sexual experiences. *The Journal of Sex Research, 37,* 76–88.

Perkins, D. F., Luster, T., Villarruel, F. A., & Small, S. (1998). An ecological, risk-factor examination of adolescents' sexual activity in three ethnic groups. *Journal of Marriage and the Family, 60,* 660–673.

Pope, L. M., Adler, N. E., & Tschann, J. M. (2001). Postabortion psychological adjustment: Are minors at increased risk? *Journal of Adolescent Health, 29,* 2–11.

Poppen, P. J. (1995). Gender and patterns of sexual risk taking in college students. *Sex Roles, 32,* 545–555.

Rodgers, J. L., & Rowe, D. C. (1993). Social contagion and adolescent sexual behavior: A developmental EMOSA model. *Psychological Review, 100,* 479–510.

Rosario, M., Rotheram-Borus, M. J., & Reid, H. (1996). Gay-related stress and its correlates among gay and bisexual male adolescents of predominantly Black and Hispanic background. *Journal of Community Psychology, 24,* 136–159.

Rosenstock, I. M. (1974). Historical origins of the health belief model. *Health Education Monographs, 2,* 328–335.

Russo, N. F., & Dabul, A. J. (1997). The relationship of abortion to well-being: Do race and religion make a difference? *Professional Psychology: Research and Practice, 28,* 23–31.

Samuels, H. P. (1997). The relationships among selected demographics and selected conventional and unconventional sexual behaviors among Black and White heterosexual men. *Journal of Sex Research, 34,* 85–92.

Santelli, J. S., Brener, N. D., Lowry, R., Bhatt, A., & Zabin, L. S. (1998). Multiple sexual partners among US adolescents and young adults. *Family Planning Perspectives, 30,* 271–275.

Savin-Williams, R. C., & Diamond, L. M. (2000). Sexual identity trajectories among sexual-minority youths: Gender comparisons. *Archives of Sexual Behavior, 29,* 607–627.

Shearer, C. L., Hosterman, S. J., Gillen, M. M., & Lefkowitz, E. S. (2005). Are traditional gender roles associated with risky sexual behavior and attitudes about condom use? *Sex Roles, 52,* 311–324.

Siegel, D. M., Klein, D. I., & Roghmann, K. J. (1999). Sexual behavior, contraception, and risk among college students. *Journal of Adolescent Health, 25,* 336–343.

Singh, S., Darroch, J. E., & Frost, J. J. (2001). Socioeconomic disadvantage and adolescent women's sexual and reproductive behavior: The case of five developed countries. *Perspectives on Sexual and Reproductive Health, 33,* 251–258, 289.

Sperber, M. (2001). *Beer and circus: How big-time college sports is crippling undergraduate education.* New York: Holt.

Sprecher, S., & Regan, P. C. (1996). College virgins: How men and women perceive their sexual status. *Journal of Sex Research, 33,* 3–15.

Stebleton, M. J., & Rothenberger, J. H. (1993). Truth or consequences: Dishonesty in dating and HIV/AIDS-related issues in a college-age population. *Journal of American College Health, 42,* 51–54.

Sullivan, H. S. (1953). *The interpersonal theory of psychiatry.* New York: Norton.

Sutherland, E. H. (1947). *Principles of criminology* (4th ed.). Philadelphia: Lippincott.

Torres, A., & Forrest, J. D. (1988). Why do women have abortions? *Family Planning Perspectives, 20,* 169–176, 255.

Udry, J., Billy, J., Morris, N., Gruff, T., & Raj, M. (1985). Serum androgenic hormones motivate sexual behavior in boys. *Fertility and Sterility, 43,* 90–94.

Ullman, S. E., Karabatsos, G., & Koss, M. P. (1999). Alcohol and sexual assault in a national sample of college women. *Journal of Interpersonal Violence, 14,* 603–625.

U.S. Bureau of the Census. (2001). *Statistical abstracts of the United States.* Washington, DC: U.S. Government Printing Office.

Waldner-Haugrud, L. K., & Magruder, B. (1995). Male and female sexual victimization in dating relationships: Gender differences in coercion techniques and outcomes. *Violence and Victims, 10,* 203–215.

Ward, S. K., Chapman, K., Cohn, E., White, S., & Williams, K. (1991). Acquaintance rape and the college social scene. *Family Relations, 40,* 65–71.

Wechsler, H., Davenport, A., Dowdall, G., Moeykens, B., & Castillo, S. (1994). Health and behavioral consequences of binge drinking in college: A national survey of students at 140 campuses. *Journal of the American Medical Association, 272,* 1672–1677.

Winer, R. L., Lee, S. K., Hughes, P. P., Adaman, D. E., Kiviat, N. B., & Koutsky, L. A. (2003). Genital human papillomavirus infection: Incidence and risk factors in a cohort of female university students. *American Journal of Epidemiology, 157,* 218–226.

Workosi, K. A., Lampe, M. F., Wong, K. G., Watts, M. B., & Stamm, W. E. (1993). Long-term eradication of chlamydia trachomatis genital infection after antimicrobial therapy: Evidence against persistent infection. *Journal of the American Medical Association, 270,* 2071–2075.

Yacobi, E., Tennant, C., Ferrante, J., Pal, N., & Roetzheim, R. (1999). University students' knowledge and awareness of HPV. *Preventive Medicine, 28,* 535–541.

Zabin, L. S., Hirsch, M. B., & Emerson, M. R. (1989). When urban adolescents choose abortion: Effects on education, psychological status and subsequent pregnancy. *Family Planning Perspectives, 21,* 248–252.

11

School, Work, and Emerging Adulthood

Stephen F. Hamilton and Mary Agnes Hamilton

Central to the argument for identifying a new stage of life between adolescence and adulthood is the lengthening time between attainment of biological adulthood and social adulthood. The age at which puberty is complete has declined in prosperous societies, presumably because of improvements in nutrition and medical care. At the same time, in those same societies shifts in labor markets toward knowledge work have extended formal education and postponed entry into full-time employment, which have in turn delayed independence from parents, marriage, and parenthood, all key markers of adulthood.

Although this particular constellation of economic influences offers the most compelling explanation for later achievement of adult status, this delay is not without precedent. Kett (1977) called attention to now-forgotten intermediate statuses between child and adult, such as that resulting from the common practice in 18th- and 19th-century farming families of young men working for a neighbor and giving their earnings to their fathers to pay them back for the cost of their rearing. Only after several years of such work was a young man free to marry and set out on his own (see also Modell, 1989).

If changes in the nature of work and consequent changes in schooling are primarily responsible for creating a new stage of emerging adulthood, then an understanding of school and work during emerging adulthood is a prerequisite to understanding the life stage. Like Arnett (2000), we believe heterogeneity is a salient feature of emerging adulthood and that its manifestations in school and work are critically important. The paths emerging adults follow through school and work differ widely and those differences strongly shape their experience of the life stage.

High school graduation comes closer than any other event to being an American rite of passage. But it differs on several counts from the archetypal rites practiced in simpler societies. First, the whole cohort is not present. Almost one quarter of all youth do not graduate with their age mates (Barton, 2002, p. 4). Second, instead of moving on together after this public ceremony, with gender as the principal distinction, the graduating cohort fragments. The most significant divide is between those who enroll in higher education and those who do not.

Moreover, each of these two directions offers a wide array of pathways, including full-time versus part-time enrollment, 4-year versus 2-year (or other) college, residential versus commuter colleges, full-time versus part-time employment, military enlistment, full-time child care or housekeeping, caring for an ill or aging parent, unemployment, and taking some time off—the list goes on. When various simultaneous and sequential combinations of these activities are added, the picture becomes dauntingly complex. However, those who quickly assume family obligations by nurturing and economically supporting children, whether married or not, become adults without the qualification as emerging. Their generally bleak economic prospects demonstrate the power of the forces postponing adulthood.

The heterogeneity of this life stage poses the greatest challenge to characterizing it with one label. For the purposes of this chapter, we accept as essentially correct for four-year college students and graduates Arnett's (2000, p. 479) portrayal of emerging adults as postponing adult commitments and responsibilities while they complete their extended education, try out and then establish careers, and explore relationships. We focus instead on young people of the same age (roughly 18–24) who do not graduate from 4-year colleges, asking whether the construct of emerging adulthood applies to them and, if so, how it is different for them. To constrain the diversity somewhat, we do not pay extended attention to high school dropouts who never return to the educational system or to those relegated to penal institutions. We want to know whether emerging adulthood is the same phenomenon for all members of a high school class when some go on through higher education and others do not.

Several questions orient this chapter, not all of which can be answered satisfactorily with available data:

- What are the career paths of emerging adults without bachelor's degrees?
- What impedes and what fosters satisfying and rewarding career paths for this group?
- What would enable more of these emerging adults to follow more favorable career paths?

Careers and Career Paths

Career can mean many things. It applies to a person's entire working life, as portrayed in a resume, for example. But it also applies to an identifiable segment of that life, as when reference is made, for example, to Louis Gerstner's career as CEO of IBM. Careers can be relatively standardized, as in the case of physicians, making it possible to describe in general terms what a career as a physician looks like. Nonstandard careers do not follow such a clear pattern. They include unusual and unexpected sequences and combinations. Such careers are often described as brilliant when they include a sequence of consistently more demanding and rewarding positions across a range of responsibilities. But nonstandard careers are called checkered when they are inconsistent and unimpressive (e.g., being at various times a short-order cook, a truck driver, an auto mechanic, and a telephone solicitor), and especially when they include spells of unemployment or activities of questionable legality and morality.

To emphasize the connections among different aspects of a career as a sequence of different occupational experiences, we use the term *career path* (S. F. Hamilton & Hamilton, 1999). The term is neutral regarding both processes and outcomes. A career path may be orderly and productive or it may be chaotic and unrewarding. Consistent with our orienting question, we are most interested in the positive side, in describing and understanding the career paths that lead high school graduates without bachelor's degrees to jobs that pay enough to support a family, provide benefits and some security, and offer prospects for advancement (i.e., jobs in the "primary labor market"; see Piore, 1971). This interest reflects a belief that employment per se is not an adequate goal for either individuals or policy; employment should yield self-sufficiency and self-respect. The distinction between being employed and earning enough to support oneself and a family has become more important over the past 30 years as earnings for male high school graduates have sharply declined.

Because of the critical importance of education to employment, we broaden the definition of career path to include the combination and sequence of education as well as employment. Including educational enrollment as well as employment in our definition of a career path recognizes not only the close connection between educational and occupational attainment but also the fact that emerging adults frequently combine employment with enrollment and frequently move between the two. The transition from school to work is not a simple one-time change that occurs when school is finished and employment commences. Rather, enrollment and employment are typically interwoven in a wide array of patterns, sequentially and simultaneously, throughout youth and emerging adulthood.

Career paths are best understood from a life-course perspective that pays attention both to the choices young people make and to the forces constraining those choices. Shanahan (2000) pointed to the need to incorporate and integrate both these dimensions, recommending and illustrating the value of considering "both young people's active efforts to shape their biographies and the structured set of opportunities and limitations that define pathways into adulthood" (p. 668).

Education and Employment Among Emerging Adults

Recognizing the challenges inherent in describing what is happening during this time of life, we first use aggregate statistics to convey something about the numbers involved and the proportions engaging in different activities. We attend to differences among genders and racial and ethnic groups and in education levels, despite the complexity introduced as a result. Then we examine more interpretive studies to see what can be discerned about the dynamics of the process. It is unfortunate that the scope of our questions exceeds the explanatory power of data we have found, leading us to repeat the scholar's inevitable plea for more research.

High School Graduation

In October 1999, 11.2% of 16- to 24-year-olds had not graduated from high school or obtained a GED (General Educational Development) certificate and were not attending high school (Kaufman, Kon, Klein, & Chapman, 2000, p. 11). It is surprising that in an era of growing emphasis on education, the high school completion rate (graduation plus GED) rose no more than 3% between 1972 and 1999 (Kaufman et al., 2000, p. 16). The current high rate has been achieved despite a decrease in actual graduation that is masked by growing reliance on high school equivalency (Kaufman et al., 2000, Table 6, p. 24). This trend is cause for serious concern and is likely to be exacerbated by higher graduation requirements and high-stakes examinations. The evidence is quite strong that earning the GED is not as beneficial as graduating; it leads to higher earnings only when it opens the door to postsecondary education (Cameron & Heckman, 1993).

Enrollment in College

In 1999, 45% of the college-age cohort, ages 18 to 24, was enrolled in college (Barton, 2002, pp. 7–8). Of the 2.5 million youth who graduated from high school in the spring of 2001, 1.6 million (61.7%) were enrolled in college by the following October (U.S. Department of Labor, 2002). As has been the case since 1988, young women enrolled at a higher rate than did young men (63.6% of women, 59.8% of men). White youth were more likely to enroll in college than were Black youth (63.1% compared with 54.8%). Hispanic youth were least likely to enroll (51.5%) and their presence among college students was further reduced by a high school dropout rate that is much higher than for other racial and ethnic groups (U.S. Department of Education, 2002, p. 73).

However, higher rates of enrollment do not translate directly into higher proportions of graduates. The percentage of entering students who graduate from 4-year colleges within 5 years of entry declined from 58% in 1983 to 51% in 2001 (Barton, 2002, p. 12). In 2001, 29% of 25- to 29-year-olds held at least a bachelor's degree (U.S. Department of Education, 2002, p. 80). Venezia, Kirst, and Antonio (2003) described the college dropout situation bluntly.

> About half of first-year students at community colleges do not continue on for a second year. About a quarter of first-year students at four-year colleges do not stay for their second year. Over 40 percent of college students who earn more than 10 credits never complete a two-year or a four-year degree. At two-year colleges, over 70 percent of students who enroll say they expect to obtain a bachelor's degree, but only 23 percent receive one. (p. 9)

The primary reason for noncompletion is low academic resources—a construct combining measures of high school curriculum intensity and quality with students' test scores and class rank (Adelman, 1999). The most hopeful implication of the importance of high school curriculum is that this factor can be directly affected by policies. Even more positive is the finding that the value of a high-intensity and high-quality curriculum is greatest for minority and low-income students. This is critical because degree completion is highly corre-lated with race and ethnicity. Whereas 49% of Asian Americans and 29% of White, non-Hispanics have earned a bachelor's degree by age 24, only 15% of African Americans, 10% of Hispanics, and 7% of Native Americans have done so (Venezia et al., 2003, Table 1, p. 10).

Enrollment in 2-Year Colleges

In the face of declining graduation among the rising proportion of youth who enroll in college, our interest in the career paths of high school graduates who do not earn bachelor's degrees must encompass not only those who never enroll in postsecondary education but also those who enroll but fail to earn a degree. As noted, those who enroll in nonbaccalaureate programs, primarily 2-year colleges, are overrepresented in this category.

Students enrolled in 2-year institutions (or less) account for almost 60% of all postsecondary students enrolled for credit; 30% of all postsecondary students and more than half of sub-baccalaureate students are in occupational programs (Bailey et al., 2003). Compared with 4-year or baccalaureate students, sub-baccalaureate students are more likely to be poor, minority, unprepared, and older. Overall, sub-baccalaureate students begin their studies later, take fewer courses, and take courses less regularly, all characteristics associated with lower completion rates.

Schneider and Stevenson (1999, p. 217) found that a student who starts in a 2-year college is 38% less likely to earn a bachelor's degree in 5 years than is a comparable student starting in a 4-year college. Interviews with 2-year college enrollees who aimed for more than an associate's degree but failed to earn one revealed three main reasons: (a) unrealistic expectations and little knowledge of what college is like, (b) poor academic preparation, and (c) costs (p. 227).

Employment

Most 2001 high school graduates (80.6%) who did not go on to college were in the labor force (i.e., either working or looking for work) in the fall after graduation; however, one fifth of those counted as in the labor force (20.9%) were unem-ployed, a substantial increase over the previous year (13.1%), reflecting a weak-ening economy (U.S. Department of Labor, 2002). Unemployment rates are very high for youth and young adults. However, the prevalence of part-time employment, often combined with part-time or full-time enrollment in educa-tion, along with frequent job changes and moves into and out of the labor force makes unemployment data less reliable and more subject to interpretation than unemployment rates for established workers. As a result, employment–population ratios rather than unemployment rates are commonly used for this age group.

Sum, Khatiwada, Pond, and Trub'skyy (2002, Chart 14, p. 26) presented data indicating that the employment–population ratio for 16- to 24-year-olds not enrolled in school rose to a high of 73.2% in 2000 before beginning to decline again as the labor market tightened. In 2001, the employment–population ratio was highest for White youth (75%), lowest for Black youth (57%), and intermediate for Hispanics (68%). In the same year, 55% of high school dropouts, 74% of graduates, 81% of those with 1 to 3 years of college, and 87% of those with a bachelor's degree or higher were employed (Sum et al., 2002, Chart 15, p. 28). Education tends to reduce racial and ethnic differences in employment rates. Among high school graduates 16- to 24-years-old in 2001, employment–population ratios were as follows: White, 76.4%; Black, 60.3%; and Hispanic, 71.8%. For college graduates the differences narrowed even further, to less than a 5% advantage for Whites over Hispanics, with Blacks in the middle (Sum et al., Chart 16, p. 29).

Women in the 16 to 24 age range are not as likely as men to be employed (76% of men compared with 67% of women in 2001, Sum et al., 2002, p. 30), reflecting in part their greater likelihood of having child-care responsibilities and being on welfare. Young men with a high school diploma had an employment–population ratio of 79% in 2001, compared with 67.8% for women. But women with 4-year degrees are as likely to be employed as men: 87.7% women compared with 87.3% of men (Sum et al., 2002, Table 9, p. 30; also Chart 17, p. 32). The higher employment–population ratio for women with more education is accompanied by their tendency to postpone childbearing and have fewer children.

Combined Enrollment and Employment

College enrollment is frequently combined with employment. Nearly 43% of full-time first-year college students were in the labor force in October 2001. Twice that proportion of part-time students, 87.5%, were either working or looking for work at that time. Combining work with enrollment is far more common in 2-year than in 4-year colleges (71.6% compared with 35.3%), a difference that also reflects the greater likelihood of part-time enrollment in 2-year than in 4-year colleges (31.3% vs. 11.3%; U.S. Department of Labor, 2002).

Young people move not only from education to work but back and forth. Using data from the 1979 National Longitudinal Survey of Youth (NLSY-79), Arum and Hout (1998, pp. 487–488) found that 19% of males and 21% of females "moved from school into the labour force, back into school and back into the labour force between 1979 and 1991." Such multiple transitions from education to work and back were most common among young adults whose highest educational attainment is a 2-year degree: 44% of women and 45% of men. High school dropouts are least likely to make multiple transitions between education and work because they are least likely to return to education.

The Diversity of Post-High-School Activities

The picture that emerges from these data of what happens after high school is one in which college attendance is far more widespread than college graduation and the majority of college students are not enrolled in 4-year residential institutions. Part-time and intermittent enrollment are common, as is combining enrollment with employment. Going to college, in other words, does not necessarily mean living on campus and being free to concentrate on academics and on an unfettered social life. In rough proportions, 60% of high school graduates enroll in college the next fall; 60% of those enrollees attend 2-year colleges; and 60% of all enrollees earn a degree, but only 23% of 2-year college students do. More than one third of 4-year students and two thirds of 2-year students also work. Less than one third of 25- to 29-year-olds have earned a bachelor's degree. White, non-Hispanic 24-year-olds are twice as likely as African Americans and three times as likely as Hispanics to have a bachelor's degree.

Earnings and Education

The perils facing high school dropouts in the labor market are well known. But the assumption that graduating from high school makes the difference between poverty and a comfortable life is sadly mistaken. Middle-class earnings increasingly require at least a bachelor's degree, and the earnings gap between college and high school graduates is large and growing. In 2000, median earnings of adult male wage and salary earners, ages 25 to 34, were $31,175 (see Table 11.1). Those with a high school diploma or GED earned much less than the median, $26,399. High school dropouts earned $19,225. Men of the same age with a bachelor's degree or higher earned $42,292, 60% more than those without a 4-year degree.

Median earnings of all female 25- to 34-year-old wage and salary earners in 2000 were $22,447. Female high school graduates and GED holders earned far less than the median, $16,573. But the premium for holding a bachelor's degree or higher was even larger than for men. Women with 4-year degrees had median earnings of $32,238, 90% higher than earnings of women

Table 11.1. Median Earnings[a] of Wage and Salary Workers (Ages 25–34) by Gender and Education, 1971 and 2000

	All	Grades 9–11	High school	Bachelor's or higher
Female				
1971	$15,985	$10,045	$15,656	$29,345
2000	$22,447	$11,583	$16,573	$32,238
change	+40%	+15%	+6%	+10%
Male				
1971	$36,564	$31,039	$36,935	$45,219
2000	$31,175	$19,225	$26,399	$42,292
change	−15%	−38%	−29%	−6%

Note. Data from the Current Population Survey reported in *The Condition of Education 2002* (Table 16–1, p. 154 [with authors' calculations of change]), by the U.S. Department of Education, National Center for Education Statistics, 2002, Washington, DC: U.S. Government Printing Office. In the public domain.

[a]In constant 2000 dollars.

high school graduates (U.S. Department of Education, 2002, Table 16-1, p. 154).

Subbaccalaureate students reap varied economic rewards. Grubb (2002, pp. 306–307) found an earnings increase over high school graduates in the range of 20% to 30% for associate's degree holders and in the range of 5% to 11% for those completing 1 year of community college, but no advantage for fewer credits. The labor market value of an associate's degree is highest in technical fields, engineering and computers for men, business and health for women. In those fields median earnings of associate's degree holders actually exceed those of bachelor's degree holders in such low-paid fields as the humanities and education (p. 313).

Reports that educational requirements in the workplace have been increasing over the past few decades are supported by the growing gap between the earnings of high school graduates and of college graduates (U.S. Department of Education, 2002, p. 67). Male bachelor's degree holders have experienced the steadiest gain in earnings compared to high school graduates; however, in 2000 female bachelor's degree holders held an advantage over female high school graduates that was even larger. Male high school dropouts have earned about 75% of what high school graduates have earned and this ratio has remained stable; for female dropouts the ratio has oscillated within the range of 50% to 75% of graduates' earnings.

Real earnings have increased somewhat for women while decreasing for men, substantially for men with no more than a high school education. In constant 2000 dollars, the median earnings of women high school graduates increased by 6% from 1971 to 2000, 10% for bachelor's degree holders or higher, and 15% for high school dropouts. For males with a bachelor's degree or more, 2000 median earnings were 6% lower than in 1971; for high school graduates and GED holders, median earnings were 29% lower in 2000 than in 1971; male high school dropouts' earnings were 38% lower.

Declining real earnings are the most important fact about the career paths of young men without a bachelor's degree. Young men who cannot earn enough to support a family are unsatisfactory mates for young women, which leads to delayed marriage and greater labor force participation among young women (Carlson, McLanahan, & England, 2004; Edin, 2000; Oppenheimer, 2003; Wilson, 1987).

Note that declining earnings have nothing to do with unemployment because only workers are included in the data. Neither can these declines be attributed to individuals failing to make educational progress; education is held constant in the cohort comparison. The declines, therefore, clearly reflect changes in the labor market, changes that have reduced the wages employers are willing to pay male workers who do not have college degrees. In simple market terms, either the demand for such workers is lower or the supply is higher, or both. The data suggest that the major change has been reduced demand for male workers with no more than a high school diploma. (Recall that reduced demand does not mean such workers are not needed, only that fewer employers are offering them jobs and, as a result, their labor may be purchased at a lower price.) Another way to characterize labor market trends is to say that the gap is widening between the primary labor market in which jobs pay well above minimum wage and provide benefits, reasonable security, and advancement opportunities, and the secondary labor market, in which jobs do not carry these advantages (Piore, 1971). Although the primary–secondary distinction is far from perfect, it is an especially important one for emerging adults without college degrees because college degrees are the most potent credentials for desirable jobs in the primary labor market.

Searching or Floundering?

Workers in their 20s, especially the early 20s, display a different pattern of employment than do older workers; they are concentrated in low-wage, low-skill positions, and they frequently change jobs, often experiencing periods of unemployment between jobs. Limited work experience and consequently limited skills easily account for young workers' lower wages. But frequent movement among jobs has two conflicting interpretations. One interpretation describes the pattern as resulting from young workers' search for the best match with their interests and abilities. The other interpretation sees it as a largely undirected and unproductive floundering process resulting from employers' reluctance to offer primary labor market jobs to emerging adults.

Topel and Ward (1992) found that two thirds of all first jobs lasted less than a year. The mean number of jobs over the first 10 years of working life was seven. Osterman (1980) revived the term *floundering period* (Davidson & Anderson, 1937) to describe the pattern of frequent movement from job to job and in and out of the labor force that he found often did not lead to better jobs. Analyzing large cohorts and intensively interviewing a small sample, he conveyed a picture of working-class emerging adults who simply look for work rather than make careers for themselves and, if they are lucky, ultimately find a job that pays enough to support them, a job they will stay in. The source of this pattern, he argued, is in employers' refusal to hire applicants younger than 25 or so, regardless of their secondary school achievements, on the grounds that they are inherently irresponsible, posing too great a risk to investment in their training.

Osterman and Ianozzi (1993) strengthened this argument with data from the NLSY-79, portraying both a widely experienced period of churning and an even more troubling pattern of some emerging adults being unable to settle down in long-term jobs. The most vivid indicator of this pattern was his finding that only 54.8% of high school graduates without college degrees who were ages 29 to 31 in 1988 had been in their current job for more than 2 years (Table 2, p. 5). (These data come from a more extensive analysis in an unpublished manuscript by Osterman, 1992.)

However, this portrayal was contested by other economists who interpret the data differently, arguing that they merely reveal a distinctively American pattern whereby young people learn about jobs and test the match between those jobs and their skills and interests by changing jobs frequently until they make the right match. Klerman and Karoly (1994) based their critique of the floundering interpretation on an analysis that also used NLSY-79 data on young men ages 25 to 32 in 1990. (Women were excluded to eliminate the complexities in employment patterns resulting from child care.) Their question was at what age young men obtain their first job that lasts for 1 year, 2 years, and 3 years. The answers, in terms of median age, were, respectively, 19, 20, and 22. They argued that these findings indicate relative stability, in contrast to floundering or churning, though they also acknowledged the great variability around these median ages. For example, the quartile with the longest time to taking a job lasting 3 years has a median age of 25. Note that these findings do not directly contradict those reported by Osterman and Iannozi (1993), who reported on the proportion of 29- to 31-year-old men currently in a job that had lasted for 2 years. Of course some people hold jobs for a year or more and then change jobs later. Klerman and Karoly concluded that the claim of widespread floundering is exaggerated but that it does apply to a portion of the youth population, especially high school dropouts and minorities.

Probably the most influential argument supporting the searching explanation has been Heckman's (1994); he concluded that frequent changes among low-skill and low-paid jobs lead ultimately to optimal matching between jobs and workers. But this conclusion, which undermined policy initiatives designed to improve the transition, can be challenged on multiple grounds. One is that Heckman relied heavily on Topel and Ward's (1992) analysis, which does not distinguish college graduates from workers without college degrees. Moreover, by examining a 10-year period it combines the period Osterman (1980) and others claim is characterized by floundering with a later period that all agree is more stable. Light and McGarry's (1998) results challenge Heckman's benign view of frequent job changes as does Neumark's (1998) finding that young workers with more stable employment during their first 5 years in the labor market receive higher wages later. But the more important point is that Heckman assumed without evidence that this job search pattern is productive, ignoring the waste of public investment in education and job training that is not put to use for several years after schooling ends. Illustrating this inefficiency is Murnane, Willett, and Levy's (1993) finding that wages showed no return for scoring better on a test of algebra until 6 years after high school graduation. It was not until that long after leaving school that graduates could find jobs that made use of their mathematical skill, which is consistent with Osterman's (1980) claim that emerging adults are handicapped in the labor market by their age; their individual capacities count for little.

It is useful to note that those contesting Osterman's (1980) floundering interpretation take two incompatible positions. Klerman and Karoly (1994) argued that most young men do not change jobs frequently, whereas Heckman (1994) accepted the reality of frequent job changes but argued that they are a constructive job search strategy.

One way out of the argument between searching and floundering is to disaggregate the population. It seems plausible that some emerging adults move purposefully through their early work experience while others get bogged down by it. The challenge is to distinguish those who are following productive career paths from those who are not, to identify their characteristics, and to compare their relative proportions in the population.

The Increasing Disadvantages of High School Graduates Without College Degrees

In the data revealing modestly declining earnings for young male college graduates and drastically declining earnings for male high school graduates is found a picture of emerging adulthood that is not nearly so positive as the one of college students and 20-something graduates exploring careers, identities, and relationships. The growing divide between the college-educated middle-class and working-class Americans manifests itself unmistakably during the stage of emerging adulthood. Increasing rates of college enrollment have extended the benefits of a prolonged period of exploration to more young people, but the near disappearance of factory jobs paying union scale that are accessible to recent high school graduates has simultaneously postponed adulthood for those who are not in college, without comparable benefits. For young men who cannot find work that pays enough to support themselves, much less a family, and for the women they might otherwise marry, postponing full adulthood may reflect painful constraints rather than welcome choices. Determining which and how many emerging adults fit this less welcome profile is quite difficult. The debate among labor economists about whether floundering or job searching characterizes employment during this period of life reflects this difficulty.

Categorizing Career Paths

It is unfortunate that the diverse array of activities that emerging adults can engage in frustrates efforts to identify categories of career paths. Zemsky, Shapiro, Iannozzi, Cappelli, and Bailey (1998) used data on the class of 1982 cohort from High School and Beyond (HSB), a representative national sample studied for 12 years beginning with their sophomore year in high school (in 1980). Recognizing the multitude of pathways young people follow, the authors defined 12 status categories based on combinations of school and work. Table 11.2 presents a simplified version of their data, consolidating several of their categories for the sake of simplicity. Most notable, both working and looking for work are counted as employment, consistent with the definition of being in the labor force; military enlistment is counted as employment, and vocational–technical training as education.

In the first column, representing the year 1982, when subjects were about 18 years old, almost all were enrolled in high school, but the majority of those in school were also either working or looking for work (66%). This year has the highest rate of combining education and employment, mainly because nearly all subjects are enrolled and almost none (8%) are only working. In each of the succeeding years, the largest proportion of the cohort is in the employment-only category (not college). The rise in the employment-only category reflects steadily decreased enrollment in education with age, whether by itself or in combination with employment. The category "neither education nor employment," which can include people who are unemployed and those committed to housekeeping and child rearing, increases steadily, peaking at

Table 11.2. Transitions of the High School and Beyond Sophomore Cohort: 1982–1992

Status	% by year (approximate age)			
	1982 (18)	1984 (20)	1986 (22)	1992 (26)
Education only (includes vo/tech)	22	27	18	6
Employment only (includes military)	8	46	54	68
Education and employment	68	18	16	14
Neither education nor employment	3	8	9	11
All others	0	2	2	1

Note. Vo/tech = vocational/technical training. Data from *The Transition From Initial Education to Working Life in the United States of America* (NCPI Project Paper 1; p. 18), by R. Zemsky, D. Shapiro, M. Iannozzi, P. Cappelli, and T. Bailey, 1998, Philadelphia: University of Pennsylvania, National Center for Postsecondary Improvement. Copyright 1998 by R. Zemsky. Adapted with permission.

11%. Comparing these data with class of 1992 HSB data, 10 years later, Zemsky et al. (1998, p. 21) found an increase of 10% in the proportion of youth enrolled in college and working 2 years after high school graduation, which reflects the growing participation in postsecondary education also shown in other data previously cited.

Zemsky et al. (1998) also provided tables showing the probabilities of moving from one of their 12 statuses to another over 2-year increments, which highlight the variability of this time of life (pp. 19–22). However, amid the changes portrayed by their tables is a thread of stability: The most likely status for a young person to hold at Time 2 is the one he or she held at Time 1.

These data are helpful for establishing the big picture, but they do not enable us to trace the progress, or lack of progress, of individuals or groups following similar pathways. Neither do they enable us to distinguish those whose education is leading them to degrees from those simply taking courses, or to distinguish those whose employment is rewarding enough to support them from those stuck in low-wage jobs.

A research network supported by the MacArthur Foundation has been examining the transition to adulthood. Two draft chapters from a book based on this work attempted to categorize emerging adults' career paths. Consistent with the broader focus on adulthood, both incorporated information about place of residence, romantic partners, and parenthood, along with education and employment. The chapter by Sandefur, Eggerling-Boeck, and Park (2005) used the same data as did Zemsky et al. (1998): from HSB of the high school class of 1982, born in 1964, and a cohort born in 1974 that was tracked in the National Educational Longitudinal Study (NELS). The authors reported on the status of the HSB sample when they were age 28 and of the NELS sample at age 26. Status was defined in terms of the combination of five markers of adulthood: educational attainment, employment, marriage, childbearing, and living independently of parents. The data indicate that by their mid-20s, most emerging adults have moved out of their parents' households and are working. The authors used latent class analysis to find five categories that fit the data

Table 11.3. Status of Adults at Ages 28 (High School and Beyond) and 26 (National Educational Longitudinal Study)

	Males		Females	
Category	HSB (%)	NELS (%)	HSB (%)	NELS (%)
Limited postsecondary education/family	36	26	40	28
Limited postsecondary education/no family	24	29	—	—
Limited postsecondary education/children	—	—	14	22
Bachelor's degree/no family	22	30	23	29
Bachelor's degree/family	18	16	23	22

Note. HSB = High School and Beyond; NELS = National Educational Longitudinal Study. Data from *On the Frontier of Adulthood: Theory, Research and Public Policy* (p. 32), edited by R. A. Settersten, F. F. Furstenberg Jr., and R. G. Rumbaut, 2005, Chicago: University of Chicago Press. Copyright 2005 by the University of Chicago Press. Adapted with permission.

best. Three of those categories apply equally to males and females but two are defined differently for women than for men (see Table 11.3). Because these categories are constructed to provide the best fit with the data, the cases included in each are not identical to each other or even to the category title.

Comparisons between cohorts reflect the well-known trend also documented by Zemsky et al. (1998) toward higher postsecondary attainment and greater participation of women in the labor force, but also toward somewhat greater rates of unwed motherhood. Most of the shifts found from the 1974 HSB cohort to the 1984 NELS show increased education and decreased propensity to marry. To the extent that additional education is associated with higher earnings and that postponing marriage allows for additional education, these trends are positive, a constructive adaptation to a labor market that rewards higher education. However, the growth in the percentage of young women without higher education but with children (14% in HSB, 22% in NELS) indicates a serious problem with that subgroup; it is growing at a time when it is also increasingly disadvantaged. Black, Hispanic, and Native American women are much more likely than Whites or Asians to have children by their mid-20s and not have college degrees.

Another chapter in the volume from the MacArthur network is similar in its topic and mode of analysis. Osgood, Ruth, Eccles, Jacobs, and Barber (2005) used the same five markers of adulthood (though they examine a range of romantic relationships, not just marriage) to assess the standing of emerging adults at age 24. They also categorized their sample using latent class analysis. However, rather than using a representative national sample, they analyzed data from a longitudinal study (Eccles's Michigan Study of Adolescent Life Transitions) that began with sixth graders in predominantly White middle-class and working-class suburbs of Detroit. Nearly all the subjects were employed at age 24 (85%). Thirty-eight percent still lived with their parents. A third had obtained a bachelor's degree or higher; 47% had attended some college

Table 11.4. Pathways Through the Transition to Adulthood at About Age 24

Category Name	% of total	% females/category
Fast starters	12	55
Parents without careers	10	71
Educated partners	19	66
Educated singles	37	53
Working singles	7	47
Slow starters	14	56

Note. Data from *On the Frontier of Adulthood: Theory, Research and Public Policy* (p.34), edited by R. A. Settersten, F. F. Furstenberg Jr., and R. G. Rumbaut, 2005, Chicago: University of Chicago Press. Copyright 2005 by the University of Chicago Press. Adapted with permission.

or received some postsecondary training; and only 21% had not gone beyond high school.

Six groups emerged from their analysis. (Recall that latent class analysis combines markers, with the result that all members of a category do not necessarily share any one characteristic, even the one used to designate the category.) The percentage of subjects in each category and the proportion female are given in Table 11.4.

Those in the first category, fast starters, had achieved the greatest number of markers of adulthood. They were most likely to be married or cohabiting, to live away from their parents, to have children, to have completed their education, and to have long-term or career-related jobs. Subjects in the last category, slow starters, were at the opposite end, having achieved the fewest of these markers. Parents without careers had the lowest educational achievement and most were either not employed or working in jobs they saw as merely short-term. Working singles had neither children nor romantic partners and most also lacked college degrees, though many had received some postsecondary education. As the category titles suggest, educated partners and educated singles were characterized by having had at least some postsecondary education. The two groups differed from each other primarily on the dimension of romantic relationships. Most partners were either married or cohabiting and lived away from their parents, but did not have children. Singles were more likely to live with their parents. They were most likely to have completed a bachelor's degree. Both groups tended to see their jobs as related to their career aspirations.

The small number of non-Whites in the sample obviates racial comparisons. It is not surprising that subjects with more education also had better educated parents, whereas those who were already parents at age 24 came from families with less educated parents. From our perspective, it is pertinent that the fast starters were more likely than those in the other groups to be employed in the skilled or technical trades. They also worked more hours per week and had the highest hourly earnings (pp. 10–11). However, their commitment to work appears to come at the price of lower longer term earnings potential because additional education is unlikely for most in this group. Working singles were also overrepresented in the skilled and technical trade; they were the most likely to be living with their parents. As in the Sandefur et al. (2005) chapter, parents without careers seemed to be in the weakest position for future earnings, having low-skill jobs, little education, and child-care obligations. The two groups defined by their higher levels of education clearly seemed best situated for the future; their jobs were most prestigious and they were most likely to be continuing their educations.

These analyses indicate that a substantial proportion of emerging adults are following career paths that we would consider productive. They are enrolled or have enrolled in postsecondary education and they are employed. Emerging adulthood appears to be a benign experience for this part of the population. At the opposite extreme, a smaller proportion is unemployed or has little or no postsecondary education. Young women are overrepresented in the less productive categories; child-care responsibilities appear to be implicated in this difference, for both those who have partners and those who do not. It remains difficult to estimate with any precision the proportion of those who are not doing well or to characterize them fully. Nor can we tell how some with unpromising backgrounds, especially lack of higher education, manage to establish themselves in stable and rewarding careers. With these limitations in mind, we turn from description to explanation.

Explaining Career Paths

What we mean by *explanation* in this context is sufficient understanding of the dynamics of career paths to guide policies and interventions to improve the progress of all emerging adults. For this purpose, the standard categories used in social science have limited value. It is quite important to know, as the studies previously cited have demonstrated, that being White and middle class is advantageous, but this social address model of explanation (Bronfenbrenner & Crouter, 1983) is inadequate to help those who are neither. To the extent that we can understand how the advantages of race and class are conferred and understand the processes through which young people find and follow career paths, we can take steps to give all of them a better chance.

The longitudinal nature of the data set that Osgood et al. (2005) used allowed them to identify some predictors, observed at age 18, of being in one of the six categories at age 24. The most important predictors of educational attainment, that is, of membership in one of the two more highly educated groups, were self-concepts of educational ability; interest in academics; and expectations for future education (p. 23). Attitudes toward employment at age 18 did not predict category membership; future members of all categories said successful employment was important and had high expectations for themselves regarding employment (p. 24). The key distinction in attitudes toward parenthood was that when they were 18 parents without careers stated an earlier age at which they expected to become parents.

A multinomial logistic regression that takes multiple predictors into account yielded an extremely important finding, described in the authors' words:

> Children whose parents are highly educated have a much greater chance of becoming educated partners and educated singles at age 24 precisely because they are more likely to have done well in high school and to expect to obtain a college degree. However, any students from poor families who do equally well in school and have the same high expectations are just as likely to arrive in those high trajectory groups at age 24. (Osgood et al., 2005, p. 342)

The encouraging finding that academic achievement can transcend family background calls for further investigation into precisely this subset of youth from poor families who succeed in school and set high expectations for themselves. How do they do it? We have not found a comprehensive empirically based answer to this question, but the rich research literature on resilience (e.g., Luthar & Cicchetti, 2000; Werner & Smith, 2001) is relevant. The central theme is that children growing up in distressed families can succeed with the right combination of personal characteristics (including intelligence, personal attractiveness, and planfulness), supportive relationships (with caregivers and others), and beneficial opportunities in a range of settings.

One of the most pertinent contributions to the explanation of why emerging adults follow different career paths is Schneider and Stevenson's (1999) finding on the importance of "aligned ambitions," meaning "educational and occupational goals that are complementary" (pp. 6–7). Ambitions are considered aligned when "how much education a student thinks he or she would like to acquire is associated with the type of job he or she would like to have" (p. 80). Although this may seem like common sense, analyzing data from the Sloan Study of 8,000 young people over 5 years, the authors documented a generalized mismatch between young people's occupational aspirations and available jobs, and an unrealistic proportion aiming for the professions as well as arts, entertainment, and professional sports (pp. 76–78). In addition, they found a distressing number of youth (56.2% of their sample, p. 81) who stated career goals that required either more or less education than they planned to pursue. Mismatch in either direction reduces chances of success because youth need "knowledge of the educational pathways to their desired occupations" (p. 79) to plan their lives.

This emphasis on life plans recalls Clausen's (1993) exceptionally long-term longitudinal study following a sample from junior high school through retirement. He concluded that "planful competence," which was visible in some young people in early adolescence, was highly associated not only with material success—more education and better paying and more prestigious employment—but also with happy marriages and life satisfaction. Clausen's findings do not indicate whether improving planful competence would also improve those outcomes or what interventions would boost planful competence. However, they strongly suggest greater emphasis on helping youth plan their career paths. As Schneider and Stevenson (1999, p. 264) carefully emphasized, the goal is not to require early and inflexible career decisions, but to help young people make choices that will leave them with more good choices to make in the future rather than with narrowed and unrewarding options. Csikszentmihalyi and Schneider (2000, p. 228), also using Sloan Study data, found that youth who transcended their class origins to succeed in college did so with support from school that included direct advice about how to prepare for and apply to college. Yet they found the availability of such advice quite limited in the schools they studied.

Approaching some of these same issues from the perspective of counseling psychology but without using the same terms, Blustein, Juntunen, and Worthington (2000, p. 459) elaborated on what it takes to achieve an adaptive transition from school to work without a college degree. Their review of the empirical literature revealed four key findings. First, competence is required, in both general and specific work-related domains. Second, personal characteristics are important—notably initiative, flexibility, purposefulness, and a sense of urgency. Third, personal relations matter, especially those with family members, peers, teachers, counselors, coworkers, and supervisors. Finally, clear links between schooling and employment are helpful. All of these factors are susceptible to intervention under the rubric of youth development (S. F. Hamilton & Hamilton, 2004; Eccles & Gootman, 2002).

Conclusions and Implications

We find considerable convergence among the factors identified in several strands of research on how emerging adults construct productive and satisfying career paths. The first factor is hardly surprising: Academic achievement is growing ever more important, not only for entry into the next level of education but also as a determinant of employment opportunities even for those who do not earn a college degree. Workers who do not earn degrees still earn more if they have better academic or vocational skills; further training, including occupational certification, which also boosts earnings, depends on a solid academic foundation. Two-year degrees, especially in fields that require math and science such as health care and computer technology, can lead to rewarding careers.

The second factor is not as well established: career directedness (also called aligned ambitions, planfulness, or planful competence). Note that career directedness is not identical to occupational choice. As Schneider and Stevenson (1999) put it, "It is not, however, consistency of occupational choice that helps adolescents organize and manage their lives but rather knowledge of the educational pathways to their desired occupations" (p. 79). Being directed need not mean prematurely foreclosing options. Indeed, we believe the greater danger by far, especially for young people who do not graduate from college, is lack of direction. Someone who plans to become an electronics technician but then discovers the actual work is unpleasant can shift in any number of other appealing directions, such as medical technology or paralegal work. But someone who had no particular career goal and simply passed the courses required for high school graduation is likely to have to take numerous remedial courses before being able to enter any of those fields. Schooling is not the only domain in which directedness is valuable. Progressively more challenging work experience in almost any type of job will open more doors than an apparently random series of low-skill jobs.

Academic achievement and career directedness are not independent. A person with a sense of career direction is more likely to persist and succeed in school than one without it. And schools can promote career directedness through instruction, counseling, and curricula linked to work and occupations. A key research question is the extent to which differences in academic performance and career direction are inherent in individuals and how much they are shaped by external factors and, therefore, can be intentionally altered.

We are especially interested in learning more about a question that the available literature appears not to address: Through what combination of education, training, work experience, other activities, and personal relationships do some high school graduates make their way into adequately paid and reasonably stable jobs in the primary labor market by age 25? We know something about the kinds of employment experiences that are most likely to be available and rewarding for this group: middle management (often in retail establishments); repair and maintenance (e.g., auto repair, electronic technology); health care (e.g., registered nurses with 2-year degrees, medical technicians); and the military. A small proportion of emerging adults surely still find well-paid factory jobs. Some may earn good sales commissions. Entrepreneurship may be another rewarding avenue. The skilled trades provide what one electrician described to us as "college pay with a high school education," but apprentices are mostly adults in their late 20s and 30s. It would be useful to know how many emerging adults find their way into such fields and how they do so.

We know that having a sense of direction to one's career path is critical, but where does that come from? Clausen (1993) treated "planful competence" as a personality trait. Schneider and her Sloan Study colleagues (Csikszentmihalyi & Schneider, 2000; Schneider & Stevenson, 1999) emphasized what schools can do but often fail to do to foster aligned ambitions. We believe high-quality work-based learning, including good mentoring, can be a powerful force (M. A. Hamilton & Hamilton, 1997) but that mentoring and work designed for learning are, like effective school counseling, far too rare. Efforts to improve all of these and other supports for academic achievement and career directedness could be informed by research on emerging adults without bachelor's degrees, with a particular examination of those who succeed in finding productive career paths, establishing families, and becoming engaged citizens. We would want to know what experiences they had that led to their success and in what institutional contexts they occurred (e.g., school, paid work, voluntary service, the military, religious organizations) and what kind of mentoring they received along the way (i.e., who mentored them, what the mentor and mentee did together, how their relationships developed). We would also want to know what motivated the youth to participate in those activities. Insight into the timing, sequences, and combinations of experiences and activities would also be valuable. The basic idea is applying to emerging adults the same approach used in studying resilient children: trying to understand how some succeed in overcoming the odds against them.

References

Adelman, C. (1999). *Answers in the tool box: Academic intensity, attendance patterns, and bachelor's degree attainment*. Washington, DC: U.S. Department of Education, Office of Educational Research and Improvement. Retrieved March 3, 2004, from http://www.ed.gov/pubs/Tool box/index.html

Arnett, J. J. (2000). Emerging adulthood: A theory of development from the late teens through the twenties. *American Psychologist, 55,* 469–480.

Arum, R., & Hout, M. (1998). The early returns: The transition from school to work in the United States. In Y. Shavit & W. Muller (Eds.), *From school to work: A comparative study of educational qualifications and occupational destinations* (pp. 471–510). Oxford, England: Clarendon Press.

Bailey, T. R., Leinbach, T., Scott, M., Alfonso, M., Kienzl, G. S., Kennedy, B., & Marcotte, M. (2003). *The characteristics of occupational sub-baccalaureate students*. Unpublished manuscript, Community College Research Center, Teachers College, Columbia University, New York.

Barton, P. E. (2002). *The closing of the education frontier?* Princeton, NJ: Educational Testing Service.

Blustein, D. L., Juntunen, C. L., & Worthington, R. L. (2000). The school-to-work transition: Adjustment challenges for the forgotten half. In S. D. Brown & R. W. Lent (Eds.), *Handbook of counseling psychology* (pp. 435–470). New York: Wiley.

Bronfenbrenner, U., & Crouter, A. C. (1983). The evolution of environmental models in developmental research. In P. H. Mussen (Series Ed.) & W. Kessen (Vol. Ed.), *Handbook of child psychology: Vol. 1. History, theory, and methods* (pp. 357–414). New York: Wiley.

Cameron, S., & Heckman, J. (1993). The non-equivalence of high school equivalents. *Journal of Labor Economics, 11,* 1–47.

Carlson, M., McLanahan, S., & England, P. (2004). *Union formation and dissolution in fragile families* (Center for Research on Child Wellbeing Working Paper 01-06-FF). Retrieved May 12, 2004, from http://crcw.princeton.edu/workingpapers/WP01-06-FF-Carlson.pdf

Clausen, J. S. (1993). *American lives: Looking back at the children of the Great Depression*. New York: Free Press.

Csikszentmihalyi, M., & Schneider, B. (2000). *Becoming adult: How teenagers prepare for the world of work*. New York: Basic Books.

Davidson, P., & Anderson, H. D. (1937). *Occupational mobility in an American community*. Stanford, CA: Stanford University Press.

National Academy Press, National Research Council, & Institute of Medicine. (2002). *Community programs to promote youth development*. Washington, DC: National Academies Press.

Edin, K. (2000). "What do low-income single mothers say about marriage?" *Social Problems, 47,* 112–133.

Grubb, W. N. (2002). Learning and earning in the middle, Part I: National studies of pre-baccalaureate education. *Economics of Education Review, 21,* 299–321.

Hamilton, M. A., & Hamilton, S. F. (1997). *Learning well at work: Choices for quality*. Washington, DC: U.S. Government Printing Office.

Hamilton, S. F., & Hamilton, M. A. (1999). Creating new pathways to adulthood by adapting German apprenticeship in the United States. In W. R. Heinz (Ed.), *From education to work: Cross-national perspectives* (pp. 194–213). New York: Cambridge University Press.

Hamilton, S. F., & Hamilton, M. A. (Eds.). (2004). *The youth development handbook: Coming of age in American communities*. Thousand Oaks, CA: Sage.

Heckman, J. (1994, Spring). Is job training oversold? *The Public Interest, 115,* 91–115.

Kaufman, P., Kon, J. Y., Klein, S., & Chapman, C. D. (2000). *Dropout rates in the United States: 1999* (NCES 2001–022). Washington, DC: U.S. Department of Education, Office of Educational Research and Improvement, National Center for Educational Statistics.

Kett, J. F. (1977). *Rites of passage: Adolescence in America, 1790 to the present*. New York: Basic Books.

Klerman, J. A., & Karoly, L. A. (1994). Young men and the transition to stable employment. *Monthly Labor Review, 117*(8), 31–48.

Light, A., & McGarry, K. (1998). Job change patterns and the wages of young men. *The Review of Economics and Statistics, 80,* 276–286.

Luthar, S. S., & Cicchetti, D. (2000). The construct of resilience: Implications for interventions and social policies. *Development and Psychopathology, 12,* 857–885.

Modell, T. (1989). *Into one's own: From youth to adulthood in the United States, 1920–1975.* Berkeley: University of California Press.

Murnane, R., Willett, J., & Levy, F. (1993). *The growing importance of cognitive skills in wage determination.* Unpublished manuscript, Harvard Graduate School of Education, Cambridge, MA.

National Research Council, & Institute of Medicine. (2002). Community programs to promote youth development. Washington, DC: National Academy Press.

Neumark, D. (1998). *Youth labor markets in the U.S.: Shopping around vs. staying put* (National Bureau of Economic Research Working Paper 6581). Cambridge, MA: National Bureau of Economic Research.

Oppenheimer, V. K. (2003). Cohabiting and marriage during young men's career-development process. *Demography, 40*(1), 127–149.

Osgood, D. W., Ruth, G. W., Eccles, J. E., Jacobs, J. E., & Barber, B. L. (2005). Six paths through the transition to adulthood: Fast Starters, parents without careers, educated partners, educated singles, working singles, and slow starters. In R. A. Settersten, F. F. Furstenberg Jr., & R. G. Rumbaut (Eds.), *On the frontier of adulthood: Theory, research and public policy* (pp. 320–355). Chicago: University of Chicago Press.

Osterman, P. (1980). *Getting started: The youth labor market.* Cambridge, MA: MIT Press.

Osterman, P. (1992). *Is there a problem with the youth labor market and if so how should we fix it? Lessons for the U.S. from American and European experience.* Unpublished manuscript, Sloan School, Massachussetts Institute of Technology, Cambridge, MA.

Osterman, P., & Iannozzi, M. (1993). *Youth apprenticeships and school-to-work transition: Current knowledge and legislative strategy* (EQW catalog number WP14). Philadelphia: University of Pennsylvania.

Piore, M. J. (1971). The dual labor market. In D. M. Gordon (Ed.), *Problems in political economy.* Lexington, MA: D. C. Heath.

Sandefur, G. D., Eggerling-Boeck, J., & Park, H. (2005). Off to a good start?: Post-secondary education and early adult life. In R. A. Settersten, F. F. Furstenberg Jr., & R. G. Rumbaut (Eds.), *On the frontier of adulthood: Theory, research and public policy* (pp. 292–319). Chicago: University of Chicago Press.

Schneider, B., & Stevenson, D. (1999). *The ambitious generation: America's teenagers, motivated but directionless.* New Haven, CT: Yale University Press.

Shanahan, M. J. (2000). Pathways to adulthood in changing societies: Variability and mechanisms in life course perspective. *Annual Review of Sociology, 26,* 667–692.

Sum, A., Khatiwada, I., Pond, N., & Trub'skyy, M. (with Fogg, N., & Palma, S). (2002). *Left behind in the labor market: Labor market problems of the nation's out-of-school, youth adult populations.* Boston: Center for Labor Market Studies, Northeastern University.

Topel, R. H., & Ward, M. P. (1992, May). Job mobility and the careers of young men. *The Quarterly Journal of Economics, 107,* 439–479.

U.S. Department of Education, National Center for Education Statistics. (2002). *The condition of education 2002.* Washington, DC: U.S. Government Printing Office. Retrieved April 30, 2003, from http://www.ed.gov/pubs/edpubs.html

U.S. Department of Labor, Bureau of Labor Statistics. (2002, May 14). *College enrollment and work activity of 2001 high school graduates* (News Release USDL 02-288). Washington, DC: author. Retrieved April 30, 2003, from http://www.bls.gov/news.release/hsgec.nr0.htm

Venezia, A., Kirst, M. W., & Antonio, A. L. (2003). *Betraying the college dream: How disconnected K–12 and postsecondary education systems undermine student aspirations.* Palo Alto, CA: Stanford University. Retrieved April 8, 2003, from http://www.stanford.edu/group/bridge project

Werner, E. E., & Smith, R. S. (2001). *Journeys from childhood to midlife: Risk, resilience, and recovery.* Ithaca, NY: Cornell University Press.

Wilson, W. (1987). *The truly disadvantaged: The inner city, the underclass, and public policy.* Chicago: University of Chicago Press.

Zemsky, R., Shapiro, D., Iannozi, M., Cappelli, P., & Bailey, T. (1998). *The transition from initial education to working life in the United States of America* (NCPI Project Paper 1). Philadelphia: University of Pennsylvania, National Center for Postsecondary Improvement.

12

Emerging Adults in a Media-Saturated World

Jane D. Brown

Young people growing up in the early part of the 21st century could become known as the new media generation. They are the first cohort to have grown up learning their ABCs on a keyboard in front of a computer screen, playing games in virtual environments rather than their backyards or neighborhood streets, making friends with people they have never and may never meet through Internet chat rooms, and creating custom CDs for themselves and their friends. This new media environment is dramatically different from the one in which their parents grew up because it is more accessible, more interactive, and more under their control than ever before. One might wonder if such unprecedented access to and use of media has affected who these young people are now and in the future.

Although a great deal of research has focused on the effects of mass media on children and adolescents over the past 50 years, little research has considered 18- to 25-year-olds, or *emerging adults* as Arnett (2001) has referred to them, as being in a developmental period worthy of study in its own right. College students in this age group have been included in some psychological studies using media as stimuli, albeit primarily because they were accessible and they could be considered cognitively mature enough to represent adult patterns of cognition and behavior. Therefore, relatively little thought has been given to how emerging adults might be using media in a way peculiar to this life stage. Most research has also focused on television as the dominant medium, although it is clear that young people today use a wide range of different kinds of media, including music, movies, magazines, newspapers, and, increasingly, the Internet for entertainment and information—and have since they were very young.

In this chapter I consider what conclusions might be drawn from existing research on this age group and extrapolate from findings with younger adolescents. I use the media practice model that my students and I have been working with as an organizing tool for studying the process of media uses and effects (Figure 12.1). One of the most important trends in mass communication research over the past couple of decades has been a turn away from what has been called the linear effects model to a model that sees individuals not as

LIVED EXPERIENCE

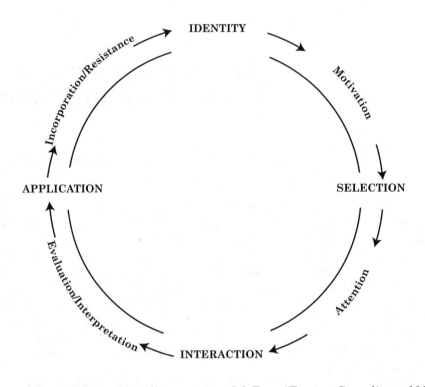

Figure 12.1. Adolescents' media practice model. From "Teenage Sexuality and Media Practice: Factoring in the Influences of Family, Friends, and School," by J. R. Steele, 1999, *Journal of Sex Research, 36,* 331–341. Copyright by Jeanne R. Steele. Reprinted with permission.

passive receivers of media messages but as more active initiators of media use. The media practice model posits that young persons' sense of who they are and where they fit in the world (identity) influences the media they attend to (selection), how they experience and make sense of that media (interaction), and the ways they incorporate or resist media messages (application) in their everyday lives (Brown, 2000; Steele, 1999).

The model assumes that the way in which people use the media in their daily lives is embedded in other contexts of their lives and what they already know and are seeking to know and feel. The media are only one of the contexts in which young people live, and individuals' use of media and the effects of what they read, see, and hear are influenced not only by personal characteristics but also by other important contexts, including families, friends, school, and work. The media also can be seen as permeating all the other contexts of an emerging adult's life: what was seen on television last night becomes the topic of conversation at work or school; going to the movies, listening to music, and communicating via instant messaging or in chat rooms are major forms of social activity; parents or roommates fight over the remote control or which movie they will rent. I refer to these other factors and contexts as *lived experience*, based on the perspective developed by Russian psychologist Vygotsky and other practice theorists, who see human development as a continual and interactive process that occurs within everyday life (Valsiner, 1991). The use of the mass media does not occur in a vacuum. Emerging adults come to mass media with different needs and different prior knowledge and understanding of themselves and their worlds, some of which was acquired through prior use of the media. This lived experience will affect how current media are selected, attended to, and incorporated in their lives.

In the next sections I look at each phase of the media practice model and consider what previous research indicates about how this process may work for emerging adults.

Identity: Who Am I?

Identity is at the top of the model because developing a sense of self is such an important aspect of what adolescents and emerging adults do. Arnett defines identity as a "conception of one's values, abilities, and hopes for the future" (Arnett, 2001, p. 370). The media may be seen as virtual tool kits of possibilities for most of the dimensions of identity work, including work, love, and ideology. The media provide a wide array of information and models from which emerging adults may draw as they continue to develop a sense of themselves in the context of the larger world. For many adolescents, and likely for emerging adults too, the kind of music they listen to, the movies they view, the television shows they watch, the magazines they read, and the Internet sites they visit are markers of who they are and who they aspire to be. Adolescent development theorists have suggested that each young person is learning in what ways he or she is like all other people, like some others, and like no others (Gallatin, 1975; Harter, 1990). One of the key motivations influencing how emerging adults make media choices may be their desire to affiliate with similar people while simultaneously distinguishing themselves from others.

Some identities are clearly marked by media use. Skateboarders, for example, are mostly White middle-class boys and young men who spend hours each day perfecting their moves on skateboards. They listen to a particular kind of rap music, rent videos of other skateboarders skating, videotape themselves and their friends skateboarding with their own video cameras, and read magazines about skateboarding. In the early 2000s, some African American girls adopted the identity of ghetto girls, on the basis of images depicted in popular rappers' songs and videos. Ghetto girls listened to a similar style of rap music, watched music videos of Black rappers on the Black Entertainment Television cable channel and Internet site, and practiced dance moves together.

Some emerging adults may be existing in what Watters (2003) called *urban tribes*—groups of single emerging adults on college campuses and in cities who cluster loosely together to socialize and provide a sense of community and connectedness between the time they leave their original families and begin their own, which for some is 20 years or longer. The hit television shows *Seinfeld* and *Friends* of the late 1990s were emblematic of the nature of these group identities. On some college campuses groups of friends congregated regularly to watch these shows together in a kind of ritual of self-recognition. MTV's path-breaking reality show *The Real World,* which threw groups of emerging adults together to live under the camera's eye, provided a distorted but compelling look at the social identity work of this age cohort.

As these examples illustrate, the media can serve as sources of the kinds of people worthy of emulation as well as provide the symbolic trappings of specific identities. These identities can be thought of as two kinds of media identification: identification by the kinds of media attended to and identification with different media characters. The latter type, identification with, is one of the main predictions of cognitive social learning theory, a theory often used by media researchers to help explain the process of media effects. The theory predicts that the more a person identifies with a particular media character, the more likely he or she will be to imitate the behavior of that character (Bandura, 1986). Research has substantiated this basic idea, especially among younger children, and increasing evidence suggests that older children and emerging adults are influenced through identification with media characters as well.

Many college students identify with media celebrities, and a surprisingly large proportion has changed their behavior to be more like their media idols. MTV capitalized on some emerging adults' obsessions with their idols by creating a show called *I Want a Famous Face* that followed young men and women as they had plastic surgery to look more like their celebrity idol. Almost all (90%) of the Canadian undergraduates participating in one study reported that they had been attracted to a celebrity idol at some point in their lives, and many (70%) had a celebrity idol at the time they completed the survey. The majority of favorite idols were movie stars and musicians (Boon & Lomore, 2001). More than one quarter of the students said they had engaged in efforts to change aspects of their personality to bring it more in line with that of their favorite idol, and more than half reported that their idols had influenced their attitudes and personal values, often in positive directions. As one student in a similar study in the United States said, "I think I have tried to be more literate ever since Oprah has done her Book Club thing. I try to read and respond differently" (Shuh, 2000, p. 134).

Selection: I Get to Choose

Such identifications affect which media and media content are chosen. Technological developments such as satellite transmission, fiber-optic cable, and the World Wide Web have provided the infrastructure for a huge array of media choices. Whereas it used to be that the average American media consumer had three television networks, a local newspaper, and a radio station, this generation of emerging adults can choose from more than 500 television channels, scores of magazines and newspapers, an almost infinite number of Web sites, and new movies, CDs, and video games coming out weekly.

In the near future it is expected that the delivery systems of today will converge into an increasingly accessible stream of visual, verbal, and print information and entertainment. As one media futurist predicted, "By the year 2020 more than 90 percent of the words, images, sounds, videos, and three-dimensional (3D) worlds produced will be located somewhere on the Internet, and much of it will be accessible for free or for some small fee" (Biocca, 2000, p. 23).

Patterns of Media Use

Young people typically are spending more of their waking hours with some form of media than in any other activity. A nationally representative survey of 8- to 18-year-olds in the United States found that the average adolescent was using some form of media 6 to 7 hours a day, often more than one simultaneously (Rideout, Roberts, & Foehr, 2005). These are the adults of the future—they have grown up surrounded by media, often in the privacy of their own bedroom, with little parental intervention or supervision of what media content they are attending to. By the turn of the past century, adolescents' bedrooms had become mini-media centers (Roberts & Foehr, 2004). Almost all U.S. adolescents had an audio system in their bedroom (CD, tape player, or radio) and two thirds had a television. More than one half had their own videocassette recorder or DVD player, and more than one third had TVs hooked up to cable or satellite reception. Almost half, primarily boys, had a video game system, and one third of all the 8- to 18-year-olds had a computer in their bedroom (one fifth had an Internet connection). The majority of teens reported spending most of their time with media either alone or with siblings or friends, almost never with parents or other adults (Rideout et al., 2005).

Although some young people are deprived of access to this ocean of information and entertainment, trends suggest that the digital divide may not last long or be as wide as originally feared, especially among emerging adults who have claimed the Internet as their medium of choice. By 2003, more than 80% of 18- to 29-year-olds were online, on average one half hour a day, e-mailing, chatting, downloading and listening to music, playing games, checking sports scores, and looking for information about products, services, or schoolwork (85% of college students in 2003 had their own computer). Hispanic, White, and Asian American young people were equally likely to have access to and be using the Internet, although African Americans lagged slightly behind in interest and use ("America's Online Pursuits," 2003; "The Internet Goes to College," 2002).

Another important aspect of the new media environment is that it provides more immediate and individualized feedback than do older media systems. As media become increasingly interactive, emerging adults are able to try on (and discard) whole new identities in relative safety, with less fear of embarrassment if they do not get it quite right (Turkle, 1997). Although early research on the impact of Internet usage suggested that prolonged use of the Internet may contribute to increased feelings of loneliness among adolescents and decreased quality of communication with family members (Kraut et al., 1998; Sanders, Field, Diego, & Kaplan, 2000), subsequent studies have shown that establishing relationships via the Internet may contribute to more intimate and longer lasting real-life relationships and may be a boon to shy, socially anxious, or physically less attractive people who can communicate initially only by text. About one in five college students in one study said they had formed a relationship online before meeting in person ("The Internet Goes to College," 2002). The Internet may provide a kind of stranger-on-the-plane situation in which people are willing to disclose more personal information more quickly than they normally would because they are anonymous. Such personal disclosure can lead to greater intimacy if the relationship moves offline. Chat rooms also allow like-minded people to find each other, and similar interests and activities typically sustain relationships (Hellenga, 2002; McKenna, Green, & Gleason, 2002; Merkle & Richardson, 2000). Some sites, such as www.friendster.com and www.tribenet.com, have been designed to promote social networks.

In the future computer-mediated communication is expected to become more embodied and interactive as it becomes less text-driven, more voice-activated, and capable of providing instant feedback. To what extent these technological developments will enhance or undermine adult development and relationships is an important new question.

Gender and Race Differences: It's About Me

Coupled with the drive for profits that compels all media institutions in the United States and an increasing number around the world, this vast array of media has already become highly specialized, designed to appeal and sell advertised products to different audience segments. It is clear that even basic social identities such as gender and race motivate different patterns of media use. Males and females, in general, live in very different media worlds at most life stages. In both the United States and Europe, studies of children and adolescents have found that males watch more television, spend more time playing video games, and use computers more than females. Females read more and listen to music more than young men. Content preferences tend to follow gender stereotypes: Females typically prefer softer music and more relationship-oriented television fare, whereas males seek action and adventure and sports programming (Livingstone, 2002; Roe, 1998; Zollo, 1995). Although there are fewer studies of the overall media use patterns of emerging adults, it is reasonable to expect that such gender differences are maintained into adulthood.

Media use patterns typically differ by race and ethnicity as well. In the United States, African American and Hispanic adolescents watch more television and movies and spend more time playing video games than their White counterparts. Some, but not all, of these differences may be related to socioeconomic status, as most studies show that time spent with screen media (television, movies, videotapes) decreases as parental education and time spent with print media and computers increases. However, studies also have consistently shown that African American youth, regardless of their family's socioeconomic status, are more screen-oriented and less print-oriented than are White Americans (Comstock & Scharrer, 1999). In the Roberts and Foehr (2004) national study, African American adolescents watched 1 more hour of television per day than did Hispanics, who, in turn, watched almost 1 hour more than did Whites.

Black and White adolescents also prefer different television shows. In a survey of more than 3,000 middle school students, Brown and Pardun (2004) found that although fewer programs on television feature African American actors, the majority of both male and female African American adolescents watched those shows regularly, whereas few of the Whites did (Table 12.1). Only 4 of 150 television shows listed on the survey were watched regularly by more than one third of all the adolescents, regardless of race or gender.

Such viewing differences call into question the presumption that all adolescents or emerging adults are attending to similar aspects of popular culture. Such fragmentation of cultural exposure has implications for current and future racial and gender understanding and interaction. If Black and White, male and female youth are growing up in highly gendered, highly racially distinct media worlds, are they learning what they will need to know to live peacefully and respectfully with each other in an increasingly multicultural world?

Emotion Regulation: How Do I Feel?

Some young people choose different kinds of media and different genres in deliberate attempts to regulate their moods and emotions. Adolescents have reported that listening to music and watching TV are things they do to cope with being angry, anxious, or unhappy (Kurdeck, 1987). Arnett (1996) found, for example, that heavy-metal fans used words such as *intense, fast,* and *powerful* to describe why they liked the music.

Whether using media is ultimately a healthy or an unhealthy way to deal with often confusing and powerful emotions is an open and important question. Larson (1995) found in time-use studies that when teens are feeling lonely and depressed, they may retreat to the privacy of their rooms and find solace in music that speaks to what they are experiencing. In studies with adolescent girls, some girls have reported using music to increase negative feelings. One girl, for example, said when she had "real problems" she liked to turn on her stereo and "just wallow in it." Another said, "When I'm sad, I tend to listen to sad music, which doesn't exactly help in cheering me up. I listen to it much louder when I'm happy" (Steele & Brown, 1995, p. 566).

Such intensification of feeling or rumination about whatever caused the sadness may not be the best way to cope with negative feelings. Although Arnett's heavy metal fans reported that listening to the fast, loud music helped them vent their anger, most studies of the effects of violent media have not found evidence of emotional catharsis but rather increased tendencies to behave aggressively. Studies of rumination among adults have found that it is related to unhappiness and depression (McIntosh & Martin, 1992; Pyszczynski & Greenberg, 1987).

More recent research points to the intriguing possibility that writing about the topic rather than only thinking about it may be beneficial because writing requires that the thoughts be put into words rather than remaining as vague images (King & Pennebaker, 1996). Thus, as Stern (2002) found in her study of girls' Web pages, those who used their Web sites to write daily journals of their confusion, sadness, and anger may have been engaged in an effective

Table 12.1. Top 10 Television Programs Watched by Black and White Adolescents

Black teens' most watched TV shows	% of Black (N = 1,338)	% of White (N = 1,604)	White teens' most watched TV shows	% of Black (N = 1,338)	% of White (N = 1,604)
Parkers	85.0**	8.3	*Simpsons*	49.4	51.5
Martin	81.4**	14.3	*Boy Meets World*	46.8	50.2
Hughleys	78.8**	12.2	*Whose Line Is It Anyway?*	25.5**	48.5
Moesha	78.8**	15.3	*Friends*	23.4**	47.8
106 and Park	78.4**	10.6	*Who Wants to Be a Millionaire?*	56.6**	43.2
Wayan Brothers	71.6**	15.9	*Seventh Heaven*	38.1	40.2
Parenthood	70.6**	12.5	*Sabrina the Teenage Witch*	48.8**	39.9
One on One	70.3**	3.2	*Malcolm in the Middle*	38.6	37.8
Steve Harvey Show	69.0**	5.4	*Survivor*	30.3**	36.7
Living Single	67.0**	11.0	*Lizzy McGuire*	33.1	35.5

Note. Average age = 13.8 years; data collected in spring 2001. From "Little in Common: Racial and Gender Differences in Adolescents' TV Diets," by J. D. Brown and C. Pardun, 2004, *Journal of Broadcasting and Electronic Media, 48,* 266–278. Copyright 2004 by the Broadcast Education Association. Adapted with permission. The Journal of Broadcasting and Electronic Media is owned by the Broadcast Education Association (www.beaweb.org) and published by Erlbaum.

**$p < .001$, χ^2

coping strategy. But such strategies may not always work, especially if it is done without guidance and if it is the only strategy the young person has. Stern learned that one of the girls whose Web site she was studying had committed suicide shortly after posting new pages of her diary.

Many studies in a number of countries have now documented a relationship between media coverage and suicide. According to Gould, Jamieson, and Romer's overview (2003, p. 1,271), "The magnitude of the increase in suicides following a suicide story is proportional to the amount, duration, and prominence of media coverage." A number of studies have found not only an increase in suicides, especially among older adolescents, but also an increase in attempts with the same method used in the suicide reported by the media or depicted in fictional accounts in television or in the movies (Stack, 2000). Adolescents and emerging adults are the primary audience for movies either at home or in theaters, and nearly 1 in 10 American films now depicts a suicide or suicide attempt. Although guidelines for news accounts of suicides have been shown to reduce copycat suicide attempts, guidelines for fictional accounts have not yet been developed (Gould et al., 2003).

In light of the increasing ability of young people to choose and create media that may reflect and affect their moods and mental states, it is important to learn more about this process and to help the media understand that some depictions may be especially harmful. Some questions to consider: Under what circumstances and with which emerging adults are media helpful or harmful in coping with emotions and recurring thoughts? Could adolescents and emerging adults be guided to choose media content and activities that ameliorate rather than exacerbate negative moods and emotions?

Interaction: What Does It Mean?

All emerging adults will not interpret the same media content in the same way. Young people come to the media with different backgrounds, motives, and identifications, and these will influence what sense they make of what is heard or seen. Scholars from both psychological and humanistic perspectives have noted the extent to which readers of the same text can extract different meaning. One striking example of differing interpretations of popular media was the study of one of Madonna's early music videos, "Papa Don't Preach." When first released in 1986, columnist Ellen Goodman called it "a commercial for teenage pregnancy," whereas the religious right said it was a stand against abortion. College students who saw the video differed in their reading of the video, too. Although most White females thought the video was about a teen girl deciding to keep her unborn child ("baby"), Black males were more likely to think the girl (Madonna) in the video was singing about wanting to keep her boyfriend "baby." Because the young men apparently were identifying primarily with the dilemma of the boyfriend in the video, they were less likely than the female viewers to see or hear the cues that suggested pregnancy (Brown & Schulze, 1990).

In a program of research designed to understand gender differences in responses to sexual content on television, Ward and her colleagues also have shown that college-age males and females respond differently to segments of popular television shows (e.g., *Martin* and *Roseanne;* Ward, Gorvine, & Cutron, 2002). They have found that the female viewers are more likely than the males to think the sexual scenes they see are realistic, are more approving of behaviors that are relationship-maintaining (e.g., a jealous husband protecting his wife), and are less approving of relationship threats (e.g., a man contemplating cheating).

Ward uses a composite theory called cognitive information processing that integrates both social learning theory and script theory to explain why males and females may be processing the same content so differently. Script theory suggests that young people observe social behavior (either in the media or in real life), then create and store scripts in their memories that will guide their subsequent behavior. They may also learn causal schemata and normative beliefs that basically suggest who should do what to whom in what circumstances and with what results. Social learning theory explains that the most salient scripts will be those with desirable consequences and attractive models. Thus, the theory would predict that females would pay more attention to the female script in the media and be less positive about scripts that jeopardize their status and security.

Increased access to sexually explicit images via the Internet and on television and cable channels has raised concern that young people may be learning an unhealthy set of sexual norms and developing unrealistic expectations about bodies and sexual performance from the media. Earlier studies with college students have found that exposure to pornography can shift expectations about the seriousness of rape and the frequency of unusual sexual behavior such as bestiality and group sex (Zillmann, 2000). Books have been written and Web sites (e.g., www.cybersexualaddiction.com) created to counsel the estimated 10% of users who become addicted to cybersex.

In light of the vast array of media materials now available, it is important to learn more about how young people are actually making sense of what they see, read, and listen to in the media. More needs to be known about the attributes of the most salient and most consistent scripts in the media and to what extent they are being adopted by emerging adults. Are the media's scripts of appropriate behavior reinforcing or undermining what emerging adults are learning in other contexts? What is the cumulative effect of being exposed to a relatively consistent set of media scripts about male–female relationships since puberty? What do emerging adults do when they have been taught one set of scripts in one context (e.g., parents and schools encourage delay of sex and practice of safe sex) and another script in the media (e.g., unprotected sexual intercourse is an important and typical part of young peoples' relationships)?

Application: How Does This Fit in My Life?

Finally, the media practice model predicts that some of what people are exposed to in the media will influence their beliefs and behaviors in the real world. This is the point in the process on which most attention has been focused in the past. Given that the impact of the media is an often subtle, conditional, and bidirectional process, it is a difficult task to identify which young people under what circumstances are influenced by the media in which domains of their lives. Nevertheless, the effects of the media on a number of kinds of attitudes and behaviors relevant to emerging adulthood, including fear and aggression, body image and obesity, occupational choice, and political ideology, have been investigated.

Fear and Aggression

Since the advent of television into most homes in the United States, researchers have been concerned about and have examined the effects of frequent exposure to depictions of violence on television. Content analyses show that violence on television is frequent and glamorized, sanitized, and trivialized. One of the most comprehensive content analyses found over a 3-year period in the late 1990s that a consistent 60% of television programming contained at least six violent incidents per hour, violent perpetrators were often the heroes of the stories, and victims rarely suffered pain (University of California, 1998). Research has shown that this persistent presence of violent acts without negative consequences on television programs is related to increased fear and aggressive behavior among children. Six major health associations, including the American Psychological Association, the American Medical Association, and the American Academy of Pediatrics, are so convinced of the evidence of a causal link between TV violence and aggressive behavior among young viewers that they issued a joint statement in 2000 on the hazards of exposing children to on-screen violence (Congressional Public Health Summit, 2000).

An often overlooked outcome of viewing on average more than 1,000 murders, rapes, and aggravated assaults per year on television is fear for personal safety in the real world. In a program of research that included retrospective case studies as well as surveys and laboratory experiments, Joanne Cantor (1998) and others found that children and adolescents frequently develop long-term fears of specific kinds of people and places from seeing just one movie or television scene that frightened them. College students have reported being afraid to live alone after seeing stalker movies when they were adolescents. Boys probably are more likely than girls to suppress such fears that may in turn cause anxiety and increased aggression (Sonesson, 1998). Gerbner, Gross, Morgan, and Signorielli (1994) speculated that the fear generated at least in part by the ubiquity of violent acts on television may contribute to Americans' reluctance to relinquish their handguns and their support for the building of more prisons and harsher penalties for criminals.

Some experimental work and a few longitudinal studies also suggest that early exposure to televised violence and identification with violent characters is related to increased aggressive behavior in emerging adulthood (Anderson, Huston, Schmitt, Linebarger, & Wright, 2001; Huesmann, Moise-Titus, Podolski, & Eron, 2003). Cantor's (1998) retrospective research with college students has shown that children's exposure to violence and scary scenes and characters on television and in the movies, such as the shark in the movie

Jaws or the murder in the shower in *Psycho,* can generate long-standing fears and influence decisions about lifestyles (e.g., don't go swimming in the ocean, always have a see-through shower curtain).

Some of the newer forms of media may contribute to continued effects of media violence in later adolescence and early adulthood as well. Although it may seem that video games are for middle school boys, recent surveys by the gaming industry claim that the average age of the gamer is 29 years old, and 40% of video game players are 18- to 35-years-old (Greenspan, 2003). Although all video games are not violent, a number of the most popular ones, such as *Grand Theft Auto: Vice City,* in which the player finds and kills prostitutes, are. The games that most concern critics are first-person shooter games in which the player becomes the perpetrator, holding, pointing, and shooting the gun and being rewarded with extra points and encouraging words for the more lethal upper body shots. Some of these games, such as the early version of *Doom,* have been found so effective in reducing inhibitions for killing through operant conditioning that they have been used as training tools by the military (Grossman & DeGaetano, 1999).

It will be important to take into account patterns of selection and interaction in studies with emerging adults, in light of the extent to which they can choose which media they want to attend to. Black and Bevan's (1992) study of the effects of violent movies is a good example of the kind of research that is needed. Researchers went to a multiscreen movie theatre and had patrons fill out a hostility inventory before or after they viewed their self-selected movie. They found that both male and female viewers who had chosen a violent movie were initially more hostile than were viewers who had selected a nonviolent movie. After participants viewed the movie of their choice, hostility levels were higher among those who had viewed the violent movie but remained at the same initial low level among those who viewed the nonviolent movie. Such evidence suggests that media effects, such as hostility, are bidirectional and that initial choice plays an important role in the effect.

Physical Attractiveness

Although physical attractiveness has always been an important component of emerging adulthood and mate selection, the media have contributed to what is now often an obsession with having the perfect body and face. In 2004, more than 4 million emerging adults posted a photograph of themselves on Internet rating sites inviting others to rate their physical appearance (Rivlin, 2004).

The media promote the idea that good looks are paramount and simultaneously present an unrealistic body ideal. Women who appear in the media are substantially thinner than the average American woman (Fouts & Burggraf, 1999; Silverstein, Perdue, Peterson, & Kelly, 1986), and young women who identify with the typical ultrathin media stars are at risk of developing unhealthy perceptions of their own bodies and may engage in unnecessary dieting and disordered eating (e.g., Hofschire & Greenberg, 2002). Some television shows have been designed to exploit such obsessions with the perfect body. Premiering in 2004, *The Swan* was billed as transforming ugly-duckling women into beauties through plastic surgery. After contestants spent 4 months under-going multiple plastic surgeries, they competed in a beauty pageant to see which one had been most successful. The media now promote an equally unat-tainable ideal image for men. In comparing the male centerfold models in *Playgirl* magazine from 1973 to 1997, Leit, Pope, and Gray (2001) found that over time the men were significantly more muscular.

The media also are paradoxically contributing to an epidemic of obesity among young people. As models and characters promote an unattainable stan-dard of beauty, advertising promotes snack food high in sugar and fat and the sheer amount of time spent sitting in front of television and computer screens reduces calorie expenditure. Following dramatic increases in obesity in the 1980s and 1990s, about one in three children and teens in the United States are either overweight or at risk of becoming overweight (Ogden, Flegal, Carroll, & Johnson, 2002). Children who are overweight tend to remain overweight in adulthood, which can have significant and long-term negative health conse-quences including diabetes and heart disease (Cook, Weitzman, Auinger, Ngu-yen, & Dietz, 2003; Pinhas-Hamiel et al., 1996). The implications of these trends for emerging adults are only just beginning to be seen. Will they remain or become couch potatoes?

Occupational Choice and Adult Roles

Exposure to and identification with media characters can also influence expec-tations about occupations and other adult roles. In the entertainment media, occupations are primarily the backdrops for dramatic storytelling. In the TV world, employed people are doctors, lawyers, and entertainers, working in the "more prestigious, glamorous, adventurous, and exciting occupations" (Signo-rielli & Kahlenberg, 2001, p. 18). The majority of the U.S. population that works in white- and blue-collar jobs (e.g., bank tellers, shopkeepers, salespeople, and factory workers) is dramatically underrepresented, except for law enforcement, which is significantly overrepresented. In the U.S. labor force, only 3% of men work in law enforcement, but on television, 25% of non-White men and 16% of White men are portrayed as police officers or detectives (Signorielli & Kahlenberg, 2001).

Although a number of studies have shown that the world of work on television is demographically unrealistic, only a few studies have directly ex-plored whether these portrayals are related to young people's own occupational expectations and aspirations (e.g., DeFleur & DeFleur, 1967; Wroblewski & Huston, 1987). The more recent research has found that high school seniors who watched more hours of television each day were more likely than those viewing less frequently to aspire to prestigious jobs that included little supervi-sion and lots of leisure time (Signorielli, 1993).

In focus groups with early adolescents (12- to 14-year-olds) in central North Carolina, more frequent media users are more likely to have occupational aspirations based on television portrayals. In one group of six African American teens, three said they wanted to have occupations based on television shows they were currently watching. One girl said she wanted to be a forensic scientist because of the popular television program *CSI* (Crime Scene Investigation), and another said she had changed her career aspiration from veterinarian to obstetrician after watching the reality shows *Maternity Ward* and *Birthday*, which feature real women having babies.

Although it is good to have high expectations and hope that these dreams will come true, these are not easily attained occupations. In a nationally representative study of middle school and high school students' occupational aspirations, Csikszentmihalyi and Schneider (2000) found even though high school seniors' expectations were more realistic than those of middle schoolers, significant proportions still overestimated their chances of becoming athletes, fashion models, doctors, and lawyers. The media may play an important role in fueling unrealistic expectations by providing only a limited variety of occupations that are rewarding in various ways and by failing to emphasize the kinds of commitments required to attain such goals.

The media can also be helpful in portraying other kinds of adult roles and transitions. During the era of reality shows, *The Apprentice* provided a fascinating look at the need for teamwork and leadership in the corporate world, and *The Wedding Story* and *The Baby Story* debunked some of the myths surrounding two important transitions from emerging adulthood to young adulthood.

Political Ideology

The media are also important agents of political socialization (McLeod, 2000). It has been traditionally thought that young people developed their ideas and loyalties about politics and the political system primarily from learning and modeling their parents' political behavior and affiliations. A small body of research suggested that attention to political news in the media, especially newspapers, increased political knowledge and participation. However, scholars have recently begun to notice that emerging adults are paying less attention to traditional sources of political news (newspaper reading among 18- to 35-year-olds is the lowest ever) and more attention to news on blogs and webzines and political humor shows such as *The Daily Show,* late night talk shows, and ideologically slanted radio talk shows. One study found that 47% of Americans between the ages of 18 and 29 obtained at least some of their political information from late night entertainment shows, such as *The Tonight Show With Jay Leno* ("The Tough Job of Communicating," 2000).

Although some critics argue that the concomitant increase in political cynicism and low levels of voting in this cohort is a reasonable response to the current state of politics (Buckingham, 1997), others are suggesting that coming of age politically in a communication environment that ridicules and makes fun of most politicians and their policies does not bode well for the future of a participatory democracy. After listening to Rush Limbaugh in one experiment, participants, regardless of race, gender, or prior political orientation, were significantly more likely to make policy judgments using the values most highly praised and endorsed by the conservative political commentator, emphasizing individualism over egalitarianism (Barker, 2002). The hit television show, *The*

West Wing, which features a strong yet humble U.S. president, has been found in experimental studies with college students to prime positive thoughts about the office of the president (Holbert et al., 2003).

In sum, emerging adults may apply content from the mass media in a number of areas of their lives and may use the mass media as reference points in resolving developmental tasks and transitions. The mass media may have an influence on emerging adults' trust in the world, fear, and aggressive behavior. Images of beauty may compel emerging adults to diet, exercise, and even undergo plastic surgery to achieve an ideal look while the sheer amount of time spent using the media may counteract efforts to be thin or muscular. Emerging adults may aspire to glamorous occupations because of what they have seen portrayed in the media and may learn more about life transitions such as marriage and children. Developing political ideologies and expectations of the government may be affected by media portrayals.

Because much of what is now known about media effects and application is based on studies with younger children and adolescents, it will be valuable to look more closely at how this works for emerging adults, who typically have more resources and may be more discriminating and more able than children and adolescents to act on what they see, hear, and read. Researchers should continue to ask, as the relatively few previous studies have, whether emerging adults use the media as part of their process of constructing who they will be as adults. Are they choosing and applying aspects of the media that are relevant to who they are or want to be?

The Future: What Could or Should Be Done?

Given that the media world is becoming simultaneously increasingly ubiquitous, interactive, and personal, emerging adults will have to become even more selective in what they attend to. Some fear that such selectivity will lead to increasing narrowness of vision and ideology because young people will tend to choose only those voices and images that reinforce their existing worldviews (Brown & Pardun, 2004). A few approaches may help young people develop the skills to negotiate more productively in this cacophony of media choices.

Media Literacy

One of the most promising strategies is what is called media literacy, or the ability to ask questions about what is watched, seen, or read. The idea is beginning to gain a foothold in the United States after years of popularity in other countries, including England, Canada, and Australia (Brown, 1991). A number of grassroots and professional groups, including the American Academy of Pediatrics and the National Education Association, have begun promoting the introduction of media literacy curricula in public schools, educating pediatricians about the importance of media in their patients' lives, and even stressing the need for antidrug programs to include media literacy components (White House Office of National Drug Control Policy, 2001). The basic idea is that some of the deleterious effects of media consumption can be reduced if youth are more aware of how media are developed, the approaches used to increase persuasion, the commercial sources and beneficiaries of advertising, and the ideology of messages contained in commercial and news media (Singer & Singer, 1998).

Unfortunately, little research has been conducted to evaluate the efficacy of media literacy interventions, but a few studies suggest that teaching youth media literacy skills can be productive. For example, evaluations of media literacy curricula focused on alcohol and tobacco advertising found increased attitudes critical of the alcohol and tobacco industries' advertising techniques and decreased intentions to drink alcohol among elementary and middle school students (Austin & Johnson, 1997; Graham & Hernandez, 1993). If media literacy education were begun early, emerging adults might be entering adulthood with a more realistic worldview and might be more capable of selecting and interpreting media in the most beneficial way.

Research Questions

Although quite a bit is known about the role of the media in the lives of children and adolescents, much still needs to be learned about emerging adults, especially as media technologies continue to evolve and become even more a part of the air everyone breathes. Here are some other research questions that might be addressed in line with the different moments in media use as outlined in the media practice model:

- Lived experience and identity. To what extent are media a kind of supercontext that permeates most other aspects of emerging adults' lives? Is creating a sense of self through identification with media celebrities different from and more or less helpful than identifying with real people?
- Selection. To what extent are emerging adults making media choices that assist or hinder their continued cognitive, social, and emotional development? Are chat rooms and instant messaging just another way to have conversations with friends and potential friends, or is there something fundamentally different in not having those conversations face-to-face?
- Interpretation. How do emerging adults make sense of what they are exposed to in the media within the other contexts of their lives? Given their greater store of knowledge and experience, are they more able than younger children to sort out the content that reinforces existing positive values and beliefs?
- Application. What is the impact of having grown up with readily accessible, increasingly computerized, and interactive entertainment and information? When and under what circumstances are media images and messages believed and acted on? Do the media set up unrealistic expectations about relationships, occupations, and the political world and contribute to relationship discord, job dissatisfaction, and political

cynicism? Or, are new-media cohorts so media savvy that they are less susceptible to media influences than are previous generations?

Appropriate Research Methods

Research on emerging adults' use of the media is difficult because it is no longer possible to study only television as the dominant medium and because media are so inextricably intertwined with the other contexts of emerging adults' lives. Multiple methods will have to be applied in innovative ways. Qualitative work may be especially helpful in understanding the ways in which emerging adults make sense of mixed and sometimes conflicting messages in the various contexts of their lives. Observation and field experiments that enhance ecological validity in media selection and interpretation also could be productive approaches.

The International Context

The extent to which the patterns seen in the United States are occurring around the globe should also be considered. As American media penetrate deeper into every nook and cranny of the world, a careful look should be taken at how these media are affecting emerging adults in other cultures. In 2001, MTV was the most-watched television network in the world, reaching 340 million households in 140 countries (Brownfield, 2001). Will the United States' domination of the world's media undermine local cultures and move young people to adopt the frequently unhealthy values and behaviors that are portrayed and promoted in Western media?

There is some evidence that this is already happening (e.g., Williams, 1986). In an ethnographic study of the Inuit (Eskimos) of the Canadian Arctic, Condon (1987, 1995) observed that after the introduction of television, the teen boys, who had rarely played competitive games in the past because of cultural traditions that discouraged competition and encouraged cooperation, began playing the games most popular on television and began to brag about their superior talents. Condon also observed that teen couples had become less secretive and private about their relationships. The adolescents told him they thought it was because of what they were seeing on television. *Happy Days*, a show about American teens in the 1950s, was one of their favorites.

Another ethnographer who was studying nutritional patterns in the South Pacific nation of Fiji found that in the 3 years after the introduction of television in 1995, including Western shows such as *Melrose Place*, admiration of women with nicely rounded bodies began to change among adolescent girls and dieting became a standard practice. One of the girls in the study said teens on television are "slim and very tall" and "we want our bodies to become like that . . . so we try to lose a lot of weight" (Becker, Burwell, Gilman, Herzog, & Hamburg, 2002).

It is clear that the media are an important context in emerging adults' lives. Close attention should continue to be paid to the possibilities as well as the potential perils of becoming an adult in such a mediated world.

References

America's online pursuits: The changing picture of who's online and what they do. (2003). Report of the Pew Research Center. Retrieved January 25, 2004, from http://www.pewinternet.org

Anderson, D. R., Huston, A. C., Schmitt, K. L., Linebarger, D. L., & Wright, J. C. (2001). Early childhood television viewing and adolescent behavior: The recontact study. *Monographs of the Society for Research in Child Development, 66*(1, Serial No. 264).

Arnett, J. J. (1996). *Metalheads: Heavy metal music and adolescent attention.* Boulder, CO: Westview Press.

Arnett, J. J. (2001). *Adolescence and emerging adulthood: A cultural approach.* Upper Saddle River, NJ: Prentice Hall.

Austin, E., & Johnson, K. K. (1997). Immediate and delayed effects of media literacy training on third graders' decision making for alcohol. *Health Communication, 9,* 323–349.

Bandura, A. (1986). *Social foundations of thought and action: A social cognitive theory.* Englewood Cliffs, NJ: Prentice Hall.

Barker, D. C. (2002). *Rushed to judgment: Talk radio, persuasion, and American political behavior.* New York: Columbia University Press.

Becker, A. E., Burwell, R. A., Gilman, S. E., Herzog, D. B., & Hamburg, P. (2002). Eating behaviours and attitudes following prolonged exposure to television among ethnic Fijian adolescent girls. *British Journal of Psychiatry, 180,* 509–514.

Biocca, F. (2000). New media technology and youth: Trends in the evolution of new media. *Journal of Adolescent Health, 27*(Suppl. 2), 22–29.

Black, S. L., & Bevan, S. (1992). At the movies with Buss and Durkee: A natural experiment on film violence. *Aggressive Behavior, 18,* 37–45.

Boon, S. D., & Lomore, C. D. (2001). Admirer–celebrity relationships among young adults: Explaining perceptions of celebrity influence on identity. *Human Communication Research, 27,* 432–465.

Brown, J. (1991). Television critical viewing skills education: Major media literacy projects in the United States and selected countries. Hillsdale, NJ: Erlbaum.

Brown, J. D. (2000). Adolescents' sexual media diets. *Journal of Adolescent Health, 27*(Suppl. 2), 35–40.

Brown, J. D., & Pardun, C. J. (2004). Little in common: Racial and gender differences in adolescents' TV diets. *Journal of Broadcasting and Electronic Media, 48*(2), 266–278.

Brown, J. D., & Schulze, L. (1990). The effects of race, gender, and fandom on audience interpretations of Madonna's music videos. *Journal of Communication, 40,* 88–102.

Brownfield, M. (2001, July 28). Sells like teen spirit. *The Business,* 28–32.

Buckingham, D. (1997). News media, political socialization, and popular citizenship: Towards a new agenda. *Critical Studies in Mass Communication, 14,* 344–367.

Cantor, J. (1998). *"Mommy, I'm scared": How TV and movies frighten children and what we can do to protect them.* San Diego, CA: Harcourt.

Comstock, G., & Scharrer, E. (1999). *Television: What's on, who's watching, and what it means.* San Diego, CA: Academic Press.

Condon, R. G. (1987). *Inuit youth: Growth and change in the Canadian Arctic.* New Brunswick, NJ: Rutgers University Press.

Condon, R. G. (1995). The rise of the leisure class: Adolescence and recreational acculturation in the Canadian Arctic. *Ethos, 23,* 47–68.

Congressional Public Health Summit. (2000, July 26). *Joint statement on the impact of entertainment violence on children.* Retrieved November 6, 2001, from http://www.aap.org/advocacy/releases/jstmtevc.htm

Cook, S., Weitzman, M., Auinger, P., Nguyen, M., & Dietz, W. H. (2003). Prevalence of a metabolic syndrome phenotype in adolescents. *Archives of Pediatrics and Adolescent Medicine, 157,* 821–827.

Csikszentmihalyi, M., & Schneider, B. (2000). *Becoming adult: How teenagers prepare for the world of work.* New York: Basic Books.

DeFleur, M., & DeFleur, L. (1967). The relative contribution of television as a learning source for children's occupational knowledge. *American Sociological Review, 32,* 777–789.

Fouts, G., & Burggraf, K. (1999). Television situation comedies: Female body images and verbal reinforcements. *Sex Roles, 40,* 473–481.

Gallatin, J. (1975). *Adolescence and individuality.* New York: Harper.

Gerbner, G., Gross, L., Morgan, M., & Signorielli, N. (1994). Growing up with television: The cultivation perspective. In J. Bryant & D. Zillmann (Eds.), *Media effects* (pp. 17–41). Hillsdale, NJ: Erlbaum.

Gould, M., Jamieson, P., & Romer, D. (2003). Media contagion and suicide among the young. *American Behavioral Scientist, 46,* 1269–1284.

Graham, J. W., & Hernandez, R. (1993). *A pilot test of the Adsmart curriculum: A report to the Scott Newman Center.* Los Angeles: Scott Newman Center.

Greenspan, R. (2003, August 29). Gamers growing up. *CyberAtlas.* Retrieved January 21, 2004, from http://www.cyberatlas.internet.com

Grossman, D., & DeGaetano, G. (1999). *Stop teaching our kids to kill: A call to action against TV, movie, and video game violence.* New York: Crown.

Harter, S. (1990). Self and identity development. In S. S. Feldman & G. R. Elliott (Eds.), *At the threshold: The developing adolescent* (pp. 352–287). Cambridge, MA: Harvard University Press.

Hellenga, K. (2002). Social space, the final frontier: Adolescents on the Internet. In J. T. Mortimer & R. Larson (Eds.), *The changing adolescent experience: Societal trends and the transition to adulthood* (pp. 208–249). Cambridge, England: Cambridge University Press.

Hofschire, L. J., & Greenberg, B. S. (2002). Media's impact on adolescents' body dissatisfaction. In J. D. Brown, J. R. Steele, & K. Walsh-Childers (Eds.), *Sexual teens, sexual media* (pp. 125–249). Mahwah, NJ: Erlbaum.

Holbert, R. L., Pillion, O., Tshida, D. A., Armfield, G. G., Kinder, K., Cherry, K. L., & Daulton, A. R. (2003). The West Wing as endorsement of the U.S. Presidency: Expanding the bounds of priming in political communication. *Journal of Communication, 53,* 427–443.

Huesmann, L. R., Moise-Titus, J., Podolski, C. P., & Eron, L. D. (2003). Longitudinal relations between childhood exposure to media violence and adult aggression and violence: 1977–1992. *Developmental Psychology, 39,* 201–221.

The Internet goes to college: How students are living in the future with today's technology. (2002). A report of the Pew Research Center. Retrieved January 26, 2004, from http://www.pew internet.org/reports

King, L. A., & Pennebaker, J. W. (1996). Thinking about goals, glue, and the meaning of life. In R. S. Wyer (Series Ed.) & R. S. Wyer (Vol. Ed.), *Advances in social cognition: Vol. 9. Ruminative thoughts* (pp. 99–106). Mahwah, NJ: Erlbaum.

Kraut, R., Patterson, M., Lundmark, V., Kiesler, S., Mukopadhyay, T., & Scherlis, W. (1998). Internet paradox: A social technology that reduces social involvement and psychological well-being? *American Psychologist, 53,* 1017–1031.

Kurdeck, L. (1987). Gender differences in the psychological symptomatology and coping strategies of young adolescents. *Journal of Early Adolescence, 7,* 395–410.

Larson, R. (1995). Secrets in the bedroom: Adolescents' private use of media. *Journal of Youth and Adolescence, 24,* 535–550.

Leit, R. A., Pope, H. G., & Gray, J. J. (2001). Cultural expectations of muscularity in men: The evolution of playgirl centerfolds. *International Journal of Eating Disorders, 29,* 90–93.

Livingstone, S. (2002). *Young people and new media.* London: Sage.

McIntosh, W. D., & Martin, L. L. (1992). The cybernetics of happiness: The relation between goal attainment, rumination, and affect. *Review of Personality and Social Psychology, 14,* 222–246.

McKenna, K. Y. A., Green, A. S., & Gleason, M. E. J. (2002). Relationship formation on the Internet: What's the big attraction? *Journal of Social Issues, 58,* 9–31.

McLeod, J. M. (2000). Media and civic socialization of youth. *Journal of Adolescent Health, 27*(Suppl.), 45–51.

Merkle, E. R., & Richardson, R. A. (2000). Digital dating and virtual relating: Conceptualizing computer mediated romantic relationships. *Family Relations, 49,* 187–192.

Ogden, C. L., Flegal, K. M., Carroll, M. D., & Johnson, C. L. (2002). Prevalence and trends of overweight among US children and adolescents, 1999–2000. *Journal of the American Medical Association, 288,* 1728–1732.

Pinhas-Hamiel, O., Dolan, L. M., Daniels, S. R., Standiford, D., Khoury, P. R., & Zeitler, P. (1996). Increased incidence of non-insulin-dependent diabetes mellitus among adolescents. *Journal of Pediatrics, 128,* 608–615.

Pyszczynski, T., & Greenberg, J. (1987). Self-regulatory preservation and the depressive self-focusing style: A self-awareness theory of reactive depression. *Psychological Bulletin, 102,* 122–138.

Rideout, V., Roberts, D. F., & Foehr, U. G. (2005). *Generation M: Media in the lives of 8–18 year-olds.* Menlo Park, CA: Henry J. Kaiser Family Foundation.

Rivlin, G. (2004, June 2). Facing the world with egos exposed: It's not hard to see the fun in rating others' looks online. What's less obvious is why people choose to be rated. *The New York Times,* p. E1.

Roberts, D. F., & Foehr, U. G. (2004). *Kids and media in America.* Cambridge, England: Cambridge University Press.

Roe, K. (1998). Boys will be boys and girls will be girls: Changes in children's media use. *Communications: European Journal of Communication, 23,* 5–25.

Sanders, C., Field, T., Diego, M., & Kaplan, M. (2000). The relationship of Internet use to depression and social isolation among adolescents. *Adolescence, 35,* 237–243.

Shuh, J. S. (2000). *False intimacy: Vicarious involvement with celebrities in the media.* Unpublished master's thesis, University of North Carolina, Chapel Hill, School of Journalism and Mass Communication.

Signorielli, N. (1993). Television and adolescents' perceptions about work. *Youth & Society, 24,* 328–342.

Signorielli, N., & Kahlenberg, S. (2001). Television's world of work in the nineties. *Journal of Broadcasting and Electronic Media, 45,* 4–22.

Silverstein, B., Perdue, L., Peterson, B., & Kelly, E. (1986). The role of the mass media in promoting a thin standard of bodily attractiveness for women. *Sex Roles, 14,* 519–532.

Singer, D., & Singer, J. (1998). Developing critical viewing skills and media literacy for children. *The Annals of the American Academy of Political and Social Science, 557,* 164–179.

Sonesson, I. (1998). Television and children's fear: A Swedish perspective. *News on Children and Violence on the Screen, 2*(1), 11–12.

Stack, S. (2000). Media impacts on suicide: A quantitative review of 293 findings. *Social Science Quarterly, 81,* 957–971.

Steele, J. R. (1999). Teenage sexuality and media practice: Factoring in the influences of family, friends, and school. *Journal of Sex Research, 36,* 331–341.

Steele, J. R., & Brown, J. D. (1995). Adolescent room culture: Studying media in the context of everyday life. *Journal of Youth and Adolescence, 24,* 551–576.

Stern, S. (2002). Virtually speaking: Girls' self-disclosure on the WWW. *Women's Studies in Communication, 25*(2), 223–253.

The tough job of communicating with voters. (2000, February 5). Retrieved December 15, 2003, from http://www.people-press.org

Turkle, S. (1997). *Life on the screen: Identity in the age of the Internet.* New York: Simon & Schuster.

University of California, Santa Barbara, Center for Communication and Social Policy. (1998). *National television violence study 3.* Thousand Oaks, CA: Sage.

Valsiner, J. (1991). Building theoretical bridges over a lagoon of everyday events. *Human Development, 34,* 307–315.

Ward, L. M., Gorvine, B., & Cutron, A. (2002). Would that really happen? Adolescents' perceptions of sexual relationships according to prime-time television. In J. D. Brown, J. R. Steele, & K. Walsh-Childers (Eds.), *Sexual teens, sexual media* (pp. 95–124). Hillsdale, NJ: Erlbaum.

Watters, E. (2003). *Urban tribes: Unhurried adventures in friendship, family, and commitment.* New York: Bloomsbury Publishing.

White House Office of National Drug Control Policy. (2001, June 1). *Helping youth navigate the media age: A new approach to drug prevention.* Rockville, MD: Author.

Williams, T. M. (1986). *The impact of television: A natural experiment in three communities.* New York: Academic Press.

Wroblewski, R., & Huston, A. C. (1987). Televised occupational stereotypes and their effects on early adolescents: Are they changing? *Journal of Early Adolescence, 7,* 283–297.

Zillmann, D. (2000). Influence of unrestrained access to erotica on adolescents' and young adults' dispositions toward sexuality. *Journal of Adolescent Health, 27*(Suppl.), 41–44.

Zollo, P. (1995). *Wise up to teens: Insights into marketing and advertising to teenagers.* Ithaca, NY: New Strategist.

Part IV _____

Conclusion

13

The Psychology of Emerging Adulthood: What Is Known, and What Remains to Be Known?

Jeffrey Jensen Arnett

Although scattered theory and research on the age period from the late teens through the 20s has taken place for decades (e.g., Bockneck, 1986; Erikson, 1968; Hogan & Astone, 1986; Keniston, 1971; Modell, 1989), only recently has scholarship in this area begun to be organized into a distinct field of study, under the term *emerging adulthood*. This book represents what will hopefully be a major step forward in scholarship on emerging adulthood. Prominent scholars from a wide range of areas were asked to summarize what is known in their area with respect to emerging adulthood and to propose new theoretical ideas and ideas for research. The chapters in this book thus provide an integrated foundation for future scholarship on emerging adulthood. The chapters not only tell us what is known about emerging adulthood today but provide an exciting and challenging research agenda.

Jennifer Lynn Tanner and I chose the subtitle *Coming of Age in the 21st Century* because emerging adulthood is when *coming of age* takes place today in America and other industrialized countries, if coming of age is understood to be the attainment of full adult status. A century ago, G. Stanley Hall published his two-volume magnum opus on adolescence, thus framing for scholars and the general public the nature of coming of age in the 20th century. Today, because adolescence begins earlier and the attainment of full adult status (by nearly any measure) comes later, it makes more sense to distinguish between adolescence (roughly ages 10–18) and emerging adulthood (roughly ages 18–25). Setting out to frame this new period of emerging adulthood is daunting, because what is known is limited in many areas, but also exciting, because this is a new field of scholarship and so many questions offer possibilities for exploration and discovery.

It was the goal of the editors and authors of this book to summarize what is known about emerging adulthood and also to direct attention to what we believe to be some of the most promising unanswered questions. My goal in this final chapter is to provide a commentary on the previous chapters, making connections across chapters and presenting an overview of what the field of emerging adulthood looks like in its present form. First, I present some thoughts about each chapter. Then I comment on what remains to be known about emerging adulthood.

Theory, Individual Factors, and Contexts in Emerging Adulthood: An Overview

My discussion of the chapters will follow the organizational structure of the book: first theory, then individual factors, and finally contexts.

Emerging Adulthood and Life Span Theory

In the first chapter I summarized my theory of emerging adulthood, discussing the various ways I believe emerging adulthood is distinctive as a developmental period. In addition to asking what is developmentally distinctive about emerging adulthood, psychologists need to understand how emerging adulthood fits into the rest of the life course. Jennifer Lynn Tanner takes on this challenge in her chapter, drawing on life span theory and developmental science. This developmental systems perspective views individual development as a function of the interaction between persons and multiple ecological contexts.

In seeking to understand development in emerging adulthood in relation to life span development, Tanner focuses on two key processes: recentering and ego development. Recentering involves a shift from dependence on parents to *system commitments* in the form of obligations to careers, intimate partners, and (for most people) children. It is during emerging adulthood that this shift takes place, and consequently these years tend to be exploratory and unstable as people try out various possibilities and learn from their experiences before making long-term commitments. The process of recentering is similar to what I have stated about emerging adulthood being characterized by identity explorations and instability (Arnett, 2000, 2004; see chap. 1, this volume), but I like Tanner's term *recentering* and I think the concept is useful as a way of describing in a dynamic way the kinds of changes that take place in emerging adulthood.

Among the notable studies that Tanner describes in her chapter is one by Grob, Krings, and Bangerter (2001), in which they surveyed adults of various ages about their most important life events and the degree of control they felt they had over those events: They found that it is during emerging adulthood that people perceive the most control over the significant events in their lives. This finding is a reflection of emerging adulthood as the self-focused age, the time when people are most likely to have the freedom to make choices as they wish. There is a distinct nadir in social and institutional control during emerging adulthood because during these years parents exercise less influence than they did in childhood or adolescence and most people have not yet entered the social or institutional roles of marriage, parenthood, and long-term employment that provide new constraints. Although there are negative aspects to the lack of social control for some people, as I discuss further later, one positive aspect of it is the freedom of this period, the peak it represents in people feeling like they have control over their own lives.

In addition to recentering, ego development is the other process Tanner proposes as central to development in emerging adulthood. This concept serves as a master trait representing qualities such as agency, self-regulation, and impulse control. Tanner sees ego development as the key to understanding the variance in developmental trajectories during emerging adulthood. Those who are relatively high in ego development tend to do well, whereas those who are relatively low tend to struggle. The absence of social and institutional control may allow for greater freedom and choice, but it also requires greater resources from individuals. Lack of constraint also means lack of guidance and support. Learning to stand alone is both an aspiration of emerging adults and an expectation for them in industrialized societies (Arnett, 1998), and a substantial amount of ego development is required for success in this developmental task.

Ego development makes possible the construction of life plans that will serve as a guide through emerging adulthood into young adulthood and beyond. As Tanner mentions, the construction of a life plan has been noted by several previous theorists as a developmental task during the 20s. Most notably, Levinson, Darrow, Klein, Levinson, and McKee (1978) argued that the novice phase that takes place during the 20s is when "the Dream" is formulated, that is, an optimistic vision of how one's adult life might be. In my theory of emerging adulthood I have proposed a related idea, that emerging adulthood is the age of possibilities, when many futures still seem possible and most emerging adults believe that adult life will turn out well for them, even if their lives in the present seem unpromising (Arnett, 2004). Perhaps emerging adulthood involves, in part, the paring down of various possibilities to settle on one Dream. Whether ego development is something that aids in this process is an intriguing question that merits further investigation.

Tanner's chapter raises the important issue of the heterogeneity of emerging adulthood and the extent to which the experience of emerging adulthood varies depending on factors such as attending college or not. She makes a case for predicting development in emerging adulthood from variables in earlier development, such as parent–child interactions or parental socioeconomic status (SES). However, I would add the caveat that even when earlier development is a significant predictor of development in emerging adulthood in longitudinal studies, such studies may not predict a substantial amount of the variance in emerging adult variables, which means that more changes than remains the same for most people from childhood to emerging adulthood. For example, parental SES is a significant predictor of emerging adults' college enrollment, but college enrollment among 18 to 21 year olds in the United States rose from less than 5% in 1900 to over 60% in 2000 (Arnett, 2004), so clearly the predictive power of SES from one generation to the next is limited and change does take place.

Once the limitations in predicting emerging adult development from earlier development are recognized, then the challenge becomes to delineate the ways that people change in emerging adulthood, and to explain why. Tanner suggests that college attendance is one crucial context that is the basis of change in emerging adulthood. What other variables matter? This is an important question for future research, and Tanner's chapter should serve as a useful basis for investigating it.

Cognitive Development

Some readers may be surprised to find a chapter on cognitive development in a book on emerging adulthood. Certainly the vast majority of research on cognitive development focuses on infancy and early childhood, with a smattering of research on middle childhood and adolescence. Isn't cognitive development pretty much over by the time formal operations are attained in adolescence—at least until cognitive abilities begin to decline in old age? The chapter by Gisela Labouvie-Vief provides a forceful corrective to this assumption. Drawing on a wide range of research, including her own, she integrates research on cognition with cognitive-related research on moral development, self-understanding, and affective changes to present a portrait of cognitive development in emerging adulthood as dynamic, diverse, and complex.

Labouvie-Vief begins the chapter by usefully emphasizing that cognitive development always takes place in a cultural context, and that the dramatic and rapid changes in Western cultures over the past century have created new cognitive challenges that require taking into account nonrational cognitive processes, the diversity of possible cognitive perspectives, and the changing nature of knowledge. She then shows evidence that emerging adulthood is a critical stage for the emergence of the complex forms of thinking required in complex societies. However, she emphasizes that emerging adults are diverse in their cognitive development, especially depending on the level of education they receive, and that the most highly developed forms of thinking in emerging adulthood are potentialities that are fulfilled only by some.

The heart of the cognitive change that (potentially) occurs in emerging adulthood is that the person decides on a particular worldview but also recognizes that there is an element of subjectivity in any worldview and diverse points of view should be recognized as adding to the total picture of what the truth is. This is not relativism that views all perspectives as equally valid, but a more complex way of thinking that chooses a worldview judged to be valid while also recognizing that other perspectives may have merit and that no one has a monopoly on the truth. The truth is sought by taking into account and coordinating multiple perspectives and by integrating subjective and objective aspects of knowledge, which requires tolerance for contradiction, diversity, and ambiguity.

The basis for this view is the cognitive–developmental theory originally proposed by Kohlberg (1969) and Perry (1970/1999), which continues to be the basis for the views of many scholars on cognitive development today. However, the major modification made by current scholars is a tendency to see cognitive development in adolescence and beyond as occurring not in *stages* that are universal and ontogenetic but as *levels* that have some relation to age but whose development depends on contextual factors, especially education. As a consequence the levels of cognitive functioning among persons at any given age are diverse. This view fits well with my emphasis on the heterogeneity of development within the emerging adult years (see chap. 1, this volume). Emerging adults are especially diverse in the types and lengths of education they obtain, and in Labouvie-Vief's view, this fact has crucial implications for their cognitive development, because higher levels of cognitive functioning in emerging adulthood and beyond tend to be related to the amount of education obtained.

Labouvie-Vief presents this case effectively. However, a thorough test of her theoretical stance will require more studies that compare emerging adults with various educational levels, those who attend college as well as those who do not, and those who attend vocational schools or community colleges as well as those who attend 4-year universities. Labouvie-Vief insightfully notes that "education is the very process or means by which culture imparts knowledge to the younger generations" (chap. 3, p. 73) and that this process of generational transmission of cognitive skills has been studied a lot between adults and young children but very little between emerging adults and older adults. Her provocative and original ideas on this topic provide a superb basis for hypotheses to guide further research in this area.

In an especially important section, Labouvie-Vief expands the field's normal thinking about the domains of cognition to include the cognitive aspects of self and emotion, considering the question of how cognition in emerging adulthood is "carried into daily experiences of individuals and expand[s] their emotions and their sense of self and reality" (chap. 3, p. 67). She presents results from her longitudinal-sequential research of persons from age 10 to 80, which shows four levels of adult emotional and self-development. At the higher levels, views of the self become more complex and show greater self-reflection and awareness that the self is something that changes over time. Movement into the higher levels takes place especially in emerging adulthood, when "individuals of the emerging adulthood period begin to profoundly restructure their sense of self" (chap. 3, p. 68).

This insight, that crucial changes take place in emerging adulthood in people's sense of self and capacity for self-reflection, opens up a wide and promising vista for future research. As someone who has interviewed both adolescents and emerging adults in research, I have been struck by how much more self-reflective and insightful emerging adults are. This is as true for noncollege emerging adults as for those who have attended college. In my view, this is one of the characteristics of emerging adults that makes them especially fun to interview and makes the interviews with them especially valuable and rich with information. Perhaps it is, in part, the self-focused nature of emerging adulthood that promotes the development of self-reflection and self-understanding during these years. Undistracted by either the peer whirl of adolescence or the family role demands of young adulthood, emerging adults are able to devote more attention to their sense of self. Labouvie-Vief's emphasis on the restructuring of the self in emerging adulthood also fits well with the idea of emerging adulthood as a time when identity issues are prominent, as these issues often entail self-reflection and the development of self-understanding. In any case, Labouvie-Vief's ideas on the topic in this chapter will hopefully inspire new research that uses her levels as well as other schemes.

Such research could also indicate how cognitive development continues past emerging adulthood into young adulthood, as Labouvie-Vief illustrates in her research on cognitive–affective differences with age. As Labouvie-Vief stresses, although important changes in cognitive development take place in emerging adulthood, some aspects of cognitive development may be substantially more developed in older adults. Furthermore, among same-age emerging adults there is a great range of individual differences in their cognitive functioning. This heterogeneity is worth keeping in mind and exploring further, here as in other areas.

Although Labouvie-Vief is clearly aware of the importance of taking into account the cultural context of cognitive development, nearly all the research she draws from is based on American samples, so it will be important in future research to examine cognitive development among emerging adults in other cultures. Patterns characteristic of the American samples used in most research may or may not apply in other cultures, particularly in cultures that value individualism and diversity relatively less and obedience and conformity relatively more. Perhaps the restructuring of the self that Labouvie-Vief has found among American emerging adults takes place in some other cultures in a way that is less self-focused and more oriented toward duties and obligations to others (Nelson, Badger, & Wu, 2004).

Identity

One of the key features I have proposed as part of development during emerging adulthood is identity explorations. In interviews with emerging adults, I have found that identity issues arise in response to a wide range of questions, which suggests that these issues are so prominent during this period that they pervade many areas of life.

How does this observation match up with the theory and research that has been done on identity formation? According to James E. Côté in his chapter on identity development in emerging adulthood, it is widely agreed among scholars that important aspects of identity development take place during the emerging adult years. He also notes that participation in higher education has greatly expanded in the past half century in countries such as the United States and Canada, and he interprets this as a sign of the spread of emerging adulthood, as the pursuit of higher education often includes identity explorations with respect to possible future work. However, he emphasizes that for emerging adults who do not obtain higher education after secondary school, their work experiences from their late teens through their 20s may involve frequent job changes, not as part of identity explorations but as part of a frustrating attempt to find an adequate job in a society that no longer offers many satisfying options for people who lack the credentials of higher education.

Côté notes, as I have, that emerging adulthood is a time of considerable freedom from institutional guidance and social control for young people in postindustrial or postmodern societies. However, his interpretation of the consequences of this self-focused freedom is somewhat darker than mine. In Côté's view the freedom of emerging adulthood is favorable for some, and they make the most of it to pursue "a life course of continual and deliberate growth," a response Côté calls *developmental individualization* (chap. 4, p. 92). But this is only part of the picture. Pursuing developmental individualization requires a substantial amount of what Côté terms *identity capital,* meaning the personal qualities of self-understanding, self-discipline, and planfulness that can be used to guide choices in love and work in the absence of social and institutional supports. Those who lack identity capital are at risk for following a course of default individualization, in which they do not engage in systematic identity explorations but instead drift along through emerging adulthood with no particular direction in mind, diverted from their anomie by the latest distractions of popular culture. Thus Côté usefully calls attention to the heterogeneity that exists among emerging adults with respect to their personal and social resources, and emphasizes the importance of studying the experiences of emerging adults who do not have the benefit of a sufficient amount of education and identity capital to thrive on the lack of structure typical of emerging adulthood.

With respect to identity status research, the amount of light this literature can cast on identity development in emerging adulthood is disappointingly meager. Vast amounts of research have been done on identity development in the emerging adulthood age period, usually with college students, but oddly, most of this research has lacked a developmental perspective. The studies seem to indicate that identity explorations in emerging adulthood are by no means normative but are experienced by only a minority of emerging adults. Still, it would be wise to hesitate before embracing this conclusion wholeheartedly. As Côté notes, the developmental validity of the identity status concept—as well as the measures used to assess it—has been called into question (Côté, 2000; Schacter, 2005; Schwartz, 2005; van Hoof, 1999).

This may be a good example of the importance of paradigms and of the potential value of the emerging adulthood paradigm for inspiring a fresh look at the developmental characteristics of the age period from the late teens through the 20s. Perhaps the assertion that emerging adulthood is distinctive developmentally and that identity explorations are one of the key features of the period will lead to new research to test this hypothesis and new measures to use in the research, informed by theory on emerging adulthood. As Côté notes, the dominant concepts and measurement approaches in identity research were formed some time ago and may not apply as well to emerging adulthood today. The new paradigm of emerging adulthood represents an opportunity to take a fresh look at identity and rethink how it is conceptualized and measured. Côté himself takes a step toward this at the end of his chapter, by presenting a number of promising theoretical ideas and by presenting his recent research. Using a measure he recently developed, he finds some (limited) support for identity development during emerging adulthood. He concedes that this step is preliminary, but hopefully it will lead to further steps. The theoretical model Côté presents should also inspire new research ideas.

Ethnic Identity

Emerging adulthood is not ontogenetic and universal but a consequence of certain cultural and historical conditions (Arnett, 2002), so it is important to explore the forms it takes in a wide variety of cultural groups. Jean S. Phinney gives this enterprise a considerable boost in her chapter on ethnic identity in emerging adulthood. She points to ways that membership in an ethnic minority group may shorten or extend the period of emerging adulthood. Often young people in American ethnic minority groups take on important family responsibilities at a relatively early age, and in some groups there may be social pressure to marry and have children relatively early. Emerging adulthood may be shortened or may not exist under these conditions. However, Phinney insightfully observes, identity formation may take longer for many members of ethnic minorities because of the challenge of working out the meaning of their ethnic identity. In this sense emerging adulthood may be extended for them, given that identity exploration is one of the key developmental challenges of emerging adulthood (Arnett, 2000, 2004).

Phinney points out that ethnic identity issues are likely to become more prominent in emerging adulthood because moving from adolescence to emerging adulthood usually means changing the contexts of daily life from family, peers, secondary school, and neighborhood to the wider world of work and possibly higher education. In this wider world there is likely to be more contact with persons from outside of one's ethnic group, leading to questions about what one's ethnic identity means and possibly to conflicts between the values of interdependence and duty learned in the family and the values of independence and self-assertion prized in the American majority culture. Phinney suggests that this exposure to other cultures may result in an identity crisis for emerging adults in minority cultures, a fascinating hypothesis that merits investigation.

Phinney also cites research suggesting that cognitive development may be involved in ethnic identity issues in emerging adulthood. Increased cognitive abilities in emerging adulthood can lead to increased abilities for reflecting on one's ethnic identity and greater capabilities for understanding how ethnicity fits into a broader sense of one's self. This observation underscores the importance of investigating cognitive development in emerging adulthood and exploring its implications for other aspects of development.

Mental Health

In their chapter, John E. Schulenberg and Nicole R. Zarrett address a striking paradox of development during emerging adulthood. They describe how mental health improves in emerging adulthood overall, as measured in terms of increasing well-being, decreasing depressive affect, and decreasing antisocial behavior. However, at the same time as these indicators turn for the better, other indicators turn for the worse, with emerging adulthood the highest risk period of the life course for the diagnosis of major psychopathology such as schizophrenia, bipolar disorder, major depression, and borderline personality disorder.

Thus, emerging adulthood appears to be a period when mental health functioning is not simply better or worse than other age periods but more diverse. As in many of the other chapters, heterogeneity is a key issue, and

Schulenberg and Zarrett emphasize the great heterogeneity of paths of mental health functioning in emerging adulthood. They attribute this heterogeneity, as I have, to the lack of institutional structure and social support during this age period. Adolescents have the institutional frameworks of living at home and attending secondary school, and most young adults enter the roles of marriage, parenthood, and long-term employment by age 30. In between, during emerging adulthood, the lack of institutional structures means that emerging adults have an exceptional amount of freedom to exercise agency and freedom of choice. These freedoms may underlie their high sense of well-being as a group, as Tanner suggests in her chapter, but those who are most in need of the guidance of institutional structures may exhibit mental health problems for the first time during emerging adulthood.

The appearance of severe psychopathology in emerging adulthood is likely to be due to more than environmental factors. Mental disorders such as schizophrenia and bipolar disorder have been shown to have a high genetic loading (Plomin, DeFries, McClearn, & Rutter, 1997), and it may be that such disorders are timed genetically to appear for the first time in the decade or so after puberty is reached. But even if this is true, it may be that the lack of institutional structure in emerging adulthood makes the expression of a genetic vulnerability to mental disorders more likely. Schulenberg and Zarrett emphasize the issue of continuity–discontinuity in mental health from adolescence to emerging adulthood and how it may be related to the transitions and events emerging adults experience. They present four categories of continuity–discontinuity, based on combinations of the descriptive (manifest) level and the explanatory (underlying meaning) level. This approach is a potentially fruitful way of understanding developmental change from adolescence to emerging adulthood and from emerging adulthood to young adulthood, not just in mental health but in other areas as well. For example, as they suggest, the changing meaning of substance use over time can be understood in terms of its functional discontinuity over time—that is, a 14-year-old adolescent who drinks a six-pack of beer every Friday and Saturday night is probably not mentally healthy and likely has a variety of other problems such as family difficulties and school problems. For a 35-year-old, the same behavior may also be a sign of poor mental health, but of a different kind, perhaps loneliness, insecurity, or self-destructiveness. However, an emerging adult who exhibits such behavior at age 21 or 22, at the height of the "prime drinking years" (Schulenberg & Maggs, 2002) in American society, may not have any mental health problems at all but be drinking out of positive motivations such as sociability and youthful exuberance. For these emerging adults, binge drinking may be a *developmental disturbance* that recedes after emerging adulthood without predicting or being predicted by enduring difficulties in development.

Throughout their chapter, Schulenberg and Zarrett emphasize the importance of identifying subgroup trajectories from adolescence to emerging adulthood. This approach to analyzing longitudinal data is extremely promising. It takes into account the heterogeneity of development in emerging adulthood because it identifies not just overall patterns but a variety of trajectories that different subsamples of emerging adults may follow. In view of the heterogeneity of emerging adulthood, I believe it would be valuable if this trajectory model became the standard methodological approach to analyzing longitudinal data that includes emerging adults.

Resilience

I have long considered resilience a promising topic with respect to emerging adulthood, partly because of my experience in interviewing emerging adults who have displayed remarkable resilience, transforming their lives in strikingly positive ways in emerging adulthood after a difficult and tumultuous childhood and adolescence. Their stories are dramatic and moving (see Arnett, 2004, chap. 9). Also, it seems that the social context of emerging adulthood offers especially rich possibilities for resilience. Unlike children and adolescents, emerging adults can leave a destructive, chaotic, or stressful family situation in pursuit of a healthier environment. Unlike older adults, emerging adults are not yet committed to long-term obligations in love and work that may lock them into an unhealthy path. The freedom of emerging adulthood, the self-focused nature of it, and the lack of social constraint seem to offer the possibility of dramatic change for the better. This is one way in which emerging adulthood is the age of possibilities.

Ann S. Masten, Jelena Obradović, and Keith B. Burt pursue this possibility in their chapter on resilience. They begin with the hypothesis that "Emerging adulthood holds particular interest for the study of risk and resilience because this period may afford important changes in functional capacity, vulnerabilities, and opportunities that may play an important role in altering the life course" (chap. 7, p. 177). They note that other longitudinal studies have found that military service, marriage and romantic relationships, higher education, religious affiliations, and work opportunities may provide turning-point opportunities in emerging adulthood. Then they examine this hypothesis using data from their landmark longitudinal study of resilience, Project Competence, which has assessed a sample in childhood, adolescence, emerging adulthood (ages 17–23), and young adulthood (ages 27–33). Looking at development from childhood to emerging adulthood, they found that emerging adults who had experienced high adversity in childhood but displayed competence in adulthood—that is, the resilient group—had resources of intelligence, personality, and family relationships not shared with their maladaptive peers who also experienced high adversity in childhood but were struggling in emerging adulthood. This finding suggests that making use of emerging adulthood as the age of possibilities depends on having the benefit of resources that provide tools for responding successfully to high adversity.

Also of interest are their findings of resilience from emerging adulthood to young adulthood. They found that the resilient group in emerging adulthood continued to function better than did the maladaptive group 10 years later, during young adulthood, in the domains of work and romantic relationships. However, of particular interest in these analyses, with respect to the question of emerging adulthood as the age of possibilities, is their finding of *late-blooming resilience* among a *turnaround group* who changed from maladaptive in emerging adulthood to resilient in young adulthood. Compared with their peers who remained maladaptive in young adulthood, the emerging adults in this turnaround group had more of what Masten and colleagues called *EA adaptive resources* of planfulness, autonomy, and adult support. But this turnaround group was small, so these findings would be worth exploring further in a larger sample, perhaps in a study focusing specifically on resilience from emerging adulthood to young adulthood.

In their research design, Masten and colleagues adapt their standard of competence to each age period, looking at *emerging domains* that have importance as developmental tasks in a specific age period as well as *core domains* that apply across age periods. They also look at predictors of resilience that are developmentally specific. With respect to emerging adulthood, these EA adaptive resources are future orientation, planfulness, autonomy, adult support, and coping skills. One notable feature of these adaptive resources is that they are largely cognitive; with the exception of adult support, all have a cognitive basis. This finding supports Labouvie-Vief's assertion that important cognitive changes take place in emerging adulthood. Although the focus of Masten and her colleagues is on resilience, their findings have important implications for cognitive development during emerging adulthood.

Also of interest is the finding that the emerging domains of work and romantic relationships in emerging adulthood did not predict future competence in young adulthood. The authors observe that this is "consistent with our developmental task theory, in that these tasks would be considered to be in an exploratory phase during EA" (chap. 7, p. 184). It is also consistent with my assertion that exploration and instability are two of the key developmental features of emerging adulthood. Work and romantic relationships are areas of life that are unsettled in emerging adulthood because of the exploration and instability that characterizes them during these years. As a consequence, an assessment of work and romantic status at any one point during emerging adulthood predicts little about what their lives will be like 10 years later.

The authors close the chapter by stating that although luck certainly plays a role in determining which emerging adults turn out to be resilient, "it would be desirable to rely less on lucky conjunctions and more on thoughtful scaffolding of this transition," through strategic interventions informed by "a better understanding of the processes that influence planful competence, future orientation, motivation to change, successful mentoring, and positive engagement in age-salient developmental tasks" (chap. 7, p. 188). The cognitive features of emerging adulthood that play such an important role in resilience are skills that can be taught. Perhaps future research will provide more information about how these skills might be taught to emerging adults or to adolescents on the verge of emerging adulthood, especially those who have experienced adverse conditions in childhood and adolescence and consequently are especially in need of the opportunity for resilience presented by emerging adulthood.

Family Relationships

Family relationships have long been regarded as the primary influence on children's social and emotional development. The influence of parents on children and adolescents is clear enough, as parents determine everything from food and clothing to where the family will live to what the rules and customs of the household will be. But what about emerging adults, who are no longer as dependent on their parents as they once were, and may not even live at home any longer? What place do family relationships have in their lives?

William S. Aquilino's chapter provides a great deal of information and insight on this question. He uses the family life-course framework to emphasize "the interdependence of family members' life paths and the constant interplay between individual development and family development." This approach is effective in drawing attention to the ways that changes not only in emerging adults but in their parents influence the relationship. For example, as emerging adults become more capable of self-sufficiency and may begin to serve as a source of support for their parents, parents may learn to recognize and adjust to their children's near-adult maturity and offer them the blessing that implicitly or explicitly encourages it. Changes on both sides allow parents and emerging adults to move toward a relationship that is less hierarchical and more like a friendship, more of a relationship between near-equals.

Aquilino reviews longitudinal studies of parent–child relationships from childhood or adolescence to emerging adulthood and finds some degree of continuity over time, especially from adolescence to emerging adulthood. However, perhaps more striking is that even when the earlier relationships are significant predictors of relationships in emerging adulthood, the effects are not strong, explaining less than 10% of the variance. This finding means that more often than not, the quality of relationships with parents is different in emerging adulthood than it was earlier. The explanation for this may lie in the changes that take place over time in the lives of both parents and emerging adults— for parents, events such as divorce, physical illness, or mental illness; for emerging adults, changes such as leaving home, obtaining full-time work, or attending college. I might add here the kinds of cognitive and identity changes described by Labouvie-Vief and Côté, which also contribute to changes in the parent–child relationship.

One of the most enduring family influences in the lives of emerging adults is a negative one, that is, the influence of parental divorce. As Aquilino describes, considerable evidence indicates that parental divorce has negative effects on relationships with emerging adults, especially between emerging adults and their noncustodial parent, usually the father. In fact, one study indicates that there may be a sleeper effect of divorce, such that the negative effects on children's mental health become more evident in emerging adulthood than they had been previously (Cherlin, Chase-Landsdale, & McRae, 1998). Furthermore, an important study by Laumann-Billings and Emery (2000) shows that even when the effects of divorce on emerging adults are not evident in their behavior, the pain of it often remains deep, even many years later. I have seen evidence of this pain often, in my interviews with emerging adults (see Arnett, 2004, chap. 3). However, I would emphasize, as many scholars on divorce have (e.g., Buchanan, 2000), that the effects of divorce are diverse and complex. It is indeed striking how deep and enduring the pain of their parents' divorce remains in the memories of many emerging adults, but parental divorce is experienced by nearly half of American children and individual differences are vast. For some, their parents' divorce is a welcome relief from constant conflict (Arnett, 2004).

Emerging adults are more capable than children or adolescents of understanding their parents' relationship, including the motivations parents may have for divorcing, and this understanding is part of a larger change. For me, the most striking quality in emerging adults' relationships with their parents is the way emerging adults come to understand their parents as persons, not just as parents (Arnett, 2004). They are much better than children or adolescents at taking their parents' perspective and understanding how life looks from that perspective. This important change in social cognition needs further exploration.

Although Aquilino acknowledges that most of the research available for his chapter is based on mostly White samples in the United States, especially college students, he emphasizes the need for studies that explore cultural variations in emerging adults' relationships with parents. I agree, and it is possible to see in the studies Aquilino reviews how the focus on European Americans has shaped certain assumptions about development in family relationships in emerging adulthood that could be challenged or filled out by research on other cultures. Assumptions are often made about the desirability of independence from parents that are based more on American individualism than on anything that is inherently part of development in emerging adulthood. In many cultures reaching adulthood means not just being able to take care of oneself but being able to take care of others. Research on perceptions of what it means to be an adult shows that European Americans typically emphasize individualistic criteria such as accepting responsibility for oneself and making independent decisions, whereas emerging adults with an Asian cultural background—for example, Asian Americans, South Koreans, and Chinese— emphasize not only these qualities but also commitments to others, especially the capacity for taking care of one's parents (Arnett, 2003; Nelson et al., 2004). As Aquilino notes, persons in minority cultures in the United States also tend to be more likely than European Americans to view it as acceptable for emerging adults to remain in their parents' household.

In addition to the need for more research on cultural variations in family relationships during emerging adulthood, Aquilino identifies several other promising "unanswered (and unasked) questions." The results of research on relationships with siblings and grandparents in emerging adulthood are intriguing, but there is very little of it. Aquilino also calls for research on how emerging adults and their parents talk about the changes occurring in their relationship, a great topic for an interview study. There is also a need for research that examines variations in emerging adults' family relationships by gender, region, socioeconomic status, and combinations of these variables. In short, an abundance of research topics awaits scholars interested in family relationships in emerging adulthood.

Friendships and Romantic Relationships

Entering emerging adulthood means leaving the setting of secondary school and the daily context it provides for peer interactions. One might expect substantial changes in friendships from adolescence to emerging adulthood because emerging adults are no longer concentrated in a context in which they are likely to see each other every school day; even emerging adults who attend college have a less concentrated, more diffuse peer environment, and of course many emerging adults do not attend college. With respect to romantic relationships one might also expect changes from adolescence to emerging adulthood, as emotional maturity develops and as the first initiation into romantic relationships gives way to more intensive exploration of emotional and sexual intimacy.

W. Andrew Collins and Manfred van Dulmen examine some of these issues in their chapter. They especially focus on the question of whether emerging adulthood can be distinguished from adolescence with respect to close relationships (i.e., friendships and romantic relationships). Their overall conclusion is that emerging adults' close relationships are similar to adolescents' in relationship motives, concerns, and expectations but that emerging adults describe their close relationships in ways that are more differentiated and complex than in adolescence. This difference provides additional support for the theme that there are distinct advances in social cognition from adolescence to emerging adulthood, as Labouvie-Vief and Aquilino described in their chapters.

A provocative finding discussed by Collins and van Dulmen is that relationships are more integrated in emerging adulthood than in adolescence, that is, relationships with family, friends, and romantic partners are more similar in quality and in the representations associated with them, and emerging adults engage in more social interactions that include diverse relationships. I would suggest that this finding might reflect greater identity development in emerging adulthood. As emerging adults develop a more integrated identity, they increasingly show the same self to others in their different relationships, which makes it easier for them to enjoy social events that include friends as well as family members or romantic partners. This may be a hypothesis worth investigating.

Collins and van Dulmen focus many of the analyses from their own data on the question of whether identity explorations in friendships and romantic relationships are a distinctive feature of development in emerging adulthood, as I have proposed. They conclude that their evidence does not generally support my distinctiveness hypothesis for identity explorations in emerging adulthood. However, they test the hypothesis by looking simply at numerical indicators such as time spent with friends and number of romantic and sexual relationships, with higher numbers indicating greater exploration. This strategy is understandable, given that they were looking for variables in their existing database to test new hypotheses about a new theory, rather than designing new measures a priori. As a result, it sheds only limited light on the question of the distinctiveness of identity explorations in emerging adulthood.

The number of friendships and romantic relationships may well decline from adolescence through emerging adulthood, as they (and others) have found, but this finding is subject to multiple interpretations. It could indicate a decline in identity explorations from adolescence to emerging adulthood, as Collins and van Dulmen suggest, if it means that changing relationships is a form of identity exploration. However, it could indicate more intensive and systematic identity exploration in emerging adulthood than in adolescence. Adolescents may change relationships frequently because their relationships are less identity-based; they choose their relationships more on the basis of criteria of companionship and status (Brown, 1999). In contrast, emerging adults may change relationships less frequently because their relationships become more identity-focused; they look more for an identity fit with another person, a deeper and more personalized attachment. In any case, Collins and van Dulmen are forthright about the limitations of existing data, and their analysis sets up a useful framework for designing studies that will allow for the examination of the relation between close relationships and identity development more directly.

Collins and van Dulmen highlight the finding in their research that measures of functioning in adolescence and even childhood significantly predict aspects of close relationships in emerging adulthood. As with the findings reported by Tanner and by Aquilino, I recommend caution in interpreting these findings. A significant finding may in fact account for only a small portion of the variance, so it should not be taken to indicate that there is more continuity than change from childhood to adolescence to emerging adulthood, whether in close relationships or other areas. On the contrary, the broad variance characteristic of emerging adults in most aspects of their lives is likely to be evident here as well, and the rich promise of future research is to examine the diversity of patterns or trajectories that people follow from adolescence to emerging adulthood to young adulthood.

Especially enlightening would be longitudinal studies that follow a sample of people closely from adolescence through emerging adulthood and chart the changes that take place in their close relationships along the way. How do they change in what they look for in friends and romantic partners? How do they meet new ones and develop relationships with them? What sorts of factors precipitate the dissolution of close relationships, and how does such dissolution influence emerging adults?

Sexuality

One part of nearly all romantic relationships among emerging adults is sexuality. A notable feature of emerging adulthood is that it is a time when it is normative for people to be sexually active, including intercourse, outside the context of marriage. This is a new phenomenon, something that never existed before in Western societies prior to the 1960s. Premarital sex has always been strongly prohibited, especially for women, who in the past were disgraced if it became known that they were no longer virgins prior to marriage, and indeed as known nonvirgins their marriage prospects plummeted. The change to widespread tolerance of premarital sex took place because of a number of factors, including the invention of the birth control pill and changes in gender role expectations for women. Now that it is generally acceptable for emerging adults to be sexually active before marriage, new opportunities are available to them as well as a number of persistent problems.

In their chapter, Eva S. Lefkowitz and Meghan M. Gillen examine a variety of aspects of sexuality in emerging adulthood. They describe emerging adults as highly diverse in their sexual behavior. Emerging adults (ages 18–24) are more likely than persons in the next older or next younger age periods to have had two or more sexual partners in the past year, but they are also more likely than 25- to 29-year-olds to have had sex a few times or not at all in the past year. Here, then, is another example of the heterogeneity of emerging adults, the broad variance in their behavior that is a consequence of their exceptional freedom of choice in combination with the lack of normative expectations for this age period.

Lefkowitz and Gillen emphasize the place of identity issues in the sexuality of emerging adults. A variety of sexual issues underscore the idea of emerging adulthood as the age of identity explorations, including deciding on one's sexual beliefs and attitudes related to premarital sex and contraception, and views of gender in relation to sexuality (e.g., the issue of male–female power in the relationship). The *hooking up* that is normative among American college students can be seen as part of the identity explorations of emerging adulthood, that is, part of obtaining a broad range of experiences before becoming committed to a particular choice. Lefkowitz and Gillen frame identity development and sexuality in emerging adulthood in terms of the development of a sexual self-schema. As they note, development of this self-schema is an especially salient issue in emerging adulthood because this is the time when most people are first incorporating their sexuality into their overall identity.

Another identity-related feature of sexuality in emerging adulthood is that, among persons who are lesbian, gay, bisexual, or transgendered (LGBT), coming out tends to occur right around the time emerging adulthood begins. Perhaps coming out is identity-related in the sense that emerging adulthood is when LGBT persons develop a more definite sense of their sexual identity, after first experiencing same-sex attractions and sexual behavior in adolescence or earlier. The timing of coming out may also be related to the beginning of emerging adulthood because this is when most young people in American society first leave home (Goldscheider & Goldscheider, 1999). Perhaps out of fear that their parents may respond aversively when they come out, LGBT persons may choose to do so only after they are about to leave home or have left home and no longer have to face their parents' dismay and disapproval on a daily basis. But the evidence on this issue is very limited; this is a hypothesis for future investigation.

Lefkowitz and Gillen seek to avoid portraying the sexuality of emerging adults strictly as problematic. As they note, "Responsible sexual behavior between two consenting emerging adults is not necessarily linked with negative psychological or physical consequences" (chap. 10, p. 236). This is a good point; the developmental differences between adolescents and emerging adults, physically, cognitively, and emotionally, make sexual involvements less problematic and potentially more positive for emerging adults. It is unfortunate that the sexual behavior of emerging adults frequently falls short of being responsible. Many of them use contraception inconsistently or use unreliable methods such as withdrawal. Rates of single motherhood, abortion, and STDs are higher in the 20s than in any other age period. Reports of unwanted sexual contact among college women are disturbingly high.

Also disturbing are the high rates of STDs such as human pappillomavirus (HPV) and chlamydia among emerging adults. Even though most emerging adults are sexually active and have a series of partners over the course of their emerging adult years, and many hook up in casual sexual episodes occasionally, few of them ever get tested for STDs. They appear to be unaware that persons with STDs such as HPV and chlamydia are often asymptomatic, and that if they remain undiagnosed and untreated they are at risk for future problems ranging from infertility to cervical cancer. There is a clear and urgent need here to educate emerging adults about the risks of STDs and the importance of regular testing.

In part, the problems associated with sexuality in emerging adulthood are the consequence of being at an age at which most people are sexually active but few are married and partners change fairly frequently. Under these circumstances, it is likely that occasionally mistakes will be made and an unintended pregnancy or an STD will result. Still, it is notable that rates of abortion, single motherhood, and STDs are considerably higher among emerging adults in the United States than in any other industrialized country. This indicates that something about the American approach to sexuality in emerging adulthood, not just sexuality in emerging adulthood per se, is problematic. What makes the problematic consequences of emerging adult sexuality higher in the United States than elsewhere? Is the answer similar to what has been found regarding adolescent sexuality, in studies comparing the United States with other Western countries (Alan Guttmacher Institute, 2001), implicating factors such as restricted access to contraception, lack of adequate sex education, and ambivalence about the morality of premarital sex? Or are there other factors specific to emerging adulthood?

These are questions for which answers are urgently needed. In their conclusion, Lefkowitz and Gillen do an excellent job of laying out an agenda for future research on emerging adult sexuality, calling for more qualitative studies, longitudinal studies, studies of couples rather than only individuals, studies that include romantic relationships as well as sexuality, and studies of nonpenetrative sexuality. I hope that many investigators will use their ideas as a road map for new research.

School and Work

Emerging adulthood is a key time for preparing the foundation for the kind of work people will be doing in their adult lives. This foundation is prepared in part through education, as many emerging adults pursue postsecondary schooling intended to provide them with skills that will be useful in the workplace, and in part through workplace experience, usually through a series of jobs rather than one job over time. In their chapter, Stephen F. and Mary Agnes Hamilton illuminate the complexity of the paths in school and work that people follow in the course of emerging adulthood.

The heterogeneity of emerging adulthood is clear with respect to school and work. Their school and work patterns are strikingly diverse, with myriad combinations of full-time or part-time school with full- or part-time work, different types of school (4-year, 2-year, General Educational Development certificate), military service, and so on. The Hamiltons' delineation of this diversity serves as a useful reminder for anyone who is accustomed to thinking about emerging adults as students at 4-year residential colleges. Such students are not a majority even among college students, as many emerging adults attend 2-year colleges or commute to 4-year schools. Nor is entering a 4-year college any guarantee of obtaining a 4-year degree; barely half of those who enroll in 4-year programs have graduated 5 years later, and only 29% of 25- to 29-year-olds in the United States hold at least a bachelor's degree. There are gaping ethnic differences, with Asian Americans and Whites far more likely than African Americans, Latinos, or Native Americans to obtain a bachelor's degree. Almost one fourth of emerging adults do not even graduate from high school on time; of these, about half obtain a GED certificate some time in emerging adulthood.

In addition to diversity, a second hallmark of emerging adults' school and work patterns is instability. The average number of jobs over the first 10 years of employment is seven, and most emerging adults hold their first job for less than a year. Many of the emerging adults who enter higher education after high school drop out before obtaining a degree, perhaps resuming some time later. Others may change from one school–work combination to another, going from full-time to part-time or vice versa in either school or work.

It seems clear that emerging adults' school and work patterns are emblematic of emerging adulthood as the age of instability, as I have called it. But what this instability means in the lives of emerging adults remains an open question. The Hamiltons describe a debate in the employment literature over whether the instability of emerging adults' work patterns indicates *searching* or *floundering*, that is, whether it indicates a search for a job that best matches their interests and abilities or whether it is indicative of lack of planning or direction. They come to the sensible conclusion that instability reflects searching for some and floundering for others. The Hamiltons recommend that scholars "disaggregate the population . . . to distinguish those who are following productive career paths from those who are not, to identify their characteristics, and to compare their relative proportions in the population." This suggestion is consistent with the identification of trajectory subgroups laid out by Schulenberg and Zarrett in their chapter on mental health, which holds promise across a wide range of areas in emerging adulthood.

As the Hamiltons emphasize, it is important not only to distinguish the searchers from the flounderers but to understand how they get that way. The usual suspects, such as parental education and income, are certainly involved, but other factors are surely involved as well. The Hamiltons describe a recent study by Osgood et al. (2005) showing that emerging adults from poor families who do well in school and have high educational expectations can do just as well in their educational or occupational attainment in emerging adulthood as those who come from backgrounds with more advantages and resources. In other words, ability and achievement motivation can trump family background. The Hamiltons tie this finding to the resilience literature, and this finding can be seen as an example of emerging adulthood as a critical period for the expression of resilience, as described by Masten and her colleagues in their chapter.

It may not be as simple as distinguishing the searchers from the flounderers. So far, floundering has been determined simply by a pattern of frequent movement between jobs and into and out of the labor force. But what if this does not feel like floundering to those who are experiencing it? Surely there is an important distinction between emerging adults who change jobs frequently and feel frustrated and despondent that they are unable to keep a job for long, as contrasted with those who move from job to job in emerging adulthood and do not mind or even enjoy the changes, perhaps because they view this as a time of life when their focus is on leisure and work is simply a necessary evil, a way to pay the bills to allow them to enjoy life outside of work. Interview research is necessary to learn more about how emerging adults experience their frequent job changes.

One thing that seems clear on the basis of what is already known is that a lot more could and should be done for emerging adults in the United States to assist them in planning a career path. As it currently stands, virtually all emerging adults have high expectations for the kind of employment they will eventually find—a testament to emerging adulthood as the age of possibilities, when optimism reigns—but relatively few of them have a clear understanding of how to develop a systematic plan to turn their hopes into reality. Instead, they hope that by falling into one job after another, they will eventually fall into one they like and want to stay in. There is no institutional school-to-work program in the United States, and consequently emerging adults must rely on what Côté calls *identity capital*: qualities such as initiative, purposefulness, and agency. But those who lack a sufficient amount of these qualities face an unpromising occupational future.

The Hamiltons offer a number of excellent suggestions to rectify this problem and move toward more structured explorations in emerging adulthood. Secondary schools and colleges can provide assistance in constructing a career plan through academic counseling and by linking their curricula to occupations. These approaches have been demonstrated to be effective. The Hamiltons also recommend work-based learning, including active mentoring, whose effectiveness has been shown through decades of their own exemplary research. Perhaps their most original and promising suggestion is to integrate research on career paths with research on resilience: "The basic idea is applying to emerging adults the same approach used in studying resilient children: trying to understand how some succeed in overcoming the odds against them" (chap. 11, p. 274). This exciting, innovative idea will hopefully inspire a great deal of new theory and research.

Media

For a variety of reasons, one might expect media to play a prominent role in the lives of emerging adults. Emerging adults spend more of their leisure time alone than do any other age group except the elderly (Larson, 1990), and one might expect that they often use media as a companion during that time alone. Emerging adults' social activities, too, often involve media; recorded music serves as a soundtrack to much of the peer social interactions of adolescents, and no doubt the same is true for emerging adults. Most emerging adults move out of their parents' household, which means they have considerably more freedom than children or adolescents to make media choices without restrictions, monitoring, or criticism from their parents. Also, today's emerging adults are what Jane D. Brown calls "the new media generation," meaning that they are the first generation to have grown up with new media that are "more accessible, more interactive, and more under their control than any other known before" (chap. 12, p. 279) such as the Internet, virtual games, and virtual friends (e.g., in Internet chat rooms).

Despite the evident importance of media in the lives of emerging adults, there is surprisingly little research on their media use. Even the ubiquitous studies on college students typically have not looked at their media use developmentally. Brown's chapter in this volume provides a valuable foundation for media research on emerging adults, as she uses the existing research on children, adolescents, and college students to generate numerous research questions on emerging adulthood.

As a framework for the chapter, she uses the media practice model that she and her colleagues have developed from their research on media uses among adolescents. This elegant model goes beyond simple assumptions of cause and effect to place media in the context of the rest of life. It recognizes that people make choices about the media content they consume, and that they are not simply the passive recipients of media but active processors who may use media for a variety of purposes, depending on characteristics they bring to it. In the course of the chapter, Brown shows that the model applies at least as well to emerging adults as it does to adolescents.

For Brown, identity is the driving force behind selection of media choices: "The media may be seen as virtual tool kits of possibilities for most of the dimensions of identity work, including work, love, and ideology" (chap. 12, p. 281). She makes a compelling distinction between "two kinds of media identification: identification by the kinds of media attended to and identification with different media characters" (chap. 12, p. 282). One might think emerging adults are beyond the age of identifying with media characters, that this is something for children and adolescents, but Brown describes a study showing that 70% of Canadian college students had a celebrity idol who had influenced their attitudes and values (Boon & Lomore, 2001). This is a good example of how research on emerging adults' media uses may be surprising and will certainly explain more not only about the role of media in their lives but about other aspects of their development as well.

Selection is a particularly interesting aspect of Brown's model, with respect to emerging adults. She aptly notes that emerging adults have "a huge array of media choices" and that what they pick from among that huge array will depend on their own identities and needs. So what do they pick? How do they divide their media time between television, music, computer games, the Internet, and other media, and what is the range of their selections within each of these media? Studies in recent years have provided excellent data on children and adolescents with respect to these questions (e.g., Roberts, Foehr, Rideout, & Brodie, 2000), but so far for emerging adults there are only isolated data here and there, such as the surprising finding that emerging adult males are enthusiastic users of violent video games. There is a clear need for a comprehensive study that will provide definitive evidence on the frequencies of media use among emerging adults.

One difference among emerging adults that may be important in their media use is between those who are involved in a romantic relationship and those who are not. I suspect that media use in emerging adulthood is especially high among those who are not in a romantic relationship, because they are likely to have more time alone that invites media use to fend off loneliness. Furthermore, it may be that certain kinds of media use are more common among emerging adults who are not currently romantically involved with someone. Internet pornography could be predicted to be especially popular among emerging adults who are currently without a partner. Also, Internet dating services may be popular among emerging adults, especially those who do not have the college environment, to provide a setting where they are likely to meet unattached people of a similar age. These are examples of the kinds of questions that are generated by thinking of media use in emerging adulthood in developmental terms, thinking about how it may be related to the rest of their lives, and reminding oneself of the heterogeneity that is likely to exist here among emerging adults, as elsewhere.

In the section entitled *Interaction: What does it mean?* Brown notes that "All emerging adults will not interpret the same media content in the same way. Young people come to the media with different backgrounds, motives, and identifications, and these will influence what sense they make of what is heard or seen" (chap. 12, p. 287). I would add that the cognitive abilities of emerging adults may make their interactions with media different from what they may be for children or adolescents. I can see the potential for a fruitful integration of what Brown describes here with the insights on emerging adults' cognitive development presented by Labouvie-Vief in her chapter. Given what Labouvie-Vief describes, that cognitive development in emerging adulthood makes possible greater abilities for understanding complexity and multiple perspectives, one might expect that emerging adults would be less easily influenced by media than children and adolescents are and more capable of recognizing and defusing media's manipulative power. But whether this is actually true awaits empirical investigation.

In her section on the portion of her model describing application of media uses, Brown herself raises a number of provocative questions about potential influences of media in emerging adulthood, on topics such as aggression, body image, occupational choice, and political ideology. There is, in that short section, enough of an agenda on media uses in emerging adulthood to keep legions of scholars busy for years to come. So, although the current lack of research information on media uses in emerging adulthood is frustrating, the vistas for research opened up by Brown's ideas offer great promise for the future in this area. Media research on children and adolescents has overwhelmingly focused on the possibility of negative effects. I hope that future research on media in emerging adulthood will explore not only the potentially negative influences of media but also its positive potential as a source of information, social interaction, and enjoyment.

Two Research Issues

Each of the chapters of the book presented ideas for new research on emerging adulthood, and together they lay out a research agenda that will provide challenges for many years to come. In this final section of the chapter and of the book, I wish to draw attention to two additional research issues: the potential of research on emerging adulthood around the world and the fruitfulness of using qualitative methods.

Emerging Adulthood Worldwide

One limitation of this book is that it focuses exclusively on emerging adulthood in the United States. All the contributors are American except for one Canadian (James E. Côté), and virtually all the studies on which the chapters are based were conducted on American samples. I have proposed that emerging adulthood is an international phenomenon, and the American focus of this book goes against the grain of my own cultural and international approach to theory and research (e.g., Arnett, 2002). However, there were practical reasons for it. As Americans, emerging adulthood in the United States is what we, the authors of this book, know best. This book is the first attempt to draw together research and theoretical ideas on emerging adulthood in a wide range of areas, so understandably we started with what we know best and what we can speak about with the most authority.

However, as the study of emerging adulthood grows, it can and should become an international enterprise in the course of the 21st century. All other developed countries have experienced the same demographic changes as I described in chapter 1 (this volume) for the United States, that is, rising median ages of marriage and parenthood and widening participation in higher education (Bynner, in press; Chisholm & Hurrelmann, 1995; Douglass, 2004). These changes are the demographic preconditions for a period of emerging adulthood, particularly a median age of marriage and parenthood in at least the late 20s, as these changes open up an emerging adulthood age period from roughly 18 to 25 that is beyond adolescence but prior to the attainment of full (even young) adulthood (Arnett, 2004).

Considerable research on this age period has taken place in Europe for decades, under the term *youth studies*. However, youth studies span an age range from the mid-teens through the mid-20s and thus fail to make what I believe to be a useful distinction between adolescence and emerging adulthood (Arnett, 2004; Bynner, in press). Also, youth studies are primarily sociological and focus mainly on transition events and socioeconomic issues, especially the transition from school to work. Applying the emerging adulthood paradigm in European countries may open up new horizons of research in the kinds of areas addressed in this book—identity issues, cognitive development, mental health, resilience, family relationships, romantic relationships, media use, and more.

This does not mean that emerging adulthood in Europe will be found to be similar to how it appears to be in the United States. For example, I do not know whether the five features of emerging adulthood I have proposed would turn up in Europe as well, as they are based on my research with Americans. However, thinking of the period between the end of secondary school (in adolescence) and the entry into adult roles (in young adulthood) as a separate period of emerging adulthood leads to an exploration of what is going on developmentally in this period in a wide range of different areas. Although sociological research in Europe on youth studies has yielded important and interesting findings, the nature of psychological development among Europeans during emerging adulthood is little explored so far and offers great promise for research.

With respect to other economically developed countries, even less is known about psychological development during the emerging adulthood age period. Japan, for example, has a median female marriage age of 27, even higher than in most Western countries (Population Reference Bureau, 2000), yet few studies have been conducted that can cast light on what is occurring in their lives between the time they leave secondary school and the time they enter marriage. Does the tradition of family obligation in Japan and other Asian countries mean that emerging adulthood has a much different psychological character there than it does in the West—that is, much less individualized—or has the impact of globalization made the Asian experience of emerging adulthood similar to the Western experience in many ways? This is the kind of compelling question that awaits researchers who wish to study emerging adulthood in economically developed countries outside the West.

With respect to developing countries, the nature of emerging adulthood is likely to be quite different than in either the West or in non-Western developed countries. In most developing countries, the majority of the people are relatively poor, receive only limited education, and enter adult work, marriage, and parenthood in their late teens or very early 20s (Brown, Larson, & Saraswathi, 2002). The majority of young people in such countries do not experience emerging adulthood. However, these countries also have an urban middle class whose young people experience an emerging adulthood that appears to be similar to that experienced by young people in developed countries, at least outwardly, with widespread entry into higher education and a median age of marriage and parenthood in at least the late 20s.

In India, for example, the majority of young people live in low-income rural families, but in the urban areas there is a thriving middle class whose young people have given India a growing reputation for excellence in information technology (Verma & Saraswathi, 2002). It cannot yet be said what the lives of these young people are like or how their experience of emerging adulthood is similar to or different from young people in developed countries, but this is certainly a compelling opportunity for research. Indeed, the changes in developing countries in the decades to come may represent a rare opportunity for researchers to chart the birth of a normative period of emerging adulthood, if researchers are foresighted enough to grasp the opportunity. In the course of the 21st century, if more of the world becomes economically developed, the proportion of the world that includes a period of emerging adulthood as part of coming of age is likely to grow steadily.

The studies conducted so far on emerging adulthood outside of North America offer provocative suggestions of what may be learned from studying emerging adulthood around the world. In Israel, the requirement of 3-year military service beginning at age 18 looms large in the lives of emerging adults, influencing everything from their attachment relationships to their emotional maturity to their views of what it means to be an adult (Mayseless, 2004; Mayseless & Scharf, 2003). In Argentina, the criteria for adulthood most valued by emerging adults reflect the mixed cultural traditions of the country as Western, urbanized, and industrialized but also Latin and Catholic. So, emerging adults widely support individualistic criteria such as accepting responsibility for one's actions and making independent decisions alongside collectivistic criteria such as making lifelong commitments to others and becoming capable of supporting one's parents financially (Facio & Micocci, 2003). Among university students in China, the criteria for adulthood they endorse most widely are a mix of criteria that reflect Chinese tradition, such as becoming capable of supporting one's parents financially, and criteria that may reflect China's growing individualism in response to globalization, such as making independent decisions (Nelson et al., 2004). These studies are suggestive of the promise of new findings that will result from studies on emerging adulthood around the world and how these studies will expand the field's understanding of the variations that take place in the development of emerging adults.

The Importance of Qualitative Methods

Because emerging adulthood is a new field of scholarship, it represents not only a new way to think about the years from the late teens through the 20s but also a chance to reexamine the methods used in research. It should not be assumed that the methods and measures used in research on adolescents should simply be transferred to emerging adults. Rather, one should think about how the characteristics of emerging adulthood might shape how the methods for studying it are devised. One of the issues to consider is the use of qualitative methods.

I am a strong proponent of qualitative methods (see Arnett, 2005) because I have used both qualitative and quantitative methods in my research on emerging adults and I have always learned more from the qualitative methods, especially structured interviews. Quantitative methods (typically questionnaires) can also be useful, and it can be especially powerful to combine qualitative and quantitative methods, as I have done. However, in research on emerging adulthood as in research on other age periods, the current balance is heavily in favor of quantitative methods, and I believe that this (im)balance is not the best way to promote knowledge of this age period.

There are several good reasons for elevating qualitative methods in the study of emerging adults. First, qualitative methods are especially valuable when studying an area in which little is known, to allow for unexpected responses (Briggs, 1989). Questionnaires typically have prestructured response options, which assumes that the researcher already knows the responses that are most likely. However, in studying emerging adults this assumption may not be warranted, because not enough is known about them in most areas to structure their possible responses. It would be a big mistake simply to take the measures used on adolescents and give them to emerging adults, because emerging adults are not adolescents and different developmental issues may apply. For example, questionnaires on relationships with parents for adolescents typically include items related to parental control that may not be appropriate for emerging adults.

Conducting interviews not only provides useful qualitative data but can lead to the development of questionnaires for emerging adults that may be more appropriate than questionnaires developed for adolescents and may more accurately cover the range of likely responses from emerging adults. I can provide an example of this from my own research. I began my studies on emerging adulthood by looking at the criteria they valued most in their conception of what it means to be an adult. I developed a draft questionnaire that was based on the available literature on this topic, drawn mainly from studies of adolescents. However, as I began to interview emerging adults, I quickly discovered that the questionnaire lacked the criterion that was mentioned most often in the interviews: accepting responsibility for the consequences of one's actions. I added this item to the questionnaire, and it has been the most widely endorsed criterion for adulthood ever since in many studies conducted by myself and others (Arnett, 1994, 1997, 1998, 2001, 2003, 2004; Facio & Micocci, 2003; Mayseless & Scharf, 2003; Nelson et al., 2004).

Qualitative interviews with emerging adults are valuable not just as a means to the end of more valid questionnaires but also in their own right. As the chapters in this volume have shown, one of the most striking characteristics of emerging adults is their capacity for social or self-cognition, that is, their insightfulness into the lives and behavior of themselves and others. This capacity is difficult to examine with a questionnaire but is abundantly evident in interviews. Whether they are talking about their relationships with parents, their sexuality, their hopes for the future, or any number of other topics, emerging adults are remarkably articulate and insightful. I am not referring just to the college students and the college graduates. As someone who has spent most of his life in middle-class suburbs, I have learned a lot more about emerging adulthood from interviewing people from the urban and rural working class than I have from interviewing people who grew up as I did. Perhaps because emerging adulthood is the self-focused age, when people spend more time alone and are intently focused on issues such as what to do with their lives, emerging adults tend to be self-reflective no matter what their backgrounds.

Furthermore, interviews provide a vivid understanding of the variance that exists among emerging adults. In psychological research, the tendency is to focus on the mean or median and examine how it compares between groups or in one group over time. Always, this focus obscures the variance that exists around the center, but this masking is especially unfortunate where emerging adults are concerned, because they are so diverse. Little is normative during emerging adulthood, so there is a great deal of variation among them in many characteristics, such as their school and work trajectories, their romantic and sexual involvements, and their identity development. Because interviews involve a human encounter, they are more vivid and memorable than mere numbers, so an investigator who has done the interviews is likely to be able to call to mind many exceptions and counterexamples when examining mean characteristics.

Of course, qualitative interviews also require much more work to analyze than do questionnaires. I am well aware of that challenge, having spent several years turning more than 300 1- to 2-hour interviews with emerging adults into a book (Arnett, 2004). Nevertheless, I think this work is necessary in the course of seeking a full understanding of the lives of emerging adults. It pays off, in terms of the satisfaction of knowing the whole person as an individual, as well as in the enjoyment of listening to their wit, insight, and emotional expressions, their everyday eloquence.

Conclusion: An End and a Beginning

This book has brought together a wealth of knowledge about the age period that comprises emerging adulthood. I hope that this volume shows the usefulness of conceptualizing emerging adulthood as a separate period of life, different in important ways from the adolescence that precedes it or the young adulthood that follows it. Bringing together research in diverse areas under the emerging adulthood framework shows that more is known about this age period than may have been realized when the research was spread out under diverse terms and without a unifying paradigm.

Nevertheless, far more remains to be known than is known today, as the authors of the chapters have demonstrated with the many provocative questions they have raised. This situation presents those who are interested in the study of this age period with an enticing prospect, the promise of many mountains to climb, each with its own discoveries (and perhaps surprises) at the top, each revealing vistas of many more mountains ahead. The end of this book also marks a beginning, as we in this new field set forth to chart the landscape of this fascinating and eventful age period, and move toward a greater understanding of what it is like to come of age in the 21st century.

References

Alan Guttmacher Institute. (2001). *Teenage sexual and reproductive behavior in developed countries: Can more progress be made?* New York: Author.

Arnett, J. J. (1994). Are college students adults? Their conceptions of the transition to adulthood. *Journal of Adult Development, 1,* 154–168.

Arnett, J. J. (1997). Young people's conceptions of the transition to adulthood. *Youth & Society, 29,* 1–23.

Arnett, J. J. (1998). Learning to stand alone: The contemporary American transition to adulthood in cultural and historical context. *Human Development, 41,* 295–315.

Arnett, J. J. (2000). Emerging adulthood: A theory of development from the late teens through the twenties. *American Psychologist, 55,* 469–480.

Arnett, J. J. (2001). Conceptions of the transition to adulthood: Perspectives from adolescence to midlife. *Journal of Adult Development, 8,* 133–143.

Arnett, J. J. (2002). The psychology of globalization. *American Psychologist, 57,* 774–783.

Arnett, J. J. (2003). Conceptions of the transition to adulthood among emerging adults in American ethnic groups. In J. J. Arnett & N. L. Galambos (Eds.), *New Directions in Child and Adolescent Development: Vol. 100. Exploring cultural conceptions of the transitions to adulthood* (pp. 63–75). San Francisco: Jossey-Bass.

Arnett, J. J. (2004). *Emerging adulthood: The winding road from the late teens through the twenties.* New York: Oxford University Press.

Arnett, J. J. (2005). The Vitality Criterion: A new standard of publication for Journal of Adolescent Research. *Journal of Adolescent Research, 20,* 3–7.

Bockneck, G. (1986). *The young adult: Development after adolescence.* New York: Gardner Press.

Boon, S. D., & Lomore, C. D. (2001). Admirer-celebrity relationships among young adults: Explaining perceptions of celebrity influence on identity. *Human Communication Research, 27,* 432–465.

Briggs, C. L. (1989). *Learning how to ask: A sociolinguistic appraisal of the role of the interview in social science research.* New York: Cambridge University Press.

Brown, B. B. (1999). "You're going out with who?" Peer group influences on adolescent romantic relationships. In W. Furman, B. B. Brown, & C. Feiring (Eds.), *The development of romantic relationships in adolescence* (pp. 291–329). New York: Cambridge University Press.

Brown, B. B., Larson, R. W., & Saraswathi, T. S. (2002). *The world's youth: Adolescence in eight regions of the globe.* New York: Cambridge University Press.

Buchanan, C. M. (2000). The impact of divorce on adjustment during adolescence. In R. D. Taylor & M. Weng (Eds.), *Resilience across contexts: Family, work, culture, and community* (pp. 179–216). Mahwah, NJ: Erlbaum.

Bynner, J. (in press). Rethinking the youth phase of the life course: The case for emerging adulthood. *Journal of Youth Studies.*

Cherlin, A. J., Chase-Lansdale, P. L., & McRae, C. (1998). Effects of parental divorce on mental health throughout the life course. *American Sociological Review, 63,* 239–249.

Chisholm, L., & Hurrelmann, K. (1995). Adolescence in modern Europe: Pluralized transition patterns and their implications for personal and social risks. *Journal of Adolescence, 18,* 129–158.

Côté, J. E. (2000). *Arrested adulthood: The changing nature of maturity and identity.* New York: New York University Press.

Douglass, C. B. (2004). *Barren states: The population "implosion" in Europe.* New York: Berg.

Erikson, E. H. (1968). *Identity: Youth and crisis.* New York: Norton.

Facio, A., & Micocci, F. (2003). Emerging adulthood in Argentina. In J. J. Arnett & N. L. Galambos (Eds.), *New Directions in Child and Adolescent Development: Vol. 100. Exploring cultural conceptions of the transitions to adulthood* (pp. 21–32). San Francisco: Jossey-Bass.

Goldscheider, F., & Goldscheider, C. (1999). *The changing transition to adulthood: Leaving and returning home.* Thousand Oaks, CA: Sage.

Grob, A., Krings, F., & Bangerter, A. (2001). Life markers in biographical narratives of people from three cohorts: A life span perspective in its historical context. *Human Development, 44,* 171–190.

Hogan, D. P., & Astone, N. M. (1986). The transition to adulthood. *Annual Review of Sociology, 12,* 109–130.

Keniston, K. (1971). *Youth and dissent: The rise of a new opposition.* New York: Harcourt Brace Jovanovich.

Kohlberg, L. (1969). Stage and sequence: The cognitive developmental approach to socialization. In D. A. Goslin (Ed.), *Handbook of socialization theory and research* (pp. 347–380). Chicago: University of Chicago Press.

Larson, R. W. (1990). The solitary side of life: An examination of the time people spend alone from childhood to old age. *Developmental Review, 10,* 155–183.

Laumann-Billings, L., & Emery, R. (2000). Distress among young adults from divorced families. *Journal of Family Psychology, 14,* 671–687.

Levinson, D., Darrow, C., Klein, E., Levinson, M., & McKee, B. (1978). *The seasons of a man's life.* New York: Knopf.

Mayseless, O. (2004). Home leaving to military service: Attachment concerns, transfer of attachment functions from parents to peers, and adjustment. *Journal of Adolescent Research, 19,* 533–558.

Mayseless, O., & Scharf, M. (2003). What does it mean to be an adult? The Israeli experience. In J. J. Arnett & N. L. Galambos (Eds.), *New Directions in Child and Adolescent Development: Vol. 100. Exploring cultural conceptions of the transitions to adulthood* (pp. 5–20). San Francisco: Jossey-Bass.

Modell, J. (1989). *Into one's own: From youth to adulthood in the United States, 1920–1975.* Berkeley: University of California Press.

Nelson, L. J., Badger, S., & Wu, B. (2004). The influence of culture in emerging adulthood: Perspectives of Chinese college students. *International Journal of Behavioral Development, 28,* 26–36.

Osgood, D. W., Ruth, G. W., Eccles, J. E., Jacobs, J. E., & Barber, B. L. (2005). Six paths through the transition to adulthood: Their predictors and consequences. In F. F. Furstenberg, R. G. Rumbaut, & R. A. Settersten (Eds.), *On the frontier of adulthood: Theory, research and public policy.* Chicago: University of Chicago Press.

Perry, W. G. (1970/1999). *Forms of ethical and intellectual development in the college years: A scheme.* San Francisco: Jossey-Bass.

Plomin, R., DeFries, J. C., McClearn, G. E., & Rutter, M. (1997). *Behavioral genetics.* New York: Freeman.

Population Reference Bureau. (2000). *The world's youth 2000.* Washington, DC: Author.

Roberts, D. F., Foehr, U. G., Rideout, V. J., & Brodie, M. (1999). *Kids & media @ the new millennium.* Menlo Park, CA: Henry J. Kaiser Foundation.

Schacter, E. P. (2005). Context and identity formation: A theoretical analysis and case study. *Journal of Adolescent Research, 20,* 375–395.

Schulenberg, J., & Maggs, J. L. (2002). A developmental perspective on alcohol use and heavy drinking during adolescence and the transition to young adulthood. *Journal of Studies on Alcohol, 14*(Suppl.), 54–70.

Schwartz, S. (2005). A new identity for identity research: Recommendations for expanding and refocusing the identity literature. *Journal of Adolescent Research, 20,* 293–308.

van Hoof, A. (1999). The identity status field re-reviewed: An update of unresolved and neglected issues with a view on some alternative approaches. *Developmental Review, 19,* 497–556.

Verma, S., & Saraswathi, T. S. (2002). Adolescence in India: Street urchins or Silicon Valley millionaires? In B. B. Brown, R. W. Larson, & T. S. Saraswathi (Eds.), *The world's youth: Adolescence in eight regions of the globe* (pp. 105–140). New York: Cambridge University Press.

Index

About the Editors

Jeffrey Jensen Arnett, PhD, of Clark University in Worcester, Massachusetts, is the originator of the term *emerging adulthood*. He has published numerous articles on emerging adulthood and is the author of the book *Emerging Adulthood: The Winding Road From the Late Teens Through the Twenties* (2004). In addition, he is the author of the textbook *Adolescence and Emerging Adulthood: A Cultural Approach* (2004). He is the editor of the *Journal of Adolescent Research* and of three forthcoming encyclopedias: the *Routledge International Encyclopedia of Adolescence* (four volumes), the *Encyclopedia of Children, Adolescents, and the Media* (two volumes), and the *Encyclopedia of Emerging Adulthood* (one volume). His other scholarly interest includes the psychology of globalization.

Jennifer Lynn Tanner, PhD, is a research assistant professor at Simmons College, Boston, Massachussetts. She is coinvestigator of the Simmons Longitudinal Study, a longitudinal study of mental health and adaptation from childhood through age 30, funded by the National Institute of Mental Health. Her work converges around the theme of mental health and adaptation across the life span, with a focus on the influence of early family experiences on pathways of adjustment during emerging adulthood. She has published work on changing relationships between fathers and adult children after parental divorce, adolescent depression and suicidal ideation, and psychiatric disorder during emerging adulthood. In addition to her studies of emerging adult development and adjustment, Dr. Tanner studies the intergenerational transmission of risk for psychopathology from emerging adult parents to their offspring.